Black and Multiracial Politics in America

Black and Multiracial Politics in America

WITHDRAWN

EDITED BY

Yvette M. Alex-Assensoh and Lawrence J. Hanks

New York University Press

NEW YORK AND LONDON

NEW YORK UNIVERSITY PRESS
New York and London

© 2000 by New York University
All rights reserved

Library of Congress Cataloging-in-Publication Data
Black and multiracial politics in America / edited by Yvette M.
Alex-Assensoh and Lawrence J. Hanks.
p.   cm.
Includes bibliographical references and index.
ISBN 0-8147-0663-0 (pbk. : alk. paper) —
ISBN 0-8147-0662-2 (cloth : alk. paper)
1. Afro-Americans—Politics and government. 2. Minorities—
United States—Political activity. 3. Immigrants—United States—
Political activity. 4. United States—Race relations—Political
aspects. 5. United States—Ethnic relations—Political aspects.
6. Group identity—Political aspects—United States.
7. United States—Politics and government—1989–
I. Alex-Assensoh, Yvette M. II. Hanks, Lawrence J., 1954–
III. Title.
E185.615 .B537 2000
305.896'073—dc21   00-009692

New York University Press books are printed on acid-free paper,
and their binding materials are chosen for strength and durability.

Manufactured in the United States of America

10 9 8 7 6 5 4 3 2 1

Contents

Foreword

Dianne Pinderhughes

Black and Multiracial Politics in America explores, in vivid detail, the intersections of race and ethnicity that stem from recent patterns of American immigration. At the end of a century prophetically described by W. E. B. Du Bois as the Century of the Color Line, there seems little doubt that current debates and conflicts over color will extend well into the twenty-first century. And so, to better understand the current racial topography in the United States, we must ask ourselves certain basic questions: What are the demographic parameters of multiracial America? Which groups are accounting for the explosion in America's nonwhite population? Where do they come from? Where do they live? How do they relate to one another? What are their politics, and how do they vote?

The diversity of America's immigrant population is such that the very catch-all term "immigrant" is of diminishing utility. The dramatic growth in the non-European population has occurred in specific regions of the country as networks of settlers from Mexico, Central and South America, Asia, and, to a certain extent, Africa have established bases of settlement, which have then expanded with the arrival of waves of new immigrants over the past several decades. Hispanics as a whole are spread relatively evenly throughout the country (although the largest proportion is in the South), but when we look closely at patterns of distribution for groups from particular nations, we find that they are much more specifically located: for instance, Mexican Americans and Asian-Pacific Islanders live primarily in the West, Puerto Ricans in the Northeast, and Cuban Americans in the South. A majority of African Americans reside in the South, and most of those not in the South live in urban areas. National politics is therefore likely to take on a regional character that is profoundly influenced by the racial/ethnic/cultural characteristics of each region's population. As the racial/ethnic, political, and cultural composition of the United States undergoes profound changes, it is imperative that we understand as best we can the tangible, quantitative realities of immigrant life and experience, and the often subtle tensions and conflicts that define the immigrant experience.

Yvette M. Alex-Assensoh and Lawrence J. Hanks present, in this volume, a collection of essays that can serve as a prism through which to view black and multiracial politics in the contemporary United States. Structuring the book around four subject areas—political incorporation, racial polarization, and interethnic discord; political and media institutions; political behavior; and race consciousness and gender, the editors have selected essays that focus on the politics of African Americans, Latinos, Asians, Africans, and, to a lesser extent, Whites, to demonstrate how we can best broaden our theoretical paradigms and methodologies. Importantly, *Black and Multiracial Politics in America* recognizes that the black political experience is central to any understanding of American racial politics; therefore, many of the essays in the volume use the scholarship on black politics as a point of departure for discussing the emerging political strategies of newer immigrant groups. Through careful scholarship and the utilization of various methodological techniques, *Black and Multiracial Politics in America* presents a fresh perspective on racial politics, one that is undergirded by sound theories and reasoned findings.

The complexities of multiracial politics will continue to push and pull at the very foundation of American politics and political institutions and at the country's racial hierarchy in the years ahead. One possible outcome of this process of national self-examination is a renewed commitment to democracy and equality for all, a commitment that both results from and is tailored to the current and future demographic realities of the United States. Consider, for instance, the ways in which African Americans have over the course of their long, tumultuous history pushed for changes that have not only benefited them as a group but ultimately improved the quality of life for all Americans. That long history suggests that Blacks as well as other racial-cum-ethnic groups will likely also meet the manifold challenges posed by *Black and Multiracial Politics in America*.

Acknowledgments

In large measure, the idea for this volume came from Larry, who suggested that we compile a series of essays that would focus on controversial issues in black politics in a form of debate. However, it soon became evident that Larry, who was then finishing the last two years of his five-year term as Dean of Afro-American Affairs at Indiana University, would be too consumed with administrative, teaching, service, and family-related commitments to serve as the lead editor for the project. Therefore, Yvette assumed the responsibility, in ample consultation with Larry, for revising the overall theme of the volume and also for inviting additional contributors, creating an edited volume that is devoted to an examination of black and multiracial politics in America. The contributing scholars, from various racial and ethnic groups and backgrounds, have discussed the implications of demographic and other shifts for the practice and process of black and multiracial politics in American society.

We are extremely excited about the end product, and we appreciate all of our colleagues and friends who have labored with us in giving birth to this edited volume. In this regard we extend much gratitude to Niko Pfund, our editor at New York University Press, who never failed to provide the necessary encouragement just as our energy was failing and who also continued to believe that we would pull the project off without a hitch. Additionally, we express a profound sense of gratitude to the NYU referees who read the entire manuscript and offered valuable suggestions for improvement.

In a similar vein, we express effusive gratitude to our contributors, including those who really meant well in agreeing to provide contributed essays but who never met a single deadline. Additionally, we are grateful to Professor Dianne M. Pinderhughes, who took time out of a very busy schedule to read the entire manuscript and to write the Foreword. Additionally for research assistance, we are grateful to Ms. Kimberly Mealy, who helped to locate relevant citation material, and to Mr. George Erhardt, who helped with proofreading, wordprocessing, locating citation information, and performing data analysis. Mrs. Margaret Anderson and Mrs. Loretta Heyen assisted with formatting the manuscript, and we also appreciate their efforts. Yet, as the coeditors, we alone bear the responsibility for any errors of commission or omission.

As we delved through the existing research to verify facts and to formulate our integrative framework, we have come to realize the debt of gratitude that we owe to scholars who have gone before us, particularly the original pioneers in the field of black politics, who received little appreciation for their work but who certainly provided a formidable foundation for later research. We also appreciate scholars in the fields of Latino politics, Asian American politics, and, in general, racial politics who have provided the theoretical and substantive foundations for our collaborative essays. Above all, we are grateful to Almighty God, who provided us with the faith and perseverance to complete this volume, even in the midst of trying personal and professional challenges.

Yvette is grateful to various scholars and friends at Indiana University and in the Bloomington-Bedford communities who have, through discussions, social events, and encouragement, facilitated this volume's completion.

Finally, Yvette thanks those who have provided the everyday love, encouragement, and patience that we needed for this project and we need for others in the future. She is extremely grateful to A. B. Assensoh, who befriended her more than fifteen years ago and who now is a great fan, cheerleader, soulmate, and husband. His constant but gentle reminder that she needed to forge ahead with the edited volume provided Yvette with the necessary encouragement and solace to persevere, even in the face of discouraging and exhaustive reminders from pessimists that an edited volume counts little. As a trained journalist-cum-editor and historian, and as an author in his own right, A. B. read a great deal of the manuscript for the volume and offered much insightful editorial assistance. The couple's sons, Kwadwo and Livingston, provided Yvette with the necessary balance that all scholars need. This scholarly project has also benefited from the encouragement given by Yvette's mother, Mrs. Thelma Coleman Alex, herself a writer of short stories, as well as from some earlier discussions about racial politics with Yvette's late father, the Reverend Livingston Alex, and with her sister, Joslyn Alex, an attorney of Breaux Bridge, Louisiana; Mrs. Enola

Thomas, her godmother and an aunt, also of Breaux Bridge; Mrs. Jean Wade, of New York; Ms. Toni Reddick; and Dr. William E. Nelson, who provided Yvette with an initial scholarly foundation in the area of Black Politics.

For Larry, his mother, Kathleen Hanks, continues to inspire him and to give his life tremendous meaning, while his father, James J. Hanks, who made the transition to the world of spirit in January 1997, continues to be a wise counselor. His siblings and their spouses, Frances and Edmond Cook, Carolyn Hanks Holley, Hasan Hanks and Julie Barbot, and Willie Paul Hanks, continue to support him personally and professionally, while also teaching him much more about the life experience. Larry's cousins Issa Jelani and Kenneth Hanks provide him with valuable insight and challenge him "to keep on keeping on." His aunts, Susan Williams and Marie Stephens, and his great-uncle, Winston Mays, provide valuable links to his ancestral past.

Above all, Larry's manifested family—in his own words, "the family that I have helped to create"—is a major source of fulfillment. His wife, Diane, continues to be beloved life partner on his life's journey. His children, Shonda, Julius, Joy, and Mahogany, help him to clearly see what is really important. His mother-in-law, Eunice Gordon, is the embodiment of human decency. Larry's extended family continue to be heavenly ambassadors, who also continue to enrich his life. His Morehouse brothers and their spouses—Adlai and Cheryl Pappy; Adverse and Iyanth Ponder; Vincent and Lorraine Cole Stovall; Oliver and Sharon Robinson; Reginald Capers; and Derrick Dunn—have been shelter in the time of storms. In Larry's words, "A wide variety of friends have been there for me and my family over the last few years. Chief among them are the following: Louis and Estella Stovall; Michael Ford and Chalmer Thompson; Lafayette and Martha Chamberlain; Charles and Rosland Greer; Michael and Thurmond Gordon; Bob and Mary Lou Morton; Brian and Tommie Easley; A. B. and Yvette Alex-Assensoh; Wayne Martin and Hanadi Al-Samman; James Mumford; and Annie Dunn."

For research and clerical work, Larry is grateful to several research assistants, including Richard Burden, Derrick Williams, Lynn McWhorter, Bala Baptiste, and Arnell Hammond.

Yvette M. Alex-Assensoh
Lawrence J. Hanks
Indiana University

Contributors

Yvette M. Alex-Assensoh is Assistant Professor of Political Science at Indiana University. Her research and teaching interests include urban politics, minority politics, and political behavior. She is the author of *Neighborhoods, Family, and Political Behavior in Urban America* (Garland 1998), as well as several articles and book chapters. Her research has been supported by grants from the Social Science Research Council, the Ford Foundation, National Academy of Education and the National Science Foundation.

Akwasi B. Assensoh received his Ph.D. in history from New York University. He is Associate Professor in the Department of Afro-American Studies at Indiana University, Bloomington. Among his many publications are *Rev. Dr. Martin Luther King, Jr.,and America's Quest for Racial Integration* (Stockwell 1986) and *African Political Leadership* (Kreiger 1998). He is currently coauthoring a book (with Yvette M. Alex-Assensoh) on the African military, ideology, and poverty.

M. Margaret Conway is Distinguished Professor of Political Science at the University of Florida. Her research interests include public opinion, political socialization, political participation, and women and politics. Among her numerous publications is *Political Participation in the United States* (3rd ed., Congressional Quarterly 1998).

José E. Cruz is Assistant Professor of Political Science at the University of Albany, State University of New York. He is the author of *Identity and Power: Puerto Rican Politics and the Challenge of Ethnicity* (Temple University Press 1998).

James W. Endersby is Associate Professor of Political Science at the University of Missouri-Columbia. He received a Ph.D. in Government from the University of Texas at Austin. His research fields include voting and elections, interest groups, and legislative behavior. He has published articles in the *Journal of Politics, Social Science Quarterly, Public Choice,* and *Legislative Studies Quarterly.*

Sekou Franklin is a Ph.D. candidate in the Department of Political Science at Howard University. His areas of interest are African American politics and American government, with an emphasis on political behavior and research methodology.

Lawrence J. Hanks is Associate Professor of political science at Indiana University. He received his Ph.D. in Political Science from Harvard University. His research and teaching interests center on African Americans and the American political system, the politics of traditionally disempowered groups (people of color, women, gays, the elderly, and the physically challenged), interest group politics, black politics in the rural South, and critical analyses of normative issues in the area of the black struggle for equity in America. He was a contributor to *A Common Destiny: Blacks and American Society* and author of *The Struggle for Black Political Empowerment in Three Georgia Counties.*

Errol A. Henderson earned his doctorate at the University of Michigan, Ann Arbor. He is Associate Professor of Political Science at Wayne State University, where he teaches courses on international relations, nationalism, and war. He is author of *Afrocentrism and World Politics* (Praeger 1995), and his recent publications can be found in *International Studies Quarterly, Journal of Conflict Resolution,* and the *Journal of Politics.*

Susan Howell is Professor of Political Science at the University of New Orleans in Louisiana and Director of the University's Survey Research Center. Her areas of specialization are American public opinion, voting behavior, and research methods. She has published articles in *Public Opinion Quarterly, American Politics Quarterly, Social Science Quarterly, Journal of Politics,* and *Political Behavior* and has written several book chapters.

Natasha Hritzuk is a Ph.D. candidate in the Political Science Department at Columbia University.

Michael Jones-Correa is Associate Professor of Political Science at Harvard University. He is the author of *Between Two Nations: The Po-*

litical Predicament of Latinos in New York City (Cornell 1998), as well as various articles on Latino identity and politics, denominational affiliation and political participation, the role of gender in shaping immigrant politics, and Hispanics as a foreign policy lobby. He is currently at work on a book that looks at civic and political responses to racial disturbances in the United States.

Pie-te Lien is Assistant Professor of Political Science and Ethnic Studies at the University of Utah. Her research interests include race, ethnicity, gender, and political participation, particularly regarding Asian Americans. She is the author of *The Political Participation of Asian Americans: Voting Behavior in Southern California* (Garland 1997), among other works.

Mamie Locke is Dean of the School of Liberal Arts and Education and Professor of Political Science at Hampton University. Her research and teaching interests include race and gender politics as well as urban and ethnic politics. She was also a member of the Hampton City Council, where she now serves as mayor.

Joseph McCormick 2d is Associate Professor in the Department of Political Science at Howard University. He is the director of the Master of Arts in Public Administration (MAPA) Program. He teaches courses in public policy process analysis and in African American politics. His areas of research interests are African American sociopolitical attitudes and the politics of racial inequality.

Charles E. Menifield is Assistant Professor in the Department of Political Science, Public Administration, and Legal Studies at Murray State University (Kentucky). He received a Ph.D. in political science at the University of Missouri—Columbia. His primary research interests are minority politics, public administration, and legislative institutions. He has published in a variety of outlets, including *Public Choice, Western Journal of Black Studies,* and *Latino Studies Journal.*

Brigitte L. Nacos, a long-time U.S. correspondent for newspapers in Germany, teaches American government and politics at Columbia University. She is the author of *The Press, Presidents, and Crises: Terrorism and the Media* and coauthor (with Lewis J. Edinger) of *From Bonn to Berlin: German Politics in Transition.*

Marion Orr is Associate Professor of Political Science at Brown University. His research interests are urban politics and urban public policy. He is the author of *Limits of Black Social Capital: School Reform in Baltimore, 1986–1998* (University Press of Kansas 1999) and coauthor of *The Color of School Reform: Race, Politics, and the Challenge of Urban Education* (Princeton University Press 1999).

Dianne Pinderhughes is Professor of Political Science and Director of the Afro-American Studies and Research Program at the University of Illinois, Urbana-Champaign. The author of *Race and Ethnicity in Chicago Politics: A Reexamination of Pluralist Theory,* she focuses her research and teaching on racial and ethnic politics, interest group politics, and voting rights policy.

Reuel Rogers is Assistant Professor of Political Science at Northwestern University. He received his Ph.D from Princeton University, where his dissertation research was funded by the Social Science Research Council and the Ford Foundation.

Introduction
In Search of Black and Multiracial Politics in America

Yvette M. Alex-Assensoh

The unprecedented growth in the populations of Latinos and Asians in the United States constitutes one of the most dramatic racial/ethnic shifts in American political history. According to the most recent demographic evidence, the number of Hispanics and Asians is increasing at a faster rate than that of African-Americans, presently considered to make up the largest single American minority group.

The implications of these demographic shifts are especially dramatic in melting-pot metropolitan areas, that is, urban centers with significant concentrations of two or more minority groups. All of the cities listed in Table I.1 (Frey 1998, p.41) have non-Hispanic white population lower than the national average of 73 percent. In addition, they have two minority groups whose share of the population exceeds those populations' national averages.[1]

Whites are now considered among the minority population in many municipalities. From William Frey's very useful demographic studies, we learn that between 1990 and 1996, as many as forty-three counties turned from "majority White" to "majority minority" (Frey 1998). Among the new majority-minority counties are Philadelphia County, Pennsylvania; Alameda Country, California; DeKalb County, Georgia; St. Louis County, Missouri; and Merced County, California. Recent evidence suggests that these trends are not as isolated as previously believed. Demographic evidence shows significant concentration of Latinos in California, Texas, Arizona, New Mexico, and Florida, while significant concentration of Asians exist in California, Hawaii, New York, New Jersey,

TABLE I.1
Melting-Pot Metropolitan Areas (Qualifying Metros and
Their Racial Distribution, 1996)

	White	Black	Hispanic	Asian	Indian/ Eskimo
Laredo, TX MSA	44%	18%	37%	2%	0%
Los Angeles-Riverside-Orange County, CA CMSA	44	7	38	10	0
Fresno, CA MSA	45	4	41	8	1
Salinas, CA MSA	46	5	40	9	1
Merced, CA MSA		4	38	9	1
Visalia-Tulare-Porterville, CA MSA	48	1	45	5	1
Stockton-Lodi, CA MSA	52	5	28	14	1
Odessa-Midland, TX MSA	53	2	38	2	5
Houston-Galveston-Brazoria, TX CMSA	54	17	24	4	0
San Francisco-Oakland-San Jose, CA CMSA	36	8	19	17	0
San Diego, CA MSA	59	6	25	9	1
Santa Barbara-Santa Maria-Lompoc, CA MSA	60	2	32	5	1
New York-Northern New Jersey-Long Island, NY-NJ-CT-PA CMSA	61	16	17	6	0
Killeen-Tempic, TX MSA	63	18	15	4	0
Chicago-Gary-Kenosha, IL-IN-WI-CMSA	64	19	13	4	0
Modesto, CA MSA	65	2	27	6	1
Washington-Baltimore, DC-MD-VA-WV CMSA	65	25	5	5	0
Yuba City, CA MSA	67	3	18	11	2
Brownsville-Harlingen-San Benito, TX MSA	68	14	15	3	0
McAllen-Edinburg-Mission, TX MSA	68	16	15	1	0
Sacramento-Yolo, CA CMSA	69	7	14		

NOTE: Melting-pot metros are those cities where the percentage of non-Hispanic Whites is lower than their U.S. share (73 percent) and where at least two minority groups constitute a larger percent of the metropolitan-area population than their national averages. CMSA is a consolidated metropolitan statistical area; MSA is a metropolitan statistical area.
SOURCE: William Frey, "The Diversity Myth," American Demographics 20, no. 5 (1998):41.

and Washington. Moreover, the migration of Latinos to southern states is currently reshaping the social and cultural landscape of many southern communities, promising to test just how much the South has learned from its racist past (Parker 1999). In fact, if current immigration patterns and birth rates continue, demographers predict that, by the year 2056, the majority of Americans will trace their ancestry to places like Africa, Asia, Hispanic nations, and the Pacific Islands (Takaki 1993).

These racial and ethnic shifts are occurring at a time of unprecedented economic expansion but also of mixed prosperity for African Americans, who will soon be replaced as America's largest minority group by Latinos. Over the past quarter century, the African American middle class has, to a significant degree, become incorporated into the mainstream of American political life, particularly with regard to electoral politics. We have seen an increase in black elected officials, greater administrative control by black Americans over urban political institutions, and the legitimation of civil rights advocacy groups in mainstream politics (Karnig and Welch 1980; Bobo and Gilliam 1990; Tate 1993; Walters 1988; Jennings 1992; Barker 1988; Stone 1989; Walton 1985, 1997; Hochschild 1995; Dawson 1994). For a growing black middle class, opportunities abound for home ownership, gainful employment, education, and the flowering of interracial social networks (Pattillo-McCoy 1999; Simpson 1998).

And yet, although some Blacks are thriving, others are not. Many Blacks remain, in the words of the sociologist Elijah Anderson, "beneath the surface of socio-economic viability" (Cose 1999). These Americans continue to suffer from grinding poverty, inadequate educational systems, deteriorating neighborhoods, government dependence, and increased involvement with the criminal justice system as persistent offenders (Alex-Assensoh 1998; Wilson 1987; Waldinger 1996; Cohen and Dawson 1993; Cohen 1999). For them, the central, agonizing question remains: How is it that American cities have offered so much hope and opportunity to new immigrants from around the globe in the past few decades, yet have offered very few opportunities for Blacks and, increasingly, for Latinos who have been caught in a web of poverty, hopelessness, and despair?

Indeed, the great waves of immigration, the political incorporation of Blacks, and the subsequent socioeconomic disenfranchisement of the black poor have not been lost on the American political scene. These phenomena have figured prominently in a number of high-profile incidents that have defined the American racial landscape late in the twentieth century.

The multiethnic racial rebellions in Los Angeles and other cities in the 1990s revealed that, while the story of racial conflict is not a novel American phenomenon, the actors in the ongoing drama are changing rapidly. In the Los Angeles uprising in 1993, for example, Korean stores bore the blunt of the property loss, while Latinos constituted the majority of those arrested (Morrison and Lowry 1994). The grinding poverty, joblessness, and disenfrachisement that prompted the Los Angeles riot remain in place, and many observers fear a repeat performance.

The O. J. Simpson trial was a case of unprecedented complexity in terms of the racial and class issues involved: a famous black football player, well assimilated into the white world, was tried by a prosecutorial team largely defined by a white female attorney (Marcia Clark) and a black male attorney (Christopher Darden) for allegedly killing his white wife, Nicole Simpson, and her white male Jewish friend Ron Goldman, and defended by a team of black and white—mainly Jewish—attorneys, before a predominantly black jury and a judge of Japanese-American descent, Lance Ito.

Or, consider the following news story from 1996, which aptly characterizes the complexity of multiracial politics at the millennium:

> At Martin Luther King Hospital, the pride of Watts, patients are disgruntled. Three fourths of them are Mexicans, Salvadorans, or Guatemalans. The vast majority of the hospital staff are black, and there's no lack of friction between staff and patients. Thus far, the hospital administrators have shrugged it off. But recently, Mark Finucane, the new health director of Los Angeles County, made things plain: Hospital recruitment must better reflect the makeup of the population and advance under-represented communities. "At present, that means Latinos," he added to make himself clearly understood. Browns versus Blacks: Latino immigrants versus the descendants of slaves. That is quite a cast of characters. (Boulet-Gercourt 1996)

At the end of the twentieth century, native Blacks and, increasingly, Latinos, who once symbolized outsider status in American society, are likely to be perceived by newer immigrant groups as representatives of the very power structures and institutions by which they were once seen as victimized. Consequently, multiethnic conflict, of a type that remains invisible to many outside these groups, abounds.

Clearly, the traditional black-white framework of white injustice no longer appropriately characterizes American racial politics. Yet, much of the research on racial politics in America, and even that on black politics, is still framed in the context of a black-white phenomenon, although a few scholars have ventured beyond the black-white paradigm (Jackson and Preston 1991; Jennings 1994; McClain and Stewart 1998; Rich 1996; Waldinger 1996; Light and Rosenstein 1995; Omi and Winant 1994; Barkan 1992; Harding 1993).

By including in this volume several essays that address the politics of African Americans, Latinos, Asians, Afro-Caribbean, and African immigrants, we hope to bridge existing gaps in the scholarship that focuses only on black politics and the emerging scholarship on multiracial politics. Making use of a wide variety of data and analytical techniques, *Black and Multiracial Politics in America* thus deliberately addresses issues from both qualitative and quantitative stances.

Moreover, while other books on multiracial politics have focused only on such specific themes as urban politics, employment issues, coalitions, and political behavior, *Black and Multiracial Politics in America* casts a wider scholarly net to explore a host of interrelated issues, among them group identity, racial polarization, interethnic discord, political and media institutions, and political behavior. Some essays focus exclusively on the black experience, while others take a broader, multiracial perspective. A conscious effort has been made to group essays with common themes, regardless of their racial perspective. After all, these racial processes occur simultaneously and very often alongside one another.

Undergirding all of the essays is the crucial understanding that the black-white paradigm, or what W. E. B. Du Bois, in the early 1900s, called the "problem of the color line, is the fundamental historical prism through which all racial and ethnic group relations are filtered. Indeed, for at least 250 years, America, in a loose sense, was a racial dictatorship, in which American identity was defined as white and also as the negation of "otherness" that was first defined as African and indigenous, most recently as Latino and Asian (Omi and Winant, 1994). Using these definitions of otherness, the distribution of political, social and economic resources was organized around a dichotomous color line, which served as the fundamental division in American society. The social construction of black subordination and discrimination was comprehensive, and it was replicated in the economic, educational, housing and political arenas (Smith and Feagin 1995).

More recently, the African American struggle for freedom, as evidenced by the abolitionist movements, the civil rights movements, the struggles for electoral power, and, most recently, the struggle for economic empowerment, has paved the way for successive political movements on the part of Native Americans, Latinos, and Asians. As such, it is often the most appropriate starting point for evaluating and analyzing racial politics in America.

Several essays in the volume address the implications of the post–civil rights movement era and the institutionalization of black politics for various political phenomena. All of the essayists enlist the black-white paradigm to explore issues that will ultimately affect other racial minorities. For example, as immigrants continue to flow into major cities that are currently dominated by Blacks, they will find many of these cities likely to be governed by black mayors. Howell's essay on black mayors reveals that the evaluation of black mayors by white citizens has little to do with quality-of-life issues and job performance but is defined by racial attitudes over which the mayor has little control. Citizen evaluations of black mayors, she argues, will become even more nettlesome as the white majority declines and other ethnic and racial groups form a bigger share of the municipal population.

In their essay on the media, Nacos and Hritzuk demonstrate how journalism shapes the way different racial and ethnic groups think about one another as well as public policy issues. Using a comparative analysis of photographs and news stories from the 1960s and 1990s, the writers demonstrate that, while the portrayal of Blacks is generally more nuanced and accurate than it was a quarter century ago, African Americans are still depicted predominantly as athletes, entertainers, or criminals, while they are sorely underrepresented in stories on politics, the sciences, and business. These discrepancies, Nacos and Hritzuk believe, are primarily the result of the corporate profit motive and of institutionalized stereotypes embedded, often unconsciously, in the minds of journalists and other members of the media. Importantly, these unconscious stereotypes affect the portrayals not only of African Americans but also increasingly of Asian and Latinos.

The multiracial blend of American politics is also redefining the meaning of partisanship and the role of party affiliation. Using the historical and contemporary experiences of Blacks in America as both yardstick and starting point, Hanks offers a persuasive argument for diversification, a more complicated understanding of how politics and racial/ethnic/group identity intersect. Marion Orr's essay offers a clear demonstration of how the preoccupation with racial hegemony has often affected the nature, substance, and timing of anticrime legislation. He argues that anticrime legislation, while traditionally aimed at the black masses, is increasingly geared toward other racial groups, including various Latino subgroups.

Building on Harold Cruse's pendulum theory, which posits that, since the mid-1800s, black leadership strategies have shifted like a pendulum between nationalist and integrationist strategies, Errol Henderson provides a theoretical framework from which to assess the role of war, the political cycles, political climate, and other factors on black leadership strategies. His analysis demonstrates that macropolitical factors were most important in determining the strategies that black leaders employed. He also discusses the implications of these findings for the resurgence of white nationalism, as well as the emerging nationalism among Asians and Latinos.

Black and Multiracial Politics in America also focuses on major contemporary racial protests and marches by Blacks in order to offer an understanding of how demographic shifts will affect the practice and process of black politics in future. In their essay on the Million Man March, Joseph McCormick 2d and Sekou Franklin survey the ideological rationale of participants in the 1995 march in an effort to discern whether African Americans are more disposed to inclusionary or exclusionary political strategies. Surprisingly, their findings demonstrate that, despite the rise in white nationalism and the backlash against race-based public policy, African Americans favor inclusionary political strategies.

Mamie Locke's essay uses the Million Woman March, which took place in Philadelphia in 1997, as a backdrop against which to focus on gender and political empowerment. Utilizing a "womanist" theory of political empowerment, she contends that before black women can formulate links with other women of color, they must deconstruct the centuries of racist and sexist oppression. While her argument does not preclude interracial alliances, she asserts that black women must make sure that they have formulated the tools for change and defined themselves in an acceptable manner before they seek linkages with other groups.

In America, the meaning and implications of race are dynamic, constructed as well as transformed sociohistorically as a consequence of competing political processes and institutions (Omi and Winant 1994). The work is thus informed throughout by a belief that the traditional theories of assimilation, political incorporation, political behavior, and public opinion, which have served as guideposts for political science research, are, as constructed, sometimes untenable when applied to Asians, Latinos, Africans and Afro-Caribbeans.

As a partial remedy to this inadequacy, Reuel Rogers, in his essay on Afro-Caribbean immigrants, assesses the assimilation and political incorporation experiences of Afro-Caribbean immigrants, mainly from the Caribbean or the West Indian islands. He finds that, because of the ethnic differences between Afro-Caribbeans and other Blacks, as well as the racial differences between Afro-Caribbeans and previous immigrant groups, such as the Irish, no current theoretical framework provides an accurate explanation for Afro-Caribbean immigrants' incorporation into American politics. Not content merely to underscore the need for a broadened theoretical framework, he offers up the concept of "differential political incorporation" and contends that voluntary immigrants may have strategic and cognitive options that are not available to African Americans.

The traditional black-white color line in American racial politics allows for virtually no distinction among Blacks, regardless of their ethnic background or country of origin. In his analysis of conflict and cooperation among Africans and African Americans, Akwasi B. Assensoh presents convincing evidence to challenge the conventional wisdom that ethnicity is unimportant among Blacks, and that black is simply Black everywhere. Furthermore, he demonstrates how macropolitical events facilitate either conflict or cooperation among African immigrants and their American-born kith and kin. As ethnicity among Blacks becomes more prominent, they will, Assensoh predicts, begin to experience problems in political mobilization and coalition building similar to those faced by their Asian and Latino counterparts.

Also challenging conventional theoretical frameworks, in this case regarding the ever controversial issue of affirmative action, M. Margaret Conway and Pei-te Lien show that the theories of symbolic racism, group interest, and ideology commonly utilized to explain public opinion differences among Blacks and Whites do not necessarily apply to Latinos and Asians. They call for broadened racial paradigms that are sensitive to the panoply of ethnic and racial groups that now makeup American society.

In other ways, the essays here demonstrate the robustness of existing theories of political behavior. For example, in their examination of the factors that affect the substantive or policy representation of Black and Hispanic congresspersons, Endersby and Menifield demonstrate that partisan identification rules.

Black and Multiracial Politics in America further seeks to apply mainstream theories about political processes to the multiracial landscape. In "Immigrants, Blacks, and Cities", Michael Jones-Correa explores the tensions between institutional stability and democratic values by focusing on how cities have responded—and are likely to respond in future—to new actors in the urban political environment. Using a new institutionalist framework in which urban governments are categorized as either hierarchical or vertically organized, the author examines the adaptability of urban political institutions. He shows that the variation in urban institutional frameworks has important effects on how cities respond to Blacks as well as to Asian and Latino immigrants. Especially useful is the author's focus on the current political reality, in which many new immigrants find themselves in conflictual situations with black political officials and bureaucrats, who frequently serve as gatekeepers in contemporary urban America.

Black and Multiracial Politics in America expands traditional concepts and measurement strategies and, in turn, reveals the lingering consequences of structural barriers to electoral participation and the extent to which the resulting impediments vary for different racial minority groups. In her analysis of the relationship between race and voter turnout, Lien begins with the contention that existing research overlooks important political processes by using a black-white dichotomy. She further illustrates that voting is a two-step process and that, for new immigrant groups, the registration aspect is the most important and, often, the most difficult hurdle to surmount. Accordingly, her conceptualization and measurement of turnout includes voter registration among voting-age citizens as well as voter turnout among the registered. Her complicated, thorough analysis reveals that race has profoundly different meanings for American Indians, Blacks, Latinos, and Asians, and that it is affected by individual orientation toward class, social networks, institutional constraints and political mobilization.

Finally, the essays assembled in this volume offer important refinements to existing theories on intergroup relations. In reality, interethnic group relations operate along a continuum that ranges from cooperation to open conflict. Yet, existing scholarship has focused not on this continuum but on the existence of conflict or cooperation, without paying much attention to the process or to the factors and situations that facilitate the so-called ambiguous or middle-ground territory in interethnic group relations. Additionally, much of the research focuses on panethnic or racial groups, with very little disaggregation of individual ethnic groups; studies focus on Blacks, Latinos, and Asians, without paying much attention to subgroups.

In "Interminority Relations in Urban Settings: Lessons from the Black–Puerto Rican Experience," José E. Cruz provides a rich analysis of the historical and contemporary relationships between Blacks and Puerto Ricans in the city of Hartford, Connecticut. The distillation of the Puerto Rican experience from the larger Latino panethnic group provides a more realistic interpretation of the political and social reality of interminority group relations. Moreover, his refinement of the theory of cooperation and conflict to include the middle ground of indecision and ambiguity elucidates another important aspect of these complex relationships.

Overall, political science as a discipline has not devoted adequate attention to issues of race and ethnicity, very often relegating minority politics to a stepchild position in the discipline. *Black and Multiracial Politics in America* takes an important step in ameliorating existing shortcomings by placing race and ethnicity front and center as an integral aspect of the mainstream of American politics.

N O T E

1. Late in the 1990s, the major racial minority groups represented the following proportions of the nation's population: Hispanics, 11%; non-Hispanic Blacks, 12%; Asians or Asian/Indians, 5% (Frey 1998).

R E F E R E N C E S

Alex-Assensoh, Yvette M. 1998. *Neighborhoods, Family, and Political Behavior in Urban America*. New York: Garland Publishing Co.

Barkan, Elazar. 1992. *The Retreat of Scientific Racism: Changing Concepts of Race in Britain and the United States between the World Wars*. Cambridge: Cambridge University Press.

Barker, Lucius J. 1988. *Out Time Has Come: A Delegate's Diary of Jesse Jackson's 1984 Presidential Campaign*. Urbana: University of Illinois Press.

Bobo, Lawrence, and Frank Gilliam. 1990. "Race, Sociopolitical Participation, and Black Empowerment." *American Political Science Review*. 84(2): 377–393.

Boulet-Gercourt, Philippe. 1996. "The New Racial Divide." *World Press Review*, July, 43–45.

Cohen, Cathy, and Michael Dawson. 1993. "Neighborhood Poverty and African-American Politics." *American Political Science Review* 87(2):286–302.

Cohen, Cathy. 1999. *Boundaries of Blackness: AIDS and the Breakdown of Black Politics*. Chicago: University of Chicago Press.

Cose, Ellis. 1999. "The Good News about Black America." *Newsweek,* 7 June, 28–39.

Dawson, Michael. 1994. *Behind the Mule: Race and Class in African American Politics*. Princeton: Princeton University Press.

Frey, William. 1998. "The Diversity Myth." *American Demographics* 20(5): 38–43.

Harding, Sandra, ed. 1993. *The "Racial" Economy of Science: Toward a Democratic Future*. Bloomington: Indiana University Press.

Hochschild, Jennifer. 1995. *Facing Up to The American Dream: Race, Class, and the Soul of the Nation*. Princeton: Princeton University Press.

Jackson, Byran, and Michael B. Preston. 1991. *Racial and Ethnic Politics in California*. Berkeley: Institute of Governmental Studies.

Jennings, James. 1992. *The Politics of Black Empowerment*. Detroit: Wayne State University Press.

———. 1994. *Blacks, Latinos, and Asians in Urban America*. Westport, Conn.: Praeger.

Karnig, Albert, and Susan Welch. 1980. *Black Representation and Urban Policy*. Chicago: University of Chicago Press.

Light, Ivan, and Carolyn Rosenstein. 1995. *Race, Ethnicity, and Entrepreneurship in Urban America*. New York: Aldine De Gruyter.

McClain, Paula, and Joseph Stewart Jr. 1998. *Can We All Get Along? Racial and Ethnic Minorities in American Politics*. Boulder: Westview Press.

Morrison, Peter, and Ira Lowry. 1994. "A Riot of Color: The Demographic Setting," in *The Los Angeles Riots: Lessons for the Urban Future,* ed. Mark Baldassare. Boulder: Westview Press.

Omi, Michael, and Howard Winant. 1994. *Racial Formation in the United States: From the 1960s to the 1990s* (2d ed.). New York: Routledge.

Parker, Suzi. 1999. "Hispanics Reshape Culture of the South." *Christian Science Monitor,* 10 June, 1.

Pattillo-McCoy, Mary. 1999. *Black Picket Fences: Privilege and Peril among the Black Middle Class*. Chicago: University of Chicago Press.

Rich, Wilbur, ed. 1996. *The Politics of Minority Coalitions*. Westport, Conn.: Praeger.

Simpson, Andrea. 1998. *The Tie That Binds: Identity and Political Attitudes in the Post–Civil Rights Generation*. New York: New York University Press.

Smith, Michael Peter, and Joe R. Feagin, eds. 1995. *The Bubbling Cauldron: Race, Ethnicity, and the Urban Crisis*. Minneapolis: University of Minnesota Press.

Stone, Clarence N. 1989. *Regime Politics: Governing Atlanta, 1946–1988.* Lawrence: University Press of Kansas.

Takaki, Ronald. 1993. *A Different Mirror: A History of Multicultural America.* Boston: Little, Brown.

Tate, Katherine. 1993. *From Protest to Politics: The New Black Voters in American Elections.* New York: Russell Sage.

Waldinger, Roger. 1996. *Still the Promised City?: African Americans and New Immigrants in Postindustrial New York.* Cambridge, Mass.: Harvard University Press.

Walters, Ronald. 1988. *Black Presidential Politics in America: A Strategic Approach.* Albany: State University of New York Press.

Walton, Hanes. 1985. *Invisible Politics.* Albany: State University of New York Press.

———. 1997. *African American Power and Politics: The Political Context Variable.* New York: Columbia University Press.

Wilson, William J. 1987. *The Truly Disadvantaged: The Inner City, the Underclass, and Public Policy.* Chicago: University of Chicago Press.

Part I

Political Incorporation, Racial Polarization, and Interethnic Discord

Chapter 1

Afro-Caribbean Immigrants, African Americans, and the Politics of Group Identity

Reuel Rogers

Pluralist theory suggests that assimilation and political incorporation are available to Americans of all racial groups and socioeconomic strata who desire these resources. For the Irish, political networks, the monopolization of certain trade unions, racial assimilation, and education went a long way toward facilitating their incorporation into society and their socioeconomic success. Eventually, the Irish, once seen as outsiders, were indistinguishable from their Anglo-Saxon counterparts in mainstream American society. Employing similar tactics, immigrants from Poland, Germany, and other European countries came to America and, in time, merged into the larger host society. As a result, it is often expected that all other willing groups can experience similar socioeconomic mobility and political integration into American society.

In her 1987 study of Chicago politics, Dianne Pinderhughes demonstrated the limits of pluralist theory, especially as it pertains to Blacks. In comparing the political experiences of Blacks, Poles, and Italians, she convincingly demonstrated that the so-called pathway of assimilation and political incorporation in American society works differently for White immigrants than it does for Blacks. Stated simply, race impedes Blacks' progress: "Blacks are not just another ethnic group . . . because the limits to their participation in the polity and economy are of a nature and character beyond anything that immigrant groups have faced." (Pinderhughes 1987, 258).

While Pinderhughes and others have demonstrated the fallacious assumptions of racial equality, America's growing racial and ethnic diversity makes the whole question of political incorporation much more complex. Unlike immigrants of the early twentieth century, contemporary immigrants are more likely to come from nonwhite countries in Asia, Africa, or Latin America. What route to political incorporation will these groups follow? Moreover, how will foreign-born Blacks from Africa and the Caribbean be integrated into the American political system? Will their experiences be similar to those of Whites or to those of their native black counterparts, or somewhere in between? The answers to these questions have important implications for the distribution of political resources, socioeconomic mobility, and the practice of politics in American society.

I. Introduction

For much of its history, America has been a nation of immigrants, although it has not always extended the ready welcome implied by popular mythology and the famous Emma Lazarus poem. Just as it was at the turn of the century, when the country absorbed unprecedented numbers of immigrants, so it remains today as the century draws to a close. Indeed, in absolute numbers, the current wave of immigration already matches and likely will soon exceed in size that earlier historic apex. A few telling details from what is by now a well-documented catalogue of immigration statistics and demographic trends will make the point. Since 1965, more than 25 million immigrants have entered the United States. First-generation immigrants currently make up roughly 10 percent of the total American population, or 24.6 million people.[1] For a more dramatic rendering, consider that one out of every ten Americans is of foreign birth, and one out of every two new American citizens is an immigrant. Even more striking is the racial and ethnic composition of the current immigration flow. For the first time since Independence, America's huddled immigrant masses are mostly non-European and nonwhite. Until the end of World War II, immigration to the United States was dominated by Europeans—German, Irish, Italian, and Polish immigrants who would eventually become the white ethnics of America's melting pot ideology. Today's immigrants, in contrast, hail predominantly from Asia, Latin America, and the Caribbean. These three regions alone account for 85 percent of all immigration to the United States since 1965 (Passel and Edmonston 1994).

Taken together, these dizzying demographic shifts and the accompanying matrix of racial and ethnic divisions present some intriguing, and perhaps nettlesome, normative and empirical questions for social scientists to ponder. Chief among them is how America's cities will absorb these recent nonwhite immigrants. Some commentators worry about the economic consequences of the new immigration. Others speculate about the cultural and social adaptation of the immigrants and how they might alter American institutions. For political scientists, one of the most urgent questions is how the increasing numbers of nonwhite immigrants will be incorporated into the American political process; more precisely, how will they mobilize and achieve representation in the cities where they constitute a significant presence? Of course, we could look to history for normative guideposts in the experiences of earlier immigrant waves to help us chart the incorporative political trajectory of the new immigrants. To be sure, earlier European immigrants were able to achieve socioeconomic mobility and political incorporation, each in turn in a relatively steady march of ethnic transition and without significant disruption to the established political system or regime. Yet, the historical parallels will go only so far. Unlike their predecessors, the current immigrants are overwhelmingly non-European and nonwhite, and America's record of incorporating non-Whites into the polity has been deeply problematic. While it is true that some early European immigrants were initially subject to stigmatizing racial ascription and viewed as separate and inferior "races" by "old-stock" white Americans, they were all ultimately accepted as white and incorporated into the American body politic.[2] Not so for nonwhite, non-European groups.

African Americans, of course, are the paradigmatic case in this regard. For them, the political incorporation process has been slow, radically tortuous, and arguably incomplete. In short, their experiences diverge dramatically from those of their white ethnic counterparts and defy all neat comparisons. Most observers agree that African Americans' racial difference and the deeply entrenched racist structures of American society have severely complicated their political incorporation. As non-Whites, the new immigrants may encounter similar barriers and therefore, follow the same tortuous path as African Americans. Yet, here too, the historical parallels are not complete. While many of the new immigrants share non-white status with African Americans, they, like earlier generations of European white ethnics, are voluntary immigrants to America. African Americans can claim no such voluntary immigrant experience; rather, theirs is a singularly bitter history of coerced importation and enslavement. Moreover, the racial obstacles they have encountered have been more systematic and entrenched than those faced by any other group in American history.[3]

The current wave of nonwhite immigrants thus has no exact historical analogy. For the first time in history, American cities must confront the challenge of integrating large numbers of nonwhite voluntary immigrants into the political system. How, then, will race complicate the political incorporation process for these new immigrants? Doubtless, the incorporative political experiences of this latest wave of immigrants will differ in some respects from those of African Americans and earlier European immigrants because of significant changes in the political culture and institutions of American cities. Nevertheless, the question remains: To what extent will race complicate the incorporation process for these new groups as they contest for power in American cities?

While very little has been written about the incorporative political experiences of the new immigrants, there is an emerging literature that takes up this problem and some of the corollary issues. Scholars generally are of two minds on the question. Some contend that recent nonwhite immigrants will follow the incorporative trajectory marked out by earlier European immigrants. Accordingly, they largely reaffirm the predictions of the pluralist model, developed a generation ago by Robert Dahl and others to describe the political incorporation process among white ethnics (Dahl 1961). Although the pluralist perspective, especially in its earliest formulations, came under criticism for its inattention to racial difference, some scholars are now resuscitating this interpretation and applying it to the new nonwhite immigrants (Portes and Stepick 1993; Portes and Rumbaut 1996; Chavez 1991). Other commentators, however, reject this model and instead argue that Latinos, Afro-Caribbeans, and other nonwhite immigrants will have incorporative political experiences much like those of African Americans. By this view, the new immigrants are destined to follow the same course and strategies as African Americans in light of the persisting patterns of discrimination against non-Whites in the United States. Recent non-white immigrants, the argument goes, encounter racial barriers comparable to those faced by African Americans, even if the obstacles are not quite as severe. Accordingly, they conclude that the new nonwhite immigrants will follow the model of political incorporation established by African Americans. In short, this "minority group" perspective stipulates that all racial minorities share in a common situation of oppression that inevitably impedes and complicates their political incorporation (Hero 1992; Barrera 1979; Henry and Munoz 1991; Browning, Marshall, and Tabb 1984; Takaki 1989).

The implications of both approaches are clear. Most scholars and commentators agree that the incorporative political experiences of black and white Americans have differed sharply. The question is where the recent nonwhite immigrants fit. If the minority group perspective is correct, then the incorporative political experiences of African Americans can be taken as a paradigm for all nonwhite groups, whether native or immigrant. If the neopluralist interpretation is more plausible, that is, if the new immigrants follow the course marked out by earlier European immigrants, then the African American case remains a singular exception, indeed a vexing anomaly, to American pluralism. Put another way, if the nonpluralist view proves accurate, then the "American dilemma" is most acutely a problem for African Americans; under the minority group formulation, the dilemma becomes an equally distressing problem for other nonwhite groups as well, whether native or immigrant. Both interpretations have troubling normative and practical implications that I will not spell out here. Yet this is an important debate that can potentially illuminate the extent to which racism remains an impediment to political incorporation for non-Whites and the modes of group politics deployed by non-Whites to achieve incorporation.

This chapter wades into that ongoing debate and concludes that neither of the two standard models readily applies to recent nonwhite immigrants. As others have observed elsewhere, pluralist and neopluralist approaches either minimize or altogether ignore the impact of race on the political incorporation process; that is, they overlook how racism might impede or complicate the incorporative trajectory. The minority group interpretation, based on the experiences of African Americans, gives due consideration to race; however, this model routinely attaches such overdetermining significance to race that it ignores important historical and contemporaneous differences between African Americans and non-white immigrants. Asian and Latino immigrants, for example, do not necessarily fit the black-white binary framework that underlies the minority group perspective. I argue that, while African Americans and nonwhite immigrants both show patterns of *differential* incorporation, the latter groups, as voluntary immigrants, may have strategic and cognitive options that are not available to African Americans. These options make for subtle, but nonetheless important, differences in the incorporative trajectory of the new immigrants. The arguments I formulate in this essay do not yet fully cohere into an alternative model and do not apply to all nonwhite immigrants; nevertheless, they provide a somewhat different lens for understanding the political incorporation process among some of the new nonwhite immigrants.

To develop this argument, I turn to the case of English-speaking Afro-Caribbeans in New York, the largest group of black immigrants in the United States. Among recent nonwhite immigrants to this country, Afro-Caribbeans furnish an intriguing and uniquely important case for exploring the impact of race on the political incorporation process. The handful of recent studies on the political experiences of nonwhite immigrants has focused mostly on groups that are not black—Latino immigrants such as Mexican and Cuban Americans and Asian American groups. Yet many researchers agree that the latter groups may not be subject to the harsh forms of racial discrimination that Blacks have tended to encounter. Already, there is evidence that Latinos and Asians face far fewer racial barriers in the housing market than Blacks, leading one pair of commentators to conclude that "it is black race, not nonwhite race per se that matters" in the United States.[4] It may be that the discrimination experienced by Latinos and Asians will prove to be less like the systematic barriers faced by Blacks and more like the prejudices encountered by earlier European immigrants.[5] Hence, discrimination may turn out to be less of a complicating factor in their political incorporation than it has been in the case of African Americans. This remains to be seen.

Afro-Caribbean immigrants, however, share a common racial classification with African Americans. Under the peculiar American system of racial ascription, both groups are subject to classification as Blacks, a category that historically has brought a host of unwanted exclusions and disadvantages to its bearers. In phenotype and in some historical experiences, the two groups are practically indistinguishable.[6] Ostensibly, then, both bear the burdens of *blackness* in American society. Unlike African Americans, however, Afro-Caribbeans are voluntary immigrants and lay claim to a separate and distinctive ethnic identity beyond their shared racial identity with African Americans. An analysis of their experiences therefore affords an unusually clear window for exploring the impact of race on the political incorporation process among recent nonwhite immigrants.[7]

This examination draws on my interviews with fifty-six Afro-Caribbean immigrants in New York City, as well as a handful of other interview-based studies on the group.[8] Although the analysis gives some attention to the outcomes of political incorporation, it is more focused on how groups navigate the process. Political incorporation is not simply an outcome measured in voting rates, representation, and policy benefits, although it is commonly treated as such in the political science literature. It is also a process. This analysis explores how that process unfolds for Afro-Caribbean immigrants. More precisely, it examines the kinds of claims the immigrants put on the political system and the group identities, interests, and ideological orientations that inform and animate those claims.[9] Accordingly, the interviews specifically sought to illumine the immigrants' perspectives on this process. The chapter begins with an overview of African American political incorporation and considers how their experiences diverge from those of white European immigrants. I then explore the case of Afro-Caribbean immigrants, focusing on their recent incorporative experiences and how they compare with those of African Americans and earlier European immigrants.

II. The Pluralist Standard and the African American Anomaly

Most scholars agree that black and white Americans have taken radically divergent paths to political incorporation. Dahl put forward the seminal account of the political incorporation process in his case study of New Haven politics, *Who Governs? Democracy and Power in an American City* (1961). Hailed as the locus classicus of pluralist scholarship, the study is based on the experiences of successive waves of European immigrants to New Haven. Though it has been subject to some criticism and challenges, Dahl's interpretation has retained considerable currency within political science. His pluralist model describes a rather neat linear path to incorporation that seems to apply to most white ethnic groups.

In brief, he argues that the process begins with the mobilization of group identity among new actors in the political system. Among European immigrants, for example, incorporation began with the emergence of ethnic group politics, with ethnicity serving as a cue for vote choice and partisan allegiance. In Dahl's view, immigrants mobilize around their shared ethnic group identity to elect coethnics to political office and win descriptive representation. Ethnic politics thus draws new groups into the political process, transforming immigrant outsiders into ethnic insiders and binding their allegiance to the system. Furthermore, as ethnic politics draws new immigrants into the political system, it has a deradicalizing effect on their ideological orientations. More precisely, even as ethnic politics binds the allegiance of new groups to the political system, it subdues their more radical political impulses. It deflects the attention of poor immigrants from their class interests and frustrations and instead focuses them on ethnic group loyalties. Hence, Dahl formulates, ethnic identity among European immigrants had no substantive ideological or political content. Indeed, he argues that ethnic politics centers on allocational policy interests and calls for symbolic recognition, while retreating from more radical or redistributive policy demands.[10] In the pluralist account, then, ethnic politics is essentially nonredistributive and conservative; it poses little threat to the status quo and pushes groups toward the ideological center of American political culture.

Finally, Dahl contends that ethnic group politics is ultimately a transitional phase in the incorporation process. As groups attain upward economic mobility and achieve political integration, ethnic identity gradually melts away, losing its salience and instrumental significance. Dahl theorizes that as groups achieve mobility, their voting behaviors, once highly informed by ethnic group identification, are instead increasingly dictated by socioeconomic or, more precisely, middle-class concerns. Among incorporated groups, then, ethnic identity becomes a nostalgic fancy or symbolic adornment to be trotted out at cultural celebrations, religious observances, and the like.[11] And, accompanying the decline in ethnic identity are other indicators of inclusion into the American mainstream, such as higher rates of residential integration and intermarriage.

Dahl predicted that all groups would achieve full political incorporation, following this basic trajectory. While a number of scholars have offered important correctives and addenda to the model, its larger assumptions and predictions have remained mostly unimpeached (Wolfinger 1965; Parenti, 1967; Erie 1988). Although the model does gloss over the prejudices and discrimination faced by the immigrant generation, it seems nevertheless to account adequately for the incorporative experiences of white ethnics. In fact, the model has become the standard theoretical perspective for understanding political integration in American cities, a continuing and relatively seamless saga of urban ethnic succession. It does not, however, apply as readily to African Americans. Indeed, their experiences pose a striking contravention to the pluralist model. Dahl himself was hard pressed to account for the anomalous political trajectory of Blacks in New Haven, largely bracketing their experiences as an unhappy, embarrassing appendage to a model that seemed to work well for everyone else. He and other pluralists tried to shoehorn African Americans into the pluralist framework by resorting to the all too common but nonetheless misguided European immigrant analogy. He predicted that African Americans would eventually achieve incorporation like their white counterparts and join in the long continuous line of ethnic group advance in American cities, albeit belatedly. His prediction, however, was more hope than confident hypothesis.

Indeed, the inconsistencies between the predictions of his model and the experiences of African Americans were plainly exposed in the harsh light of the civil rights movement and the racial upheaval of the 1960s. No white ethnic group in American history had been compelled to press for integration by means of such a radical episode of group mobilization. Nor had any faced racial barriers to mobility as deeply entrenched as those confronted by African Americans. A fundamental weakness of the pluralist model lay in its failure to take these racial differences, and race more generally, into serious account. In recent decades, several scholars have addressed this troubling lacuna in the pluralist literature, with works that explain the peculiar incorporative trajectory of African Americans (Dawson 1994b; Pinderhughes 1987; Reed 1988). Taken together, their studies advance an alternative model for understanding African American political incorporation, one that stands in sharp contrast to the pluralist interpretation put forward by Dahl and other scholars. Let me outline the significant differences.

The political incorporation process for African Americans, as with European immigrants, begins with the mobilization of group identity. The similarities, however, practically end there. While ethnic politics among Whites is typically nonreformist, racial group politics among African Americans has had a far more radical or progressive content. African American politics has been marked by redistributive and reformist demands, as well as by the usual calls for symbolic recognition and allocational policy benefits. Mindful of their unequal racial status, African Americans have tended to reject the standard pluralistic, nonreformist politics practiced by white ethnics. As Reed (1988, 154) observes, "The black regime typically comes to power in a spirit of reform, surrounded by images of redress for long-standing [racial] inequities and breaking through the walls of entrenched privilege" (see also Pinderhughes 1987; Gurin, Hatchett, and Jackson 1989, 156–162). That account of African American group politics contrasts almost diametrically with Dahl's description of the nonredistributive, nonreformist ethnic group politics of European immigrants.

Furthermore, racial group politics has had very different ideological consequences for African Americans than the ethnic group politics of European immigrants had for that group. Among European newcomers to this country, ethnic politics tended to deradicalize group members and bind their support for the political system. Racial group politics among African Americans, however, has often had a *radicalizing* effect on group members and has not necessarily inspired or reinforced their allegiance to the political system. Much of the research on black American political life shows that persistent discrimination has pushed African Americans leftward on the American ideological spectrum.[12] And, as Pinderhughes (1987, 140) has observed, black political attitudes and beliefs often reject the legitimacy of American political institutions and authority symbols, which in turn produces the demand for systemic reform. Hence, unlike the ethnic group politics of most white Americans, African American racial group politics has tended to carry a distinctly liberal or radical ideological agenda.

There are other striking inconsistencies between the incorporative experiences of African Americans and the predictions of pluralist model. Dahl predicts that as group members move into the middle class, they lose their attachment to their ethnic group identity and begin to base their political decisions on class or economic calculations. One would perhaps expect that predicted pattern to be especially pronounced among African Americans, what with the sharp trends toward economic polarization between middle- and lower-class segments of the population in recent decades. Counter to Dahl's formulation, however, group identity among African Americans does not decline in political salience as group members attain middle-class status. In fact, many studies have found that middle-class African Americans have an even greater attachment to their racial identity than do their poor and working-class counterparts (Dawson 1994b; Tate 1994; Hochschild 1995). Dahl would expect a decline in group identity, but these findings confound that bit of pluralist logic.

Throughout the incorporative process, group identity also assumes far greater political and ideological significance among African Americans than it does among Whites. The salience of race in the United States and long-standing patterns of antiblack discrimination have combined to elevate the political importance of racial identity among African Americans. According to Dawson (1994b, 56–63), this strong sense of shared racial group identity encourages perceptions of a *linked racial group fate*. This linked-fate outlook often informs African Americans' political attitudes and policy preferences, giving them a distinctly liberal hue. Further, Dawson observes that this heightened sense of group identity disposes African Americans to evaluate their political prospects and economic status vis-à-vis those of Whites. Racial group identity has thus served as an interpretive device to help African Americans make sense of their political world. Ethnic identity among white Americans, however, generally has not assumed such acute and sustained political significance and cognitive utility; recall, in fact, that ethnic group identity loses much of its political significance for Whites as they achieve upward socioeconomic mobility.[13]

The African American incorporative trajectory differs from the pluralist model and the European immigrant experience in one other important respect. Among white ethnics, political incorporation was accompanied by other signs of inclusion in the wider society—occupational mobility, increased residential integration, higher rates of intermarriage with other groups, and so on (Lieberson 1980; Lieberson and Waters 1988; Farley and Allen 1987). As middle-class arrivistes, the formerly stigmatized European immigrants and their progeny overcame any initial barriers to mobility and melted almost imperceptibly into the American mainstream, in keeping with the predictions of Dahl's model. Not so with African Americans. Although they have achieved some measure of political incorporation in many cities across the United States, African Americans have not been able to escape racial considerations. Even upwardly mobile, middle-class African Americans find their progress stymied in some arenas of American life.[14] Incorporation has thus proven somewhat hollow and incomplete for African Americans, leading some to speak despairingly of the "permanence of racism" and the "impermanence" of African American gains in the post–civil rights era. All in all, the African American experience is an obvious case of *differential political incorporation,* contrasting starkly with the white ethnic experience and contravening the predictions of the pluralist model.

Scholars of black political life generally agree that severe discrimination and the continuing significance of race account for the anomalous political trajectory of African Americans. They reject the pluralist tendency to assimilate race to ethnicity and to represent the African American experience as a variant of the traditional European immigrant experience.[15] Rather, they insist that "[r]ace unlike ethnicity is so distinct as to make the process of political integration considerably more difficult for African Americans than it was for European immigrants" (Pinderhughes 1987, 20).[16] Other researchers have come to share this view. Peterson (1981, 158–159), for example, asserts,

> Color changes the character of ethnic politics. The visibility of the minority group is much greater and therefore group members are assimilated into the larger society more slowly and more painfully. . . . African Americans have been the most militant minority ever to surface in urban areas. . . . Only the particularly severe economic and political deprivations of black Americans would account for a radicalism more characteristic of Europe than North America.

That explanation is useful as far as it goes, but it is incomplete.

First, "color" or subordinate racial classification does not confer ipso facto uniform modes of political thinking or behavior. Such arguments tend toward analytical determinism and show traces of essentialist thinking about racial categories. Second, the experience of discrimination by itself does not necessarily compel a group to radical political action or attitudes. After all, early European immigrants were subjected to some forms of discrimination; indeed, although they never faced barriers as formidable as those encountered by African Americans, some European groups were "racially" marked victims of prejudice. Yet, as Dahl and others have shown, they made no sustained radical claims on the political system and only occasional demands for redistribution. The differences in the political trajectories of African Americans and white ethnics, then, is not simply a result of the greater discrimination faced by African Americans.[17] Discrimination, or any oppressive social condition for that matter, does not inevitably produce radical political sensibilities in its victims. More formally, discrimination is a necessary, but hardly sufficient, condition for the emergence of radical political demands. Sociologists have long argued that groups that suffer discrimination and hardship will demand political remedy or mount resistance only insofar as they find their situation unfair, illegitimate, or unjust (McAdam 1982; Conover 1988; Brown 1986). The political response of the group is determined by the subjective meanings they attach to their experiences.

Therein lies the other important factor that explains the kinds of claims that African Americans have placed on the political system; it accounts for why they were more inclined than their white ethnic counterparts to place reformist and redistributive demands on local and national government. African Americans made political sense of their racially oppressive experiences by reference to a specific historical memory. That historical memory informed the subjective meanings they attached to their experiences with discrimination in northern cities, and this, in turn, shaped their political responses. As Dawson (1994b, 51, 58) has correctly argued, racial identification among African Americans has to do with a specific collective memory rooted to their history of racial suffering in the United States and transmitted across generations. He writes, "[T]he collective memory of the African American community continued to transmit from generation to generation a sense that race was the defining interest in the individual's lives and that the well-being of Blacks individually and as a group could be secured only by social and political agitation . . . [that memory] has been reinforced historically." That collective memory and shared group identity has helped African Americans make sense of the political world, disposing them to make radical or progressive demands to redress antiblack discrimination.

Of course, that sense of shared racial fate and collective memory is not static or uniformly held by all African Americans. Some members of the group identify with that memory only weakly or perhaps not at all, especially as racism diminishes. Again turning to Dawson (ibid.,

63), "differences [in the strength with which the identity is held] can be explained by different conditions of socialization and by the severity and salience of individual experiences with discrimination. . . . [Further,] just as African American identity was forged in response to racial oppression, as conditions and institutions within the black community change, so should the nature of racial identity." Nevertheless, that specific collective memory has informed and shaped African American political choices and behavior along the course of their incorporative trajectory. European immigrants, in contrast, had no similar long-standing historical memory of oppression in the United States. As I argued earlier, their collective ethnocultural attachments, although at times stigmatized, never hardened into sustained political identities with radical implications. The African American incorporative political trajectory is thus the result not simply of discrimination but also of a specific history and a collective memory that inform the group's racial identity and infuse it with political content.

III. Political Incorporation and the New Nonwhite Immigrants: The Afro-Caribbean Case

Perhaps, then, we should not necessarily assume that the new nonwhite immigrants will follow the same incorporative trajectory as African Americans. Scholars who subscribe to the minority group perspective assume, rather deterministically, that the nonwhite racial status of the new immigrants and their vulnerability to racism will place them on the same incorporative path as African Americans. As the foregoing discussion suggests, however, the experience of discrimination and subordinate racial classification do not automatically radicalize a group or lead to a common set of political choices and behavior. Nor should we readily endorse the neopluralist view that recent nonwhite immigrants will replicate the incorporative patterns of earlier European immigrants. This interpretation glosses over or ignores the potentially complicating impact of racism on the incorporation process. Racial discrimination against Blacks and other non-Whites has diminished significantly in the past four decades, to be sure. Yet there have been recent rollbacks in the legal remedies for discrimination. More generally, racism and racial discrimination persist, albeit often in more subtle, less flagrant forms (Bobo and Smith 1998). Doubtless, the new immigrants will encounter some forms of discrimination, which may complicate their political incorporation; however, those complications may manifest differently than they did for African Americans.

Of all the recent nonwhite immigrants, Afro-Caribbeans are arguably the most predisposed to following the incorporative model established by African Americans. Comparisons between the two groups yield obvious and analytically significant parallels. For other nonwhite immigrants, specifically Asians and Latinos, the parallels with African Americans are fewer and more difficult to sustain. As I noted earlier, Asian and Latino immigrants generally seem to face less discrimination than Blacks;[18] moreover, Latinos pose an especially complicated case, because a notable plurality identify as white, rather than nonwhite, and are often viewed as white by other groups (Rodriguez and Cordero-Guzman 1992; Alonso 1987; Waldinger 1989; Skerry 1993). Those differentiating factors qualify the racial minority status of Asian and Latino immigrants and counsel against facile comparisons between the two groups and African Americans. The racial minority status of Afro-Caribbeans, and hence the basis for comparisons between them and African Americans, is far more unequivocal. As *black* immigrants, they, like African Americans, wear the "racial stigmata of subordination" in their black features or phenotype. As Charles Mills (1998, 84) has written, "Blacks are identifiable by phenotype no matter how they try to assimilate; permanent subpersonhood is written in their faces." Ostensibly, then, African Americans and Afro-Caribbeans are vulnerable to the same forms of discrimination. Furthermore, although there are important differences in their historical experiences, to which I will attend shortly, both groups share a historical memory of the slave experience. In light of these similarities, it would not be surprising if Afro-Caribbeans followed the tortuous incorporative political trajectory marked out by African Americans and, in so doing, confirm the minority group interpretation.

There are, however, important differences between the two groups that bear consideration. Unlike African Americans, Afro-Caribbeans are voluntary immigrants to the United States and claim a distinctive *ethnic* identity separate from their shared *racial* status with African Americans. Even as the immigrants share a common racial identity with African Americans, they also identify around a unique ethnocultural identity. They are thus *black ethnics* with ties to countries other than the United States. Furthermore, while the historical commonalities between the two groups are substantial, there are also important divergences. Perhaps most notably, the immigrants hail from countries where the population is predominantly black, or at any rate nonwhite, and largely unfamiliar with the historical experience of Jim Crow and more contemporary American patterns of racial segregation.[19] Second, racial classificatory schemes in the immigrants' home countries have historically been far more fluid than the dichotomous racial categorizations that have prevailed in the United States (Patterson 1972; Alonso 1987; James and Harris 1993). The question, then, is whether these factors, that is, their immigrant status, ethnic identity, and distinctive group history, disposes Afro-Caribbean immigrants to an incorporative path different from the one African Americans have taken. For example, some scholars have argued that, as voluntary immigrants, Afro-Caribbeans share greater affinity with earlier European immigrants than with African Americans;[20] hence, this neopluralist viewpoint goes, they might be expected to follow the incorporative political patterns of previous immigrant waves from Europe.

We can assay the relative validity of both the minority group and the neopluralist approaches by turning to the case of Afro-Caribbean immigrants in New York City. Appreciable numbers of Afro-Caribbean immigrants have lived in New York since the turn of the century, but their ranks have increased almost exponentially since the 1965 immigration reforms. The 1990 census reported that there were approximately 1.5 million foreign-born Blacks in the United States, most of them from the Caribbean. Almost half of these Caribbean immigrants live in New York.[21] Recent estimates put their numbers in New York at roughly 700,000, or almost 40 percent of the city's black population.[22] If the current immigration and demographic trends continue, first- and second-generation Afro-Caribbean immigrants will soon constitute a majority of the city's black population, their numbers exceeding those of African Americans.[23]

Despite their significant and growing numbers, Afro-Caribbeans have been mostly overlooked in scholarly analyses of ethnic and racial politics in New York City. More generally, they have not been considered in studies of black political development in the United States.[24] Until quite recently, most researchers have simply grouped Afro-Caribbean immigrants with the African American community, thus treating New York's black population as a homogeneous group.[25] Such monolithic categorizations have become increasingly untenable in recent decades, however, as the numbers of Afro-Caribbeans have grown and, even more important, as they have begun to articulate a self-conscious ethnic identity. Since the 1970s, Afro-Caribbeans have publicly asserted a distinct ethnic identity and a collective consciousness beyond their shared racial group identification with African Americans. This development is especially noteworthy because, prior to this period, Afro-Caribbeans showed no similar inclination to mobilize their ethnic identity in the public sphere. Indeed, earlier cohorts of Afro-Caribbean immigrants, that is, those who immigrated to New York before 1965, tended to deemphasize their ethnicity in public activities.[26] As Philip Kasinitz (1992, 8) has observed, "despite maintaining strong ties to their nations of origin, [Afro-Caribbeans] generally played down their ethnic separateness as far as North American affairs were concerned." This is not to say that these earlier immigrants had tenuous or inconsequential ties to the Caribbean cultures of their home countries. On the contrary, "[m]any maintained strong ties to [Afro-Caribbean] culture, what we might term ethnic culture, in their private lives" (ibid., 55). Yet they identified with African Americans and thus emphasized their racial group identification in public activities.

Among this earlier cohort of Afro-Caribbean immigrants, the tendency to deemphasize ethnicity was especially pronounced in New York City politics. Prior to the 1970s, Afro-Caribbean political entrepreneurs entered politics not as representatives of New York's Afro-Caribbean population but as leaders of the city's wider black constituency. There is a long tradition of Afro-Caribbean participation in New York's black political establishment. Indeed, some researchers contend that Afro-Caribbeans were disproportionately "overrepresented" among New York's black political elites between 1935 and 1965. Kasinitz (ibid., 215–216) describes this period as one of "[Afro-Caribbean] ascendancy in New York black Democratic politics" (also see Holder 1980; Lewinson 1974; Watkins-Owens 1996). Nevertheless, these early Afro-Caribbean politicians could hardly be taken as representatives of the Afro-Caribbean population per se. Indeed, before the 1970s, there was no Afro-Caribbean ethnopolitical constituency to speak of, in the strict pluralist sense of the term. Afro-Caribbean politicians marketed themselves as representatives of the black community at large and made no special ethnic appeals to the Afro-Caribbean population.[27] The immigrant community was small, to be sure, but their numbers were hardly insignificant. On the contrary, their numbers were enough to make them a potentially influential bloc of voters, whose collective clout might factor in the citywide electoral calculus for Blacks, at least. Yet the immigrants exhibited no interest in mobilizing Afro-Caribbean ethnic identity, largely refraining from ethnic modes of identification in politics and other public activities.

IV. The New Afro-Caribbean Politics

Since the 1970s, there has been a radical departure from the earlier pattern of racial identification among Afro-Caribbean immigrants. Over the past two decades, ethnographers and other researchers of New York City life have noted the very public crystallization of Afro-Caribbean ethnic identity among post-1965 immigrants. If ethnic identity was mostly a sub rosa attachment for earlier cohorts of Afro-Caribbeans, it is, in contrast, very much on bold display among the current wave of immigrants. Throughout New York, signs of a blossoming, vibrant ethnic consciousness among Afro-Caribbean immigrants are widely apparent. I cannot exhaustively catalogue the evidence here, but the mobilization of Afro-Caribbean ethnic identity has been widely recognized (Kasinitz 1992; Foner 1987).[28] Within the past two decades, symbols of this burgeoning ethnic identity have been deployed in the group's social, civic, business, educational, and political enterprises. These symbols are most pronounced in parts of Brooklyn, the Bronx, and Queens, New York City boroughs where Afro-Caribbean residential enclaves have emerged over the past two decades. The immigrants have established Afro-Caribbean–styled schools and academies, and a number of ethnic press organs have been launched to address the interests and concerns of a specifically Afro-Caribbean readership. Afro-Caribbean voluntary associations have also proliferated since the 1970s. While these associations have been a perennial fixture in New York's Afro-Caribbean community, according to Kasinitz, they have assumed a far more public role in the lives of post-1965 immigrants.

While the newly mobilized Afro-Caribbean ethnic identity is everywhere apparent, the most striking evidence of this development has come in New York City politics. Increasingly since the 1970s, Afro-Caribbeans have begun to use explicitly ethnic cues as a basis for political organization. Numerous Afro-Caribbean political groups and civic organizations have emerged over the past two decades. Although ethnic and racial groupings have always been pronounced in New York City politics, there were no such politically minded organizations for Afro-Caribbeans prior to the mid-1970s. Kasinitz devotes a considerable portion of his study to detailing these recent ethnopolitical developments in the Afro-Caribbean population. According to the author, the first signification of a distinct Afro-Caribbean political presence came in 1977 with the formation of "Caribbeans for Sutton," a group established to support the mayoral candidacy of Manhattan borough president Percy Sutton. As Kasinitz (1992, 223–224) recounts, "It was the first time such a group had publicly declared itself to be Caribbeans for anything. The new strategy asserted, if perhaps not completely intentionally, that a Caribbean constituency existed and was able to use the political process to support [Afro-Caribbean] interests." The launching of this group in support of Sutton's candidacy marked the first time in the city's electoral politics that Afro-Caribbean political leaders had publicly identified with their own distinctive ethnic constituency and had articulated an identity apart from their shared racial group identification with African Americans.

Interestingly enough, this first tentative step in the mobilization of Afro-Caribbean ethnic identity was taken outside of New York's hegemonic Democratic party organization. Although traditional pluralist interpretations portrayed parties, and political machines more specifically, as vital institutions for encouraging political participation among immigrants, that view has been challenged by more recent scholarship. According to the traditional account, machines were immigrant mobilizers par excellence, encouraging participation in the political process through voter registration efforts, ethnic politicking, and patronage. New studies by scholars like Erie (1988), Jones-Correa (1998), and Mollenkopf (1992), however, convincingly show that machines typically function as gatekeepers rather than as mobilizers. In less competitive or one-party regimes, like New York, especially, hegemonic machines keep core constituencies satisfied and invariably ignore newcomers. The Afro-Caribbean experience lends credibility to the latter view. New York's party organizations have been slow to court the immigrants and have taken a largely reactive posture to Afro-Caribbean ethnic mobilization.

After the launching of "Caribbeans for Sutton," a number of similar developments ensued. Unlike this first effort, however, several of the more recent organizations have been established with a view toward institutional longevity (Kasinitz 1992). Moreover, New York's white politicians have hastened to make symbolic appeals to the growing immigrant population. African American politicians have come more belatedly to making ethnic appeals to the Afro-Caribbean constituency. Many of the earliest attempts by Afro-Caribbean political entrepreneurs to organize a distinct ethnopolitical bloc engendered fiercely disapproving reactions from African American politicians, and there have been occasional rifts between the city's African American and Afro-Caribbean leadership.[29] More recently, however, African American politicians have worked increasingly to establish stronger liaison with the Afro-Caribbean community. For example, in his 1989 campaign for mayor, David Dinkins openly courted the Afro-Caribbean media and won endorsement from the community's key press organs.

Even more striking than these organizational efforts is the growing descriptive presence of Afro-Caribbeans in New York's electoral politics. Parting with the pre-1965 pattern, Afro-Caribbean politicians have begun to make bids for elective office specifically as representatives of the Afro-Caribbean population. The first forays came in the early 1980s when reapportionment decisions created a number of predominantly black districts. Several of these districts encompassed heavily Afro-Caribbean neighborhoods in Brooklyn and Queens.[30] In 1982, Afro-Caribbean candidates made bids in three districts but lost to incumbents in all three races (Kasinitz 1992). Yet the campaigns helped to crystallize the emerging Afro-Caribbean ethnopolitical identity. More recent electoral bids by Afro-Caribbean have proven successful. The 1992 redistricting decisions created more Afro-Caribbean districts, which have considerably enhanced the group's prospects for descriptive representation.[31] Afro-Caribbeans currently hold two seats in the city council and three in the state legislature. Several immigrant leaders are also active in Brooklyn's Democratic county organization. Finally, Afro-Caribbeans have also secured seats on school and community boards in both Brooklyn and Queens.

Still, Afro-Caribbeans have yet to achieve a level of descriptive representation proportionate to their numbers. As Mollenkopf (1992) notes, however, immigrant populations in New York are younger than native groups, and their naturalization rates are rather low. Hence, their participation rates lag well behind those of native groups. One recent study put the naturalization rate among Afro-Caribbean immigrants at a modest 38 percent, a figure consistent with those for most other recent nonwhite immigrants except Asians, who naturalize at higher rates. Nevertheless, naturalization rates are expected to increase dramatically in the wake of the recent Draconian legislation limiting the availability of social services to unnaturalized immigrants.[32] Perceived as an assault on the immigrant community, the legislation galvanized a number of Afro-Caribbean organizations, most notably Caribbean Immigrant Services, to redouble their efforts to urge immigrants to acquire U.S. citizenship. Now many of these same organizations are turning some of their focus to political participation.[33]

V. Assessing Afro-Caribbean Political Incorporation

Taken together, these developments signal the emergence of a distinctive Afro-Caribbean ethnic bloc in New York City politics. The political mobilization of Afro-Caribbean ethnic identity marks a key moment in the group's political incorporation. That fact, by itself, however, does not arbitrate decisively in favor of either the standard pluralist interpretation or the minority group model based on the African American experience. Under both approaches, the mobilization of group identity is a critical starting point in the incorporation process for new or marginalized groups. The two interpretations diverge, however, in their accounts of the ensuing group politics, the role of identity in the process, and the ideological and political outcomes. Hence, a closer examination of the content and consequences of Afro-Caribbean group politics and the cognitive underpinnings of the newly mobilized ethnic identity are in order if we are to determine where these black immigrants fit. More precisely, we need to examine the kinds of claims they place on the political system and how their group identities and ideological preferences inform or shape those claims.

Unlike African American group politics, the emerging Afro-Caribbean ethnic politics has yet to put forward any especially radical claims, at least not with any consistency. Rather, the new Afro-Caribbean politics has focused primarily on symbolic recognition and heightened visibility for the immigrant community. As I noted earlier, African American racial group politics has tended to combine the usual calls for group recognition with demands for systemic reform and redistribution. Thus far, however, Afro-Caribbean politics has been confined mostly to issues of recognition and access to government power.

Kasinitz's (1992, 196, 202) conversations with a number of Caribbean community leaders yielded this same insight.

> [Afro-Caribbean political leaders] have produced nothing like [an Afro-Caribbean] political program, but they share a common view of their own activity, which is first and foremost intended to promote the idea of [an Afro-Caribbean] community. . . . Caribbean identity politics is as much a strategy for gaining access to government power as an expression of distinct community needs. One of my respondents, himself a community organizer, characterized the political aims of Afro-Caribbeans this way. The goal is to get on the inside. . . . You have to learn the system. You live here. We have to live here. Just learn the system.[34]

Interestingly, he stops short of advocating any major systemic reform. Rather, he and other Afro-Caribbean leaders insist on recognition for the community. Such rhetoric implies that their goal, at least for now, is to win serious political acknowledgment of the Afro-Caribbean ethnic presence.

This is not to say that Afro-Caribbean ethnic group politics is contentless or devoid of substantive issues, as Wolfinger might argue (Wolfinger 1974, 65). Many of my respondents were acutely concerned about immigration, especially in light of the recent legislative reforms that limit the availability of welfare services to immigrants. Even more important, they tended to see racialistic overtones in these retrenchment measures. The Afro-Caribbean City Councilman Lloyd Henry denounced the legislation as racist and discriminatory.[35] Another interview respondent defined immigration as a civil rights issue meriting the same urgent attention as the antidiscrimination concerns of African Americans. "African Americans are deeply concerned about race, as are we. But we also face immigration. Both are civil rights."[36] Interestingly, some respondents linked their anxieties about immigration to other issues, such as police brutality. Male respondents, in particular, complained that police target young Caribbean men. They speculated that unnaturalized Caribbean immigrants who encountered police brutality or ran afoul of the law were especially vulnerable because of the threat of deportation. One respondent offered, "Police brutality is a big issue. It is, it is, it is. Now more so than ever. You see, what is happening, especially from the immigration standpoint, a number of our youth have been caught up in the system, and they get a record, which makes them more liable for deportation."[37] What is notable about these observations is how respondents factor their immigrant status into their political thinking.[38]

All in all, however, the emergent Afro-Caribbean ethnic group politics has yet to take on the pronounced liberal or radical cast of African American incorporative politics. To be sure, Afro-Caribbean immigrants in New York largely vote Democratic, even slightly more so than their native counterparts (Mollenkopf et al. 1999). And concerns about discrimination and racism often surfaced in the interviews. Yet, there was less talk of advancing racial democracy or combating discrimination through government intervention than is usually found among African Americans. Of course, some might argue that these findings tend to support the standard pluralist or neopluralist model of political incorporation. One common line of reasoning is that Afro-Caribbean immigrants outperform African Americans on most socioeconomic indicators, and thus are less inclined to look to government for redress or relief (Sleeper 1993; Sowell 1978). That inference, however, is not supported by the evidence. As I noted earlier, recent scholarship has challenged previous claims about the socioeconomic disparities between Afro-Caribbeans and African Americans (Kalmijn 1996; Model 1991; Kasinitz 1992; Farley and Allen 1987). Census data indicate that New York's Afro-Caribbean immigrants show higher labor force participation and lower public assistance levels than African Americans; however, the two groups have similar patterns of performance on most other indicators (see Table 1.1). And both lag well behind Whites on most measures of socioeconomic well-being.

Another plausible explanation favored by neopluralists emphasizes the post–civil rights decline in racism and the political and economic gains achieved by African Americans in recent decades. The racial barriers to incorporation, the argument goes, have diminished, and African Americans—once the most stigmatized and subordinated group in the American polity—have secured virtually full inclusion. In this view, the post–civil rights successes of African Americans and the decline in racism obviate the minority group model or at least render it anachronistic for the new nonwhite immigrants. More precisely, recent nonwhite immigrants, like Afro-Caribbeans, have no need for the incorporative political strategies employed by African Americans, because most of the racial impediments have been eliminated. For example, neopluralists might cite the political gains of African Americans in New York as confirmation that pluralism now works for everyone.

A closer examination of the evidence, however, counsels against such sanguine conclusions. As Mollenkopf (1992) observes, although African Americans have achieved a substantial degree of political representation in New York, they and other nonwhite groups are nonetheless disadvantaged relative to Whites in the electorate. Despite their considerable numbers, Blacks are relegated mostly to subordinate positions in key decision-making bodies, while Whites continue to dominate the policy-making process at most levels of government. Moreover, racial conflict remains a palpable source of tension in the city's politics (Mollenkopf 1992). In the late 1980s and early 1990s, for example, New York was convulsed by a series of racial bias incidents, including several violent attacks against Blacks. All but one of the antiblack attacks involved an Afro-Caribbean victim. Not surprisingly, then, most of my Afro-Caribbean interview respondents cited racial discrimination as one of the city's more pressing problems. One despaired, "Racism is a big problem. Yes, without a doubt . . . because the playing field is not level for blacks."[39] In Milton Vickerman's (1994, 80) study of Jamaican men in New York, one man soberly concludes, "I am living as a second-class citizen [in America]." Contrary to the pluralist formulation, then, the immigrants, like African Americans, view racism as an obstacle to their incorporation.

Nevertheless, Afro-Caribbean immigrants and many other nonwhite newcomers have not exactly followed the incorporative political pattern established by African Americans, per the minority group perspective. How do we account for this? I argued earlier that subordinate racial classification and the experience of discrimination do not produce ipso facto uniform modes of political thinking or behavior; nor do they necessarily compel a group to radical or progressive political action, as the minority group perspective predicts. Rather, the political response of the subordinated group is determined by the subjective meanings members attach to their experiences. African Americans' incorporative political strategies were informed by their sense of a *linked racial fate* and a unique collective memory of long-standing racial oppression in the United States. Most of the recent nonwhite voluntary immigrants, however, do not share in that memory and thus do not necessarily attach the same set of political meanings to their experiences with discrimination as African Americans. For example, while black racial group identity has strong political significance among African Americans, researchers have yet to find any consistent political meaning in Latino panethnicity among Latinos.[40]

Afro-Caribbean immigrants are a unique case. While they share a common racial group identity with African Americans, they are also voluntary immigrants who claim a distinct ethnic identity. As it turns out, that distinction makes for the crucial difference in how the two groups make sense of their political world and negotiate the political incorporation process. Afro-Caribbean ethnicity is a transnational identity that orients the immigrants toward their home countries and divides their emotional and cognitive attachments "between two nations"—the United States and the country they left behind. Transnational identities are not unique to Afro-Caribbeans and indeed have been attributed to immigrants in general, especially post-1965 immigrants (Basch et al. 1994; Massey 1986; Portes and Grosfoguel 1994; Jones-Correa 1998). As one researcher (Piore 1979, 65) has observed, "However settled [immigrants] actually become, they continue to see themselves in a certain sense as belonging to some other place and retain an idea, albeit increasingly vague and undefined, of returning 'home.'" Hence, transnational identities encourage a "sojourner mentality" among immigrants and fuels the "myth of return." Transnational attachments are especially pronounced among Afro-Caribbean immigrants (Kasinitz 1992; Basch et al. 1994; Toney 1986). Most of my respondents reported strong ties to their home countries, evinced in frequent trips back and forth, remittances to family and friends "back home," and even property holdings and assets on the islands.[41] Moreover, most Caribbean countries allow dual citizenship, a key institutional mechanism that ultimately facilitates transnational attachments.[42] The immigrants seem to prize this transnational identity and retain an attachment to it over many years. As one respondent proudly avowed, "I have been in this country [the United States] for many years, but I am a natural Jamaican and a naturalized American."[43]

This transnational ethnic identity among Afro-Caribbean immigrants factors into their political thinking and behavior and explains why they have not exactly replicated the incorporative political patterns of African Americans. Although the two groups share a common racial identity and the experience of discrimination, Afro-Caribbeans and African Americans map their identities on different, albeit overlapping, cognitive fields. African Americans anchor their identities primarily in the United States. In contrast, Afro-Caribbeans, as voluntary immigrants with transnational attachments, conceive of their identities on a somewhat wider cognitive map that includes both the United States and their home countries in the Caribbean. In short, they straddle that divide, alternating between transnational attachments, as well as between their racial and ethnic identities. This is a critical distinction, because it ultimately informs the immigrants' political decisions, providing them with cognitive and strategic options that are not available to African Americans. As Jones-Correa argues in his illuminating study of Latino immigrants, transnational identities inform the political decisions—and nondecisions—of immigrants.[44] Both the pluralists and those who endorse the minority group perspective overlook the significance of transnationalism, but it is absolutely critical for understanding the incorporative political experiences of first-generation immigrants. In the case of Afro-Caribbeans, it accounts for the subtle, but nonetheless important, differences between their incorporative experiences and those of African Americans.

Most Afro-Caribbeans prize their transnational ethnic identity and typically choose it as their primary group identification. Most of my interview respondents chose a national origin or ethnic label—for instance, Jamaican or Caribbean American—as their primary source of self-identification. The following response, given by a Jamaican immigrant, is typical.

> *Q:* How would you describe yourself to someone who asked about your social background or identity?
> *A:* I'm a Jamaican. There is a mixture there, because I know that my racial ancestry is that of Africa . . . but my most immediate is that of the Caribbean. I'm from Jamaica. Jamaica is my home. Not Ethiopia, not South Africa. Those are the homes of my foreparents. I respect that. Jamaica is from whence I came. I now live in the United States. Those are my homes.[45]

The tendency of Afro-Caribbean immigrants to emphasize this transnational ethnic identity has been well documented. Kasinitz (1992), Waters (1996), and Vickerman (1994) all report similar findings. This identity, which they hold in conjunction with their racial group identity, informs their political thinking and provides them with cognitive options not available to African Americans. Consider, for instance, how African Americans tend to measure their status in American society. They typically compare themselves to Whites and are justifiably frustrated with their subordinate racial status and the persisting racial disparities (Cohen and Dawson 1993; Pinderhughes 1987). Afro-Caribbean immigrants, in contrast, compare themselves not only to groups in the United States but also to compatriots "back home." Or, as Vickerman (1994, 123) notes, "they . . . measure success by comparing their present condition with their lives in the [Caribbean]."

Simply by migrating, the immigrants secure a higher status in their home countries, where they are likely to be viewed as a highly motivated and self-selected. If they experience even incremental upward mobility in the United States, they can compare themselves favorably with those "back home." And, whether the comparisons ultimately prove favorable or no, many Afro-Caribbeans make evaluations from this transnational frame of reference. While the immigrants are saddled with racial minority status upon their arrival in the United States, they also derive status and self-definition from their transnational attachments to their home countries.[46] They can simply draw on this alternate frame of reference. Their political decisions, then, are not necessarily guided by the black-white dialectic that informs African American political behavior. Thus, they should not be expected to respond to racial frustrations in exactly the same manner as African Americans. More precisely, they will not necessarily be as disposed as African Americans to demand systemic reform, redistribution, or other liberal forms of redress.

Other researchers have taken this argument even further, suggesting that the transnational frame of reference disposes immigrants to dismiss or minimize racial barriers as temporary inconveniences. John Ogbu (1990a, 526), for instance, contends that "immigrants tend to interpret the economic, political, and social barriers against them as more or less temporary problems, as problems they will overcome or can overcome with the passage of time and with hard work." He contrasts the immigrants' outlook with that of African Americans, who, as "involuntary minorities," had a far more radical or militant response to these barriers. While Ogbu's emphasis on the immigrants' alternate frame of reference is correct, he reaches the wrong conclusion, at least in the case of Afro-Caribbean immigrants. Afro-Caribbeans' transnational frame of reference, that is, their ethnic identity, affords them an important strategic option for responding to discrimination that is not available to African Americans. It is not that they view discrimination as temporary or insignificant, hardly. Rather, they recognize that they have unique options for alleviating it.

In the case of earlier European immigrants, transnationalism, that is the focus on conditions in their countries, may very well have tempered their frustrations with the harsh inequalities of American life and thus may have made them less inclined to demand radical political reforms. Transnationalism has a far more instrumental significance in the case of Afro-Caribbeans. Transnational identities and attachments among European immigrants gradually declined as the immigrants gained entrée to all arenas of American life, per the predictions of Dahl's model. Ethnocultural identities tied to the home country declined, and the myth of return evaporated. If Afro-Caribbean immigrants find their mobility blocked by insuperable racial barriers, however, they will likely retain their transnational attachments and keep the myth of return alive. In such instances, the myth of return becomes an option for escape or exit, which coincidentally may also dampen the immigrants' interest in political participation generally, or in radical political action or systemic reform more particularly. Rather than make costly political demands for systemic reform, the immigrants can simply exit the American polity. This is not to say that Afro-Caribbeans will inevitably retreat from making radical claims on the American political system. After all, many of them will be radicalized by their experiences with discrimination; yet, with their ties to other countries, the immigrants have recourse to what is perhaps the most radical political response to oppression, that is, the option to exit.

The immigrants often speak of this option. When I asked one woman how she copes with racism in the United States, she responded, "If things get impossible, I can always go home to Jamaica."[47] The choice to return to the Caribbean remains a viable option for her, although she has been in the United States for well over thirty years. Similarly, Vickerman (1994, 90) reports that the Jamaican immigrants he interviewed "were 'birds of passage' in the sense that though they evinced little desire to actually return to Jamaica, they wanted to feel that the option was always there for them. As they expressed it to the writer, they could always return to Jamaica if conditions became intolerable in the United States." Hence, it is not that the immigrants are inclined to ignore or even minimize discrimination, as Ogbu has argued. Rather, it is that they have an important, albeit seldom utilized, strategic response—the option to exit. Even if they never resort to that option, it necessarily informs their approach to political incorporation.

African Americans, in contrast, have no similarly viable option for escape or exit. With very few real options, save the occasional abortive attempt at separatism, African Americans have been compelled to demand systemic reform and major redistribution as they pressed for political integration.[48] Their incorporative experiences are thus unique, and they remain a vexing anomaly to American pluralism. They are far more rooted in the American experience than are recent voluntary immigrants (Falcon 1988). While racial discrimination is certain to complicate the incorporative path for Afro-Caribbean immigrants, they have strategic and cognitive options that have not been available to African Americans. Scholars who make facile comparisons between African Americans and Afro-Caribbeans or other recent nonwhite voluntary immigrants overlook this important distinction.

Nor should we conclude that Afro-Caribbeans are more like earlier European immigrants and hence apt to follow the standard pluralist trajectory to incorporation. As Blacks, Afro-Caribbeans immigrants are subject to the same forms of racial discrimination as African Americans. Racial barriers have already complicated their incorporation in ways not anticipated by the pluralist model. Specifically, their transnational ethnic identity has taken on far more instrumental significance than such identities ever carried among European immigrants. Ethnic group attachments typically lost their salience among Whites as they achieved middle-class status; contrastingly, for Afro-Caribbean immigrants, ethnic identity is a significant source of group identification, even among middle-class cohorts. The Afro-Caribbean immigrants I interviewed were almost all middle class, and most of them expressed a strong attachment to their transnational ethnic identity. Waters (1990) found the same pattern in her research; indeed, she concludes that the identity may actually be more pronounced among middle-class immigrants. This is a clear contravention of the pluralist model and the pattern observed among earlier European immigrants.

A number of scholars have argued that Afro-Caribbeans stress their ethnic identity in an effort to distance themselves from African Americans and avoid stigmatization as Blacks in the United States. Indeed, that argument is now the gathering consensus (Waters 1990; Vickerman 1994).[49] We should not assume, however, that the immigrants' attachment to their ethnic identity is a rejection of their shared racial group identity with African Americans. The two poles of identity are not mutually exclusive. Although they were quick to emphasize cultural differences between themselves and African Americans, most of my Afro-Caribbean respondents expressed a shared racial group identification with their native counterparts. Furthermore, though they observed that Whites sometimes compare them favorably to African Americans, they had no illusions about their own vulnerability to discrimination in this country. One respondent deftly conveyed these sentiments.

> *Q:* Do you feel close to African Americans?
> *A:* Oh, yes . . . because we have the same racial background. Our histories are similar. It just so happens that some got dropped off here, and some in the West Indies. Yes, and how we are viewed in this country today. It's a matter of color. We, basically, face the same kinds of stigmas.[50]

Several of the respondents also spoke admiringly of African Americans' history of radical resistance to American racism and their struggles for civil rights. The same woman who had lived in the United States for more than thirty years offered, "You have to respect black Americans. They knocked down doors to make it easier for the immigrants who come today."[51] Interestingly, the most emphatic declarations of respect for African Americans and the greatest identification with their antidiscrimination struggles came from immigrants, like this woman, who had resided in the country for the longest periods. That pattern is consistent with recent research findings on Latino and Asian immigrants. That is, older generations of immigrants—those who have lived in the United States longer—tend to express views on racial discrimination more in line with the liberal attitudes of African Americans than those of their more recently arrived counterparts (Uhlaner 1991; Garcia et al. 1996; de la Garza et al. 1992).

Nevertheless, Afro-Caribbean immigrants draw a subtle, but nonetheless important, distinction between their group history and that of African Americans. As I noted earlier, African Americans draw on a unique collective memory of long-standing racial oppression in the United States. Afro-Caribbeans do not completely share in that historical memory, although they viscerally appreciate it. Noting that distinction, Vickerman (1994) speculates, "The fact that black [Caribbean immigrants] are a numerical majority in their homelands had freed them from some of the brutal racist repression with which African Americans have had to deal. As outsiders to the system, [Afro-Caribbeans] are free of some of the baggage which African Americans have had to carry." Although somewhat indelicate, the observation highlights a critical difference between the two groups. Some of my respondents noted the same distinction, with perhaps less grace. "We [Afro-Caribbeans] are concerned about racism. But basically we don't walk around with a chip on our shoulders like African Americans. Although, like you said, we experience a lot of racial prejudice." He goes on to observe, "America owes African Americans something . . . more opportunity. We feel less owed. For us, the opportunities of this country are a luxury."[52]

The implications fairly shout from these reflections. Afro-Caribbean immigrants alternate between a shared racial group identification with African Americans and their transnational ethnic identity. Unlike African Americans, however, they do not have reference to a collective memory of long-standing racial suffering in the United States. Afro-Caribbeans may therefore be less inclined than African Americans to place radical or reformist claims on the political system during the course of their political incorporation, not when they have recourse to an exit option. When these immigrants are radicalized by their own encounters with discrimination, they often contemplate exit, just as readily as African Americans have chosen voice. Their transnational ethnic identity disposes them to an outward orientation, which ultimately infuses their political thinking and behavior. Reflecting on a past encounter with racism, one of Vickerman's (1994, 102) respondents sums up this outward-looking perspective: "[T]his redneck guy looked around and told us that . . . he used to . . . kill people like us, meaning he used to kill black people! That only crystallized my resolve to leave here [the United States] and go home." The cognitive and instrumental utility of the exit option among Afro-Caribbean immigrants sets them apart from both African Americans and white ethnics. Whites developed *loyalty* to the political system on the way to full incorporation. African Americans were galvanized to *voice* radical claims against that system when they found their path to incorporation blocked by racial barriers. Afro-Caribbean immigrants turn to the *exit* option in the face of similar obstacles.[53]

VI. Conclusion

In sum, neither the pluralist approach nor the minority group perspective definitively captures the incorporative political experiences of

Afro-Caribbean immigrants. The pluralist interpretation fails to anticipate how racial obstacles complicate the incorporative process for this
group. Though more attentive to race, the minority group perspective
assumes, rather deterministically, that Afro-Caribbeans and other nonwhite immigrants, will simply replicate the incorporative patterns of
African Americans; that view glosses over subtle but important differences between Afro-Caribbeans and African Americans that are reflected in the incorporation process for each group.

Nevertheless, so long as racism remains a disfiguring scar on the
American body politic, Blacks, both native and immigrant, will be
subject to differential political incorporation. What is more, the cognitive and strategic options available to Afro-Caribbean immigrants
may lose their significance over time. Consider the prospects for the
children of these immigrants, the second generation. It may be that
they will have little or no connection to their parents' transnational
ethnic identity and hence no cognitive or practical recourse to an exit
option. Moreover, the political attitudes, policy concerns, and strategic inclinations of the second generation may draw even closer to
those of African Americans if they continue to encounter racial hur-
dles that hamper their mobility and prevent them from doing better
than their parents. Already, there is some evidence of "second-generation decline" among the children of some nonwhite immigrants.[54] In
short, any distinctions that we can now draw between African Americans and Afro-Caribbeans may be erased within another generation
or two.[55] There is a distinct possibility, then, that the promises of
American pluralism will prove elusive for yet another group of Blacks
in this country.

TABLE 1.1
*Selected Socioeconomic Characteristics of Native and Foreign-Born
Blacks and Whites, New York City, 1990*

	% High School or GED	% 4-Year College	% Labor Force Unemployed	% Receiving Public Assistance
Native Blacks	71.37	13.97	10.90	13.32
Foreign-Born Blacks	70.60	15.16	8.37	3.97
Native Whites	90.69	43.53	4.17	2.53
Foreign-Born Whites	70.63	27.56	6.38	3.14

SOURCE: U.S. Bureau of the Census

NOTES

My thanks to Jennifer Hochschild, Tali Mendelberg, John Mollenkopf, Michael Hanchard, Jane Junn, Hawley Fogg-Davis, and Janelle Wong for their helpful comments on this chapter.

1. Figures are from the 1996 *March Current Population Survey*, U.S. Bureau of the Census.

2. Some Southern and Eastern European immigrants were subject to severe racial stigmatization upon their arrival on American shores; yet, within a generation or two, most of these groups shed their ascriptive racial status and became simply white Americans or white ethnics. Racial stigmas have clung far more stubbornly to African Americans and other non-European groups. For the classic work on the racialization of early European immigrants, see John Higham, *Strangers in the Land: Patterns of American Nativism, 1860–1925* (New Brunswick: Rutgers University Press, 1963). On how these same immigrants became white, see David R. Roediger, *The Wages of Whiteness: Race and the Making of the American Working Class* (London: Verso, 1991); Noel Ignatiev, *How the Irish Became White* (London: Verso, 1995); Richard D. Alba, *Ethnic Identity: The Transformation of White America* (New Haven: Yale University Press, 1990).

3. Definitive claims about the unique severity of African American racial suffering sometimes invite disagreement or calls for qualification. After all, other groups have faced racial barriers and felt the sting of discrimination. As Jennifer Hochschild reminds me, "Asian immigrants could not become citizens until forty years ago; Asians could not own property in some states; some Asians were put in virtual concentration camps in our lifetime." And this is just one case. Here, then, is my caveat. The historical record clearly shows that some immigrant groups suffered serious discrimination after their arrival on American shores—some for a generation or two, others for much longer. But African Americans' history of enslavement and their continued suffering from racial discrimination and poverty over successive generations set them apart from all voluntary immigrants to this country. Acknowledging the severity and persistence of their racial suffering is hardly a denial of the prejudice and exclusion that other groups have faced. Conversely, however, the historical reality of discrimination against these other groups ought not lead to the mistaken conclusion that they and African Americans have all borne equivalent racial disadvantages.

4. See Douglass Massey and Nancy Denton, *American Apartheid: Segregation and the Making of the Underclass* (Cambridge, Mass.: Harvard University Press, 1993). Like African Americans, Afro-Caribbeans and black Hispanics are much more residentially segregated than nonblack Hispanics and

Asians. The latter two groups also intermarry with Whites at much higher rates than Blacks.

5. Peter Skerry, for instance, argues that the obstacles and difficulties encountered by Mexican newcomers are hardly different from those faced by earlier European immigrants. I am inclined to disagree with the author, but space does not permit a full engagement with his argument here. See Peter Skerry, *Mexican Americans: The Ambivalent Minority* (Cambridge, Mass.: Harvard University Press, 1993).

6. My reference to phenotype or skin color is not an endorsement of biologistic definitions of race. I recognize that such definitions have been soundly debunked in the scientific literature; moreover, the view that race is "social constructed" is by now the gathering consensus among social scientists—so much so that the observation is almost de rigeur in some circles. Nevertheless, in the United States, skin color has been the long-standing physical marker for distinguishing between Blacks and Whites. Although socially constructed, that distinction has deep experiential meaning. For an illuminating philosophical discussion of racial constructivisim, see Charles W. Mills, "' But What Are You Really': The Metaphysics of Race," in *Blackness Visible: Essays on Philosophy and Race,* ed. Charles W. Mills (Ithaca: Cornell University Press, 1998).

7. To keep that analytical window clear and to better isolate the effects of race on the incorporation process, I focus exclusively on English-speaking Afro-Caribbean immigrants. By doing so, I eliminate the potentially confounding effect of foreign language, which is typically a key barrier to incorporation for non-Anglophone immigrants.

8. The interview respondents were predominantly middle and working class. The interviews are still ongoing; hence, the analyses presented here are mostly preliminary.

9. I take my cues here from the line of urban political analysis prescribed by Michael Peter Smith. He writes, "[U]rban [scholars] could benefit from a closer examination of the cultural and ideological processes that determine how people in particular national and local . . . settings come to define their values and interests, prior to the point where interests are either mobilized into politics or deflected from consideration." See Smith, *City, State, and Market: The Political Economy of Urban America* (New York: Oxford University Press, 1984), 79–81.

10. Dahl 1961, 52–59. Also see Raymond Wolfinger, *The Politics of Progress* (Englewood Cliffs, N.J.: Prentice-Hall, 1974). Skerry and Paul Peterson both offer similar descriptive accounts of white ethnics politics. See Skerry 1993; Peterson 1981, especially chapter 8. Allocational policies address public employment and the housekeeping functions of government; they have little or no impact on prevailing systemic arrangements. Redistributive policies are intended to redress inequality and often entail systemic reform.

11. See Mary Waters, *Ethnic Options: Choosing Identities in America* (Berkeley: University of California Press, 1990).

12. Pinderhughes 1987, 121; Dawson 1994b, 55. We should not assume that the pronounced liberal slant of African American public opinion produces complete consensus within the group. See Dawson 1994b, chapters 6, 8; Pinderhughes 1987, chapter 5.

13. Some scholars have theorized that the immigrants' access to a *white racial identity*, assumed during the course of their incorporation, ultimately had far greater political implications than their ethnocultural identity. Others also argue that the immigrants achieved incorporation by distancing themselves from Blacks. While I am inclined to give weight to such arguments, they are beyond the scope of my discussion here. For examples, see Charles Mills, *The Racial Contract* (Ithaca: Cornell University Press, 1997); Roediger 1991; Rogers M. Smith, *Civic Ideals: Conflicting Visions of Citizenship in U.S. History* (New Haven: Yale University Press, 1997); Hochschild 1995.

14. For example, while middle-class status leads to higher levels of residential integration among Whites, middle-class African Americans have remained residentially segregated. See Massey and Denton 1993. Also see Farley and Allen 1987; Joe R. Feagin and Melvin P. Sikes, *Living with Racism: The Black Middle-Class Experience* (Boston: Beacon Press, 1994); Gerald Jaynes and Robin Williams, *A Common Destiny: Blacks and American Society* (Washington, D.C.: National Academy Press, 1989). For poor and working-class African Americans, the material rewards of political incorporation have been practically nonexistent (Browning, Marshall, and Tabb 1997; Reed 1988).

15. The tendency to conflate race and ethnicity actually typifies much of the influential pluralist scholarship on political incorporation. See, for example, Peter K. Eisinger, *The Politics of Displacement* (New York: Academic Press, 1980); Edward C. Banfield, *The Unheavenly City* (Boston: Little, Brown, 1970). For critiques of this practice, see Stephen Steinberg, *The Ethnic Myth: Race, Ethnicity, and Class in America* (Boston: Beacon Press, 1981); Michael Omi and Howard Winant, *Racial Formation in the United States: From the 1960s to the 1980s* (New York: Routledge & Kegan Paul, 1986).

16. Pinderhughes and other scholars of black political life also reject the standard pluralist recitation about the structure of the American polity—that is, that inequalities are dispersed, and hence the obstacles to incorporation are few, transitory, or otherwise insignificant. On the contrary, studies on African American political incorporation show that this group, unlike European immigrants, has faced cumulative inequalities and long-standing barriers to integration.

17. While the reality of severe discrimination against African Americans is undeniable, that explanation alone does not suffice. To posit discrimination as the single radicalizing factor in African American political incorporation only

begs another question: When does discrimination become so severe as to compel political action? Is there some threshold of discriminatory harm or victimization that African Americans exceeded but European immigrants and other groups did not? Obviously so, but how do we specify that threshold for any one group?

18. There are also obvious historical differences among the groups. Furthermore, within the Asian and Latino groups, there are differences of nationality and socioeconomic status.

19. This is not to say that these island countries have been completely free of white or European domination since the abolition of slavery. Europe left its mark on the islands through years of colonial rule.

20. For the best-known example, see Thomas Sowell, "Three Black Histories," in *Essays and Data on American Ethnic Groups,* ed. Thomas Sowell (Washington, D.C.: Urban Institute, 1978). Sowell argues that Afro-Caribbeans outperform African Americans on most socioeconomic indicators. He concludes that their mobility patterns look more like those of earlier European immigrants. Recent scholarship, however, has challenged and partially debunked Sowell's arguments. See Philip Kasinitz, *Caribbean New York: Black Immigrants and the Politics of Race* (Ithaca: Cornell University Press, 1992); Suzanne Model, "Caribbean Immigrants: A Black Success Story?" *International Migration Review* 25 (1991): 248–276; Matthijs Kalmijn, "The Socioeconomic Assimilation of Caribbean American Blacks," *Social Forces* 74 (1996): 911–930; Farley and Allen 1987.

21. Another 17 percent live in Florida. See Kalmijn 1996.

22. The 700,000 figure is cited in Milton Vickerman, "The Responses of West Indians to African-Americans: Distancing and Identification," *Research in Race and Ethnic Relations* 7 (1994): 83–128. The percentage derives from my calculations based on New York population estimates from the 1990 census.

23. Since the 1970s, Caribbean immigrants have accounted for the largest share of New York City's total immigrant influx. Of course, this includes immigrants from both the Hispanic and the nonHispanic Caribbean. Source: U.S. Census Microdata Sample, prepared by New York City Department of City Planning.

24. Notable exceptions include Kasinitz (1992); Winston James, *Holding Aloft of Ethiopia: Caribbean Radicalism in Early Twentieth Century America* (London: Verso, 1998); Irma Watkins-Owens, *Blood Relations: Caribbean Immigrants and the Harlem Community, 1900–1930* (Bloomington: Indiana University Press, 1996). Mollenkopf's work on New York City politics gives passing attention to the Afro-Caribbean immigrants, but they are outside the scope of his larger inquiry.

25. Criticizing this oversight, Roy Bryce-Laporte has called Afro-Caribbeans the "invisible immigrants." See Bryce-Laporte, "Black Immigrants: The

Experience of Invisibility and Inequality," *Journal of Black Studies* 3 (1972): 29–56. The tendency to treat the black population monolithically is a critical flaw that typifies much of the influential scholarship on racial and ethnic politics. Blacks are routinely viewed as just another ethnic group, while ethnic divisions or other differences *within* the black population are overlooked.

26. Researchers distinguish among three cohorts of Afro-Caribbean immigration to New York. The first sizable wave came in the first three decades of the century. The second, much smaller group entered between the end of the Depression era and the early 1960s. The third and largest wave began in 1966 and continues today. See Kasinitz 1992.

27. The political career of former congresswoman Shirley Chisholm is instructive. She was one of the few Afro-Caribbean politicians who made public references to her ethnic background, and yet she was emphatic about her role as a representative of the larger black constituency. See Chisholm, *Unbought and Unbossed* (New York: Houghton Mifflin, 1970).

28. The media have also taken notice of the growing strength of the Afro-Caribbean ethnic presence. See, for example, Thomas Morgan, "Caribbean Verve Brightens New York," *New York Times,* 3 June 1988, B1, B5; Celia Dugger, "Immigrant Voters Reshape Politics," *New York Times*, 10 March 1995, 1, 28.

29. Formalized Afro-Caribbean support for Mayor Edward Koch in his 1985 bid for reelection generated tensions between Afro-Caribbean and African American political elites. "Caribbeans for Koch" marked the first time that a segment of the Afro-Caribbean political leadership had assumed a posture diametrically opposed to that of the city's African American leadership. I shall return shortly to the question of divisions between Afro-Caribbeans and African Americans.

30. Brooklyn is home to the city's largest Afro-Caribbean population, but there are rapidly expanding Afro-Caribbean neighborhoods in Queens and the Bronx as well. Source: U.S. Census Microdata Sample, prepared by New York City Department of City Planning.

31. By creating opportunities for minority enfranchisement, legal mechanisms, such as the Voting Rights Act, arguably have done more to facilitate immigrant political incorporation than local party organizations in the post–civil rights era. Nevertheless, legal measures alone are hardly adequate to ensure immigrant participation. Organizational and institutional strategies to encourage immigrant mobilization are crucial; as I noted earlier, however, the record of contemporary party organizations on that score is rather weak. For more on the merits and limitations of the Voting Rights Act in this regard, see Frank Macchiarola and Joseph Diaz, "Minority Political Empowerment in New York City: Beyond the Voting Rights Act," *Political Science Quarterly* 108 (1993): 37–57.

32. In the spring of 1997, *Carib News,* the leading Afro-Caribbean newspaper in New York, carried a series of articles documenting the precipitous

increase in naturalization requests among Caribbean immigrants. See, for example, *Carib News*, March 4, 1997. Of course, such developments raise the troubling specter of immigrants choosing citizenship under duress or coercion.

33. Interview, November 29, 1996. Here again, we see that political parties have played almost no role in these efforts to mobilize the immigrant population. The interview respondent dismissed the parties as largely unresponsive to recent immigrants.

34. Interview, November 29, 1996.

35. *Carib News,* 20 August 1997, 6.

36. Interview, April 17, 1997.

37. Interview, April 23, 1997.

38. This is a key point to which I shall return shortly.

39. Interview, November 29, 1996.

40. See Michael Jones-Correa and David L. Leal, "Becoming 'Hispanic': Secondary Panethnic Identification among Latin American-Origin Populations in the United States," *Hispanic Journal of Behavioral Sciences* 18 (1996): 214–254. On Asians and Mexicans, see Carol J. Uhlaner, "Perceived Discrimination and Prejudice and the Coalition Prospects of Blacks, Latinos, and Asian Americans," in *Racial and Ethnic Politics in California,* eds. Bryan O. Jackson and Michael B. Preston (Berkeley: IGS Press, 1991).

41. Of my fifty-six respondents, forty-seven reported that they make a trip to their home country at least once a year. Most also indicated that they read Caribbean newspapers regularly to stay abreast of developments back home and throughout the Caribbean region.

42. According to one community organizer, many Afro-Caribbean immigrants are unaware of the dual-citizenship privilege. Unwilling to renounce the citizenship rights of their home countries, the immigrants are initially reluctant to pursue naturalization. Knowledge of the dual citizenship privilege usually eases their reluctance, though not always. Interview, November 29, 1996. For a sensitive account of similar anxieties among Latino immigrants, see Jones-Correa (1998).

43. Interview, May 2, 1997.

44. In Jones-Correa's formulation, Latino immigrants base a key political nondecision—that is, the refusal to acquire U.S. citizenship—on transnational attachments. See Jones-Correa 1998.

45. Interview, May 6, 1997. Note the respondent's pluralization of the word "home" to signify his transnational attachments.

46. Similarly, in his discussion of European immigrants, John Ogbu writes, "[T]he immigrants did not measure their success or failure primarily by the standards of other white Americans, but by the standards of their homelands. . . . Even when they were restricted to menial labor, they did not consider themselves to be occupying the lowest rung of the American status system." Of

course, what Ogbu fails to mention is that these European immigrants did not occupy the lowest rung, because that dubious distinction was reserved for Blacks. See Ogbu, "Minority Status and Literacy in Comparative Perspective," *Daedalus* 119 (1990): 150.

47. Interview, April 1, 1997.

48. Of course, African Americans can choose to exit the American polity, and a few have on occasion. Consider the numbers of individual African Americans, prominent and otherwise, who have become expatriates. W. E. B. Du Bois and Richard Wright, for example, renounced their ties to America and chose self-imposed exile. Expatriation is not, however, a viable option for most African Americans, who have strong, abiding ties to the United States despite its sins against them. Immigrants, in contrast, have ties to other countries. Furthermore, the emotional and practical costs of expatriation are much higher than those associated with repatriation. Interestingly, the most well-known attempt by Blacks to exit the American polity was led by Marcus Garvey, himself an Afro-Caribbean immigrant.

49. For other views, see Kasinitz 1992; Foner 1987; Rogers forthcoming.

50. Interview, November 29, 1996.

51. Interview, April 1, 1997.

52. Interview, November 29, 1996.

53. This analytic framework loosely reinvents Albert Hirschman's classic model. See Albert Hirschman, *Exit, Voice, and Loyalty: Responses to Decline in Firms, Organizations, and States* (Cambridge, Mass.: Harvard University Press, 1970).

54. See Alejandro Portes, ed., *The New Second Generation* (New York: Russell Sage, 1996). Socioeconomic backsliding by the new second generation contravenes the predictions of the pluralist model and the pattern established by the children of earlier European immigrants. On second-generation Afro-Caribbean immigrants, see Mary C. Waters, "Ethnic and Racial Identities of Second-Generation Black Immigrants in New York City," in Portes 1996; Andrea Simpson, *The Tie That Binds: Identity and Political Attitudes in the Post–Civil Rights Generation* (New York: New York University Press, 1998).

55. As one of my interview respondents pointed out, these distinctions are also becoming increasingly meaningless as Afro-Caribbeans and African Americans intermarry and intermingle socially.

REFERENCES

Alba, Richard. *Ethnic Identity: The Transformation of White America.* New Haven: Yale University Press, 1990.

Alonso, William. "Identity and Population," in *Population in an Interacting*

World, ed. William Alonso. Cambridge, Mass.: Harvard University Press, 1987.

Banfield, Edward. *The Unheavenly City.* Boston: Little, Brown, 1970.

Barrera, Mario. *Race and Class in the Southwest: A Theory of Racial Inequality.* Notre Dame: University of Notre Dame Press, 1979.

Basch, Linda, Nina Glick Schiller, and Christina Szanton Blanc. *Nations Unbound: Transnational Projects, Postcolonial Predicaments, and Deterritorialized Nation-States.* Amsterdam: Gordon and Breach, 1994.

Bobo, Lawrence, and Ryan Smith. "From Jim Crow Racism to Laissez-Faire Racism: The Transformation of Racial Attitudes," in *Beyond Pluralism: The Conception of Groups and Group Identities in America,* eds. Wendy Katkin, Ned Landsman, and Andrea Tyree. Urbana: University of Illinois Press, 1998.

Brown, Roger. *Social Psychology,* 2d ed. New York: Free Press, 1986.

Browning, Rufus P., Dale Rogers Marshall and David H. Tabb. 1984. *Protest Is Not Enough: The Struggle of Blacks and Hispanics for Equality in Urban Politics.* Berkeley: University of California Press.

Bryce-Laporte, Roy. "Black Immigrants: The Experience of Invisibility and Inequality." *Journal of Black Studies* 3 (1972): 29–56.

Chavez, Linda. *Out of the Barrio: Toward a New Politics of Hispanic Assimilation.* New York: Basic Books, 1991.

Chisholm, Shirley. *Unbought and Unbossed.* New York: Houghton Mifflin, 1970.

Cohen, Cathy, and Michael Dawson. "Neighborhood Poverty and African-American Politics." *American Political Science Review* 87(2)(1993): 286–302.

Conover, Pamela. "The Role of Social Groups in Political Thinking." *British Journal of Political Science* 18 (1988): 51–76.

Dahl, Robert. *Who Governs? Democracy and Power in an American City.* New Haven: Yale University Press, 1961.

Dawson, Michael. "A Black Counterpublic? Economic Earthquakes, Racial Agenda(s), and Black Politics." *Public Culture* 7 (1994a): 195–223.

———. *Behind the Mule: Race and Class in African American Politics.* Princeton: Princeton University Press, 1994b.

de la Garza, Rudolfo, Louis DeSipio, R. Chris Garcia, John Garcia, and Angelo Falcon. *Latino Voices: Mexican, Puerto Rican, and Cuban Perspectives.* Boulder: Westview Press, 1992.

Dugger, Celia. "Immigrant Voters Reshape Politics." *New York Times,* 10 March 1995, 1, 28.

Eisinger, Peter. *The Politics of Displacement.* New York: Academic Press, 1980.

Erie, Stephen. *Rainbow's End: Irish-Americans and the Dilemmas of Urban Machine Politics, 1840–1985.* Berkeley: University of California Press, 1988.

Feagin, Joe R., and Melvin P. Sikes. *Living with Racism: The Black Middle-Class Experience.* Boston: Beacon Press, 1994.

Falcon, Angelo. "Black and Latino Politics: Race and Ethnicity in a Changing Urban Context," in *Latinos and the Political System,* ed. F. Chris Garcia. Notre Dame: University of Notre Dame Press, 1988.

Farley, Reynolds, and Walter Allen. *The Color Line and the Quality of Life in America.* New York: Russell Sage, 1987.

Foner, Nancy. "The Jamaicans: Race and Ethnicity Among Migrants to New York City," in *New Immigrants in New York,* ed. Eric Foner. New York: Columbia University Press, 1987.

Gans, Herbert. "Symbolic Ethnicity: The Future of Ethnic Groups and Cultures in America." *Ethnic and Racial Studies* 2 (1979): 1–20.

Garcia, F. Chris, Angelo Falcon, and Rodolfo de la Garza. "Ethnicity and Politics: Evidence from the Latino National Political Survey," *Hispanic Journal of Behavioral Sciences* 18 (1996): 91–103.

Gerstle, Gary. "The Working Class Goes to War." *Mid-America* (October 1993): 303–322.

Glazer, Nathan, and Daniel Moynihan. *Beyond the Melting Pot: The Negroes, Puerto Ricans, and Irish of New York City.* Cambridge: MIT Press, 1963.

Gurin, Patricia, Shirley Hatchett, and James S. Jackson. *Hope and Independence: Blacks' Response to Electoral and Party Politics.* New York: Russell Sage, 1989.

Halter, Marilyn. *Between Race and Ethnicity: Cape Verdean American Immigrants, 1860–1965.* Urbana: University of Illinois, 1993.

Henry, Charles, and Carlos Munoz Jr. "Ideological and Interest Linkages in California Rainbow Politics," in *Racial and Ethnic Politics in California,* eds. Bryan O. Jackson and Michael B. Preston. Berkeley: IGS Press, 1991.

Hero, Rodney. *Latinos and the U.S. Political System: Two-Tiered Pluralism.* Philadelphia: Temple University Press, 1992.

Hirschman, Albert O. *Exit, Voice, and Loyalty: Responses to Decline in Firms, Organizations, and States.* Cambridge, Mass.: Harvard University Press, 1970.

Higham, John. *Strangers in the Land: Patterns of American Nativism, 1860–1925.* New Brunswick: Rutgers University Press, 1963.

Hochschild, Jennifer. *Facing Up to the American Dream: Race, Class, and the Soul of the Nation.* Princeton: Princeton University Press, 1995.

Holder, Calvin. "The Rise of the West Indian Politician in New York City." *Afro-Americans in New York Life and History* 4 (1980).

Ignatiev, Noel. *How the Irish Became White.* London: Verso, 1995.

James, Winston. *Holding Aloft of Ethiopia: Caribbean Radicalism in Early Twentieth-Century America.* London: Verso, 1998.

James, Winston, and Clive Harris, eds. *Inside Babylon: The Caribbean Diaspora in Britain*. London: Verso, 1993.

Jaynes, Gerald, and Robin Williams. *A Common Destiny: Blacks and American Society*. Washington, D.C.: National Academy Press, 1989.

Jones-Correa, Michael. *Between Two Nations: The Political Predicament of Latinos in New York City*. Ithaca: Cornell University Press, 1998.

Jones-Correa, Michael, and David L. Leal. "Becoming 'Hispanic': Secondary Panethnic Identification among Latin American–Origin Populations in the United States." *Hispanic Journal of Behavioral Sciences* 18 (1996): 214–254.

Kalmijn, Matthijs. "The Socioeconomic Assimilation of Caribbean American Blacks." *Social Forces* 74 (1996): 911–930.

Kasinitz, Philip. *Caribbean New York: Black Immigrants and the Politics of Race*. Ithaca: Cornell University Press, 1992.

Langberg, Mark, and Reynolds Farley. "Residential Segregation and Asian Americans in 1980." *Sociology and Social Research* 69 (1980): 51–61.

Lewinson, Edwin. *Black Politics in New York City*. New York: Twayne, 1974.

Lieberson, Stanley. *A Piece of the Pie: Blacks and White Immigrants since 1880*. Berkeley: University of California Press, 1980.

Lieberson, Stanley, and Mary Waters. *From Many Strands: Ethnic and Racial Groups in Contemporary America*. New York: Russell Sage, 1988.

Macchiarola, Frank, and Joseph Diaz. "Minority Political Empowerment in New York City: Beyond the Voting Rights Act." *Political Science Quarterly* 108 (1993): 37–57.

Massey, Douglass. "The Social Organization of Mexican Migration to the United States." *Annals of the American Academy of Political and Social Science* 487 (1986): 102–113.

Massey, Douglass, and Nancy Denton. "Racial Identity among Caribbean Hispanics: The Effect of Double Minority Status on Residential Segregation." *American Sociological Review* 54 (October 1989): 790–808.

———. *American Apartheid: Segregation and the Making of the Underclass*. Cambridge, Mass.: Harvard University Press, 1993.

McAdam, Doug. *Political Process and the Development of Black Insurgency, 1930–1970*. Chicago: University of Chicago Press, 1982.

McNickle, Chris. *To Be Mayor of New York City: Ethnic Politics in the City*. New York: Columbia University Press, 1993, 277–292.

Mills, Charles. *The Racial Contract*. Ithaca: Cornell University Press, 1997.

———. *Blackness Visible*. Ithaca: Cornell University Press, 1998.

Model, Suzanne. "Caribbean Immigrants: A Black Success Story?" *International Migration Review* 25 (1991): 248–276.

Mollenkopf, John H. "The Postindustrial Transformation of the Political Order in New York City," in *Power, Culture, and Place*, ed. John H. Mollenkopf. New York: Russell Sage Foundation, 1988.

————. *A Phoenix in the Ashes: The Rise and Fall of the Koch Coalition in New York City Politics.* Princeton: Princeton University Press, 1992, 81–87.

Mollenkopf, John, Timothy Ross, and David Olson. "Immigrant Political Participation in New York and Los Angeles." Paper prepared for the Project on Negotiating Difference, International Center for Migration, Ethnicity, and Citizenship, New School University, 27 May 1999.

Morgan, Thomas. "Caribbean Verve Brightens New York." *New York Times,* 3 June 1988, B1, B5.

Ogbu, John. "Cultural Model, Identity, and Literacy," in *Cultural Psychological: Essays on Comparative Human Development,* eds. James W. Stigler, Richard A. Schweder, and Gilbert Herdt. New York: Cambridge University Press, 1990a.

————. "Minority Status and Literacy in Comparative Perspective." *Daedalus* 119 (1990b): 141–148.

Omi, Michael, and Howard Winant. *Racial Formation in the United States: From the 1960s to the 1980s.* New York: Routledge & Kegan Paul, 1986.

Parenti, Michael. "Ethnic Politics and the Persistence of Ethnic Political Identification." *American Political Science Review* 61 (September 1967): 717–726.

Park, Robert. *Race and Culture.* Glencoe: Free Press, 1950.

Passel, Jeffery S., and Barry Edmonston. "Immigration and Race: Recent Trends in Immigration to the United States," in *Immigration and Ethnicity: The Integration of America's Newest Arrivals,* eds. Jeffrey S. Passel and Barry Edmonston. Washington, D.C.: Urban Institute Press, 1994.

Patterson, Orlando. "Toward a Future That Has No Past—Reflections on the Fate of Blacks in the Americas." *Public Interest* 27 (1972): 25–62.

————. "The Emerging West Atlantic System: Migration, Culture, and Underdevelopment in the United States and the Circum-Caribbean Region," in *Population in an Interacting World,* ed. William Alonso. Cambridge, Mass.: Harvard University Press, 1987.

Peterson, Paul. *City Limits.* Chicago: University of Chicago Press, 1981.

Pinderhughes, Dianne. *Race and Ethnicity in Chicago Politics: A Reexamination of Pluralist Theory.* Urbana: University of Illinois Press, 1987.

Piore, Michael. *Birds of Passage.* New York: Cambridge University Press, 1979.

Portes, Alejandro, ed. *The New Second Generation.* New York: Russell Sage, 1996.

Portes, Alejandro, and Ramon Grosfoguel. "Caribbean Diasporas: Migration and Ethnic Communities." *Annals of the American Academy of Political and Social Science* 536 (1994): 48–69.

Portes Alejandro, and Ruben Rumbaut. *Immigrant America: A Portrait* Berkeley: University of California Press, 1996.

Portes, Alejandro, and Alex Stepick. *City on the Edge: The Transformation of Miami.* Berkeley: University of California Press, 1993.

Reed, Adolph. "Black Urban Regime: Structural Origins and Constraints." *Comparative Urban and Community Research* 1 (1988): 138–189.

Reid, Ira. *The Negro Immigrant: His Background, Characteristics, and Social Adjustments, 1899–1937.* New York: AMS Press, 1939.

Rodríguez, Clara E., and Hector Cordero-Guzman. "Placing Race in Context." *Ethnic and Racial Studies* 15 (October 1992): 523–542.

Roediger, David. *The Wages of Whiteness: Race and the Making of the American Working Class.* London: Verso, 1991.

Rogers, Reuel. "Black Like Who? Afro-Caribbean Immigrants, African Americans, and the Politics of Group Identity," in *West Indian Migration to New York: Historical Contemporary and Transnational Perspectives,* ed. Nancy Foner. Berkeley: University of California Press, forthcoming.

Rosenstone, Steven, and John Mark Hansen. *Mobilization, Participation, and Democracy.* New York: Macmillan, 1993).

Shefter, Martin. "Political Incorporation and Extrusion of the Left: Party Politics and Social Forces in New York City." *Studies in American Political Development* 1 (1986): 50–90.

Simpson, Andrea. *The Tie That Binds: Identity and Political Attitudes in the Post–Civil Rights Generation.* New York: New York University Press, 1998.

Skerry, Peter. *Mexican Americans: The Ambivalent Minority.* Cambridge, Mass.: Harvard University Press, 1993.

Sleeper, Jim. "The End of the Rainbow? America's Changing Urban Politics." *New Republic,* 1 November 1993, 23.

Smith, Michael Peter. *City, State, and Market: The Political Economy of Urban America.* New York: Oxford University Press, 1984.

Smith, Rogers M. *Civic Ideals: Conflicting Visions of Citizenship in U.S. History.* New Haven: Yale University Press, 1997.

Sonenshein, Raphael. "Post-Incorporation Politics in Los Angeles," in *Racial Politics in American Cities,* eds. Rufus P. Browning, Dale Rogers Marshall, and David H. Tabb. New York: Longman, 1997.

Sowell, Thomas. "Three Black Histories," in *Essays and Data on American Ethnic Groups,* ed. Thomas Sowell. Washington, D.C.: Urban Institute, 1978.

Steinberg, Stephen. *The Ethnic Myth: Race, Ethnicity, and Class in America.* Boston: Beacon Press, 1981.

Takaki, Ronald. "Reflection on Racial Patterns in America: An Historical Perspective," in *Ethnicity and Public Policy,* vol. 1, eds. Winston Van Horne and Thomas V. Tonnesen. Madison: University of Wisconsin System, 1982.

———. *Strangers from a Different Shore: A History of Asian Americans.* Boston: Little Brown, 1989.

Tate, Katherine. *From Protest to Politics: The New Black Voters in American Elections.* Cambridge, Mass.: Harvard University Press, 1994.

Toney, Joyce Roberta. "The Development of a Culture of Migration among a

Caribbean People: St. Vincent and New York, 1838–1979." Unpublished Ph.D. dissertation, Columbia University, 1986.

Uhlaner, Carol J. "Perceived Discrimination and Prejudice and the Coalition Prospects of Blacks, Latinos, and Asian Americans," in *Racial and Ethnic Politics in California*, eds. Bryan O. Jackson and Michael B. Preston. Berkeley: IGS Press, 1991.

Verba, Sidney, and Norman H. Nie, *Participation in America: Political Democracy and Social Equality*. New York: Harper & Row, 1972.

Vickerman, Milton. "The Responses of West Indians to African-Americans: Distancing and Identification," in *Research in Race and Ethnic Relations* 7 (1994): 80–128.

———. *Crosscurrents: West Indian Immigrants and Race*. New York: Oxford University Press, 1999.

Waldinger, Roger. "Race and Ethnicity," in *Setting Municipal Priorities, 1990,* eds. Charles Brecher and Raymond D. Horton. New York: New York University Press, 1989.

Waters, Mary C. *Ethnic Options: Choosing Identities in America*. Berkeley: University of California Press, 1990.

———. "Ethnic and Racial Identities of Second-Generation Black Immigrants in New York City," in *The New Second Generation*. New York: Russell Sage, 1996.

———. *Black Identities: West Indian Immigrant Dreams and American Realities*. Cambridge, Mass.: Harvard University Press, 2000.

Watkins-Owens, Irma. *Blood Relations: Caribbean Immigrants and the Harlem Community, 1900–1930*. Bloomington: Indiana University Press, 1996.

Woldemikael, Tekle. *Becoming Black American: Haitians and American Institutions in Evanston, Illinois*. New York: AMS Press, 1989.

Wolfinger, Raymond. "The Development and Persistence of Ethnic Voting." *American Political Science Review* 59 (December 1965): 896–908.

———. *The Politics of Progress*. Englewood Cliffs, N.J.: Prentice-Hall, 1974.

Chapter 2

Racial Polarization, Reaction to Urban Conditions, and the Approval of Black Mayors

Susan Howell

The election of black mayors has generated both elation and conflict among scholars of black politics. On the one hand, a black mayor serves as a symbol that many of the barriers to electoral participation have been dismantled, and that Blacks—often with the help of other racial minorities and Whites—have been able to elect a candidate of their choosing to political office. The thinking was that, once in office, black elected officials would be able to utilize the mechanisms of government to positive effect for Blacks and other supportive constituents. Yet, it is on this point that many scholars of black politics disagree.

The optimists, for example, argue that black mayors have performed admirably under difficult circumstances. Black mayors, they contend, have increased black and overall minority representation in municipal institutions, utilized progressive economic policies to offer an efficient integration of Blacks and other minorities into previously impenetrable social and economic institutions, bestowed economic resources on schools, and weakened the stronghold of police brutality.

Less optimistic scholars, however, have maintained that the black mayoral office is little more than a hollow prize. They point to the limited gains that cities controlled by black mayors have achieved in the areas of employment, public housing, crime control, education, and community stability. These scholars also stress the impotence of business-oriented strategies, by which mayors pro-

mote a trickle-down version of economic growth, which ultimately serves more to increase corporate profits than to improve the lot of their constituents, most of whom happen to be Blacks. Others have stressed the problems of deracialization and the extent to which the efforts of black mayors to minimize racial themes have also weakened the effectiveness of their offices.

A largely overlooked question is how black mayors are evaluated by white and black citizens. Using a performance model of approval typically enlisted for the evaluation of presidents and governors, Susan Howell demonstrates the extent to which race influences the evaluation of urban conditions and, most important, the mayor. In doing so, she provides a starting point for our understanding of the myriad ways in which black mayors are judged, not only by Whites and Blacks but by other racial minorities as well.

Introduction

Over the past twenty years there has been dramatic growth in the number of African American mayors. Research has documented the positive effects of electing a minority mayor on the attitudes and participation of minority citizens (Bobo and Gilliam, 1990; Howell and Fagan, 1988; Abney and Hutcheson, 1981), as well as the racially polarized voting that results in the election of many of these black mayors (Browning and Marshall, 1986; Browning et al., 1984; Huckfeldt and Kohfeld, 1989; Kleppner, 1985; Vanderdeeuw, 1990; Engstrom and Kirkland, 1995). Other changes have also accompanied the election of minority mayors in many cities: crime and drug epidemics, dwindling urban economic opportunities, accelerated middle-class flight, and a general decline in the quality of life. Recently, some cities have been successful in reversing the crime trend by using innovative policing methods or increasing the police presence, and some cities' economic climates have improved, in keeping with the national economic upturn. Regardless of the direction of the change, these urban environments present an interesting opportunity to examine the cognitive responses of both black and white citizens, the new majority and the new minority, to the quality of life in their cities, and the consequences of these responses for black mayors.

In this research we propose a performance model of approval for black mayors and hypothesize that race plays a pivotal role by both directly influencing performance evaluations and approval of mayors, and by conditioning the relationship between the two, that is, the relationships within the model operate differently for Blacks and for Whites. Cognitive theory stipulates that people develop their perceptual viewpoints over a lifetime of experiences (Fiske and Linville, 1980; Axelrod, 1973) and that groups with different relevant "life experiences" can and do perceive the same event differently. There is ample evidence that black and white Americans constitute distinctive subcultures within the American public, in terms of both political opinions (Milburn, 1991: 28–29; Erikson and Tedin, 1995: 188–195; Kinder and Sanders, 1996) and participation (Rosenstone and Hansen, 1993: Ch. 3); therefore, it is reasonable to expect that urban Blacks and Whites will have different reactions to the urban changes I have described.

The research has theoretical and practical implications. Most of the large body of literature on presidential approval is based on a performance model that emphasizes citizen evaluations of conditions in the country, most notably economic conditions (Hibbs, 1982; Kernell, 1978; MacKuen, 1983; Ostrom and Simon, 1985; MacKuen et al., 1989). This model has also been successfully applied to governors of states (Neimi et al., 1995; Howell and Vanderdeeuw, 1990). However, all of the presidents and governors have been White (with the exception of Governor Wilder of Virginia); thus, they have not been subjected to the intense racial polarization that faces many black local elected officials. The performance model may well operate differently under conditions where two groups of citizens react differently to their evaluations of conditions in the city and where other considerations may overpower performance evaluations in judging the elected official.

The race-driven and race-conditioned performance model for black mayors has practical implications. If approval of the mayor and the criteria for judging the mayor differ from one racial group to another, it diminishes the ability of the mayor to forge a truly biracial coalition for governing. Perry (1990) has described the difficulties black officials face when attempting to "deracialize" their campaigns, and differing criteria for perceived success can only exacerbate those difficulties. Second, determinants of white approval of a black mayor have implications for urban revival. If white voters are more eager than black voters to hold the mayor accountable for urban decline, it will make governing even more difficult than it already is in many of these cities (see Reed, 1988; Barnes, 1994; Preston, 1990; and Nelson, 1990 for problems facing black mayors).

A Model of Mayoral Appeal

The model of mayoral approval to be tested is fundamentally a performance model and is presented in Figure 2.1. The exogenous variables are citizen evaluations of seven specific city services, all of which have the potential to influence general evaluations of quality of life in the city. Perceptions of the quality of life and a general assessment of government services, in turn, are the intervening variables that connect the specific evaluations to approval of the mayor. The two-stage nature of the model represents a more complete elaboration than is found in most models of presidential or gubernatorial approval. In the national or state models, researchers have tended to use general perceptual measures alone (Neimi et al., 1995), leaving unanswered questions about the relationship between specific conditions and general perceptions. In cities with minority mayors, race may have an impact on general perceptions of the quality of life that is independent of any specific conditions. Nonetheless, this model represents a fairly simple performance model when applied to local executives.

The Inoculation Hypothesis

Researchers who have studied cities with minority mayors have consistently found positive attitudinal and behavioral effects on the cities' black citizens, including higher trust in local government (Abney and Hutcheson, 1981; Howell and Fagan, 1988) and higher levels of political knowledge, efficacy, and participation (Bobo and Gilliam, 1990). Furthermore, the more positive citizen orientations have been linked empirically to approval of the black mayor (Howell and Fagan, 1988). These studies, in combination with the research on the racial polarization cited earlier, form the justification for the *Inoculation Hypothesis,* the expectation that, *in the presence of a black mayor, all relationships in the performance model are weaker for black citizens than for white citizens.* That is, because of the high level of black citizen identification with the minority mayor, he is somewhat "inoculated" from the effects of negative conditions in the city. The Inoculation Hypothesis predicts, in the first stage of the model, that Blacks' general perceptions of conditions in the city will not be as sensitive to specific conditions as are Whites' general perceptions and, in the second stage of the model, that mayoral approval is not as responsive to general perceptions of the quality of life in the city. That is not to say that black urban residents will approve of a black mayor regardless of performance; there is already evidence to the contrary (Howell and Marshall, 1998). Rather, the Inoculation Hypothesis predicts that relationships in the model will be weaker for black citizens than for white citizens.

The Racial Polarization Hypothesis

Race-based voting in biracial mayoral contests lends support to a *Racial Polarization Hypothesis* about white support for black mayors. Stated simply, *citizens' perceptions of conditions in the city and their approval of the black mayor are partly a function of their race.* As a result of traditional racial stereotypes, Whites perceptions of conditions in the city are likely to worsen, regardless of the actual conditions, as the percentage of minority residents in the city increases. A Racial Polarization Hypothesis is also supported by experimental research on white voters' perceptions of black candidates. Colleau et al. (1990) and Williams (1990) found that white voters attributed different traits to white candidates and to black candidates. White candidates were perceived as more likely to possess certain positive traits, such as intelligence, competence, strength, fairness, and experience. There is reason to suspect that these perceptions apply to public officials as well as to candidates.

The Racial Polarization Hypothesis makes the following predictions: (1) individuals' race will have a significant effect on their perceptions of the general quality of life in the city and on their evaluations of government services, and this effect will occur independent of individuals' perceptions of any specific conditions in the city, and (2) race will have a direct impact on citizens' approval of a black mayor, independent of the citizens' perceptions regarding the quality of life, and the quality of general government services or any specific services. In sum, with the two hypotheses, we expect race to have both additive and interactive effects in a model of black mayoral approval.

Data and Measures

The model of black mayoral approval is best tested using longitudinal data in order to observe greater variation in conditions in the city. This approach requires the researcher to measure residents' perceptions of the quality of life and their evaluations of specific services and services in general and to determine the mayor's approval ratings over time in the same city. Fortunately, such data are available from three public opinion surveys of the New Orleans electorate, the earliest of which was taken in 1994 and the most recent in 1997 (see Appendix A). During that time, perceptions of conditions in the city and evaluations of certain city services varied considerably, as will be seen shortly.

The City of New Orleans is a majority minority city; 63 percent of registered voters are black. It has a mayor/council form of government, with five district council seats and two at-large seats. The city has had three black mayors since 1978, and during the years of this study five of the seven city council members were black. Like many urban areas, New Orleans experienced a sharp increase in crime during the late 1980s and early 1990s, the trend climaxed in 1994 when the city had the highest murder rate in the nation. Thus, the first year covered in this study was understandably a year of great dissatisfaction with conditions in the city.

All three public opinion surveys measured citizens' general perceptions of the quality of life and government services in the city and sought their specific evaluations of police, crime control, traffic, parks, street conditions, public safety, and transportation and their opinions of the mayor. The general Quality-of-Life Scale is composed of three items: a retrospective evaluation of whether life in the city has become better or worse, a future-oriented evaluation of whether city life is expected to become better or worse, and the respondents' overall satisfaction with life in the city. The scale possesses a reliability estimate (Cronbach's Alpha) of .585 and ranges from one to seven, with one representing the least favorable perception of the quality of life and seven the most positive perception. Government services are measured by a single indicator that asks the respondents to rate "government services in general" as excellent, good, fair, or poor. Five of the specific services (police, traffic, street conditions, parks, and public transportation) were also measured by the same excellent-to-poor rating. Perception of crime is measured by a single indicator: whether crime has increased, decreased, or remained the same over the past few years. Safety is measured by an additive index containing two items: how safe respondents feel around their homes at night and how safe they feel around home during the day (reliability = .860). (See Appendix B for the exact wording of the questions.) The survey results were pooled, creating a composite file with 569 (39 percent) white respondents and 892 (61 percent) black respondents.

Racial Polarization and Perceptions of Conditions in the City

Before I present the multivariate analysis, a short description of racial polarization in perceptions of conditions in the city is in order. Figures 2.2 through 2.8 present black and white perceptions of the specific services covered in the model; it is apparent that *racial polarization does not consistently characterize any of these seven evaluations.* Both Blacks and Whites are fairly negative about services in their city, with the exception of public transportation. Police activity, traffic conditions, and street conditions are seen as particularly inadequate, although ratings of the police and of street conditions show some improvement in the most recent survey; substantial minorities of respondents of both races do not feel safe around their homes at night. In one instance of racial polarization, white citizens are more positive about the parks in the first two years of the survey, but that difference disappears in the third survey. The other two instances of racial polarization were higher white evaluation of public transportation in the first year (possibly because Whites do not use public transportation) and lower white evaluation of street conditions in the third year.

Blacks and Whites are in remarkable agreement about whether crime is increasing or decreasing (Figure 2.8). At the beginning of the mayor's term, there was virtually unanimous agreement that crime was increasing in the city, but, as actual crime rates decreased, both racial groups recognized that reality, and the percentage perceiving an increase in crime dropped precipitously.

Turning to the intervening variables in the model, again there is very little evidence of consistent racial polarization over the three years (Figures 2.9 and 2.10). Both Blacks and Whites have negative evaluations of the general level of government services, and both races become increasingly positive about the general quality of life in the city over time.[1] These descriptive results suggest that the Racial Polarization Hypothesis may not be valid for the first stage of the model.

However, racial polarization is quite evident in the approval ratings of the mayor; *in all three years there is more than a 30 percent gap between Blacks' and Whites' approval ratings of the mayor* (Figure 2.11). This pattern stands in sharp contrast to the insignificant black/white differences on the specific and general evaluations of conditions of the city, suggesting that the factors that influence constituents' judgements on the mayor are more complex than the performance model would suggest.

Specific Services and General Evaluations

The first stage of the model, illustrated in Figure 2.1, involves an estimate of the effects of evaluations of specific services on citizens' overall perceptions of the quality of life and government services in the city, and the role of race in that relationship. Table 2.1 presents three models of the general quality of life and two models of the quality of government services. The first model includes only the specific services as explanatory factors, the second model adds race, and the third model adds any statistically significant interaction terms with race.

Three conclusions emerge from the results in Table 2.1. First, the specific services do a respectable job of predicting assessments of the quality of life and the general quality of government services, with explained variances of .299 and .291. However, quality of life in general and government services are influenced by slightly different sets of specific government services. General quality of life is more closely associated with crime, police, public safety, and street conditions, while views of general government services are affected by citizens' evaluations of parks, traffic, and public transportation, as well as by their opinions on crime, police, and street conditions. It makes intuitive sense that citizens' evaluations of the general quality of life would be heavily influenced by the crime and the safety dimensions, since these are among the most pressing problems facing urban areas today. On the other hand, when asked about government services, respondents might also think of concrete things that the city is expected to provide, such as attractive parks and public transportation.

The second conclusion to be drawn from Table 2.1 is that race does have an independent effect on both of the general evaluations but that the effect does not eliminate the explanatory power of citizens' views on specific services. Nor does race overwhelm the specific services in terms of explanatory power; the general assessments are still more a function of views of specific services than they are a function of race. The third conclusion one can draw from Table 2.1 is that, in all but one instance, race does not condition the relationships between the specific services and the general evaluations. That is, the relationships between these constructs are similar for Blacks and for Whites. The one exception, and it is an important one, is the evaluation of crime. The sign of the statistically significant interaction term indicates that evaluations of crime have a greater impact on Whites' evaluations of the quality of life than on Blacks'. The direction is consistent with the hypothesis, but the lack of other significant interactions (thirteen others were insignificant) leads us to reject race as an important conditioning variable in predicting general evaluations.

In sum, these urban citizens seem to be using a "rational" utility in coming to their general evaluations about conditions in the city. They are influenced primarily by specific services and conditions that they observe or read about. Race also has independent effects on the general evaluations, but it does not add much explanatory power to the models. Thus, the Racial Polarization Hypothesis receives only weak support, while the Inoculation Hypothesis receives virtually no support.

General Evaluations and Mayoral Approval

The estimates of the second stage of the model are presented in Table 2.2, and it is clear that race plays a larger role when the mayor himself is involved. The first model includes the two general evaluations, a few demographics, and two dummy variables for year. These variables explain 21.8 percent of the variation in mayoral approval. As predicted by the model, the two general evaluations have significant effects, as do all of the demographic and year variables. Younger people, those less educated, and males are more likely to approve of the mayor. The year dummies reflect changes in mayoral support resulting from events specific to that year and not captured by the other explanatory variables.

Adding race to the model of mayoral approval increases its explanatory power by 9 percent (from 21.8 percent to 30.9 percent). Reflecting the racial polarization we saw earlier in the table, race is the best predictor of whether a citizen approves of the mayor when general evaluations of the quality of life and government services are controlled for; thus, the Racial Polarization Hypothesis is confirmed. The magnitude of the coefficient (.64) is twice as large as its magnitude in the Quality-of-Life model (.34); the significance of the difference is even greater when one considers that the mayoral approval scale has only four points, while the quality of life scale has seven points.

The Inoculation Hypothesis is also confirmed in the model of mayoral approval (Models 3 and 4). The signs and significance of the interaction terms indicate that both quality-of-life assessments and evaluations of government services have more impact on Whites' judgements about the mayor than they do on Blacks' judgements. This is consistent with the prediction that black voters, because of their racial identification, are more likely to approve of the mayor regardless of their evaluations of general and specific city conditions. Furthermore, specific judgements of the incidence of crime have a direct effect on mayoral approval ratings over and above the general evaluations, attesting to the centrality of this issue in urban life.

To test the robustness of these findings over time, Model 4 was estimated for each of the three years (Table 2.3). The Racial Polarization Hypothesis is strongly confirmed; in all three years, race is the most influential predictor of approval of the mayor. The Inoculation Hypothesis is also confirmed for all three years, albeit through different constructs. Of the six conditional effects tested, four are significant and in the direction that indicates their greater impact on white voters. General quality of life is influential in all three years, and evaluation of government services is significant in two of the three years. We suspect that government services lacked impact in 1994 because the mayor had just been elected and was thus not held responsible for government services. In sum, the findings of the pooled surveys are not a function of a single year.

Discussion

Performance models have been the norm in research on approval of elected executives, particularly presidents and governors. It seems reasonable to generalize this model to the local level, especially since performance, or lack of performance, is quite easily observed firsthand. However, in the case of minority mayors, the performance model may not operate in so straightforward a manner.

In our analysis of citizens' evaluations of three years of the administration of a minority mayor in a major southern city, we found that Whites and Blacks were in general agreement about conditions and services in the city. Both racial groups noticed the drop in crime, improvements in police work, and improvements in the parks, and both groups translated these specific observations into general evaluations of the quality of life and government services. However, while in multivariate models that predict general quality of life and government services race has an impact independent of respondents' evaluations of specific services, we found the impact of race to be considerably less than the impact of specific services. That is, while Blacks had a more positive view of the general quality of life and government services, racial polarization was a minor factor in predicting general evaluations of conditions in the city.

However, when the model was used to predict approval ratings for the minority mayor himself, racial polarization was quite evident. Race is the single most powerful predictor of mayoral approval, even though the general performance evaluations were also quite influential. Race did not detract from the performance model, it simply added its own predictive power. We had hypothesized that the performance model would be more predictive for white voters than for black voters (the Inoculation Hypothesis), and this was indeed the case in the model of mayoral approval. Both general performance evaluations had more impact among Whites than among Blacks, although the differences were not great. This is probably a result of the high level of popularity of the mayor among minority voters, some of which was not directly related to minority voters' evaluations of the mayor's performance.

Black mayors already face formidable obstacles in governing, given the conditions in many majority minority cities. These difficulties are complicated by racial polarization in the electorate, which can overwhelm performance considerations when citizens are evaluating the mayor. Among the black electorate, a sense of identification with the minority mayor can provide the mayor with some protection against negative performance evaluations, but among the white electorate the mayor may begin with a deficit of support that is difficult to overcome, regardless of his performance in office. Since this study was conducted in a city that has had minority mayors for twenty years, we suspect that this pattern is not likely to change in the near future.

A similar phenomenon may occur as other urban areas experience growing populations of Hispanics and elect Hispanic mayors. The displaced former Anglo majority may not adjust well to its new minority status and the Hispanic/Anglo distinction may then become a powerful predictor of mayoral approval ratings, regardless of the mayor's performance. This model needs to be tested in other settings with other ethnic combinations.

Appendix A: *The Surveys*

The two Quality-of-Life surveys and the Early Look at the Mayor's Race survey were conducted by the Survey Research Center at the University of New Orleans. All surveys included only registered voters and were stratified by race to ensure exact representation on that variable. Samples, drawn by Survey Sampling of Fairfield, Connecticut, were a random-digit dialing procedure to which the SRC applied a screen for registered voters. Response rates in the surveys were 36 percent, 56 percent, and 50 percent. The low response rate in the 1994 Quality-of-Life Survey was a result of the use of a commercial phone bank. The final sample was weighted on gender and race to accurately represent the registered voters on those variables, but other consequences of the low response rate are unknown.

Interviewers for the other two surveys, which were also conducted in the early 1990s, were students at the University of New Orleans who were paid or worked as part of a course assignment. Students were trained in two sessions on interviewing techniques and the goals of the survey. They were required to practice mock interviews in the presence of a supervisor. The interviews were conducted from a central phone

TABLE 2.A1
Number of Respondents in Surveys Pooled for This Study

Year	Survey	Black (n)	White (n)	Total (n)
1994	Quality of Life	289	206	495
	Quality of Life	246	155	409
	Early Look at Mayor	357	208	565

bank with constant supervision by a graduate student in political science. The graduate supervisors were all trained in the field of political behavior and had prior experience with SRC surveys. Interviewers made three to four attempts on different nights to reach a registered voter before moving on to the next potential respondent. A second attempt was made to convert refusals. The final number of respondents for each survey is shown in Table 2.A1.

Appendix B: Question Wording

General Quality of Life

Now I'd like to ask you about a few issues facing the City. Thinking back over the past five years, would you say that Orleans Parish has become a better or worse place to live, or hasn't there been any change?

And thinking ahead over the next five years, do you think Orleans Parish will become a better or worse place to live, or won't there be much of a change?

How satisfied are you with life in Orleans Parish? Are you very satisfied, satisfied, dissatisfied, or very dissatisfied?

Mayor Approval

In general, do you approve or disapprove of the job Mayor XX is doing? (Pause) Is that strongly or not very strongly?

Strongly approve
Approve
Disapprove
Strongly disapprove
Don't know

Crime

Would you say that the amount of crime in New Orleans has increased, decreased, or remained about the same over the last several years?

Safety

How safe do you feel around your home during the day—very safe, safe, not very safe, or not safe at all?
How safe do you feel around your home during the night—very safe, safe, not very safe, or not at all safe?

Government Services, Police, Traffic, Streets, Parks, and Public Transportation

How would you rate the following aspects of government services in New Orleans: first, the overall level of government services—are they excellent, good, fair, or poor?

The quality of police protection
Conditions of the streets
Parks and recreation
Control of traffic congestion
Availability of public transportation

FIGURE 2.1
Model of Mayoral Approval

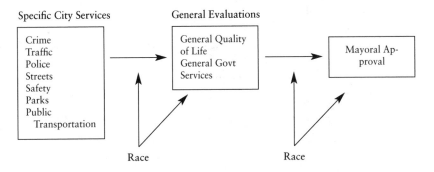

FIGURE 2.2
*Percentage of Respondents Who Perceive Parks
as Good or Excellent*

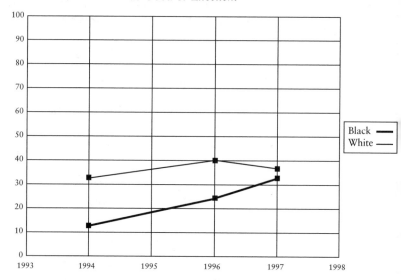

FIGURE 2.3
*Percentage of Respondents Who Perceive Public
Transportation as Good or Excellent*

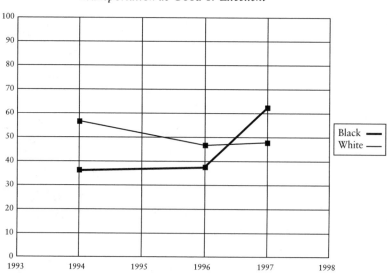

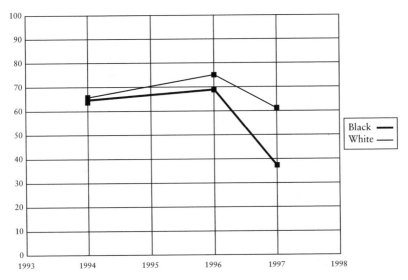

FIGURE 2.4
*Percentage of Respondents Who Perceive
Street Conditions as Poor*

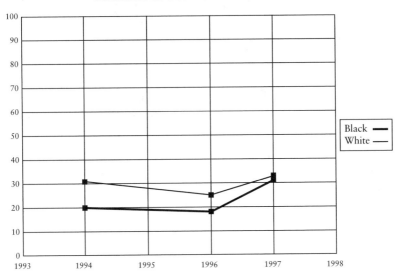

FIGURE 2.5
*Percentage of Respondents Who Perceive Traffic
Conditions as Good or Excellent*

FIGURE 2.6
*Percentage of Respondents Who Do Not Feel Safe
at Home at Night*

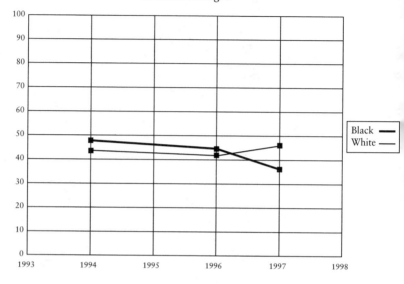

FIGURE 2.7
*Percentage of Respondents Who Perceive Quality of
Police Protection as Good or Excellent*

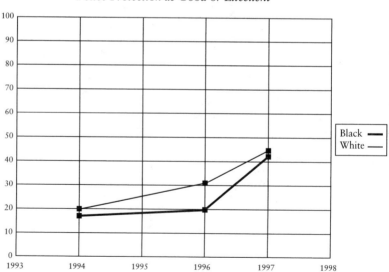

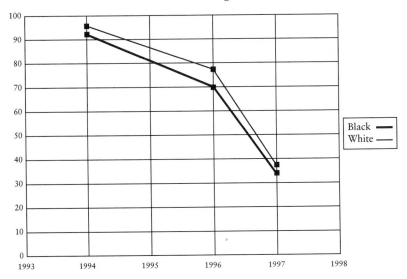

FIGURE 2.8
*Percentage of Respondents Who Perceive
Crime as Increasing*

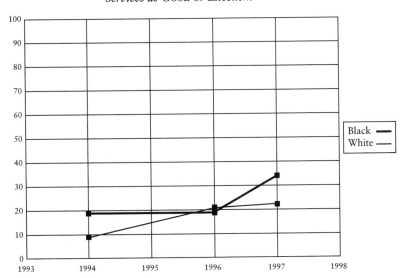

FIGURE 2.9
*Percentage of Respondents Who Perceive Government
Services as Good or Excellent*

FIGURE 2.10
*Percentage of Constituents Who Believe
Parish Has Become Worse Place
(Quality of Life)*

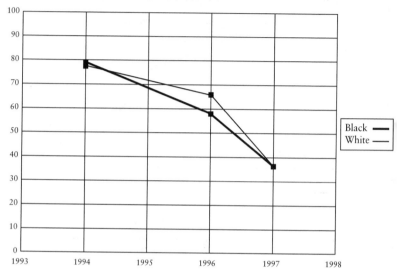

FIGURE 2.11
Percentage of Constituents Who Approve of Mayor

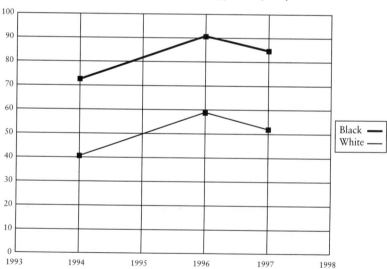

TABLE 2.1
Specific and General Conditions in the City
(Unstandardized Regression Coefficients)

	Quality of Life			Evaluation of City Services	
	Model 1	Model 2	Model 3	Model 1	Model 2
Specific Services:					
Crime	.36***	.35***	.63***	.04**	.03*
Traffic	.01	.01	.02	.09***	.10***
Police	.37***	.38***	.37***	.28***	.28***
Streets	.16**	.13*	.14*	.10***	.08**
Safety	.14***	.14***	.14***	−.01	−.01
Parks	.07	.09	.11*	.14***	.16***
Pubtrans	.03	.05	.66***	.07**	.08**
Race	—a	.34***	.66***	—	.19***
Race*Crime	—	—	−.17**	—	—
Y96	−.18	−.19	−.20	.01	−.00
Y97	−.29*	−.30*	−.33**	−.02	−.03
Age	.04	.08	.08	−.05*	−.03
Gender	.06	.07	.07	−.06	−.06
Education	−.14***	−.09*	−.09*	−.04*	−.01
N	1059	1059	1059	1160	1160
R^2	.299	.307	.311	.291	.303
Sig. of F	.000	.000	.000	.000	.000

a Variable not included in the model.
*P ≤ .05, **P ≤ .01, ***P ≤ .001

TABLE 2.2
General Evaluations and Approval of the Mayor
(Unstandardized Regression Coefficients)

Y = Mayoral Approval	Model 1	Model 2	Model 3	Model 4
Quality of Life	.18***	.16***	.31**	.31***
Govt. Services	.24***	.22***	.57**	.55***
Race	—a	.64***	1.39**	1.39***
Race*Qual. of Life	—	—	−.10**	−.11***
Race*Govt. Serv.	—	—	−.21**	−.20**
Crime	—	—	—	.06**
Y96	−.20**	−.17*	−.17*	−.19**
Y97	−.51***	−.47***	−.47*	−.57***
Age	−.09***	−.02	−.01	−.01
Education	−.14***	−.05	−.06	−.05*
Gender	−.21***	−.17***	−.16*	−.18***
N	1044	1044	1044	1034
R^2	.218	.309	.324	.330
Sig. of F	.000	.000	.000	.000

a Variable not included in the model.
*P ≤ .05, **P ≤ .01, ***P ≤ .001

TABLE 2.3
Model of Mayoral Approval by Year
(Unstandardized Regression Coefficients)

Y = Mayoral Approval	1994	1996	1997
Quality of Life	.44***	.39***	.27**
Government Services	.31	.61**	.82***
Race	1.11***	.69***	1.67***
Race*Qual. of Life	−.20**	−.16*	−.07
Race*Govt. Services	−.12	−.26[b]	−.31**
Crime	.01	.02	.06*
Y96	—[a]	—	—
Y97	—	—	—
Age	.01	−.05	.01
Education	.03	−.14**	−.01
Gender	.01	−.14	−.23**
N	259	320	455
R^2	.174	.334	.391
Sig. of F	.000	.000	.000

[a] Variable not included in the model.
[b] $p = .056$
*$p \leq .05$, **$p \leq .01$, ***$p \leq .001$

NOTE

1. The Quality-of-Life Scale is composed of three variables—direction of the city in the past five years, prospects for the next five years, and satisfaction with life in the city currently. Because scale scores are difficult to interpret in charts, we have presented one of the three variables, which generally tracks the other two.

REFERENCES

Abney, R. G., and J. Hutcheson Jr. 1981. "Race, Representation, and Trust: Changes in Attitudes after the Election of a Black Mayor." *Public Opinion Quarterly* 45: 91–101.

Alvarez, R. M., and J. Brehm. 1997. "Are Americans Ambivalent Toward Racial Policies?" *American Journal of Political Science* 41: 345–374.

Axelrod, R. 1973. "Schema Theory: An Information Processing Model of Perception and Cognition." *American Political Science Review* 67: 1248–1266.

Barnes C. 1994. "Atlanta's Post–Civil Rights Political Economy: Demobilization and Economic Dependency." Paper presented at the annual meeting of the SPSA, Atlanta, Georgia, November.

Bobo, L., and F. D. Gilliam, Jr. 1990. "Race, Sociopolitical Participation, and Black Empowerment." *American Political Science Review* 84: 377–393.

Browning, Rufus P., and Dale Rogers Marshall, eds. 1986. "Black and Hispanic Power in City Politics: A Forum." *Political Science* 19: 573–640.

Browning, Rufus P., Dale Rogers Marshall, and David H. Tabb. 1984. *Protest Is Not Enough.* Berkeley: University of California Press.

Carmines, Edward G., and Richard A. Zeller. 1979. *Reliability and Validity Assessment.* Beverly Hills: Sage.

Carsey, Thomas M. 1995."The Contextual Effects of Race on White Voter Behavior: The 1989 New York City Mayoral Election." *Journal of Politics* 57: 221–228.

Chubb, Jon. 1988. "Institutions, the Economy and the Dynamics of State Elections." *American Political Science Review* 82: 133–154.

Colleau S. M., K. Glynn, S. Lybrand, R. M. Merelman, P. Mohan, and J. E. Wall. 1990. "Symbolic Racism in Candidate Evaluation: An Experiment." *Political Behavior* 12: 385–402.

Engstrom, Richard L., and Willie Kirkland. 1995. "The 1994 New Orleans Mayoral Election: Racial Divisions Continue." *Urban News* 9: 6–9.

Erikson, R., and K. Tedin. 1995. *American Public Opinion: Its Origins, Content, and Impact.* 5th ed. Boston: Allyn and Bacon.

Fiske, S., and P. W. Linville. 1980. "What Does the Schema Concept Buy Us?" *Personality and Social Psychology Bulletin* 6: 543–557.

Giles, Michael W., and Melanie A. Buckner. 1993. "David Duke and Black Threat: An Old Hypothesis Revisited." *Journal of Politics* 55: 702–713.

Hibbs, Douglas A. 1982. "The Dynamics of Political Support for American Presidents among Occupational and Partisan Groups." *American Journal of Political Science* 26: 312–332.

Howell S. E., and D. Fagan. 1988. "Race and Trust in Government: Testing the Political Reality Model." *Public Opinion Quarterly* 52: 343–350.

Howell, S. E., and B. K. Marshall. 1998. "Crime and Trust in Local Government: Revisiting a Black Empowerment Area." *Urban Affairs Review* 33: 361–381.

Howell, S. E., and J. M. Vanderdeeuw. 1990. "Economic Effects on State Governors." *American Politics Quarterly* 18: 158–168.

Huckfeldt, Robert, and Carol Weitzel Kohfeld. 1989. *Race and the Decline of Class in American Politics.* Urbana: University of Illinois Press.

Kernell, Samuel. 1978. "Presidential Popularity." *American Political Science Review* 72: 506–522.

Kinder D., and L. Sanders. 1996. *Divided by Color: Racial Politics and Democratic Ideals.* Chicago: University of Chicago Press.

Kinder D. R., and D. O. Sears. 1981. "Prejudice and Politics: Symbolic Racism versus Racial Threats to the Good Life." *Journal of Personality and Social Psychology* 40: 414–431.

Kleppner, Paul. 1985. *Chicago Divided: The Making of a Black Mayor.* DeKalb: Northern Illinois University Press.

MacKuen, Michael. 1983. "Political Drama, Economic Conditions, and the Dynamics of Presidential Popularity." *American Journal of Political Science* 27: 165–192.

MacKuen, Michael, Robert Erikson and James A. Stimson. 1989. "Macropartisanship." *American Political Science Review* 83: 1125–1142.

McConahay J. B., and J. C. Hough. 1976. "Symbolic Racism." *Journal of Social Issues* 32: 23–45.

Meertens, R. W., and T. F. Pettigrew. 1997. "Is Subtle Prejudice Really Prejudice?" *Public Opinion Quarterly* 61: 54–71.

Milburn, M. 1991. *Persuasion and Politics: The Social Psychology of Public Opinion.* Pacific Grove, Calif.: Brooks/Cole.

Moore, J. 1988. "From Dreamers to Doers." *National Journal* 20: 372–377.

Neimi, Richard, Harold Stanley, and R. J. Vogel. 1995. "State Economies and State Taxes: Do Voters Hold Governors Accountable?" *American Journal of Political Science* 39: 936–957.

Nelson, W. 1990. Black Mayoral Leadership *National Political Science Review* 2: 188–195.

Ostrom, Charles, and Dennis Simon. 1985. "Promise and Performance: A Dynamic Model of Presidential Popularity." *American Political Science Review* 79: 334–358.

Perry, H. L. 1990. "The Relection of Sidney Barthelemy as Mayor of New Orleans." *PS: Political Science and Politics* 23: 56–157.

Preston, M., ed. 1990. "Symposium—Big-City Black Mayors: Have They Made a Difference?" *National Political Science Review* 2: 129–195.

Reed, A. 1988. "The Black Urban Regime: Structural Origins and Constraints." *Comparative Urban Research* 1: 139–189.

Rosenstone, S., and J. M. Hansen. 1993. *Mobilization, Participation, and Democracy in America.* New York: Macmillan.

Sears, D. O., and D. R. Kinder. 1971. "Racial Tensions and Voting in Los Angeles," *Los Angeles: Viability and Prospects for Metropolitan Leadership,* ed. W. Z. Hirsch. New York: Praeger.

Sears, D. O., C. Van Laar, M. Carrillo, and R. Kosterman. 1997. "Is It Really Racism? The Origins of White Americans Opposition to Race-Targeted Policies." *Public Opinion Quarterly* 61: 16–53.

Sonenshein, R. 1989. "Can Black Candidates Win Statewide Elections?" *Political Science Quarterly* 105: 219–241.

Stroh, Patrick K. 1995. "Voters as Pragmatic Cognitive Misers: The Accuracy-Effort Tradeoff in the Candidate Evaluation Process," in, *Political Judg-*

ment: Structure and Process, eds. Milton Lodge and Kathleen M. McGraw. Ann Arbor: University of Michigan Press.

Vanderdeeuw, James. 1990. "A City in Transition: The Impact of Changing Racial Composition on Voting Behavior." *Social Science Quarterly* 71: 326–328.

Williams, L. F. 1990. "White/Black Perceptions of the Electability of Black Political Candidates." *National Political Science Review* 2: 45–64.

Chapter 3

Interminority Relations in Urban Settings
Lessons from the Black–Puerto Rican Experience

José E. Cruz

Television images of conflict styled as Black versus Korean, Latino versus Korean, or Black versus Jewish often present the fallacious impression that interethnic conflict is a recent phenomenon in American history. Yet, as Ronald Takaki has shown, interethnic conflict is as old as the American Union. Before liberal migration policies facilitated the migration of racial minorities to American shores, interethnic conflict occurred primarily among Whites for reasons similar to those that explain current-day interethnic strife.

The most infamous examples of early interethnic conflict occurred between white Anglo-Saxon Protestants and the Irish. Almost every stereotype applied to black Americans was initially associated with the Irish, who were called lazy, idle, intellectually inferior, immoral, and incapable of keeping up their homes. In early urban America, the Irish and the English were in conflict over scarce resources, including housing, jobs, and political representation. With the arrival of Blacks in cities, however, the Irish emphasized their commonalities with the English (or British), especially where skin color was concerned. Subsequently, they made use of their limited status to exclude Blacks from trade unions and other economic opportunities.

Today, interethnic conflict revolves around similar issues of political representation, employment, housing, and geographical boundaries. Yet, the players are often poor racial minorities, since the vast majority of Whites and middle-class minorities have moved to the suburbs. Furthermore, today's urban residents are native Blacks, as well as immigrants from Africa, the Caribbean, Asia, and Latin America. How will these groups get along in multiethnic America? Relatedly, what factors promote conflict or cooperation among urban ethnic groups?

In addition to the foregoing queries, there is also limited information about how political elites from different ethnic and racial groups bargain and vie for political resources. Using the case study of Hartford, Connecticut, where Whites, Blacks, and Puerto Ricans predominate, José E. Cruz provides a descriptive assessment of interminority relations among political elites. With the emerging multicultural landscape of American urban society, the possibilities for ethnic and racial group cooperation and conflict are seemingly endless. Yet, the author demonstrates that the choices available to inner-city ethnic groups include not only cooperation or conflict but also the middle ground of indecision and ambiguity. Toward that end, Cruz offers a set of contextual and relational factors to account for various positions along the continuum of conflict and cooperation.

The reality of most settings where Blacks and Puerto Ricans concentrate is that neither group has the numbers to achieve, by itself, control of local governments or to tip the balance of power in its favor. The demographics of just a few places—large and small—illustrate the point well. In New York City, Puerto Ricans were 12 percent of the total population in 1990, compared to 29 percent for Blacks; in Chicago, the proportions were 4 and 39 percent, respectively. In Boston Puerto Ricans were close to 5 percent of the population; African Americans were 26 percent. In Paterson, New Jersey, where at 20 percent the proportion of the total city population that was Puerto Rican in 1990 was one of the highest in the Northeast, Puerto Ricans still cannot dispense with the support of other groups, especially African Americans, who account for 36 percent of the city's total population. The same is true of Hartford, Connecticut, the city that is the focus of this chapter, where Puerto Ricans represent 27 percent of the total residents and African Americans 39 percent.[1]

Table 3.1 provides a fuller picture of this urban reality. In Hartford, in Camden and in Paterson, New Jersey, African Americans and Puerto

TABLE 3.1
Puerto Rican and Black Concentrations in Selected Northeastern Cities, 1990

City and State	Total Pop.	Number of Puerto Ricans	% of Total	Number of Blacks	% of Total
Boston, MA	574,000	29,000	5	149,000	26
Bridgeport, CT	142,000	30,000	21	38,000	27
Camden, NJ	87,000	23,000	26	49,000	56
Chicago, IL	2,784,000	111,000	4	1,086,000	39
Hartford, CT	140,000	38,000	27	54,000	39
Lancaster, PA	56,000	11,000	19	7,000	12
Lawrence, MA	70,000	15,000	21	4,000	6
Newark, NJ	275,000	41,000	15	162,000	59
New Haven, CT	130,000	14,000	11	47,000	36
New York, NY	7,323,000	879,000	12	2,124,000	29
Passaic, NJ	58,000	12,000	20	12,000	21
Paterson, NJ	141,000	28,000	20	51,000	36
Philadelphia, PA	1,586,000	63,000	4	634,000	40
Springfield, MA	157,000	24,000	15	30,000	19
Waterbury, CT	109,000	12,000	11	14,000	13
Yonkers, NY	188,000	13,000	7	26,000	14

SOURCE: U.S. Department of Commerce, Bureau of the Census.

Ricans together constitute a majority of the population. Because of residential patterns or at-large electoral systems, they must work together to achieve political power in these cities. In Hartford, collaboration is particularly difficult because no coalition can be successful without the support of Whites. In places like Lancaster, Pennsylvania, or Lawrence, Massachusetts, the fact that Blacks and Puerto Ricans constitute close to one-third of the population is offset by the groups' low levels of registration and voting. In Bridgeport, Chicago, and New York, they are also weak within the electorate, despite their constituting almost half of the cities' residents. In many of these cities, Blacks and Puerto Ricans are either indifferent to each other or work at cross-purposes. But, whatever the specifics of each situation, in city after city the numbers suggest that, to achieve political power, minorities must work in collaboration while avoiding or minimizing conflict. The purpose of this essay is to shed some light on the specific aspects of interminority relations that prevent this from happening.

According to McClain and Karnig, cooperation or conflict among minorities will prevail depending on the result of "power contests which exist when there is rivalry and groups have roots in different cultures."[2] The problem with this view is that cooperation would require the absence of rivalry and/or the presence of cultural homogeneity, a prospect that is not realistic. Peter Eisinger, on the other hand, suggests that conflict results from "differences among groups regarding the goals to be won through politics."[3] This is true; yet, in conditions of relative scarcity or if groups disagree over strategy, similarity of goals is a poor remedy against rivalry. Eisinger's point that conflict cannot be understood outside the context in which it emerges is equally valid. However, given that he defines context in terms of the goals, behavior patterns, and integrative attitudes of elites, it is unclear whether the result would be a precise appraisal of the likelihood of conflict rather than a better understanding of the kind of elites that develop in particular contexts.

Thus, to better appreciate the process of interminority relations as opposed to the characteristics of groups or individual participants, it is necessary to know what specific pressures bear on political actors as they contemplate the prospect of collaboration. In other words, what are the specific barriers that political elites need to overcome in order to fashion purposive coalitions?

On the basis of secondary research, interviews, and participant observation, this essay describes some of the contextual and relational factors that shape the formation and maintenance of interminority coalitions, using the case of Blacks and Puerto Ricans as an example. Unlike other studies that examine the mobilization of voters across racial and ethnic lines,[4] my focus is on concrete, purposive relations between elites seeking access to governing bodies. This not only distinguishes this study from those oriented toward the electorate but also corrects for the failure of the literature to separate the elite and group levels in systematic fashion. Using black–Puerto Rican relations in Hartford as a springboard, I develop a set of hypotheses about interminority relations in urban settings, paying special attention to the conditions that hinder political alliances. As will be demonstrated, interminority relations in Hartford provide a negative example. As a result, they are suggestive of what political elites need to avoid in order to achieve successful coalition building.

The Research Context: Hartford, Connecticut

For most of its twentieth century history, Hartford, Connecticut has had a business-dominated political culture.[5] During the 1930s, the city became more liberal, in part as a consequence of New Deal policies. In this context, Republican preeminence was offset by the resurgence of the Democratic party. After the Second World War, when business forces regained momentum, the city adopted nonpartisan elections, establishing a nine-member city council elected at large. This decision, made on 3 December 1946, gave the council the power to select a deputy mayor from its ranks. This deputy mayor, along with a city manager, a treasurer, and a corporation counsel, effectively ran the city. The mayor became a figurehead, his power determined by personal attributes and by circumstances, and it is this condition that continues to prevail.

Economically, Hartford transformed from a manufacturing and insurance center to a postindustrial city. Between 1965 and 1975, manufacturing jobs went from 20 to 9 percent of the total nonagricultural employment in the city, while service jobs climbed from 19 to 23 percent. In 1980 service jobs were 24 percent of the total, compared to 32 percent by 1990. In contrast, the proportion for manufacturing jobs was 9 percent in 1980 but only 4.4 percent in 1990. Changes in the proportion of jobs in the financial, insurance, and real estate sectors were also significant during this period. Jobs in these sectors climbed from 24 percent of the total in 1965 to 31 percent in 1975. By 1990 their proportion had decreased to 28 percent, but this was offset by increases in the proportion of other service and public sector jobs.

The consequences of these shifts were manifold, but among the most significant was the decreasing capacity of city residents to get jobs in the city. Between 1960 and 1970 city jobs increased by 16 percent, while the number of such jobs held by Hartford residents decreased by a whopping 24 percent. Two decades later, the proportion of city jobs held by commuters was an amazing 78 percent.[6]

During the past three decades, social unrest has coincided with political change in the city. Partisan elections were restored in 1967, and in 1971 the Democrats took full advantage of this change. In that year, the party achieved control of the mayoralty and of the city council. Nearly two-thirds of the voters had been registering as Democrats since 1966, making Hartford a de facto one-party city way before the formal electoral takeover of 1971. In this context, interparty competition waned and intraparty divisions waxed. Electoral contests began to be fueled by race and ethnicity, making relations between Blacks and Puerto Ricans especially important. In 1981 Hartford elected its first African American mayor, and in 1991 the city council was controlled by a multiracial coalition. In this governing coalition, Puerto Ricans exerted considerable influence and held key positions.[7] By 1993 the alliance had broken apart, and its members were ousted from the mayoralty and from the city council by a group of conservative challengers.

Black–Puerto Rican Relations in Hartford

What is the pattern of black–Puerto Rican relations in Hartford? To answer this question, it is useful to first know what defines the context of black–Puerto Rican relations more generally. Even though extant analyses are mostly focused on New York City, the pattern that emerges from these studies provides a model against which other experiences can be compared. The literature suggests a set of features that include compartmentalization, racial ambivalence, resentment, paternalism, and a mix of cooperation and conflict between the two groups.

With minor exceptions, my research confirms the applicability to Hartford of this model. But the Hartford case speaks not just to the question of black–Puerto Rican relations. In addition, it sheds light on the question of coalitional behavior beyond the basic notion that cooperation and conflict coexist. In that sense, the black–Puerto Rican experience in the insurance city is useful in that it points to some of the contextual and relational factors that hinder purposive coalition-building processes among political elites.

Compartmentalization and Ambivalence

Historically, the context for black–Puerto Rican relations has not been hospitable to political collaboration. The immigration history of both groups is not only different from the experience of other immigrants but also differs from that of the other in significant ways.[8] These differences led many observers to wonder how Puerto Ricans would relate to other groups, while concluding in no uncertain terms that the paths of Puerto Rican and Black history would be distinct.[9] "By and large," wrote Carey McWilliams in 1964, "there has never been much, if any, solidarity between Caribbean Negroes and American Negroes."[10] In his view, the differences between the two groups in terms of history and attitudes toward each other suggested not only a spatially shared yet compartmentalized experience but also that the twin would never meet.

Residential segregation between these groups is high. The resulting social distance has been an objective obstacle to cooperation. The resulting boundaries, however, have been permeable. For example, when central city jobs are abundant, the level of black–Puerto Rican segregation tends to decline.[11] Like black-white segregation, Puerto Rican–white segregation is largely explained by race rather than class.[12] Yet African Americans and Puerto Ricans have experienced segregation in different ways.

Puerto Rican identity not only is bifurcated in terms of ancestry and place of birth but also lacks a racial center.[13] According to McWilliams, Puerto Ricans were not eager to be identified as Blacks "and the latter unfortunately share many of the prejudices of the white majority."[14] Writing about Puerto Ricans in New Haven during the 1970s, Lloyd Rogler identified a similar pattern concerning racial identity. The basic response of Puerto Ricans to discrimination was "to call themselves Spaniards—Hispanos—to avoid being labeled black."[15] Some have argued that the racial ambivalence of Puerto Ricans is not so much about color but about "the denial of personal identity and the receipt of discriminatory treatment."[16] Yet this issue continues to puzzle researchers. In fact, the relationship between racial self-identification and the state of intergroup relations is not straightforward.[17]

Even though the presence of Puerto Ricans in the insurance city can be dated to the 1940s, they became demographically significant as recently as 1970 (see Table 3.2). By 1990, Puerto Ricans made up almost one-third of the city's population (see Table 3.3). This demographic reality buttressed Puerto Ricans' claim to parity in political representation, but it did not translate into a low level of social distance from Blacks, nor did it automatically promote collaboration.

The political experience of Blacks in the city—which goes back more than a hundred years—has run parallel to that of Puerto Ricans. For example, black representation was achieved in 1955 at a time when Puerto Ricans had barely begun to settle in Hartford. The Spanish Action Coalition (SAC), a group established in 1967, tried to provide some cross-pollination of efforts among Puerto Ricans, Blacks, and other groups, but its presence was short-lived. By 1970 SAC had transformed into La Casa de Puerto Rico, an antipoverty agency controlled by Puerto Ricans.

TABLE 3.2
*Estimated Population Growth of Puerto Ricans
in Hartford, 1954–1970*

Year	U.S. Census	Local Estimate	% Change
1954	—	500	—
1956	—	2,000	300
1957	—	3,000	50
1958	—	4,500	50
1959	—	6,000	33
1961	—	7,000	17
1969–70	8,543	20,000	186

NOTE: Census figures before 1970 not available.
SOURCES: Culled by José E. Cruz from the *Hartford Courant* and the
Hartford Times (1958 only); U.S. Bureau of the Census.

TABLE 3.3
*Total, White, Puerto Rican, and African American Population
in Hartford, 1950–1990*

Year	Total	Number of Whites	% of Total	Number of Puerto Ricans	% of Total	Number of African Americans	% of Total
1950	177,397	164,743	93	*	*	12,774	7.2
1960	162,178	108,334	67	*	*	25,138	15.5
1970	158,017	105,383	67	8,543	5.4	44,091	27.9
1980	136,392	52,180	38	24,615	18.0	46,186	33.8
1990	139,739	55,869	40	38,176	27.3	54,338	38.8

*Census data not available.
NOTE: The figures for Whites and Puerto Ricans are not entirely reliable. The 1956 *County and City Data Book* distinguishes only "non-Whites" from the total. Puerto Ricans may be included in the "white" category. The 1962 edition disaggregates the total as "non-Whites" and "foreign-born." Puerto Ricans may be counted as either one. The 1970 figure is considerably lower than local estimates, as are subsequent figures. This table, however, illustrates well the dominant demographic trend since 1950.
SOURCES: U.S. Department of Commerce, Bureau of the Census, *County and City Data Book* 1956, 1962, 1977, 1983, 1994. Figures for Puerto Rican population for 1970 and 1980 from Hartford Capitol Region Council of Governments.

Most important, black–Puerto Rican residential segregation has been historically high in Hartford. In 1980, for example, the index of dissimilarity—the statistical measure that indicates the proportion of persons who would have to move from one area to another in order to achieve residential integration—for the two groups was .576. To be sure, the distance of Puerto Ricans from Whites was significantly higher (.832), but, compared to other metropolitan areas with similar Puerto Rican concentrations, Hartford stood at the apex of black–Puerto Rican measures of segregation. In Boston, the index was .543;

in Paterson, New Jersey, it was .464, and in nearby Bridgeport, it was only .461.[18]

Even during the time of radical politics, the compartmentalization of the black–Puerto Rican experience was significant. For example, the initial group of members of the People's Liberation Party (PLP), an organization of Puerto Rican youth created in 1969, was fascinated by the radical rhetoric and the flamboyant posturing of the Black Panthers. Like the Panthers, they donned berets and military garb, held marches and rallies to protest police brutality, and also provided community services such as free food and clothing, often seizing vacant buildings where they set up distribution and community information centers. Their rallying cry was "Power to the People!" and in their view only through education could the people be empowered.[19]

Yet the PLP never had any contact with Black Power organizations. The group started as a chapter of the Young Lords Party (YLP) after José Claudio, the PLP's seventeen-year-old chairman, was authorized to do so by Pablo "Yoruba" Guzmán, the YLP's Minister of Information in New York City.[20] The YLP connection, however, was severed rather quickly, and the stylistic emulation of the Panthers did not last long. PLP members developed the slogan "*se acabó el ay bendito*" [no more mister nice guy], which, although militant, was a far cry from the explicit references to armed struggle and militia-style self-defense typical of the Panthers. During the riots that took place in Hartford in 1969, PLP members asked city officials, "Is this what you want to see in Hartford?" Upon getting the predictable negative answer, they rejoined, "Give us a voice, a vote, representation, and Hartford will not follow in the footsteps of New York, Chicago, and LA."[21]

This integrationist stance did not match the approach of radical black groups such as the Black Caucus, in which some members used obscene language to urge Blacks to resort to violence.[22] In fact, most Puerto Rican radicals never even heard of the Black Caucus. According to Aida Claudio, a member of the local chapter of the Puerto Rican Socialist Party, Puerto Rican radicals "received a lot of support from the leftist movement within the white community. . . . [But] it was different with the African American community. . . . Although we might be fighting for the same goals, we didn't want to do it, mainly because the black community did not want to get involved with us."[23] Puerto Ricans did work with individual black radicals, but this was done under the umbrella of the white/ethnic left.[24]

Puerto Ricans in Hartford have not been ambivalent about their *ethnic* identity. This is true at both the elite and the community levels, despite class, gender, ideological, neighborhood-based, and generational divisions. According to Florencio Morales, a social worker, "The Hartford community must understand Puerto Ricans as Puerto Ricans. . . . Yes, we are Americans, but we don't look like Americans. Americans must look for what the Puerto Rican has to offer."[25]

Puerto Ricans knew that blackness was part of their experience, but they also understood that culturally they were not black. This was an important distinction, especially in the context of competition for political power. Thus, when in 1985 an African American councilman sought to replace a Puerto Rican incumbent with a black candidate of mixed ethnic background, the Puerto Rican leadership did not accept the implicit conflation of ancestry and identity. As Edwin Vargas, a Puerto Rican leader and activist, put it: "Charlie Mathews and Frank Borges were riding high on the North End. They made the fatal mistake of trying to replace [Nancy] Meléndez with Abe Giles's son, [Radames,] who . . . was born of a Puerto Rican mother but culturally was black. We were sympathetic with Mathews, but we didn't like the idea of black power at Puerto Rican expense."[26]

Resentment and Paternalism

The counterpart to Puerto Rican ambivalence about race has been black resentment over Puerto Rican racial identification. This pattern was identified early on by McWilliams, who concluded that the Puerto Ricans' emphasis on their Spanish origin was a source of irritation for Blacks.[27] Rogler, however, found elements within the black community that neither resented nor rejected the Puerto Ricans. They did not like the idea of Puerto Ricans organizing and developing their own groups and felt that Puerto Ricans should join existing black organizations. Their claim was that ethnic-based organization would only perpetuate Puerto Rican isolation. Collaboration was considered a better alternative, but Puerto Ricans were not encouraged to join Blacks from a position of equality and strength.[28] This paternalistic attitude made Puerto Ricans cautious about alliances at best or suspicious of Blacks at worst.

In her 1978 study of Puerto Rican political participation in New York City, Rosa Estades noted that one area of tension between Puerto

Ricans and Blacks was the latter's monopoly of the antipoverty establishment. Puerto Ricans were said to resent this situation.[29] According to the more recent literature, Blacks and Latinos resent each other over access to affirmative action programs and other forms of job displacement.[30] On the other hand, survey data reveal that the attitudinal foundation for a black-Latino coalition in support of affirmative action does exist.[31] Nevertheless, Latinos are wary of black "dominance of the civil rights agenda, frequently to the exclusion of issues important to Hispanics."[32]

One weakness of this literature is its failure to distinguish between Latino subgroups. Thus, it is not clear the degree to which black–Puerto Rican resentment persists or what it looks like. The limited evidence that is available shows that among Latinos, Puerto Ricans are the most supportive of governmental programs designed to assist Blacks.[33] But it is uncertain how or to what extent this could assist coalition-building efforts, especially since one of the conditions that is considered necessary for such efforts to come to fruition is "enlightened political leadership,"[34] which among Puerto Ricans is lacking.[35]

In Hartford, the perceived paternalism of Blacks did not entice Puerto Ricans to collaborate. Initially, some Puerto Rican leaders assumed that, as minorities, they and Blacks were destined to work together.[36] Eventually, many realized that this was a questionable assumption. The problem was not that solidarity was impossible but that it could not be taken for granted. In 1969, at the height of a riot involving Puerto Ricans and white ethnics, the statements of an NAACP official became emblematic of the patronizing attitudes of Blacks. His words were: "If you don't think you're colored like me, you've got something to learn."[37] In his view, the problem with Puerto Ricans was that they did not accept their blackness. They considered themselves different, he noted, implying that "different" meant "better than" Blacks. However, he did not tell Puerto Ricans to follow the example of Blacks. Instead, he invited them to join the NAACP and to follow their leadership; otherwise, they would be left behind.

As in other cities, black paternalism in Hartford was often couched in resentment over the perception of racial ambivalence on the part of Puerto Ricans. In turn, Puerto Ricans resented their subordination to Blacks. An example of social subordination was the nearly monopolistic control of the distribution of program services that Blacks exerted during the 1960s. About this Olga Mele, a Puerto Rican resident since 1941, said:

Blacks care only about blacks, and they use us. All this time they have used us. They work for themselves, not for us. At CRT [Community Renewal Team, an antipoverty agency] I worked with Blacks for a long time and I noticed that. I had a program for the families of alcoholics, and the Blacks looked for money for their programs but not for mine. With all the antipoverty programs, Blacks would always overlook us. Every time there was a new program, Blacks would give us nothing.[38]

In 1971, at a meeting sponsored by the Hartford Foundation for Public Giving, foundation officials were told by a group of Puerto Rican community leaders that, in funding the Black-controlled CRT, they would be wasting their money. They protested the fact that no Puerto Ricans were involved in CRT's decision-making process and also that, "even though CRT serves many Puerto Ricans," there was no Puerto Rican delegate agency.[39]

The association between two community notables—the Puerto Rican María Sánchez and Abe Giles, an African American party regular—is a good example of political subordination of Puerto Ricans by African Americans. For well over a decade, Sánchez did the bidding of Giles, supporting his leadership of their district's Democratic town committee. Despite this, in 1988 Sánchez was unceremoniously ousted from the committee because of her absence from meetings and her failure to sign a consent slip that would allow for an extension of her tenure. According to Giles, the exclusion was a mistake that could have been easily corrected except that "nobody seemed to want to."[40]

Yet, Sánchez perceived the ousting as intentional. She saw it as a betrayal and as a sign that Blacks were intent on squashing Puerto Rican aspirations. In a fit of ethnic indignation and personal anger, Sánchez decided to mount a primary challenge against Giles. Her victory did not come easy, and it was obtained by a slim thirty-three vote margin. Still, it was seen by many as a clear sign of the emergence of Puerto Ricans from the political shadow of Blacks.[41]

Cooperation and Conflict

As far as coalitional behavior is concerned, extant discussions are more speculative and exhortative than analytical. To be sure, prospective discussions are not necessarily meaningless. The important point here is that in these studies speculation and exhortation are not grounded in the analysis of actual instances of coalitional behavior.[42]

One exception to this rule is the analysis by Angelo Falcón of the 1989 mayoral election in New York City. Using Puerto Ricans as an example, he suggests that the disposition of minority elites to build coalitions will be high or low depending on (1) how they interpret the behavior of their counterparts, (2) the level of elite coherence, and (3) how elites perceive the structure of opportunities available to them. In addition, if the political cues exchanged by elites regarding issues, policies, and/or incumbents are mixed or inconsistent, they will be less willing to engage in unified concerted action. And, if they are internally divided, collaboration is less likely.[43] Interestingly, governmental structure might also play a role in this process. If large councils are more likely to have minority incumbents,[44] it is logical to assume that the disposition of elites to build coalitions in places where councils are small might be minimal and competition might be fierce, or both.

Puerto Ricans are the Latino subgroup most sympathetic to black interests, but they have also competed strenuously for control over community corporations, local school boards, and party organizations at the district level.[45] This has been a feature of Puerto Rican history from the very beginning of migration to the United States.[46] Further, this pattern has been observed in communities outside New York where relations were marked by tensions over busing[47] and deliberate social distance,[48] as well as by violent confrontations.[49] Conflict over neighborhood-, community-, and electoral-level issues has coexisted with solidarity.[50] In fact, in some instances Latino elites have bent over backwards to accommodate black concerns.[51] Yet, a characterization of black–Puerto Rican relations as harmonious and marked by periodic political solidarity[52] simply reflects a decision to see them as a glass of water that is half-full rather than half-empty.

But the pattern is complex beyond a simple polarity, because the terms of collaboration affect the outcomes and because collaboration among elites can be punctuated by conflict at the grass roots.[53] In Philadelphia, for example, the subordinate status of Puerto Ricans in Wilson Goode's coalition negatively affected the level of the Mayor's responsiveness to Puerto Rican needs.[54] Support for Goode was dichotomous, that is, more pronounced at the elite level than at the grass roots, but the split was determined in part by cultural rather than political factors. The weakness of the black–Puerto Rican coalition at the grass-roots level was partly a result of the unfortunate perception of Blacks as "lazy troublemakers."[55] A similar situation developed in Chicago during Harold Washington's regime,[56] although it is not clear how Puerto Ricans fared vis-à-vis Mexicans. Washington's focus on the tensions within his governing coalition prevented him from paying adequate attention to the needs of his overall electoral constituency, creating a racial/ethnic dichotomy in the level of support for his regime.

Many of these themes and issues can be found in the experience of Blacks and Puerto Ricans in Hartford. There, cooperation and conflict among elites were structured by a set of premises, assumptions, and inferences about status, worthiness, and political expectations. Black elite behavior was shaped by the following premises: (1) Blacks came to Hartford first and therefore should not be upstaged by more recent arrivals; (2) they had a longer and more tormented history of suffering, and the plight of Puerto Ricans paled by comparison; (3) they had worked hard to achieve positions of leadership and influence, and no upstart group was going to benefit without paying its dues, especially since black suffering was not yet a thing of the past. Puerto Ricans, for their part, assumed that (1) as minorities, Puerto Ricans and Blacks were all "in the same boat"; (2) black activism could and ought to embrace Puerto Rican interests. Yet, somewhat paradoxically, they also believed that Puerto Rican interests should be represented directly in community agencies and elected bodies. Blacks expected deference and Puerto Ricans expected solidarity, but not all Puerto Ricans agreed that solidarity was enough.[57]

One key aspect of black–Puerto Rican relations in Hartford was that Blacks were simultaneously powerful and oppressed. Politically, Blacks were above Puerto Ricans but below Whites. Therefore, what under conditions of equality could have been a relationship based mostly on solidarity in the context of inequality became a relationship charged with ambivalence, at times cordial and cooperative but often conflictive and wracked by suspicion and hostility. In 1981, for example, the support of Puerto Ricans, through the Greater Hartford Labor Council, contributed to the election of Thirman Milner, the city's first African American mayor. On the other hand, when African American leaders challenged the Democratic party's Irish leadership in 1985, Puerto Ricans withdrew their support, afraid that a black victory might undermine their position within the city council.[58]

African Americans often perceived Puerto Ricans as disloyal, sometimes with reason. For example, it is likely that when Dolores Sánchez, a Puerto Rican, ran for the State Senate to represent Hartford's Second Senatorial District, he was being used by the Republican party to undermine a black aspirant.[59] This, admittedly, was in 1966, and much has changed since. Yet, as recently as 1992, black–Puerto Rican relations were wracked by questions of loyalty. These concerns were compounded by fear and disagreement over the intentions of protagonists. In that year conflict pitted the city's black Mayor, Carrie Saxon Perry, against one of her most prominent Puerto Rican supporters, Edwin Vargas Jr., then president of the Puerto Rican Political Action Committee of Connecticut (PRPAC), a group that was instrumental in Perry's 1991 reelection. In this conflict, involving the chairmanship of the Democratic party, Vargas emerged victorious. In order to win, he allied himself with one of Perry's opponents. His intent was to show the Mayor that he was a player in his own right, but the means he chose to achieve his goal confused many and raised questions about his trustworthiness to Perry.[60]

During this episode a subset of Perry's supporters within the black community did all they could to promote reconciliation and trust between the Mayor and Vargas and, more generally, between Puerto Ricans and African Americans.[61] In contrast to those who perceived Vargas as narrowly concerned with Puerto Rican interests, this subset understood that, while the two groups had different priorities, a mutually beneficial coalition was possible and desirable. In the heat of conflict, however, almost no one remembered the history of black–Puerto Rican efforts and accomplishments such as the election of Hartford's first black mayor, the appointment of the first black city treasurer, and Carrie Saxon Perry's own victory in November 1991. Perry in particular began to decry what she called "backroom stuff" and "package deals,"[62] apparently forgetting that her coalition had been the product of backroom negotiations and deals among the various racial and ethnic players.

Coalitional Behavior: Push and Pull Factors

The preceding discussion reveals a context for coalitional behavior between Blacks and Puerto Ricans marked by compartmentalization, racial ambivalence, paternalism, resentment, and conflict over goals, interests, achievement, and status. The following statements recapitulate that discussion in abstract form to offer a set of hypotheses about the factors that are likely to bring minorities together or pull them apart.

First, conflict is likely as a result of *incongruent attitudinal frameworks* that stem from divergent historical experiences. A minority group with a longer history of settlement whose experience is singularly oppressive will place itself above other minorities in the hierarchy of social and political expectations, as Blacks did with Puerto Ricans in Hartford and elsewhere. Other minorities, for their part, will assume that similarities of status make the coincidence of interests and advocacy automatic and unproblematic. This is how many Puerto Rican leaders felt until the confrontation of 1969 suggested otherwise. The combination of such divergent frameworks is a sure recipe for tensions and confrontation.

Second, once it becomes clear that the relationship between interests and interest representation is problematic, minorities need to negotiate the *dilemma between direct and virtual representation*. The tug of war between the two alternatives is another source of dissidence, at best, or of division, at worst, and Blacks and Puerto Ricans in Hartford had a taste of both. The worst-case scenario occurs when the benefits of virtual representation are grudgingly recognized by some—like those who were grateful for services provided by black-controlled agencies—while emphasizing that the absence of direct representation is unacceptable— which was the stance this same group took when it urged the creation of a Puerto Rican-controlled agency. In this scenario, indirect paths to redistribution, such as virtual representation, are often considered a waste of energy and resources.

Third, *when minority elites represent a group that is simultaneously powerful and oppressed*, a context of ambiguous relations develops that exacerbates disagreement. The elites will compensate for their subordination to the politically dominant group by using other, less powerful minorities for their own purposes—as did Abe Giles with María Sánchez for more than a decade. In doing so, they exact a psychological wage that alleviates their subjective plight, and when the rewards are political in nature, such as elected office, the prize is deeply appreciated, even if it is hollow. In other words, even if access to power does little to improve objective conditions in ways that might help the elites and other groups, it is still perceived as beneficial.

Fourth, *discrepancies in different minorities' intentions, actions, and perceptions* often undermine the possibility for both immediate and prospective cooperation. Such discrepancies are at times rooted in the inability of actors to determine which category is the better predictor of behavior, for example, the failure to figure whether partisanship or ethnicity can better foretell electoral support. For example, when Dolores Sánchez emerged as a candidate, Blacks assumed he would be supported by Puerto Ricans because of his ethnic identity, when in fact he was rejected for being a Republican candidate. Alternatively, conflict is frequently the result of the inability of elites to dispel incorrect perceptions—as Falcón suggests and the conflict between Vargas and Mayor Perry illustrates. In these situations, clarification is often possible only in retrospect. And the problem with retrospective clarity is that it is absent when it is most needed: in the present.

Fifth, *the lack of a historical memory* is a serious condition whose negative effects are felt markedly even when the distance between present and past does not stretch very far. By being short and selective, the collective memory of a recently successful minority group will tend to airbrush the record of solidarity and cooperation that made success possible. The clash between Vargas and Perry over the Democratic chairmanship is a good illustration of this. What is baffling about these cases is not so much that decade-old events are less easily remembered than more recent ones but that immediacy is no guarantee of memory, that the events of *last week* can be as easily forgotten as those that are removed from consciousness by one or two generations.

Finally, conflict or cooperation will closely follow the contours of the *distribution of responsibilities as much as the distribution of rewards*. In other words, racial and ethnic minorities will come together and fight over participation in the decision-making process as much as over the size of their distributive shares. In Hartford, Blacks had to contend with an unresponsive power structure dominated by Whites and white ethnics, while Puerto Ricans had to wrestle Blacks to increase their access to power. Thus, the problem of interminority relations and, more generally, of politics is not just determining who gets what, where, and when but reaching the point where decision-making structures incorporate all legitimate parties. In this case, "who decides" can be as important as "what one gets."

Whither Interminority Relations?

Minority political elites seeking to develop the political alliances that many think will be indispensable for years to come face a daunting challenge. According to Samuel Betances, the remedy for compartmentalization is purposive contact.[63] Yet it is not certain that contact fosters a greater disposition toward coalitional behavior among minorities.[64] For some the antidote against racial ambivalence is a focus on class[65] or the confluence of class, race, and ethnicity.[66] Class is also supposed to minimize resentment, substitute equality for paternalism, and promote collaboration across racial and ethnic lines.[67] The fact is, however, that class as the basis for coalition building efforts is far from an ideal category. Are there instances where, instead of promoting alliances, class interacts with other factors to increase the likelihood of conflict? The answer, alas, is yes.[68]

The case of black–Puerto Rican relations adds to this already complex picture a set of contextual and relational factors that can cause purposive coalition-building to run amuck. If the historical premises of interelite attitudes are incongruent and the level of dissonance between actions and perceptions is high, it will be difficult for purposive coalition building either to get started or, once initiated, to succeed. How minorities negotiate the dilemmas of representation, especially in the context of relative degrees of empowerment status among groups will also be an important factor. Once the initially difficult process of building a coalition is set in motion, it will succeed or fail depending on the strength or weakness of collective memory. Additionally, the distribution of responsibilities, particularly the opportunity to exercise power, will be as critical as the distribution of social and economic rewards.

In a general sense, the Hartford story applies to any city with a similar racial and ethnic mix. Insofar as minorities are forced to seek collaborative arrangements to achieve political goals, they will have to negotiate differences in background, intentions, empowerment status, and so on. At the same time, it is unlikely that the Hartford experience could be replicated in any other city. In other words, even in places with a similar political system, economy, size, and demographic mix, it is likely that minorities will respond to issues of representation, historical memory, the exercise of power, and so on in specific, divergent, and unpredictable ways. Part of the problem here is that by definition case studies are not equipped to allow for conclusive or predictive generalizations. Yet, to the extent that individual cases validate previous research, one can be more confident about the larger applicability of findings.[69] In that sense, the case of Blacks and Puerto Ricans in Hartford is useful because it confirms the model of black–Puerto Rican relations that emerges from extant analyses, while adding features to it that might be of critical importance beyond Hartford. Nevertheless, this expanded model should be applied to other cities and other minority populations with caution. The Hartford case is not a blueprint for comparable settings, but it does offer a road map for research and action.

NOTES

1. If Census Bureau estimates are any guide, it is likely that current proportions for minorities in urban centers in the Northeast are higher. Nationally, the Bureau estimates that the Hispanic population grew by 39 percent between April 1, 1990, and April 1, 1999, from 22 to 31 million residents. The increase for non-Hispanic Blacks during that period is estimated to be 13 percent, from 29 to 33 million inhabitants. Estimates at the county level also show significant increases. For example, in Hartford county the estimates show an increase of 18 percent for Hispanics and 4 percent for Blacks between April 1, 1990, and July 1, 1997. Unfortunately, the county-level data do not account for differences by Hispanic subgroup. Further, no counts or estimates are available after 1990 to gauge population changes by race or Hispanic origin at the city level.

2. Paula D. McClain and Albert K. Karnig, "Black and Hispanic Socioeconomic and Political Competition," *American Political Science Review* 84 (1990): 536.

3. Peter K. Eisinger, *Patterns of Interracial Politics, Conflict and Cooperation in the City* (New York: Academic Press, 1976), p. 18.

4. Recent examples of this type of analysis are Dianne M. Pinderhughes, "Racial and Ethnic Politics in Chicago Mayoral Elections," 37–61, and Byran O. Jackson and Michael B. Preston, "Race and Ethnicity in Los Angeles Politics," 85–104, both in George E. Peterson, ed., *Big-City Politics, Governance, and Fiscal Constraints* (Washington, D.C.: Urban Institute Press, 1994). For a discussion of the limitations of the literature on de facto electoral coalitions, see Karen M. Kaufmann, "Racial Conflict and Political Choice: A Study of Mayoral Voting Behavior in Los Angeles and New York," *Urban Affairs Review* 33: 5 (May 1998): 655–685.

5. A recent analysis characterizes Hartford during this period as a bifurcated economy and a paternalistic society. See Stephen Valocchi, "Hartford

Voices: Race, Ethnicity and Neighborhood During the Great Depression," unpublished manuscript, Trinity College, September 1993.

6. Connecticut Department of Labor statistics assembled by Louise Simmons; Department of Planning, Hartford, Conn., *Hartford, The State of the City, September 1983* and *State of the City 1995*; Census data on commuter employment in 1990 provided by Benjamin Barnes, Planning Department, City of Hartford.

7. The politics of this most recent period are analyzed in detail in Louise Simmons, *Organizing in Hard Times* (Philadelphia: Temple University Press, 1994); José E. Cruz, "A Decade of Change: Puerto Rican Politics in Hartford, Connecticut, 1969–1979," *Journal of American Ethnic History* 16:3 (Spring 1997): 45–80; Louise Simmons, "Dilemmas of Progressives in Government: Playing Solomon in an Age of Austerity," *Economic Development Quarterly* 10 (May 1996): 159–171; José E. Cruz, *Identity and Power: Puerto Rican Politics and the Challenge of Ethnicity* (Philadelphia: Temple University Press, 1998); Louise Simmons, "A New Urban Conservatism: The Case of Hartford, Connecticut," *Journal of Urban Affairs* 20:2 (1998): 175–198.

8. Oscar Handlin, *The Newcomers: Negroes and Puerto Ricans in a Changing Metropolis* (New York: Doubleday, 1959), pp. 2–3.

9. Nathan Glazer and Daniel P. Moynihan, *Beyond the Melting Pot: The Negroes, Puerto Ricans, Jews, Italians, and Irish of New York City* (Cambridge, Mass.: MIT Press, 1963), pp. 301, 315.

10. Carey McWilliams, *Brothers under the Skin* (Boston: Little, Brown, 1964), p. 219.

11. Anne M. Santiago, "Patterns of Puerto Rican Segregation and Mobility," *Hispanic Journal of Behavioral Sciences* 14:1 (February 1992): 117, 128.

12. Douglas S. Massey and Nancy A. Denton, *American Apartheid* (Cambridge, Mass.: Harvard University Press, 1993), pp. 146–147.

13. See Douglas S. Massey, "Latinos, Poverty, and the Underclass," *Hispanic Journal of Behavioral Sciences* 15:4 (November 1993): 449–475. This article does not analyze Puerto Ricans specifically, but its general outline of differences between Blacks and Latinos applies to all Latino subgroups.

14. McWilliams, *Brothers under the Skin*, p. 219.

15. Lloyd H. Rogler, *Migrant in the City: The Life of a Puerto Rican Action Group* (New York: Basic Books, 1972), p. 15. Rogler uses the pseudonym "Maplewood" to refer to New Haven.

16. Clara E. Rodríguez, *Puerto Ricans, Born in the U.S.A.* (Boston: Unwin Hyman, 1989), p. 59. See also Clara E. Rodríguez, "Puerto Ricans: Between Black and White," 25–35, and Pablo "Yoruba" Guzmán, "Puerto Rican Barrio Politics in the United States," 144–151, in Clara E. Rodríguez and Virginia Sánchez Korrol, eds., *Historical Perspectives on Puerto Rican Survival in the United States* (Princeton: Marcus Wiener, 1996).

17. See respectively, Clara E. Rodriguez, "Racial Classification among Puerto Rican Men and Women in New York," *Hispanic Journal of Behavioral Sciences* 12:4 (November 1990): 366–379, and Angelo Falcón, "Puerto Ricans and the Politics of Racial Identity," in Herbert W. Harris, Howard C. Blue, and Ezra E. H. Griffith, eds., *Racial and Ethnic Identity: Psychological Development and Creative Expression* (New York: Routledge, 1995), pp. 193–207.

18. Santiago, "Patterns," p. 118.

19. W. Edward Wendover, "Puerto Rican Group Seizes Vacant Store," *Hartford Courant,* 24 November 1970, p. 1.

20. José Claudio, interview, 30 September 1995. For background information on the Young Lords Party, see Hilda Vazquez Ignatin, "Young Lords, Serve and Protect," *The Movement* (May 1969), p. 4, reprinted in Clayborne Carson, ed., *The Movement 1964–1970* (Westport, Conn.: Greenwood Press, 1993), p. 196. For an account of the group's origins and development in New York City see two interviews with Pablo "Yoruba" Guzmán in *The Movement,* also reprinted in Carson's book, pp. 739, 744, 805–806, and 818, and his recent account, "La Vida Pura: A Lord of the Barrio," *Village Voice,* 21 March 1995, pp. 24–31. For a recent assessment of the theory and practice of the group, see Agustín Lao, "Resources of Hope: Imagining the Young Lords and the Politics of Memory," *Centro* 8:1 (1995), 34–49.

21. Jackie Ross, "City Community Center Opened by People's Liberation Party," *Hartford Courant,* 16 December 1970, p. 38.

22. Herbert F. Janick Jr., *A Diverse People: Connecticut 1914 to the Present* (Chester, Conn.: Pequot Press, 1975), p. 94.

23. Aida Claudio, interview, 29 September 1995.

24. For a more detailed analysis of Puerto Rican radicalism in Hartford see José E. Cruz, "Pushing Left to Get to the Center: Puerto Rican Radicalism in Hartford, Connecticut," in Andrés Torres and José E. Velázquez, eds., *The Puerto Rican Movement, Voices from the Diaspora* (Philadelphia: Temple University Press, 1998), pp. 69–87.

25. Gerald A. Ryan, "Need for Involvement in Community Is Seen," *Hartford Courant,* 20 November 1965, p. 1.

26. Edwin Vargas, Jr., interview, 30 July 1991. See also "Nancy Meléndez Va a la Reelección," *Qué Pasa* (Hartford, Conn.), July 1985, p. 3; Juan Daniel Brito, "Comité de la Ciudad Apoya Candidatura de Meléndez," *Qué Pasa* (Hartford, Conn.), July 1985, p. 16.

27. McWilliams, *Brothers under the Skin,* p. 219.

28. Rogler, *Migrant in the City,* p. 14.

29. Rosa Estades, *Patterns of Political Participation of Puerto Ricans in New York City* (Rio Piedras, P.R.: Editorial Universitaria, 1978), p. 45.

30. Rodolfo O. de la Garza, "Latino Politics: A Futuristic View," *National Political Science Review* 3 (1992): 141; Andrés Torres, *Between Melting Pot*

and Mosaic: African Americans and Puerto Ricans in the New York Political Economy (Philadelphia: Temple University Press, 1995), p. 85.

31. F. Chris Garcia, "Latinos and the Affirmative Action Debate: Wedge or Coalition Issue?," in F. Chris Garcia, *Pursuing Power: Latinos and the Political System* (Notre Dame: University of Notre Dame Press, 1997), pp. 387–388.

32. Charles Kamasaki and Raul Yzaguirre, "Black-Hispanic Tensions: One Perspective," *Journal of Intergroup Relations* 21:4 (Winter 1994–95): 33.

33. See Rodolfo O. de la Garza et al., *Latino Voices* (Boulder: Westview Press, 1992), p. 91.

34. Garcia, "Latinos and the Affirmative Action Debate," p. 388.

35. See Angelo Falcón, "Puerto Ricans and the 1989 Mayoral Election in New York City," *Hispanic Journal of Behavioral Sciences* 11:3 (August 1989): 251, and José E. Cruz, "Unfulfilled Promises: Puerto Rican Politics and Poverty," in Luis M. Falcón and Edwin Meléndez, eds., *Recasting Puerto Rican Poverty* (Philadelphia: Temple University Press, forthcoming).

36. Antonio Soto, interview, 5 August 1991.

37. Edward Rudd, "Angry Meeting Airs Complaints on Police Tactics in Disorders," *Hartford Courant,* 20 August 1969, p. 35.

38. Olga Mele, interview, 6 August 1992.

39. Janet Anderson, "Foundations to Seek Methods to Aid Puerto Rican Students," *Hartford Courant,* 2 November 1971, p. 25.

40. Abe Giles, interview, 3 August 1991.

41. Mark Pazniokas and Bill Keveney, "Puerto Ricans Show Power in City Primaries," *Hartford Courant,* 16 September 1988, p. 1.

42. See James Jennings, "Future Directions for Puerto Rican Politics in the U.S. and Puerto Rico," in F. Chris Garcia, ed., *Latinos and the Political System* (Notre Dame: University of Notre Dame Press, 1988), p. 492; Raul Yzaguirre, "Keys to Hispanic Empowerment," in Roberto E. Villareal and Norma G. Hernandez, eds., *Latinos and Political Coalitions* (Westport, Conn.: Praeger, 1991), p. 183; Samuel Betances, "African-Americans and Hispanics/Latinos: Eliminating Barriers to Coalition Building," *Latino Studies Journal* 6:1 (January 1995): 9.

43. Falcón, "Puerto Ricans and the 1989 Mayoral Election," pp. 249–250.

44. Nicholas O. Alozie and Lynne L. Manganaro, "Black and Hispanic Representation: Does Council Size Matter?" *Urban Affairs Quarterly* 29:2 (December 1993): 276–298.

45. Estades, *Patterns,* pp. 45–46.

46. McWilliams, *Brothers under the Skin,* p. 205.

47. Rogler, *Migrant in the City,* pp. 31–32.

48. Rogler, *Migrant in the City,* p. 201.

49. Rogler, *Migrant in the City,* pp. 151–152, 241.

50. James Jennings, "Conclusion: Racial Hierarchy and Ethnic Conflict in

the United States," in James Jennings, ed., *Blacks, Latinos, and Asians in Urban America* (Westport, Conn.: Praeger, 1994), pp. 143–144.

51. Kamasaki and Yzaguirre, "Black-Hispanic Tensions," p. 17. For variation in Latino attitudes toward black interests and concerns, see de la Garza et al., *Latino Voices,* pp. 91, 93; Keith Jennings and Clarence Lusane, "The State and Future of Black/Latino Relations in Washington, D.C.: A Bridge in Need of Repair," 57–77, and Daryl Harris, "Generating Racial and Ethnic Conflict in Miami: Impact of American Foreign Policy and Domestic Racism," 79–94, in Jennings, *Blacks, Latinos and Asians in Urban America.*

52. James Jennings, "New Urban Racial and Ethnic Conflicts in the United States," *SAGE Race Relations Abstracts* 17:3 (August 1992): 20, 26.

53. In her recapitulation of research on forty-nine cities with populations of 25,000 or more in which Blacks and Latinos were at least 10 percent of the total, Paula D. McClain came to a similar conclusion. See "Coalition and Competition: Patterns of Black-Latino Relations in Urban Politics," in Wilbur C. Rich, ed., *The Politics of Minority Coalitions, Race, Ethnicity, and Shared Uncertainties* (Westport, Conn.: Praeger, 1996), pp. 57–58.

54. Judith Goode and Jo Anne Schneider, *Reshaping Ethnic and Racial Relations in Philadelphia* (Philadelphia: Temple University Press, 1994), p. 57.

55. Goode and Schneider, *Reshaping Ethnic and Racial Relations,* p. 140. The quote is from Goode and Schneider; the inference about grass-roots support is mine.

56. Larry Bennett, "Harold Washington and the Black Urban Regime," *Urban Affairs Quarterly* 28:3 (March 1993): 435.

57. See "Las Posibilidades de Trabajo Conjunto entre la Comunidad Negra e Hispana," Editorial, *Qué Pasa* (Hartford, Conn.) November 1981, p. 7; Anderson, "Foundations to Seek Methods"; Soto, interview, 5 August 1991. Also, the idea of black suffering and entitlement was expressed to me by a local activist in a conversation that took place in 1993. She argued that a Puerto Rican had no prior right to be the chair of the city's Democratic party because Blacks had settled in Hartford first and had suffered more.

58. "Historico Triunfo de Milner," *Qué Pasa* (Hartford, Conn.), November 1981, p. 1; Vargas, interview, 30 July 1991.

59. José Cruz, interview, 27 January 1993 (informant no relation to the author).

60. Steve Walsh, "Town Committee Races Rip Mayor's Coalition," *Hartford News,* 5:6 (12–19 February 1992), p. 3; Edwin Vargas Jr., interview, 17 September 1993; Carrie Saxon Perry, interview, 20 July 1994.

61. "Get Rid of the Baggage," *Hartford News,* 5:11 (18–25 March 1992), p. 4.

62. Steve Walsh, "Perry Slate Divided over Next City Manager Appointment," *Hartford News,* 4:36 (20 November–4 December 1991), p. 1; Steve

Walsh, "Council Removes Shipman, Appoints Interim Manager," *Hartford News,* 4: 39 (18 December 1991–8 January 1992), p. 1.

63. Betances, "African Americans and Hispanics/Latinos," p. 9.

64. Jaclyn Rodriguez and Patricia Gurin, "The Relationships of Intergroup Contact to Social Identity and Political Consciousness," *Hispanic Journal of Behavioral Sciences* 12:3 (August 1990): 248.

65. James Jennings, "Conclusion: Puerto Rican Politics in Urban America—Toward Progressive Electoral Activism," in James Jennings and Monte Rivera, eds., *Puerto Rican Politics in Urban America* (Westport, Conn.: Greenwood Press, 1984), p. 143. In 1988 Jennings declared that, even though an exclusive focus on class was "simplistic and inappropriate," progressive coalitions based on racial/ethnic issues and concerns were less likely to succeed than those based on class. See Jennings, "Future Directions," pp. 485, 491–494.

66. Felix Padilla, *Puerto Rican Chicago* (Notre Dame: University of Notre Dame Press, 1987), pp. 230–31.

67. Torres, *Between Melting Pot and Mosaic,* pp. 19–20, 167.

68. Angelo Falcón, "Black and Latino Politics in New York City: Race and Ethnicity in a Changing Urban Context," in F. Chris Garcia, *Latinos and the Political System,* 171–194.

69. For useful discussions of this issue, see Joe R. Feagin, Anthony M. Orum, and Gideon Sjoberg, eds., *A Case for the Case Study* (Chapel Hill: University of North Carolina Press, 1991), and John Walton, "Theoretical Methods in Comparative Urban Politics," 243–257, in John R. Logan and Todd Swanstrom, *Beyond the City Limits* (Philadelphia: Temple University Press, 1990.

REFERENCES

Alozie, Nicholas O., and Lynne L. Manganaro. 1993. "Black and Hispanic Representation: Does Council Size Matter?" *Urban Affairs Quarterly* 29:2 (December): 276–298.

Anderson, Janet. 1971. "Foundations to Seek Methods to Aid Puerto Rican Students." *Hartford Courant,* 2 November, p. 25.

Bennett, Larry. 1993. "Harold Washington and the Black Urban Regime." *Urban Affairs Quarterly* 28:3 (March): 423–440.

Betances, Samuel. 1995. "African Americans and Hispanics/Latinos: Eliminating Barriers to Coalition Building." *Latino Studies Journal* 6:1 (January): 3–26.

Brito, Juan Daniel. 1985. "Comité de la Ciudad Apoya Candidatura de Meléndez." *Qué Pasa,* Hartford, Conn. July, p. 16.

Bullock III, Charles S., and Bruce A. Campbell. 1984. "Racist or Racial Voting in the 1981 Atlanta Municipal Elections." *Urban Affairs Quarterly* 20 (December): 149–164.

Claudio, Aida. 1995a. Recorded interview, 29 September.

Claudio, José. 1995b. Recorded interview, 30 September.

Cruz, José. 1993. Recorded interview, 27 January.

————. 1997. "A Decade of Change: Puerto Rican Politics in Hartford, Connecticut, 1969–1979." *Journal of American Ethnic History* 16:3 (Spring): 45–80.

————. 1998. *Identity and Power: Puerto Rican Politics and the Challenge of Ethnicity.* Philadelphia: Temple University Press.

————. 1998. "Pushing Left to Get to the Center: Puerto Rican Radicalism in Hartford, Connecticut," in *The Puerto Rican Movement, Voices from the Diaspora,* eds. Andrés Torres and José E. Velázquez, pp. 69–87. Philadelphia: Temple University Press.

————. Forthcoming. "The Missing Link: Puerto Rican Politics and Poverty," in *Recasting Puerto Rican Poverty,* eds. Luis M. Falcón and Edwin Meléndez. Philadelphia: Temple University Press.

————. Forthcoming. "Unfulfilled Promises: Puerto Rican Politics and Poverty," in *Recasting Puerto Rican Poverty,* eds. Luis M. Falcón and Edwin Meléndez. Philadelphia: Temple University Press.

de la Garza, Rodolfo O. 1992. "Latino Politics: A Futuristic View." *National Political Science Review* 3:141.

————, et al. 1992. *Latino Voices, Mexican, Puerto Rican, and Cuban Perspectives on American Politics.* Boulder: Westview Press.

Department of Planning, Hartford, Conn. 1983. *Hartford, The State of the City, September 1983.*

————. 1995. *State of the City 1995.*

Eisinger, Peter K. 1976. *Patterns of Interracial Politics, Conflict, and Cooperation in the City.* New York: Academic Press.

Estades, Rosa. 1978. *Patterns of Political Participation of Puerto Ricans in New York City.* Rio Piedras, P.R.: Editorial Universitaria.

Falcón, Angelo. 1988. "Black and Latino Politics in New York City: Race and Ethnicity in a Changing Urban Context," in *Latinos and the Political System,* ed. F. Chris Garcia, pp. 171–194. Notre Dame: University of Notre Dame Press.

————. 1989. "Puerto Ricans and the 1989 Mayoral Election in New York City." *Hispanic Journal of Behavioral Sciences* 11:3 (August):245–258.

————. 1995. "Puerto Ricans and the Politics of Racial Identity," in *Racial and Ethnic Identity: Psychological Development and Creative Expression,* eds. Herbert W. Harris, Howard C. Blue, and Ezra E. H. Griffith, pp. 193–207. New York: Routledge.

Feagin, Joe R., Anthony M. Orum, and Gideon Sjoberg, eds. 1991. *A Case for the Case Study*. Chapel Hill: University of North Carolina Press.

Garcia, F. Chris. 1997. "Latinos and the Affirmative Action Debate: Wedge or Coalition Issue?" in *Pursuing Power: Latinos and the Political System*, F. Chris Garcia, pp. 368–400. Notre Dame: University of Notre Dame Press.

"Get Rid of the Baggage." 1992. *Hartford News* 5:11 (18–25 March): 4.

Giles, Abe. 1991. Recorded interview, 3 August.

Glazer, Nathan, and Daniel P. Moynihan. 1963. *Beyond the Melting Pot: The Negroes, Puerto Ricans, Jews, Italians, and Irish of New York City*. Cambridge: MIT Press.

Goode, Judith, and Jo Anne Schneider. 1994. *Reshaping Ethnic and Racial Relations in Philadelphia*. Philadelphia: Temple University Press.

Guzmán, Pablo "Yoruba." 1995. "La Vida Pura: A Lord of the Barrio," *Village Voice*, 21 March, pp. 24–31.

———. 1996. "Puerto Rican Barrio Politics in the United States," in *Historical Perspectives on Puerto Rican Survival in the United States*, eds. Clara E. Rodríguez and Virginia Sánchez Korrol, pp. 144–151. Princeton: Marcus Wiener.

Handlin, Oscar. 1959. *The Newcomers: Negroes and Puerto Ricans in a Changing Metropolis*. New York: Doubleday.

Harris, Daryl. 1994. "Generating Racial and Ethnic Conflict in Miami: Impact of American Foreign Policy and Domestic Racism," in *Blacks, Latinos and Asians in Urban America*, ed. James Jennings, pp. 79–94. Westport, Conn.: Praeger.

"Historico Triunfo de Milner." 1981. *Qué Pasa*, Hartford, Conn. November, p. 1.

Jackson, Byran O., and Michael B. Preston. 1994. "Race and Ethnicity in Los Angeles Politics," in *Big-City Politics, Governance, and Fiscal Constraints*, ed. George E. Peterson, pp. 85–104. Washington, D.C.: Urban Institute Press.

Janick Jr., Herbert F. 1975. *A Diverse People: Connecticut 1914 to the Present*. Chester, Conn.: Pequot Press.

Jennings, James. 1984. "Conclusion: Puerto Rican Politics in Urban America—Toward Progressive Electoral Activism," in *Puerto Rican Politics in Urban America*, eds. James Jennings and Monte Rivera, pp. 139–143. Westport, Conn.: Greenwood Press.

———. 1988. "Future Directions for Puerto Rican Politics in the U.S. and Puerto Rico," in *Latinos and the Political System*, ed. F. Chris Garcia, pp. 480–497. Notre Dame: University of Notre Dame Press.

———. 1992. "New Urban Racial and Ethnic Conflicts in the United States." *SAGE Race Relations Abstracts* 17:3 (August): 3–36.

Jennings, James. 1994. "Conclusion: Racial Hierarchy and Ethnic Conflict in the United States," in *Blacks, Latinos, and Asians in Urban America,* ed. James Jennings, pp. 143–157. Westport, Conn.: Praeger.

———. 1994. "Changing Urban Policy Paradigms: Impact of Black and Latino Coalitions," in *Blacks, Latinos, and Asians in Urban America, Status and Prospects for Politics and Activism,* ed. James Jennings, pp. 3–16. Westport, Conn.: Praeger.

Jennings, Keith, and Clarence Lusane. 1994. "The State and Future of Black/Latino Relations in Washington, D.C.: A Bridge in Need of Repair," in *Blacks, Latinos, and Asians in Urban America, Status and Prospects for Politics and Activism,* ed. James Jennings, pp. 57–77. Westport, Conn.: Praeger.

Kamasaki, Charles, and Raul Yzaguirre. 1994–95. "Black-Hispanic Tensions: One Perspective." *Journal of Intergroup Relations* 21:4 (Winter): 17–40.

Kaufmann, Karen M. 1998. "Racial Conflict and Political Choice: A Study of Mayoral Voting Behavior in Los Angeles and New York." *Urban Affairs Review* 33:5 (May): 655–685.

Lao, Agustín. 1995. "Resources of Hope: Imagining the Young Lords and the Politics of Memory." *Centro* 8:1: 34–49.

"Las Posibilidades de Trabajo Conjunto entre la Comunidad Negra e Hispana." 1981. *Qué Pasa,* Hartford, Conn. November, p. 7.

McClain, Paula D. 1996. "Coalition and Competition: Patterns of Black-Latino Relations in Urban Politics," in *The Politics of Minority Coalitions, Race, Ethnicity, and Shared Uncertainties,* ed. Wilbur C. Rich, pp. 53–63. Westport, Conn.: Praeger.

McClain, Paula D., and Albert K. Karnig. 1990. "Black and Hispanic Socioeconomic and Political Competition." *American Political Science Review* 84: 535–545.

McWilliams, Carey. 1964. *Brothers under the Skin.* Boston: Little, Brown.

Massey, Douglass S. 1993. "Latinos, Poverty, and the Underclass." *Hispanic Journal of Behavioral Sciences* 15:4 (November): 449–475.

———, and Nancy A. Denton. 1993. *American Apartheid.* Cambridge, Mass.: Harvard University Press.

Mele, Olga. 1992. Recorded interview, August 6.

"Nancy Meléndez Va a la Reelección." 1985. *Qué Pasa,* Hartford, Conn. July, p. 3.

Padilla, Felix. 1987. *Puerto Rican Chicago.* Notre Dame: University of Notre Dame Press.

Pazniokas, Mark, and Bill Keveney. 1988. "Puerto Ricans Show Power in City Primaries." *Hartford Courant,* 16 September, p. 1.

Perry, Carrie Saxon. 1994. Recorded interview, 20 July.

Pinderhughes, Dianne M. 1994. "Racial and Ethnic Politics in Chicago Mayoral Elections," in *Big-City Politics, Governance, and Fiscal Constraints,* ed. George E. Peterson, pp. 37–61. Washington, D.C.: Urban Institute Press.

Rodríguez, Clara E. 1989. *Puerto Ricans, Born in the U.S.A.* Boston: Unwin Hyman.

———. 1990. "Racial Classification among Puerto Rican Men and Women in New York." *Hispanic Journal of Behavioral Sciences* 12:4 (November): 366–379.

———. 1996. "Puerto Ricans: Between Black and White," in *Historical Perspectives on Puerto Rican Survival in the United States,* eds. Clara E. Rodríguez and Virginia Sánchez Korrol, pp. 25–35. Princeton: Marcus Wiener.

Rodriguez, Jaclyn, and Patricia Gurin. 1990. "The Relationships of Intergroup Contact to Social Identity and Political Consciousness." *Hispanic Journal of Behavioral Sciences* 12:3 (August): 235–255.

Rogler, Lloyd H. 1972. *Migrant in the City: The Life of a Puerto Rican Action Group.* New York: Basic Books.

Ross, Jackie. 1970. "City Community Center Opened by People's Liberation Party." *Hartford Courant,* 16 December, p. 38.

Rudd, Edward. 1969. "Angry Meeting Airs Complaints on Police Tactics in Disorders," *Hartford Courant,* 20 August, p. 35.

Ryan, Gerald A. 1965. "Need for Involvement in Community Is Seen." *Hartford Courant,* 20 November, p. 1.

Santiago, Anne M. 1992. "Patterns of Puerto Rican Segregation and Mobility." *Hispanic Journal of Behavioral Sciences* 14:1 (February): 107–133.

Simmons, Louise. 1994. *Organizing in Hard Times.* Philadelphia: Temple University Press.

———. 1996. "Dilemmas of Progressives in Government: Playing Solomon in an Age of Austerity." *Economic Development Quarterly* 10 (May): 159–171.

———. 1998. "A New Urban Conservatism: The Case of Hartford, Connecticut." *Journal of Urban Affairs* 20:2: 175–198.

Soto, Antonio. 1991. Recorded interview, August 5.

Torres, Andrés. 1995. *Between Melting Pot and Mosaic: African Americans and Puerto Ricans in the New York Political Economy.* Philadelphia: Temple University Press.

Valocchi, Stephen. 1993. "Hartford Voices: Race, Ethnicity and Neighborhood during the Great Depression." Unpublished manuscript, Trinity College, September.

Vargas Jr., Edwin. 1991. Recorded interview, 30 July.

———. 1993. Recorded interview, 17 September.

Vazquez Ignatin, Hilda. 1993. "Young Lords, Serve and Protect." *The Movement* (May 1969), p. 4. Reprinted in Clayborne Carson, ed., *The Movement 1964–1970.* Westport, Conn.: Greenwood Press.

Villarreal, Roberto E., and Norma G. Hernandez, eds. 1991. *Latinos and Political Coalitions, Political Empowerment for the 1990s.* Westport, Conn.: Praeger.

Walsh, Steve. 1991. "Perry Slate Divided Over Next City Manager Appointment." *Hartford News* 4:36 (20 November–4 December): p. 1.

―――. 1991–1992. "Council Removes Shipman, Appoints Interim Manager." *Hartford News* 4:39 (18 December–8 January), p. 1.

―――. 1992. "Town Committee Races Rip Mayor's Coalition." *Hartford News* 5:6 (12–19 February), p. 3.

Walton, John. 1990. "Theoretical Methods in Comparative Urban Politics," in *Beyond the City Limits,* eds. John R. Logan and Todd Swanstrom, pp. 243–257. Philadelphia: Temple University Press.

Wendover, W. Edward. 1970. "Puerto Rican Group Seizes Vacant Store." *Hartford Courant,* 24 November, p. 1.

Yzaguirre, Raul. 1991. "Keys to Hispanic Empowerment," in *Latinos and Political Coalitions,* eds. Roberto E. Villareal and Norma G. Hernandez, pp. 178–184. Westport, Conn.: Praeger.

Chapter 4

Conflict or Cooperation?
Africans and African Americans in Multiracial America

Akwasi B. Assensoh

Research on black politics has devoted very little attention to the political orientations and political behavior of Africans in the American diaspora, particularly when it comes to interactions between Africans and African Americans. This relationship will be a crucial one in the coming decades as increasing numbers of African immigrants migrate to American shores. Yet, native (or American-born) Blacks and their African-born kith and kin have been lumped together as researchers often fail to make important distinctions between them, assuming that they implicitly share similar policy dispositions, political orientations, and behavior.

American-born Blacks and their African counterparts, however, disagree on a range of issues and vary widely in cultural norms and, to some extent, racial attitudes. Using histopolitical analysis, A. B. Assensoh shows how the relationship between Africans and African Americans ranges from cooperative to conflictual, depending on the issue at hand.

"There is one basic fact that is very true for all time. It is the fact that all black people originated from Africa. Which part of Africa each black person originated from is another issue entirely. But the fact that the 'Dark Continent' is the root of the family tree of all black peoples worldwide is unquestionable. Even, some researchers have traced the root of all humankind to Africa."[1]

"So, excuse me if I sound cynical, jaded. I'm beaten down, and I'll admit it. And it's Africa that has made me this way. I feel for her suffering, I empathize with her pain, and now, from afar, I still recoil in horror whenever I see yet another television picture of another tribal slaughter, another refugee crisis. But most of all I think: Thank God my ancestor got out, because, now, I am not one of them. In short, thank God I am an American."[2]

The foregoing statements—the first made by an African writer from the continent and the second culled from the work of an African American journalist—provide a snapshot of the conventional wisdom regarding the relationships that have, over the years, existed between Africans and African Americans. On the one hand are scholars, who argue that Africans and African Americans are inextricably linked by virtue of their common ancestry and, indeed, that their ties are durable across historical time periods, continental divides, and political differences. In contrast are those scholars who argue that their American identity is much more important and central than the mere common ancestry and skin color that seem to bind the two groups. In the midst of these controversial and opposing perspectives, what is the nature of the relationship between Africans and African Americans? Most certainly, the answer to this question is important as an ever-increasing number of Africans, from various countries on the continent, migrate to predominantly black-populated communities to coexist in the current environment of scarce social, economic, and political resources.

This essay demonstrates that the relationship between Africans and African Americans takes no one particular form. Instead, the relationship can be most adequately characterized as a pendulum that swings from conflict to cooperation, depending on the time, the histopolitical and economic context, media images, and cultural norms. Yet, as the essay also underscores, the increasing migration of Africans to predominantly black inner-city communities provides increased opportunities for conflict and that, in the end, when Blacks from every nook and corner of the world unite, they both show strength and make progress.

Nationalist and Civil Rights Movements: The Pendulum Swings toward Cooperation

Historically and sociopolitically, nothing is known to bind and promote both collaboration and cooperation more than years and shared experience of fighting common and easily identifiable enemies. Indeed, that has been the plight that Africans, on the continent, and Blacks in America faced in the 1950s as they fought separate but similar battles against the common foes of colonialism and Jim Crowism. Therefore, it is no surprise that, in the midst of battles against these common and very similar enemies, continental Blacks (in Africa) and those in the diaspora transparently supported each other with firebrand rhetoric, laced with axioms and slogans, and with their physical presence via travels to Africa and America, respectively, as well as through revolutionary proposals to work together to enhance the technological skills of Africans and to protect the common good of the black race worldwide.

For example, as a great proponent of Pan-Africanism, Ghana's late President Kwame Nkrumah linked his country's freedom from colonial rule to "the total liberation of Africa and with the projection of the African [black] personality in the international community."[3] Nkrumah firmly believed that Africa was the root of all blackness and that it should serve as the fountain of black solidarity and Pan-Africanism. With his firm belief in Pan-Africanism and the unity of black people, Nkrumah wished to see an increased collaboration between Africans and Blacks in the diaspora; thus, in June 1951, in his capacity as the nominal Ghanaian (or Gold Coast) leader,[4] he extended an invitation to African Americans (then called Negroes) to return to Africa with their technological as well as their intellectual expertise so that they could share in the rebuilding of the continent after years of colonial subjugation and exploitation.

In a commencement speech at Lincoln University, in Pennsylvania, Nkrumah's alma mater, the Ghanian leader appealed to the democracies of America and Great Britain for technicians, machinery, and capital to help develop Ghana, then called the Gold Coast, adding, "I said that there was much for the Negro people of America to do to help their ancestral country both then and in the future and that upon the attainment of independence, it was the intention of my [political] Party to re-name the country Ghana."[5]

It has been shown that collaborative efforts emanated not only from postcolonial African leaders but from African American leaders as well. To a large extent, many African American intellectual and political leaders always saw the interconnectedness of Africans on the continent and African Americans; hence, several of them had a burning desire either to visit the continent or to live and die there, as Dr. W. E. B. Du Bois, from America, and George Padmore, from the Caribbean, did in the 1960s. As Professor Herbert Aptheker wrote in his introduction to Dr. W. E. B. Du Bois's *Africa and Its Place in Modern History* (1977), Dr. Du Bois was principally a black diasporan leader. Aptheker wrote:

> Among Du Bois' earliest memories was that of his grandmother singing lullabies to him in an African tongue; his final years from 1961 to 1963 found him a resident of Africa and he lies buried in Ghana. The central meaning of his life was the effort to assist in the liberation of his people, the Afro-American people, and certainly by 1900 he saw it as tied to the struggle for the liberation of all Africa. In the next generation, and increasingly as the time of his death approached, he believed that the freeing of Black people throughout the world was a part of the process of the freeing humanity itself.[6]

Not only did Dr. Du Bois live in Africa, attain Ghanaian citizenship, and die to be buried there in 1963, around the time that Dr. King was leading the historic March on Washington, but he also became the founding editor of the *Encyclopedia Africana* in order to document African culture-cum-history. He also wrote forcefully about European encroachment on the continent. In this respect, Dr. Du Bois used his powerful pen and his intellectual skills to provide a positive image of the African continent and its people.

Not only did postcolonial African and postmodern civil rights African American leaders seek to collaborate by encouraging one another with rhetoric and writing, but they also backed their words with action. These leaders offered much-needed advice to leaders of emerging independent African nations and often traveled to the continent to attend important conferences. They also participated in new nations' celebrations of their newly won independence, as Mrs. Coretta Scott King discussed in her published memoirs about her trip to the former Gold Coast, in the company of her husband, on the eve of its independence as the nation of Ghana. Among the several important historical details she recorded, Mrs. King wrote:

On March 3, 1957, Martin and I boarded a plane with the other black leaders whom Nkrumah had invited [to attend Ghana's independence ceremonies on March 6, 1957], including Ralph Bunche, Adam Clayton Powell, A. Phillip Randolph, Roy Wilkins, Lester Granger, and Prime Minister Norman Washington Manley of Jamaica.[7]

Additionally, in 1958, barely a year after Ghana's independence—the celebration of which was witnessed by the Kings and many other diasporan black leaders—a delegation of ten black leaders traveled from America to Ghana to attend that year's All-African Peoples Conference in Accra, the capital; it included Lincoln University President Horace Mann Bond, Etta Moten, Claude Barnett, Marguerite Cartwright, Mercer Cook, John Davis, St. Clair Drake, George McCray, Maida Spinger, and Camilla Williams.[8]

As expected, the 1958 conference both provided the nucleus and served as the springboard for the 1963 conference held in Ethiopia, that created the Organization of African Unity (OAU), with the sole aim of seeking continental political unity for Africa. At the least, the presence of the diasporan black luminaries and other dedicated Pan-Africanists, mostly from the continent and the Caribbean, gave a much-needed boost to an idea about the future unification of a continent that was and continues to be torn asunder by interethnic (or tribal) strife.

Then, in 1991, from America, the Reverend Leon Sullivan, a black religious leader from Pennsylvania, launched a biennial summit that was aimed at helping move Africa forward as it had never moved before. According to Sullivan, he devised the concept of a summit as an intense series of workshops and conference sessions designed to promote trade, tackle social problems, and stimulate investment in Africa. The first summit convened in Abidjan, Ivory Coast, where three hundred African American civil rights leaders accompanied Sullivan to meet with African leaders. Subsequent summits were held in Libreville, Gabon, in 1993; Dakar, Senegal, in 1995; Harare, Zimbabwe, in 1997; and, most recently, in the Ghanaian capital of Accra in 1999.

When boarding the plane to travel to the 1999 summit in Ghana, the Rev. Sullivan declared: "This is not a conference. This is not a convention. This is not a vacation. This is a SUMMIT! Our work is to help nudge a continent ahead and to show the world what Africans and

African Americans can do." (Whitaker 1999). The 1999 summit has been described as the largest of all of the summits. More than one thousand African Americans traveled to the West African nation to meet with leaders from nineteen African nations, educators, and business leaders. The summit attracted also nearly four thousand African delegates from across the continent. The overall achievement of the summit were described in a statement by Dr. Edith Irby Jones, the former president of the National Medical Association:

> We just didn't sit around and talk about the health problems affecting Africa. We actually put down a plan of attack and timetables for addressing those issues. So that within weeks we will have people on committees, people procuring vaccines and people actually working to eradicate and stop the spread of things like AIDS and tuberculosis and some of these other preventable diseases.[9]

Not only have the summits led by Sullivan revolutionized the relationship between African and African American leaders, but they have also played an indisputable role in shedding light on the need for economic development and sociopolitical reform in Africa. Therefore, it was not surprising that, in 1998, President Bill Clinton, with an entourage of black political and social leaders, visited several African nations in an effort to encourage and stimulate economic development and partnership. Moreover, it was on this continent that Clinton issued a feeble apology for the ravages of slavery, although he had earlier refused to offer a substantive apology with reparations to be paid to the descendants of slaves, as black leaders in and outside Africa had demanded.

Any viable assessment of African and African American relationships must devote some attention to the very important role that the Trans-Africa Forum, based in Washington, D.C., and its leader, Dr. Randall Robinson, have played in drawing international attention to the tragedy of apartheid in South Africa. Robinson and his African American organization helped formulate anti-apartheid strategies, focus media attention on the ongoing dehumanizing conditions and, on the practical side, organize anti-apartheid boycotts and protests, which eventually contributed to the overwhelming anti-apartheid pressure that led to the release of Mr. Nelson Mandela after years of imprisonment and subsequently paved the way for Mr. Mandela to become the first elected President in post-apartheid South Africa. As a leader who believes in true democracy, Mr. Mandela chose to rule South Africa for only one term, which ended in 1999.

It is not an exaggeration to suggest that African and African American leaders have worked together to dismantle the power of racist, colonial and, to an extent, neocolonial institutions in Africa and America. As is amply detailed elsewhere in this study, both groups have also worked together to facilitate strong educational institutions from which both Africans and African Americans can benefit.

Collaboration and Conflict on the Educational Front

In varied ways, American black educational institutions have played crucial roles in efforts to ensure that African leaders, first as students in America and, later, as nationalist leaders struggling against colonialism and imperialism, were given the fullest support. For example, as Marika Sherwood of London, the author of a recent biography of Nkrumah, wrote in her study, published in 1996, of Nkrumah's years abroad (1935 to 1947), that the Phelps-Stokes Fund was "the most important of the few American charitable foundations with an interest in Africa." It became one of the major sources of financial assistance to Nkrumah and several other African students studying in America.[10] The distinguished author and history professor John Hope Franklin, with his coauthor, Alfred A. Moss, Jr., and Edwin W. Smith have both noted that the Phelps-Stokes Fund was set up through a generous bequest in the final 1909 Will and Testament of Miss Caroline Phelps Stokes.[11]

Speaking of what he saw as the "good old days" for African students and their diasporan cousins in America, the late Professor Lawrence Dunbar Reddick, a University of Chicago-educated historian who was a close friend of Nkrumah, of Nigeria's first president, Nnamdi Azikiwe, and of other African leaders who studied in America, said:

> My contacts with Kwame Nkrumah came during the "good old days" when American Blacks and Africans who came to Black colleges in the U.S.A. to study were close friends and admirers. Howard, Fisk and Lincoln were institutions where the student bodies were enthusiastic about two objectives: 1. American Blacks were to aid and support the liberation of Africa from European domination; and 2. Our African brothers were to join with us over here in the U.S.A. in destroying Jim Crow.[12]

It is reassuring that, as far back as in 1909, Miss Stokes would inscribe in her will that part of her bequest should be used to assist African and other black students, with the instruction that the income be used "for the education of Negroes, both in Africa and the United States, North American Indians and needy and deserving white students."[13] Indeed, predominantly black colleges and universities continue to play a role in educating African Americans as well as Blacks from both African and Caribbean countries. The United Negro College Fund (UNCF) has also become a catalyst for ensuring that Blacks generally receive quality academic and professional training.

Indeed, as briefly noted earlier, Blacks in America were to aid and support the liberation of Africa from European domination so that, later, their sisters and brothers from liberated Africa could join with today's African Americans in their own fight against Jim Crow and other forms of institutional racism. It is in remembering the early stalwart, radical, and forward-looking mutual support that Du Bois, Reddick, and other diasporan Blacks extended to black nations on the continent that, very sadly, many Africans and African Americans these days wonder about the seeming disconnectedness between the two sets of Blacks.

The question, then, is this: What happened to create the measure of animosity and, sometimes, mutual suspicion that Africans and American Blacks harbor against each other? As discussed later, some writers and the news media have played a large role in presenting negative stereotypes that have damaged relations between Africans and African Americans.

As the Pendulum Swings toward Conflict: The Power of the Pen

Professor Inez Smith Reid, one of the leading scholars on Africa, undertook research on the relationship between today's Africans and African Americans. She wrote: "Little wonder, then, that black Americans were ripe to swallow much of the propaganda on Africa disseminated by Whites reputed to be men of letters. . . . With the circulation of such writings, interest in Africa was bound to dim."[14]

Louis Agassiz, a Harvard University scientist and anthropologist quoted in 1996 by Reid, a Barnard College professor, described Africans as "indolent, playful, sensual, imitative, subservient, good na-tured, versatile, unsteady in their purpose, devoted, and affection-ate."[15] Very worried by the negative writings, Dr. Du Bois reportedly "correlated the flagging black American interest in Africa in the nine-teenth century to the rise of the cotton industry and to a simultaneous effort on the part of the church and American society in general to de-grade African culture and history."[16]

In spite of Du Bois's worries, several prominent African American scholars continued to write negatively about Africa. For example, in 1882, George Washington Williams, although a black historian of note, had the effrontery to write, among other demeaning details, that "the Negro type is the result of degradation. It is nothing more than the lowest strata of the African race."[17]

In retrospect, it is not surprising that some of the black leaders shied away from anything African. For example, Adelaide Hill, trying to den-igrate Africa, wrote, "In all candor it should be admitted that Ameri-can Negroes as a group were not at an early date enthusiastic in their desire for knowledge about Africa. For too long Africa and things African seemed to relate to their position of inferiority in American life."[18] Rayford Logan put it diplomatically in writing, indeed as if he were merely offering the following explanation, "Equally important, and concomitant with the growth of imperialism, was the intensifica-tion of campaigns to portray 'Black Africa' as a land of heathens, sav-ages, and cannibals. As a result, some American Negroes were ambiva-lent about their identity as Negroes in America and rejected any associ-ation with the 'dark continent.'"[19]

While Africans are often undermined and even degraded in the eyes of their African American "cousins," African Americans are, in turn, presented to Africans in the most distasteful ways. In some cases, they are seen as spies and agents of the "divide-and-conquer" syndrome of the white or nonblack political establishment. One prominent example is a former American Ambassador to Ghana, the late Dr. Franklin Williams, who was accused by Nkrumah and others—although erro-neously—of being a spy who worked to overthrow the Ghanian gov-ernment in February 1966 on behalf of the Central Intelligence Agency (CIA).[20] Ambassador Williams later left Ghana to become the president of the Phelps-Stokes Fund in New York.

In a mild defense of Ambassador Williams, given the circumstances of his few weeks' stay in Ghana before Nkrumah's overthrow, I documented in *Kwame Nkrumah: Six Years in Exile, 1966–1972* that it was not logistically possible for the African American envoy, the first black U.S. diplomat to serve in Ghana in that high capacity since the African nation's independence in 1957, to be involved in such an elaborately planned coup. I elaborated further: "According to the existing records, the envoy arrived in Ghana on January 8, 1966 and the *coup* took place on February 24, 1966."[21]

Unfortunately, Ambassador Williams, who returned home after his tour of ambassadorial duty, died of cancer and could not finish his memoirs, as he often told me that he hoped to do, to defend himself against the unfortunate accusation that he, as an African American diplomat and former Peace Corps deputy director, was involved in the overthrow of a progressive African government headed by a graduate of his own alma mater, Lincoln University. However, the idea that many African Americans serve as spies for the American government has become a popular stigmatizing refrain that is utilized by some Africans.

Also sad is the fact that in the aftermath of the overthrow of Nkrumah's regime in Ghana, very unfriendly and unflattering assessment of Nkrumah and other African leaders were published by the Western news media. Some of these publications were either edited or written by African American scholars who had benefited tremendously from the generous invitations from African leaders for their fellow Blacks outside the continent to return to their ancestral home. One such unfortunate publications was Leslie Alexander Lacy's *The Rise and Fall of a Proper Negro* (1970), written by an African American scholar who, with St. Clair Drake and several other African American intellectuals, had accepted Nkrumah's invitation, moved to Ghana, and taught for many years at University of Ghana, Legon. Apart from casting aspersions on Nkrumah's character and ridiculing several aspects of his leadership, Lacy, playing on words, described the overthrow of Nkrumah's regime as "the end of Negro existentialism."[22] Also, in concluding his writing about Nkrumah's "downfall," Professor Lacy recalled:

> The rest is history. I survived for six months. I left for Nigeria to get a job at the University of Lagos. They were having a *coup* there, and the [Nigeria-Biafra] civil war was easily predictable. It finally occurred to me, sitting in Lagos, that it was time to return to America. And so, after four years away [mostly in Ghana and briefly in Nigeria]—years crowded with discoveries—years of struggling and despairing to develop a new me, of contemplating school, of fashioning a new image of the world, of

seeing Africa and participating in her revolution, of partial success and added recognition, I arrived at Kennedy Airport in late summer 1966, ending my exile in Mother Africa.[23]

Although it was the general feeling of many intellectuals that most of the negative reports about Africans and their diasporan black "cousins" would be found in small-circulation publications or, possibly, in the tabloid press, that has not been the case. Instead, several sophisticated publications have, in the recent past, made it their business to specialize in degrading publicity about either Africa in general or specific African countries in particular.

For example, in its "Sunday" column, in the January 17, 1999, edition of the *New York Times Magazine,* Edmund J. Pankau, described as a private investigator and the author of *Hide Your Assets and Disappear* (Regan Books), poked intriguing but very degrading fun at Nigeria that many Africans did not find amusing. In "Questions for Edmund J. Pankau," a reader had written to ask about where the Yugoslav President and his wife should run "if The Hague [the Tribunal on War Crimes or Genocide] suddenly decided to go after Slobodan Milosevic and the Serb strongman decided to skip."[24] Pankau's answer was:

> He [Milosevic] may want to go to Nigeria. They offer new identities and will even stage your death for you. They'll blow up a boat or arrange a "fatal" car accident, then give you the name of someone who really did die. Explosions are preferred because there's no body left. . . . They do the whole thing in Nigeria for about $1,000. Often a person falls into a river and is eaten by crocodiles. An explosion on a boat costs extra.[25]

Surely, poking such fun—which, sadly, borders on defamation at times—does not improve the image of Africa for the young African Americans who are still deciding whether to look on Africa as an ancestral home. Happily, however, as earlier stated, there is still one basic fact that remains true—that the ancestors of all black people originated in Africa. As observed in the quotation at the beginning of this essay, the only sadness arises from the fact that knowing which "part of Africa each black person originated from is another issue entirely."[26] Yet, not knowing where an African American came from in Africa should not be a problem but, instead, a challenge for the African American interested in researching his or her ancestry, as Alex Haley of *Roots* fame did.

Not only are anti-African publications being written by non-Blacks, but African Americans and even Africans are also authoring such works. In a recent book, *Out of America*, Richard Richburg, quoted at the beginning of this essay, described his abominable experiences in Africa and, in the end, reported that he was glad to be an American.

Also, for at least a decade, Professor George Ayittey, a Ghana-born economist with a conservative ideological bend, has written several books and newspaper articles that have been labeled as anti-African. In fact, on the back cover of the cloth edition of *Africa in Chaos* (St. Martin's Press, 1998), Ayittey, with whom I have had ideological, philosophical, and other differences, agreed with his publishers to associate me with his work by quoting, out of context, a one-paragraph statement from a lengthy *Africa News Weekly* column that I wrote on the Ghanaian's published work.

For African American writers and journalists, the interesting question is how far American Blacks should go in confronting African despots and deplorable socioeconomic conditions on the continent. This question is especially important in contemporary Africa, where the elected leaders and those who have foisted themselves on various nations there through coups d'état are usually Black. Although Randall Robinson of the Trans-Africa Forum concedes that it is disquieting and uncomfortable to address these issues in a racist environment, he further argues that human rights ought to be judged by one yardstick: "When it's wrong, it's wrong."[27]

Therefore, African and African American writers are increasingly putting aside their rose-colored glasses in an effort to see other Blacks as they really are, rather than accepting myths and dreams. While these efforts to create honest dialogue are admirable and may, in the end, lead to cooperative healing, they are also certain to create conflict and misunderstanding along the way.

Propinquity and the Politics of Conflict

While distance and the fight against a common enemy facilitated cooperative relationship between Africans and African Americans, it appears that propinquity in the form of the migration of Africans to America has facilitated a measure of conflict. This is especially so with respect to politics, public policy, and the quest for opportunity in race-conscious American society. An example of the extent to which more recent black immigrants have disagreed with other Blacks, especially those at lower income levels, is in the arena of immigration. Recent immigrants from Africa, the Caribbean, and elsewhere are more likely to support liberal immigration policies but to disapprove of anti-immigration legislation like Proposition 187, the anti-immigration law in California, which sought to deny welfare and other benefits to both legal and illegal immigrants.

On the other hand, however, lower-income, native Blacks often perceive immigrants as fierce competitors for low-skilled jobs and adequate housing. As a result, support for nonrestrictive immigration policies among Blacks largely derive from a sense of shared ethnic identity. A second issue is the extent to which naturalized Caribbean and African immigrants are competing with indigenous African Americans for electoral positions. For example, in 1995–96, Mr. Joe Aidoo, a Ghana-born, naturalized resident of New Orleans, almost unseated a long-term African American state legislator in Louisiana. Aidoo, a hard-working Loyola University student leader, lost the election narrowly. Also, in New York, there have been several local elections in which naturalized African and Caribbean-born Blacks have competed with native Blacks for positions. While intraracial competition is not new in American politics, it does complicate the already tenuous public policy agenda among the black political elite.

Additionally, research on inner-city communities has revealed a strong bias against native black labor in favor of immigrant labor from Mexico, Asia, and Africa. In "We'd Love to Hire You But . . .", the authors convincingly demonstrate that employees prefer to hire immigrant black labor rather than African Americans, a situation that the latter find frustrating and irritating.

Not only is conflict between Africans and African Americans evident in American communities, but it exists also in African countries, where some American Blacks have gone in search of entrepreneurial opportunities. According to Nokwanda Sithole, the deputy editor of *Enterprise*, a black business magazine based in Johannesburg, "there's a sense of solidarity, a sort of black thing, but there's also a lot of jealousy on behalf of South African black businessmen. They fear the African Americans are coming to take jobs from local professionals. That is a widespread view."[28]

Moreover, while American-born Blacks in South Africa have some commonalities with their South African brothers and sisters, it is evident that political and social struggles, customs, and linguistic differences can present limitations to cooperation and collaboration. However, many American-born black businessmen confess that they are not bothered by these limitations. Perhaps the words of Mr. Roland Pearson, executive director of Ebony Development Alternatives, adequately summarizes the sentiments of many African American sojourners in Africa:

> Whatever the emotional fascination Africa may hold, the major motivation for being here is simple—making money. It was a business thing, but I have always been interested in this region and country. It was a nice marriage of my personal ambition and the country's needs.

Conclusion

Thus, as we return to the question posed at the beginning of this essay, the evidence suggests that there is no straightforward way to assess the relationship between Africans and African Americans. Most certainly, African American and African leaders have made every effort to ensure that their respective struggles for freedom and justice on the continent and in the United States benefited from the other's rich experiences and strategies; hence the interactive connections through regular pilgrimage-like trips to and from Africa. Many African Americans have traveled to Africa, very often to break bread with their "cousins" and also to see the "Motherland."

While many African Americans genuinely have a sense of belonging to and consider Africa a true "Motherland," some Africans on the continent have met African Americans with either a sense of superiority or outright contempt. In fact, some U.S.-born Africans of African parentage have begun to call themselves American-Africans, as opposed to being labeled African Americans. When it comes to criticisms of Africa and Africans by African Americans, many black scholars agree that, while the substance may be true, in the words of the Loyola University Professor Tunde Adeleke, "the color line mandates racial solidarity under all circumstances."[29] Indeed, the same yardstick should be used in measuring African criticisms of African America and African Americans, especially if conflict is to be replaced with cooperation between continental Africans and African Americans. Above all, there should be an end to the romanticized view of the place that African Americans occupy in America and, most certainly, on the African continent that diasporan Blacks refer to, with much reverence, as the "Motherland."

NOTES

1. Robert O. Awolabi, *An African's View of the American Society* (Chapel Hill, N.C.: Professional Press, 1996), p. 61.

2. Keith B. Richburg, *Chronicle of Higher Education* 43(27): B11.

3. Kwame Nkrumah, *Axioms of Kwame Nkrumah* (London: Thomas Nelson and Sons, 1967), p. 3.

4. Kwame Nkrumah's position as Leader of Government Business before his country's independence in 1957 was considered nominal and not substantive because the ruling British colonial authorities still occupied several of the nation's most important cabinet positions, including those of defense and finance.

5. Kwame Nkrumah, *The Autobiography of Kwame Nkrumah* (London: Thomas Nelson and Sons, 1957), p. 164.

6. Herbert Aptheker, Introduction to W. E. B. Du Bois, *Africa and Its Place in Modern History* (New York: Kraus-Thomas Publishers, 1977), p. v.

7. Coretta Scott King, *My Life with Martin Luther King, Jr.* (New York: Holt, Rinehart, and Winston, 1969), p. 54.

8. Inez Smith Reid, "Black Americans and Africa," in Mabel M. Smythe, ed., *The Black American Reference Book* (Englewood Cliffs, N.J.: Prentice-Hall, 1976), p. 671.

9. Charles Whitaker, "Ghana's Summit Success," *Ebony,* August 1999, p. 108.

10. Marika Sherwood, *Kwame Nkrumah: The Years Abroad, 1935–1947* (Legon, Ghana: Freedom Publications, 1996), pp. 55–60.

11. Edwin W. Smith, *Aggrey of Africa: A Study in Black and White* (London: Student Christian Movement Press, 1929), p. 143; also in John Hope Franklin and Alfred A. Moss Jr., *From Slavery To Freedom* (New York: Knopf, 1994), p. 266.

12. A. B. Assensoh, *Kwame Nkrumah of Africa* (Devon, U.K.: Stockwell, 1989), p. 247.

13. Smith, *Aggrey of Africa,* p. 143.

14. Reid, "Black Americans," p. 649.

15. Ibid.

16. Ibid.

17. George Washington Williams, *History of the Negro Race in America*

from 1619–1880 (New York: Arno Press & the New York Times, 1968), p. 109; also quoted in Reid, "Black Americans," pp. 648–649.

18. Reid, "Black Americans," p. 648.

19. Rayford W. Logan and Michael R. Winston, *The Negro in the United States,* vol. 2 (New York: Van Nostrand Reinhold, 1971), pp. 92–93; also in Reid, "Black Americans," p. 648.

20. For a detailed discussion of Nkrumah's views on the alleged American involvement in his overthrow, readers may consult Kwame Nkrumah, *Dark Days in Ghana* (New York: International, 1968). A book that discusses the coup from an American perspective is John Stockwell, *In Search of Enemies: A CIA Story* (New York: Norton, 1978). In my own book on Nkrumah, I discuss several aspects as well: A. B. Assensoh, *Kwame Nkrumah: Six Years in Exile, 1966–1972* (Devon, U.K.: Stockwell, 1978).

21. Assensoh, *Six Years in Exile,* p. 48.

22. Leslie Alexander Lacy, *The Rise and Fall of a Proper Negro* (New York: Macmillan, 1970), p. 13.

23. Ibid., p. 247.

24. Edmund J. Pankau, "Questions for Edmund J. Pankau," *New York Times Magazine,* January 17, 1999, p. 13.

25. Ibid., p. 13.

26. Awolabi, *An African's View,* p. 61.

27. Michel Marriott and Lucy Shackelford, "Brother against Brother," *Newsweek,* May 22, 1995, p. 47.

28. Judith Matloff, "South African Blacks Wary of US 'Kin,'" *Christian Science Monitor,* November 2, 1995, p. 1.

29. Tunde Adeleke, "The Color Line as a Confining Restraining Paradigm: Keith Richburg and His Critiques Analyzed," *Western Journal of Black Studies* 23, no. 2 (summer 1999): 97.

BIBLIOGRAPHY

Books

Adeleke, Tunde. 1999. "The Color Line as a Confining Restraining Paradigm: Keith Richburg and His Critiques Analyzed." *Western Journal of Black Studies* 23, no. 2 (summer): 97.

Aptheker, Herbert. 1977. Introduction to W. E. B. Du Bois, *Africa and Its Place in Modern History.* New York: Kraus-Thomas Publishers.

Assensoh, A. B. 1978. *Kwame Nkrumah: Six Years in Exile, 1966–1972.* Devon, U.K.: Stockwell.

———. 1989. *Kwame Nkrumah of Africa.* Devon, U.K.: Stockwell.

———. 1998. *African Political Leadership: Jomo Kenyatta, Kwame Nkrumah, and Julius K. Nyerere*. Malabar, Fl.: Krieger.

Awolabi, Robert O. 1996. *An African's View of the American Society*. Chapel Hill, N.C.: Professional Press.

Du Bois, W. E. B. 1977. *Africa And Its Place In Modern History*. Millwood, N.Y.: Kraus-Thomas.

King, Coretta Scott. 1969. *My Life with Martin Luther King, Jr.* New York: Holt, Rinehart, and Winston.

Kirschenmann, Joleen, and Kathryn M. Neckerman. 1991. "We'd Love to Hire Them, But . . . : The Meaning of Race for Employers." Christopher Jencks and Paul Peterson, *The Urban Underclass*. Washington, D.C.: Brookings.

Lacy, Leslie Alexander. 1970. *The Rise and Fall of a Proper Negro*. New York: Macmillan.

Logan, Rayford W., and Michael R. Winston. 1971. *The Negro in the United States*. vol. 2. New York: Van Nostrand Reinhold.

Marable, Manning. 1987. *African and Caribbean Politics: From Kwame Nkrumah To Maurice Bishop*. London: Verso.

Marriott, Michel, and Lucy Shackelford. 1995. "Brother against Brother." *Newsweek*, May 22, p. 47.

Matloff, Judith. 1995. "South African Blacks Wary of U.S. 'Kin.'" *Christian Science Monitor*, November 2, p. 1.

Nkrumah, Kwame. 1957. *The Autobiography of Kwame Nkrumah*. London: Thomas Nelson and Sons.

———. 1967. *Axioms of Kwame Nkrumah*. London: Thomas Nelson & Sons.

———. 1968. *Dark Days in Ghana*. New York: International.

Pankau, Edmund. 1999. "Question for Edmund J. Pankau." *New York Times Magazine*, January 17, p. 13.

Richburg, Keith. *Chronicle of Higher Education* 43 (27): B11.

Rodney, Walter. 1968. *How Europe Underdeveloped Africa*. Washington, D.C.: Howard University Press.

Sherwood, Marika. 1996. *Kwame Nkrumah: The Years Abroad, 1935–1947*. Legan, Ghana: Freedom Publications.

Smith, Edwin W. 1929. *Aggrey of Africa: A Study in Black and White*. London: Student Christian Movement Press.

Smythe, Mabel M., ed. 1976. *The Black American Reference Book*. Englewood Cliffs, N.J.: Prentice-Hall.

Stockwell, John. 1978. *In Search of Enemies: A CIA Story*. New York: Norton.

Whitaker, Charles. 1999. "Ghana's Summit Success." *Ebony*, August p. 108.

Williams, George Washington. 1968. *History of the Negro Race in America from 1619–1880*. New York: Arno Press and the *New York Times*.

Wright, Richard. 1954. *Black Power*. New York: Harper & Row.

Journals, Magazines, and Newspapers

Proteus Journal.
The New York Times.
The Western Journal of Black Studies.
West Africa Magazine (London).

Part II

Political and Media Institutions

Chapter 5

Immigrants, Blacks, and Cities

Michael Jones-Correa

Since the 1950s, cities have been at the forefront of various social, economic, and political triumphs for American Blacks. While cities have, of course, been the site of conflict and social change on a massive scale, and have experienced riots in three of the past four decades, it is important to recall that the first civil rights bus boycott occurred in Baton Rouge, the capital of Louisiana, on June 19, 1953, when Blacks demanded that the city honor its own ordinance allowing all riders—Blacks and Whites alike—to be seated in city buses on a first-come, first-served basis. Also, black mayoral power was initially demonstrated in cities such as Cleveland, Ohio, and Gary, Indiana, where, in 1967, Carl Stokes and Richard Hatcher, respectively, mobilized Blacks and their white allies around successful mayoral campaigns. Given the size of their municipal workforces, cities have also provided Blacks with an opportunity to work in white-collar industries and thereby facilitated their economic and socioeconomic elevation.

But Blacks are not the first racial-cum-ethnic group to benefit from the transformative power of cities, their resources and institutions. Decades before them, the Irish took advantage of trade unions, racial tactics, and the political machine to catapult themselves from outsider to insider status. In this respect, they provide a preview of sorts of the logistics and obstacles faced by Blacks— although the Irish have obviously been able to assimilate to a much greater extent than their black counterparts.

As American cities experience a new generation of immigration, from Asia, Africa, and Latin America, the role of municipal

133

institutions in bringing about or impeding the political incorpora-
tion of the new citizens, has been little investigated. Relying on
the new institutionalist framework, Michael Jones-Correa pro-
vides a framework to explain how different types of cities and
their various institutions respond to the needs of Blacks and more
recent immigrant groups.

Over the past thirty years, cities in the United States have undergone a series of swift and dramatic changes. Not the least of these has been the departure from the nation's largest cities of native Whites, who have left for the suburbs; the incorporation of African Americans into the governing coalitions of a number of cities, and concentrated, large-scale immigration. The cast of urban actors has become increasingly diverse and the dynamics of urban politics increasingly complex. This chapter explores the tension between institutional stability and democratic values by focusing on the adaptability of local, particularly urban, political institutions to the introduction of new political actors. How have cities dealt with rapid demographic changes, which have taken place in a relatively short period of time? How have they responded as new actors have been introduced to the urban mix? How has the incorporation of new ethnic minorities been complicated by the presence of older minorities, whose own incorporation into the social, economic, and political structure remains in many ways incomplete? What do these cities' responses, or their absence, say about the possibilities for the political incorporation of new urban actors?

I begin with the assumption, following the arguments of the "New Institutionalists", that urban institutions, like institutions more generally, are basically conservative. Once in place, they are resistant to change. However, the structure of urban institutions varies systematically. Basically, local governments are either "horizontally" or "vertically" organized. This variation in the urban institutional framework has important effects on how cities respond to new urban actors, such as Blacks and immigrants, and what form that response will take. This is particularly true when, as was the case in the late 1980s, intergovernmental transfers to cities were at a low point and cities themselves were experiencing severe budgetary crises.

The implications of this variance in urban institutions are evident in cities' response to interethnic disturbances in the 1980s and 1990s. Together with structural variables—the economic context and the demographics of each city—institutions are critical intermediary variables in interethnic conflict and in the renegotiation of political access, representation, and resources that takes place following ethnic conflict. This chapter, then, explores demographic and structural shifts that affect cities, seeing them through the lens of interethnic civil disturbances and the manner in which cities respond to these changes.

New Institutionalism

Over the past fifteen years, there has been a resurgence of interest in the manner in which institutions structure political behavior. Institutions are increasingly recognized as laying out the "rules of the game" for players in the political arena, guidelines that set the parameters for allowable action, constrain strategies, and structure choices (Martin 1997). The basis of institutions' influence lies in the fact that, whether formal or informal, they are "relatively stable, routinized arrangements."[1] Institutions last beyond the immediate deployment of power and interests that create them. The understanding is that institutions are not simply propelled by the tides of power and interest but rather help to shape both. Power and interests are themselves partly the result of institutional variables (Pierson 1994: 31).

Once institutions are in place, their very existence creates the conditions for their continued stability (Pierson 1994: 42–45). Given the sunk costs in a given institution, switching to an alternative set of institutions is usually prohibitively costly in the short run, even if other possibilities offer a better return in the long run. The reason for this is in part that new institutions may have large startup costs that are likely to outweigh the costs of any inefficiencies in the existing institutions (North 1990: 92–104; Arthur 1989). In addition, institutions generate commitments and create interests that profit from the perpetuation of these institutions. If these institutions are threatened, these interests mobilize in their defense.[2] Finally, given the imperfection and the high cost of information in the political world, "decision makers lean heavily on preexisting policy frameworks, adjusting only at the margins to accommodate distinctive features of new situations" (Pierson 1994: 42). All these factors together ensure that institutions tend to be "path dependent," that is, the initial choices of institutional design have long-term implications. Once institutions are in place, they tend to stay in place.

What the "New Institutionalists" have developed over the past few years is a set of theories about why institutions matter. These theories rest largely on arguments that institutions are inherently conservative, meaning that they resist change of any kind. Once in place, institutions are difficult to dislodge; if there is any change, that change will occur mostly at the margins.[3] The very persuasiveness of the institutionalist argument, however, raises some concerns. The primary concern explored in this essay is that the stability of institutions itself may be problematic. Some degree of change may be normatively desirable. From the perspective of democratic theory, we would want representative institutions to reflect the changing views of citizens. Elections, for example, are one means of achieving this goal. That is why democratic institutions in general are designed with some leeway for change. In the United States, for instance, the Constitution has an amendment process, and electoral districts undergo adjustments in the number of representatives and the boundaries of the districts they represent on the basis of the decennial census. The more inflexible the institution, then, the less likely it is to reflect democratic principles. Thus, institutional stability may be at odds with democratic values.

Cities as Institutions

The tension between institutional stability and democracy is evident in many areas, but perhaps nowhere as starkly as in urban areas in the United States. If we look at ethnic and racial minorities, for instance, on the one hand urban areas often provided these actors with their first experience of government—of its role in policing, housing, health care, education, and the job market. Historically, minorities' first experience with the state has been local. It is their participation in this local context that provide racial and ethnic minorities with the tools and skills of citizenship, that leads to management of their relationships with their neighbors, and that serves as a gateway into participation in the larger national polity. Urban institutions therefore have a critical role as political institutions.

On the other hand, urban institutions have never straightforwardly translated the interests of new actors into political influence and representation.[4] The old political machine, which some still romanticize as having taken immigrants up and thrust them into politics, rarely lived up to its reputation. Machines mobilized new actors only as long as they were in competition for political dominance. Once that dominance was established, machines had very little incentive to mobilize new actors who would demand their share of scarce resources.[5] Turning out the vote was only a means to an end; when it could be dispensed with, it often was (Erie 1988; Jones-Correa 1998: ch. 4). Reform regimes, which were established to counter the perceived flaws of the urban machine, were specifically designed to deflate voter turnout and to insulate urban administration from the machinations of elected politicians. By creating appointed city managers to replace elected mayors, by establishing firewalls between administrators and elected officials (and by reducing the powers of the latter), and by creating at-large districts instead of single-member districts, Progressive-era reforms made it much more difficult for new actors at the margins to mobilize effectively and have their voices heard in the day-to-day running of the city's affairs.

Both the urban political machine, which first appeared in the nineteenth century, and the reform regime, which was introduced at the beginning of the twentieth century, were designed for institutional continuity, not for political mobilization. They were both conservative, in the sense I have posited: They resisted change and made every effort to perpetuate themselves. These attempts were largely successful. Though true political machines hardly exist anymore and Progressive reforms have been transmuted over time so that cities are characterized more by the diversity of their forms of government than by any allegiance to a particular set of principles of governance, these initial designs of city government have had a lasting effect. Once these institutions were set in place, they successfully entrenched themselves.

For example, even as cities underwent racial succession in the 1960s and 1970s, with African Americans acquiring proportionally greater weight in the governance of cities and with more Blacks being elected both as mayors and as council members, urban institutions themselves were relatively immune to change. Blacks achieved descriptive representation while making relatively little headway with substantive policy-oriented changes that would improve the lot of most black residents in urban areas (Karnig and Welch 1980). In large part the reason for this was that capturing top locally elected positions gave African Americans little leverage over broader institutional and structural problems. Elected officials were tightly constrained by the fiscal crises of cities, local civil service bureaucracies, the decline of the urban manufacturing economy, and the erosion of the tax base with white middle-class flight (Patterson 1974; Preston 1976; Nelson and Meranto 1977; and Nelson 1978). Black politicians had perforce to work within the institutions that bound them.

The persistence of institutional forms underscores the fact that while cities today are not easily classified as "machine" or "reform," and while there are almost as many hybrid models of local government as there are cities, nevertheless, the institutional pedigree of cities is still important in understanding how cities respond and adapt to change. Reform and machine traditions have left institutional legacies. These are increasingly not in cities' choice of chief executive (larger cities, in particular, have moved toward some form of elected mayor, away from the appointed city manager) or in their mode of electing officials (since the passage of the Voting Rights Act many cities have abandoned at-large districts in favor of single-member districts). The relevant distinction is between "horizontally" organized and "vertically" organized governing institutions. Vertically organized cities, descendants of the strong-party cities of the nineteenth century, have a dense network of local representative bodies that link every level of government, from neighborhood associations on up. Horizontally organized cities isolate each level of government from the others, a legacy of the Progressive reform movement.

The differences between horizontally and vertically organized cities has implications for the way in which they adapt to change and, by extension, the manner in which they function as democratic institutions. Although institutions are resistant to change (and urban institutions are no exception), they respond when obliged to by conditions outside their control. Given the necessity of change, cities respond differently and, in fact, have different capacities to respond, depending on their institutional setup. We would expect vertically organized cities to channel the new demands through the networks that link levels of local organizations together. Similarly, given the absence of these linkages in horizontally organized cities, we would expect these demands to be shunted elsewhere.

Pressures for Institutional Change:
The New Urban Landscape

In 1996 the Census Bureau announced that almost 10 percent of the U.S. population was made up of first-generation immigrants, the highest proportion since the 1940s and more than double the percentage in 1970 (4.8 percent). Four and a half million immigrants arrived between 1990 and 1994; 8.3 million arrived in the 1980s, and 9.8 million before 1980 (see Jaret 1991; Portes and Rumbaut 1990; Waldinger 1989). By the early 1990s, almost one out of every two new Americans was an immigrant. The foreign-born population is not distributed evenly throughout the country. In 1990, 76 percent of immigrants arriving to the United States resided in one of only six states: California, New York, Florida, Texas, New Jersey, and Illinois. California and New York alone attract more than 40 percent of new immigrants (Smith and Edmonston 1997: 59). The distribution of the foreign-born is very similar to that of new immigrants. California is home to 7.7 million foreign-born persons—more than one-third of all immigrants to the United States and nearly one-quarter of all California residents. New York ranks second, with 2.9 million, and Florida ranks third, with 2.1 million foreign-born. Three other states have more than one million foreign-born residents—Texas, Illinois, and New Jersey. Immigrants are concentrated in a relatively few states and, within these states, in selected metropolitan areas (see Figure 5.1).

According to the 1990 census, more than 93 percent of the foreign-born population resides in metropolitan areas, compared with 73 percent of native residents. As a result, major urban areas, and, increasingly, secondary urban and suburban areas as well, have gone through rapid demographic shifts. About one-half of new immigrants entering the United States in the 1980s live in one of eight metropolitan areas: Los Angeles, New York, Miami, Anaheim, Chicago, Washington, D.C., Houston, and San Francisco (Smith and Edmonston 1997: 61) (see Figure 5.2). It is impossible, walking through these cities today, to ignore the signs of transformative change. These can be seen in the lettering of signs over the storefronts, which are not just in English but in a panoply of other languages as well; in the faces of store owners, street vendors, waiters, pedestrians, passengers on the bus lines; and in the astonishing mix of national origins among the students in the schools.

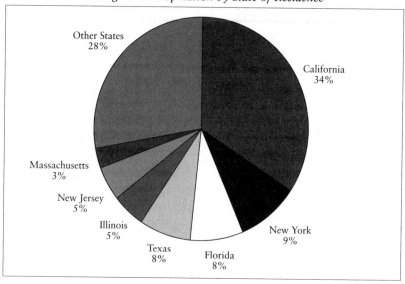

FIGURE 5.1
Foreign-Born Population by State of Residence

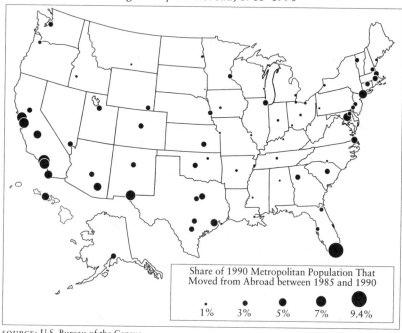

FIGURE 5.2
Migration from Abroad, 1985–1990

Share of 1990 Metropolitan Population That
Moved from Abroad between 1985 and 1990

1%   3%   5%   7%   9.4%

SOURCE: U.S. Bureau of the Census.

These three facts at least are clear: There are more first-generation immigrants residing in the United States than ever before; the vast majority of these immigrants settle in a handful of states; and within these states they are overwhelmingly concentrated in urban areas. (See Table 5.1.) Urban areas in these states, therefore, are in the midst of accelerated demographic transitions. Dramatic demographic change is not new in the American experience—certainly previous waves of immigration, rapid urbanization, the migration of Blacks from the South, and the postwar move to the suburbs have all brought massive change in relatively short periods of time. In one sense, then, the new wave of

TABLE 5.1
Cities with Populations of 200,000 or More Ranked by Percent Foreign-Born and Percent Speaking Language Other Than English

	Percentage of Persons Foreign Born, 1990		Percentage of Persons Speaking Language Other Than English at Home, 1990	
	Percent	Rank	Percent	Rank
Miami, FL	59.7	1	73.3	1
Santa Ana, CA	50.9	2	69.2	2
Los Angeles, CA	38.4	3	49.9	4
San Francisco, CA	34.0	4	42.4	6
New York, NY	28.4	5	41.0	9
Anaheim, CA	28.4	5	37.4	11
San Jose, CA	26.5	7	38.5	10
Jersey City, NJ	24.6	8	41.3	8
Long Beach, CA	24.3	9	32.8	16
El Paso, TX	23.4	10	66.7	3
Stockton, CA	22.6	11	36.5	13
Honolulu, HI	21.4	12	33.8	14
San Diego, CA	20.9	13	29.2	18
Boston, MA	20.0	14	25.6	22
Oakland, CA	19.8	15	27.3	20
Newark, NJ	18.7	16	36.8	12
Houston, TX	17.8	17	30.7	17
Fresno, CA	17.1	18	33.1	15
Chicago, IL	16.9	19	29.1	19
Riverside, CA	15.5	20	25.0	24
Sacramento, CA	13.7	21	23.8	25
Seattle, WA	13.1	22	15.4	32
Dallas, TX	12.5	23	22.2	27
Tuscon, AZ	10.7	24	27.1	21
Las Vegas, NV	10.3	25	15.2	33
Washington, DC	9.7	26	12.5	37
San Antonio, TX	9.4	27	47.3	5
Fort Worth, TX	9.0	28	19.4	28
Phoenix, AZ	8.6	29	18.7	29
Austin, TX	8.5	30	22.4	26

SOURCE: U.S. Census Bureau

immigration into urban areas is simply one more in a chain of demographic transformations that have continually made and remade the United States. What is new is the context in which these demographic shifts have been taking place. Many of these new immigrants arrived into multiethnic urban areas that were already undergoing fundamental economic transitions while facing severely constrained public resources. In the midst of economic downturn, the institutional response demanded by these demographic changes was complicated by two additional factors: competing claims at the local level, where immigrants from Asia and Latin America were directly or indirectly competing with native African Americans for both public and private resources, and the withdrawal of support by the state and federal government.

New Actors and Competition over Resources

The influx of immigrants into cities over the past thirty years has overshadowed an equally striking movement: the exodus of middle-class Blacks from central cities (see Farley 1987; Galster 1991; and Culver 1982). While the suburbanization of African Americans began in the late 1960s, it accelerated in the 1970s and 1980s. Middle-class and working-class black suburbs appeared, for instance, around predominantly African American cities like Detroit, Gary, and Atlanta, as well as around cities like Chicago, Los Angeles, Miami, and Washington, D.C. African American populations in many cities have remained flat, with migration outward either to the suburbs or, in a reversal of patterns earlier in the century, back to the South. The 1970s and 1980s were characterized by the suburbanization not only of Whites but of other ethnic groups as well (Frey 1995). Without immigration, many cities, particularly those in the northeastern United States, would have had significant (or significantly higher) population losses. New York City in the early 1990s, for instance, lost half a million residents; however, these were replaced by at least an equal number of immigrants.

The suburbanization of the black middle class should not obscure the fact that significant African American populations remain in cities. There is a continued concentration of African Americans in urban areas, despite suburbanization (see Tobin 1987; Orfield 1986; Massey and Denton 1993). But much of the black population that remains in central cities is substantially cut off from the larger urban economy, unlike the urban black population of the 1950s and 1960s (see Wilson 1987, 1997).

Not every city that has a substantial black population has been affected by immigration—Atlanta, Baltimore, Cleveland, Detroit, Gary, and Pittsburgh, for instance, have not—but the major cities that have been *most* impacted by immigration—Los Angeles, New York, Anaheim, Chicago, Washington, D.C., Houston, Miami, and San Francisco—all have significant native Black populations. In these cities Blacks have been joined by sizable contingents of first-generation immigrants who have moved into adjacent, and at times even the same, neighborhoods. While many immigrants have moved directly into outlying suburban areas, many others, particularly those with less economic and social capital, move into central cities. Searching for cheap housing and access to transportation and jobs, they may compete with African Americans for the same scarce resources.

Although a consensus seems to be emerging that immigration is not, as a whole, detrimental to the job prospects of the native, this may not hold true for those at the very bottom of the ladder. A study by the National Research Council indicated that workers with lower levels of education are particularly vulnerable to the effects of immigration. Because new immigrants increase the supply of low-skilled labor and compete for the same jobs, immigration account for a significant portion of the erosion of wages among native high-school dropouts (Smith and Edmonston 1997: 236). According to the study, immigration led to about a 5 percent wage reduction in the 1980s for this group. High-school dropouts account for less than 10 percent of the American workforce but make up a significantly larger percentage of the resident central-city workforce. The wage effects of immigration are concentrated, therefore, in the areas where lower-skilled immigrants and native workers are themselves concentrated—in inner cities.

In addition to these wage effects, there may be some job displacement going on as well. Recent research in the New York and Los Angeles metro areas suggests that immigrant social networks serve to lower the information costs immigrants face in the job market, giving immigrants an advantage in the marketplace for lower-skilled jobs and driving out competitors—particularly African Americans (Waldinger 1996). In addition, the National Research Council study notes that several studies have found that employers may also strongly prefer to hire immigrants over inner-city Blacks (Smith and Edmonston 1997: 394. See also Kasinitz and Rosenberg 1994; Kirschenman and Neckerman 1991; Neckerman and Kirschenman 1991; and Wilson 1987).

Competition does not occur only in the private sphere. Indeed, there is every indication that the more intractable competition takes place in the areas of political representation and public-sector hiring (Waldinger 1995). While contestation in the job market may be detrimental to some, outcomes are more open-ended, so a loss of a job in one sector may be offset by opportunities in others. This is less likely to be the case in the public sector, which depends on relatively fixed resources. Giving new ethnic groups a share of public jobs means existing jobs—in city agencies, public schools, and other civil service positions—must be redistributed away from the current holders. This zero-sum situation applies as well to elected representatives: If representation is seen as descriptive,[6] a gain for one ethnic group entails a loss for another.

Friction among ethnic groups occurs when the actors involved believe they are engaged in a zero-sum game, rather than a situation that may have mutually beneficial outcomes. In Los Angeles, for instance, Bobo and Hutchings (1996: 958) found that Blacks and Latinos both perceived Asian competition as a zero-sum game and that "Asian Americans and Latino respondents who are foreign born tend to perceive greater competition with blacks than do their native born co-ethnics." The influx of immigrants thus presents significant challenges for urban institutions. Grievances, both real and perceived, have the potential for triggering sometimes violent conflict.

The Erosion of Federal Support

If cities had the resources to address some of the issues that underlay the existing ethnic tension, and the willingness to use them, some conflict might have been avoided. The recent demographic shifts in cities began, however, at a time when cities were undergoing their worst recessions in memory and the broad institutional context of American intergovernmental relations was undergoing change. In the initial postwar period, the federal government was more than willing to help fund local programs, becoming an increasingly important player in local affairs.[7] Over the next thirty years, though, this willingness to shoulder the fiscal burden of cities eroded. One can trace the path of federal disengagement from cities from direct federalism under President Johnson, through the new federalism of Nixon, to the devolution of responsibilities to the states under Reagan.

Under Johnson, the federal government developed a direct relationship with cities through a variety of grants programs that essentially bypassed the states. By the late 1970s, between 25 and 30 percent of all federal intergovernmental aid bypassed states and was negotiated directly with cities (Walker 1995: 111–113). During the Nixon administration, regulations that restricted the use of federal grants were loosened, and cities were increasingly given block grants, allowing them considerable freedom in allocating funds. With the arrival of the Reagan administration, federal grants-in-aid to localities and states fell to $88.2 billion in 1982, the first decline in constant dollars in federal outlays to localities and states since the 1960s. By 1989, grants-in-aid were reduced to less than 11 percent of federal outlays and constituted only 17 percent of state and local budgets (Ross and Levine 1996: 403). The Reagan administration not only cut back its funding to both cities and states but also shifted urban funding through the states and allowed states increasing flexibility on how to spend those funds. As states dealt with the economic downturn of the early 1980s, they chose to channel the available money away from cities to deal with their own budget shortfalls. Cities were hit with a double blow: The federal government cut back on intergovernmental aid and re-directed much of what was left to states, and states chose to keep this money from cities.

Cities dealt with the fiscal shortfalls of the 1980s by cutting back services, neglecting capital improvement, and turning their attention to cost-cutting measures like the subcontracting and privatization of city functions (Ross and Levine 1996: 388). However, even as the immediate crises passed—first in the late 1980s and again in the mid-1990s—and cities turned their attentions once again to basic structural issues, privatization proposals only gained greater currency. This has been true at the federal level as well: Clinton's proposals in his first term to "reinvent" government, giving greater leeway for experimentation to the states, were a symptom of this trend. Government at every level has been reluctant to propose any new spending initiatives to address urban issues. Rather than embark on grand schemes, state and federal governments have instead proposed programs designed to harness private energies without spending public resources. As a result, the cutting edge of federal urban policy is now on the tax side rather than on the spending side.[8]

Beginning in the early 1980s, then, the trend in urban financing has been away from directly funding metropolitan areas and toward giving block grants to the states, and away from grants and toward tax breaks and loans. These shifts—the increased role of the states, the emphasis on privatization, the reliance on the tax structure rather than spending to shape urban policy—continue to define the philosophy of intergovernmental relations in the United States and to delimit the scope of municipal action. In general, these shifts give cities fewer external resources they can rely on and hence fewer degrees of freedom in responding to structural changes in cities and their consequent crises. Left to their own devices, local elected officials have had to come up with their own solutions to the structural changes brought about by immigration and a globalizing economy.

The Eruption of Tensions: Institutions Put to the Test

Given that in the 1980s many of the nation's major cities went through rapid demographic transformations while government cutbacks left both immigrants and African Americans in poorer areas of these cities vulnerable to economic restructuring and openly engaged in competition for scarce resources, it shouldn't have come as a surprise that four of the top eight immigrant-receiving metropolitan areas had serious civil disturbances by the early 1990s. Los Angeles, New York, Miami, and Washington, D.C., were the destination for almost one in three immigrants settling in the United States in this period; the rapid influx of immigration into poor, inner-city neighborhoods had an enormous impact, even as these cities' economies shuddered under the strain of adapting to a radically changing economy. Riots were centered in Miami's Liberty City and Overtown neighborhoods in 1980, 1982, 1984, and 1989; in Washington, D.C.'s Mt. Pleasant and Adams Morgan sections in 1991; in Crown Heights, New York, in 1991; and in the South-Central area of Los Angeles in 1992. These civil disturbances, all involved a mix of recent immigrants and resident minorities, though each had their own distinct dynamic and resolution.

Much of the subsequent attention by policymakers and scholars has been, understandably enough, on the riots themselves, which together caused dozens of deaths and billions of dollars worth of damages. But these disturbances are less interesting for the headlines they produce than for what they indicate about the state of interethnic relations in American cities and about the manner in which institutions respond to the structural problems exposed by civil strife. Unlike the response to the riots in the 1960s, the rebuilding efforts in the aftermath of the disturbances have received relatively little attention and scant funding from the federal government. These four riot cities, then, provide examples, albeit extreme ones, of the roles of urban institutions in the context of massive structural changes.

Cities' Institutional Response

Of the four cities where riots occurred in the 1980s and 1990s, two—Washington, D.C., and New York City—are vertically organized cities, characterized by relatively dense organizational networks that link different levels of government, and connect the public, nonprofit, and private sectors. The second pair, Miami and Los Angeles, are horizontally organized, with relatively few organizational links between levels of government, or between government and other sectors. The brief case studies that follow outline institutional responses in two of these cities—New York and Los Angeles—to the civil disturbances of the 1980s and 1990s.[9]

New York City

In the 1950s and 1960s the Crown Heights section of Brooklyn experienced white flight, as the children of an earlier generation of immigrants began moving further out in Brooklyn or to Long Island or New Jersey. The neighborhood shifted over to native Blacks. The exception was the area where the Jewish Lubavitch community had established itself in the late 1930s and expanded with an influx of refugees from Europe before and after the Second World War. Beginning in the 1970s there was a very rapid demographic shift in the areas around Crown Heights and Flatbush, as Caribbean immigrants from the English- and French-speaking islands moved into these neighborhoods. By the late 1980s, the neighborhood was predominantly Afro-Caribbean.

These demographic changes led to certain tensions, which were reflected in disputes over public space and political access. Examples of disputes over public space included the blocking off of Eastern Parkway in front of the main Lubavitch synagogue every Saturday, the use of motorcades on public streets, the yearly Caribbean Festival, which also goes down Eastern Parkway, the use of civic patrols by the Lubavitch community, competition over scarce housing (amid accusations of block-busting on the part of Blacks), and different notions of appropriate dress, demeanor, and manners on public streets. Should one acknowledge one's neighbor on the street? Lubavitch often did not greet their neighbors, leading to a certain frostiness of relations. Should one be allowed to play loud music? Caribbean Americans thought this was perfectly natural. The Lubavitch did not.

Disputes over inequalities in political access arose when it was often Lubavitch notions of public access that were, according to Blacks in the neighborhood, upheld by the authorities. The Lubavitch got police protection for their headquarters, but black churches did not. The Lubavitch at one time had a police escort for the Rebbe; black pastors did not have a similar escort. The police supposedly responded faster to calls from the Lubavitch and were more lenient toward them when they were involved in criminal incidents themselves. In 1977 Lubavitchers succeeded in petitioning Mayor Abraham Beame into partitioning Crown Heights into two community boards, North and South Crown Heights. The Lubavitch allegedly got preference in state-financed housing loans and financing.

There was a fairly long history, then, of tension between the Lubavitch and the surrounding African American and Caribbean American population that preceded the disturbances that took place in 1991. These were precipitated by the accidental death of Gavin Cato, a young boy of Guyanese parentage. The boy was run over by a car in the motorcade of the Lubavitch Rebbe as it returned to the Lubavitch headquarters on Eastern Parkway. The first ambulance on the scene belonged to the Lubavitch emergency service and left without picking up the boy. The rumor quickly circulated that the ambulance had refused treatment for any of the injured Blacks on the scene. This brought people out onto the streets and led from there to four days of confrontations among Blacks, Jews and police.

In the aftermath of the disturbances, Borough President Howard Golden explicitly rejected any "meddling," as he saw it, from the Manhattan-dominated mayoral office and city agencies. He invoked the oldest rule in New York City politics, the turf rule. Then-Mayor David Dinkins, being an old-school former borough president himself, backed off. It's striking how absent the Mayor was from any role in the aftermath (this is true of the current mayor, Rudolph Giuliani, as well, but here the dynamics are different, party differences being paramount). (It also goes without saying that the Lubavitch community rejected most offers of aid. Relations between the Lubavitch community and the broader mainstream Jewish community continue to be strained.)

Once it was clear that the city agencies were going to play a minimal role in the aftermath, this left the Borough President to marshal his own resources. The resources he had at his disposal were primarily political. The Borough President has leverage over the community groups in the county through the budget process. Though the budget directly under his control is nominal, his support is necessary for proposals for funding to city, state, and federal agencies. The Borough President is also a key player in appointing many of the county's officials, as well as supporting nominations to elected office. The Borough President's office has a gatekeeping function. As a result, the Borough President's staff have close working relationships with many of the more established nonprofits. In the aftermath of the Crown Heights disturbances, the Borough President called the African American, Lubavitch, and Caribbean American leadership together in the "Crown Heights Coalition" to establish a discussion on the issues surrounding the riots. It was clear to the participants that attendance was not optional.

On the one hand, the Coalition was a classic cooptation strategy, which operated at little or no cost to the Borough President. Other than expending some political capital and incurring some day-to-day administrative costs for staff, the Borough President has not had to bear any costs at all working with the Crown Heights Coalition. Whatever direct funding for programs was allocated came directly from the city or state. And very little of that was ever spent. The Coalition, once in place, kept communication going among the most tractable representatives of the various factions. This was useful both to keep the Borough President's office informed about what was going on and to keep a pressure valve open for the continuing, unresolved disputes. There was an added bonus—the Coalition has been used to address other possible ethnic flash points, like the Williamsburg neighborhood, where tensions existed between Hasidim and Puerto Ricans, or the Louima affair, in which a Haitian immigrant was brutally assaulted by police officers. In short, the Coalition—which is the main positive outcome of the disturbances—has essentially served to maintain things the way they were.

On the other hand, the actions the Borough President and other actors took to address the Crown Heights aftermath made sense in their own way, playing to their strengths, which were political strengths. The Crown Heights Coalition *did* reduce tension by opening up lines of communication across communities that simply had not been talking to one another (it also meant that some members of these communities ended up being ostracized by their own communities for talking to the other sides). Some issues were addressed, notably inequalities in police protection. Tensions around community policing were reduced. There was some clearing up of misconceptions: that the Lubavitch did not, in fact, get much more in the ways of city services and, that in fact, all these communities were underserved. Given that conclusion, however, the next step would be to see to it that services and opportunities would improve. This was not done.

Los Angeles

The "Rodney King" disturbances of April 1992 were preceded, as in the other cities, by rapid economic and demographic shifts that weakened the already brittle state of interethnic relations in Los Angeles. Between 1980 and 1990 the numbers of Latinos in Los Angeles county increased by 62 percent to a total of 38 percent of the county's population; the numbers of Asian Americans increased by 119 percent or 10 percent of the total. South-Central Los Angeles, which for decades had been the heart of the city's African American neighborhoods, went through a stunning transformation between 1980 and 1990. In 1980 South-Central was 90 percent native Black; in 1990 it was 50 percent Latino. The effects of these demographic shifts were only magnified by the fact that in the early 1990s southern California was still struggling to recover from the effects of deindustrialization and recession.[10] The tensions between the various ethnic groups made the acquittal of Rodney King's police assailants particularly explosive.

Responses to the civil disturbances of 1992 were structured by the horizontal nature of city politics. If New York City is organized vertically, Los Angeles is horizontally stratified. Los Angeles has not *one* politics but a series of parallel politics, the various layers of politics in the city having little to do with one another. The city's executive branch, its administration, and the city's nonprofit organizations all have little contact with one another. In part this reflects the city's history as a reform city, with its characteristic nonpartisan, managerial-style politics, a city characterized by an antigovernment political style. Political authority is dispersed and, if possible, rendered impotent. The city seems to have taken the philosophy of 'every tub on its own bottom'—a call for fiscal and organizational self-sufficiency—to heart. Interestingly, the city's reformist history is reflected as much in its nongovernmental institutions as in its governing structures. The city's political design encourages minimal government and the privatization of communal efforts, rather than the channeling of these efforts through public channels. As a result, community-based organizations orient themselves, on the whole, away from city politics and toward an alternative political vision of their own.

This is particularly evident in the response to the disturbances in April 1992, when each sector had independent—and divergent—responses. These distinct responses were not simply a matter of playing to the strengths of each sector—each sector working in the area that maximized its comparative advantage—but of fundamentally different visions of the city. The response of the city's administration—the mayor's office and the city's administrative agencies—emphasized an economic vision of the city, while the nonprofit sector focused on racial and ethnic tension. These visions are not mutually exclusive, by any means. Many "progressive" nonprofits have economic programs of their own. But, again, the interesting thing here is that both the city's and the nonprofits' responses to the disturbances were largely private-sector rather than public-sector responses.

The dominant response to the events of April 1992 was the city's decision to form a private-sector organization, Rebuild Los Angeles (RLA), and to pass responsibility for dealing with the aftermath of the crisis to this entity. RLA initially was almost entirely composed of corporate members, under the leadership of Peter Ueborroth, who had overseen Los Angeles' last grand public/private venture, the 1984 Olympics. The corporate board interpreted the underlying cause of the riots as the lack of economic investment and development in South-Central. Given that government had washed its hands of the whole thing, investment capital would have to come from the private sector.

RLA's primary goal was to drum up pledges of investment, which it did quite successfully. As the pressures for more tangible responses mounted, however, RLA took on additional tasks, including addressing racial and ethnic dialogue in the city, which ultimately ended up driving out many of the original corporate sponsors (who had already reaped the public relations benefits of being portrayed as the city's saviors) and making the organization increasingly unwieldy. Ultimately, RLA spun apart and reorganized itself as an economic development agency (for more critical accounts see Regalado 1994: 206–207; Chang 1995: 140–141).

If one were cynical, one might conclude that Rebuild Los Angeles was an attempt by the city's administration to foist responsibility for dealing with the crisis on someone else and, to let the city, particularly the mayor's office, walk away free and clear. While there may be some truth to this, the fact is that RLA fit in with the city's style—turning to the private sector to deal with this civic emergency did not seem an unnatural thing to do.

Institutional Response: New York and Los Angeles

The difference in response to these urban crises by vertically and horizontally organized cities was not in the magnitude of the resources involved. It's clear that in all four cases, cities were unwilling to expend additional fiscal resources to address the issues underlying these disturbances. As noted earlier, the late 1980s were a time of severe constraints on municipal budgets. The ineffectiveness of appeals to federal and state government, each dealing with its own budgetary crises, left cities on their own. Given these constraints, in each of these four cases cities proved unwilling to redistribute resources among various urban actors.[11] Instead, cities chose to mobilize, reallocate, or create resources that fell outside public sector budgets. In the case of New York City (and, to a lesser extent, Washington, D.C.), this meant mustering political resources to bring actors together to discuss points of contention. The vertical model, then, creates space for discourse. The horizontal model works very differently. In the cases of Miami and Los Angeles, the response was to turn to the private sector, counting on business to generate resources where the public sector was clearly incapable of doing so. The response to ethnic conflict was private economic investment, rather than ethnic dialogue. It seems clear that the response to structural and demographic shifts (seen through the lens of crisis, the aftermath of interethnic civil disturbances) are constrained by the institutional framework of cities and that this response varies with differences in cities' institutional frameworks. Again, focusing on two of these cities, New York and Los Angeles, highlights these differences.

In New York, for instance, the choice of action—calling on political ties and obligations to bring all parties to the table and then keeping them there even six years later (which is very unusual—most coalitions formed in the aftermath of disturbances fall apart after a couple of years)—depended on a particular kind of political environment. The City of New York, with its constituent boroughs, which are technically separate counties, delivers services directly, as well as through a web of private-service providers. These private-service providers, along with religious institutions, are the primary community-based organizations in the city. Private-service providers are almost entirely funded through public moneys—most get 90 percent or more of their funds directly from state or city sources. This gives city officials enormous leverage over these organizations.

For their part, these community-based organizations (CBOs) have little incentive to look for money elsewhere. Their funding is often fairly stable, even in times of cutbacks. Even during the height of the city's recession in the early 1990s, there was no sign that community organizations were being closed as a result of cutbacks in city funds. This was not the case in Los Angeles, where CBOs have had to find funding from other sources apart from the city. What this means, however, is that there are very few *additional* resources to be found. The political structure of New York City and its client CBOs are locked into their relationship, with little maneuvering room. Unlike Los Angeles, the Borough of Brooklyn did not experiment with public/private partnerships to raise additional resources in the aftermath of the civil disturbances. Nor did CBOs feel that they had to forge new relationships with private funders that could have led to experimentation with new programs. Whereas the primary effort in Los Angeles was privately launched, in New York City the main engine of response was governmental.

As noted earlier, after the 1992 riots Los Angeles' main response was to turn to the private sector for a solution. It's no surprise that the current mayor of Los Angeles is a fan of privatization. In an interview during his reelection campaign, Richard Riordan talked, for instance, about the formation of neighborhood groups under his administration and particularly their presence in South Los Angeles. He said, "For two years I've been speaking with them and saying damn near the same thing: 'If you want to solve problems in the community, you have to organize and take responsibilities.' At our meetings, somebody will ask me a question about 'what are you, as mayor, going to do about the tree that's overhanging my driveway.' I'll say, 'Organize, get something going. Then you go to the council office or come to me as an organization, or better yet, do what I would do. Cut the tree down without asking anybody.'"[12] What's surprising is that community-based organizations in Los Angeles seem to believe this as well. Nonprofits in Los Angeles are not generally oriented toward city government, or toward altering city policy, but rather see themselves as an *alternative* to government, perhaps at times as a kind of substitute for government, stepping in to do what government can't do, or won't do. Perhaps this comes of working in a system where access to government is difficult and where, even with access, one finds the government generally unresponsive.

Whatever the reason, in many ways, nonprofits *accept* the city's ethos of private endeavor. This is partly the result, or at the very least made possible, by the fiscal independence of community-based organizations. The city plays a minor role in financing community organizations and other nonprofits in the city. Unlike other cities, such as New York, where council members have a significant pool of funds at their disposal to use as they wish to fund projects in their communities, Los Angeles city council members have a proportionately much smaller fund to contribute to community groups in their districts. The funds, usually disbursed five hundred dollars at a time, serve mostly as a symbolic token of the council member's support—again, unlike New York, where councilmanic funds can sustain nascent community organizations.

In addition, service organizations in New York receive much of their state funding through borough or county organizations in the city; city and county functions overlap. In New York City, this has the effect of tying nonprofits into patronage politics in the city, where organizations are beholden to elected officials. In Los Angeles, state funds are allocated through the county board of supervisors, so community-based organizations are largely independent of the city's institutional politics. On the plus side, this has the effect of weaning nonprofits from any dependence on city funding and giving them significant leeway in their actions. Unlike in New York, nonprofits in Los Angeles can choose to operate largely independent of local political considerations. On the negative side of the ledger, the nonprofit universe in the city is considerably more fragile than New York's; it does not have available the public resources that can make the difference between viability and insignificance.

For nonprofits that can find alternative sources of funding—from federal or county government, from foundations, or from the private sector—Los Angeles's lack of institutional ties can seem liberating. It can mean having a separate power base from which to play a role in local affairs, a chance to play the role of mediators among the city's feuding factions. An example of this is the role that MALDEF, the Mexican American Legal Defense and Education fund, played in redistricting in 1992, bringing city and state politicians to the table to construct a coordinated strategy when no elected official had the status or perceived impartiality to bring together the city's various feuding Latino political factions. On the negative side, CBOs' distance from formal politics results in a relative marginality in city politics, a weak bargaining position when it comes to lobbying city government and little leverage over elected officials. Except in some very clearly defined cases—the intervention, for instance, of the Coalition Against Substance Abuse against the rebuilding of liquor stores in riot-damaged areas—CBOs have stayed clear of city politics. In short, the lack of institutional linkages between the city's formal and informal political sectors is very much a double-edged sword.

The strengths of a city's institutions are in a way also its weaknesses. New York City depends heavily on its public institutions and so provided a political solution to its crisis. Los Angeles's political institutions are almost nonexistent, but the city has a strong entrepreneurial ethos. So Los Angeles turned to a public/private partnership after the 1992 riot. Both approaches have their strengths and weaknesses. The point is that, in each case, the city's institutions mattered. In an odd kind of way, this supports my contention that cities are significant actors in spite of the lack of economic resources and the impossibility of appealing to the federal government.

Institutional Response: Where Are Cities Headed?

Given the trends traced in this chapter, particularly the manner in which intergovernmental aid has been moving away from direct grants and toward loans and tax breaks, a shift that appears to benefit the private sector and to disadvantage the public and nonprofit sectors, it might seem that government at all levels is moving away from the kind of response favored by vertically organized cities like New York and toward the responses favored by entrepreneurially inclined horizontally organized cities like Los Angeles. In the absence of public commitment to urban areas and their problems, the trend has been toward generating programs outside the public sphere. Whether through enterprise zones, business improvement districts, or local development corporations, urban problem-solving would be delegated to both for-profit and nonprofit private institutions. The Los Angeles case simply seems to be, then, a harbinger of what is happening around the nation: the retreat of government and the privatization of public space and governmental functions. However, the truth is a bit more complicated.

In the name of efficiency and their own "reinvention," governments have turned over the provision of services to private subcontractors. This has meant the spinning off or subcontracting out of garbage collection, recycling, day-care centers, emergency medical service, and public relations functions to private vendors. "Spinning off" or subcontracting services are two very different options, however. The spinning off of government functions implies that governments are permanently ceding authority to private entities. It may be the case, for instance, that municipal governments no longer want to be in charge of running sports arenas or recreation facilities, which are then sold off. Once these are sold off, local government has no say (except through its general powers of taxation and regulation) on the operation of these facilities. Subcontracting, on the other hand, still allows for municipal control: CBOs or private companies are chartered by city governments to take over development activities and service provision, but municipal service bureaucracies ultimately determine funding and level of services. In this model, municipal responsibilities are only delegated, not abrogated. Contracts with private providers continue at the discretion of municipalities (Ross and Levine 1996: 238).

This is true even in the case of Business Improvement Districts (BIDs) and other quasi-public entities that appear to have complete independence of action within their circumscribed realms. Although BIDs often have their own governing boards, the authority to tax and spend moneys, and the capacity to provide services, they exist at the behest of metropolitan governments. They are not private voluntary agencies and can take on only those responsibilities that have been granted to them by city government.[13]

Given the choice, most municipalities choose to subcontract rather than spinoff their services, allowing them to maintain their leverage over service providers. True privatization is the exception, not the rule. Even Los Angeles, in many ways the prototypical entrepreneurial city, the response is certainly not to turn over government functions to private actors, however much that may be part of the political rhetoric. The more common result has been the creation of public-private partnerships. Contrary to the spirit of the turn-of-the-century reform movement, the partnerships that have been developing do not guarantee private-sector independence from the patronage politics of more institutionally integrated cities. For community-based organizations in particular, subcontracting can actually mean a *loss* of independence.

The irony, then, is that cities are *not* becoming more like Los Angeles but rather more like New York. What does this mean? Cities are becoming more like New York not in the sense of maintaining one-party political institutions but rather in developing networks of public-private partnerships. Most people would not think to characterize the City of New York in this way, but, in reality, New York City has a decades-long history of subcontracting its services through private providers, mostly CBOs, and this has led to a very dense web of public-private partnerships and a complicated relationship between the public and the private spheres and between the nonprofit and the political worlds. Given that cities are basically on their own but have a number of pressing issues to be addressed, these kinds of private-public partnerships are much more likely to be the model for urban developmental coalition building than either a dominant government or the old reform tradition's picture of minimal, aloof city government.

Institutions and the Democratic Incorporation of New Actors

Cities are under enormous pressures to adapt to the structural and demographic changes that have only accelerated over the past two decades. But political institutions resist change and in particular are designed to resist drastic change. Even when at times in the 1980s and the early 1990s these changes have manifested themselves more dramatically as interethnic disturbances, cities have avoided responses that would entail a redistribution of resources or the raising of new resources through their powers of taxation. Nor do the aftermaths of ethnic disturbances result in huge political shifts. Instead, cities respond by mobilizing cheaper resources at their disposal. These resources vary by the institutional framework of cities. With their dense organizational linkages, vertically organized cities tend to turn to political rather than economic responses. Horizontally organized cities, for their part, try to make up for the lack of resources in the public sector by tapping slack resources in the private sector. In neither case, however, are cities willing to expend scarce public resources, namely money. These patterns have held even as cities returned to relative prosperity in the mid-1990s; the response to ethnic and racial shifts is not simply a matter of budgets but also a matter of the institutional framework in place at the time of transition.

What does this say about the capacity of political institutions to adapt to the demands of new actors? Institutions' unwillingness to change, even in times of severe crisis, raises questions about the incorporation of new actors. Institutions do not, as democratic pluralists might have envisioned, offer perfect translations of interests. As new interests appear, institutions tend to resist any kind of redistributive change. This means that institutional incorporation of new actors takes place more slowly and painfully than democratic theory allows. Although this institutional foot dragging reinforces the findings of the "New Institutionalists," it should also serve to warn us that the role of institutions is not neutral. The stability of institutions should raise concerns about the transparency and openness of democratic institutions to actors on the margins of the political process.

As African Americans increasingly share urban space with new ethnic minorities, whether Latino, Asian, or Caribbean, issues of institutional responsiveness will continue to come to the fore, but in increasingly complicated ways. Urban institutions will have to adjudicate demands from sometimes competing ethnic groups. For African Americans, the issue of institutional responsiveness has a double edge. On the one hand, Blacks are still relatively new urban actors and as a group still have many unmet needs in the areas of health, education, and social services, which local government provides. In this sense, African Americans remain on the outside, pressing claims on tightfisted institutions. On the other hand, African Americans have made great strides in gaining representation in local government and bureaucracy since the

1960s and now often staff the very institutions that their fellow-ethnics petition for services. By the same token, it is now African Americans who are sometimes seen by new immigrants as wielding power and as reluctant to share it. That both scenarios are true, sometimes simultaneously, only adds to the complex web of interethnic relations in American cities today.

NOTES

1. Pierson 1994: 31; for other influential examples of the "new institutionalism" see Evans et al. 1985; March and Olsen 1989; and Skowronek 1982.

2. This is what Pierson means by "policy feedback" (Pierson 1994: 47–48).

3. Pierson 1994: 44. See also Lindblom 1959.

4. Dahl. The pluralist argument was twofold: first, that political competition would lead representative institutions to incorporate the interests of new actors, and, second, that while interests might not be equally represented in every arena, given the profusion of public arenas, they would be represented somewhere. See Robert Dahl's classic portrayal of this view in *Who Governs? Democracy and Power in an American City* (1961).

5. On African Americans and political machines, see Kilson 1971. On Blacks and the machine in New York, see Osofsky (1966); on Chicago, see Gosnell's classic *Negro Politician: The Rise of Negro Politics in Chicago* (1935).

6. Hanna Pitkin draws a distinction between descriptive and substantive representation. Representation is descriptive if representatives share ascribed characteristics with their constituents: race, ethnicity, gender, or religion. Substantive representation implies that representatives and their constituents share similar views of issues, ideology, or principles, which may supersede ascribed characteristics. The two modes of representation are not mutually exclusive (Pitkin 1969).

7. In 1932, only about $10 million in federal grants was given to cities; by 1960 federal aid to state and local governments reached $7 billion, representing 7.6 percent of total federal budget outlays and 14.5 percent of state and local budgets. By 1980, grants totaled $91 billion, amounting to nearly 16 percent of federal spending and 26 percent of state and local outlays. These figures declined under the Reagan administration but rebounded under Bush. When Clinton came into office in 1992, grants-in-aid totaled $178 billion and represented 12.9 percent of federal outlays (Ross and Levine 1996: 400–403).

8. The best indication of this is that the only major urban proposal to emerge in the 1990s was the creation of "enterprise" or "empowerment" zones. The one exception to this has been crime control and prevention. Budgets for policing and incarceration both increased substantially in the 1980s and 1990s.

9. The discussion and arguments presented here are drawn from fieldwork and interviews conducted in 1997 in Los Angeles, New York, Miami, and Washington, D.C., for a larger project on ethnic relations in the aftermath of civil disturbances.

10. The economic transformation of southern California has been documented extensively. For instance, see Oliver et al. (1993); Soja et al. (1983).

11. For a further discussion of the difficulties of redistributive strategies in cities, see Paul Peterson's *City Limits* (1981).

12. Tim Rutten and Peter Y. Hong, "Candidates' Complex Views on Race Issues," *Los Angeles Times*, March 30, 1997, p. A1.

13. See Houston (1996) and Bradley (1995) on the establishment of BIDs. See Briffault (1997) for a discussion of BIDs and their implications for local government.

BIBLIOGRAPHY

Arthur, Brian. 1989. "Competing Technologies, Increasing Returns and Lock-In by Historical Events." *Economic Journal* 99(394): 116–131.

Bobo, Larry, and Victor Hutchings. 1996. "Perceptions of Racial Group Competition: Extending Blumer's Theory of Group Position to a Multiracial Social Context." *American Sociological Review* 61(6): 951–973.

Bradley, Richard. 1995. "Downtown Renewal: The Role of Business Improvement Districts." *Public Management* 77 (Fall): 9–13.

Briffault, Richard. 1997. "A Government for Our Time? The Business Improvement District and Urban Governance." Unpublished manuscript.

Chang, Edward. 1995. "The Impact of the Civil Unrest on Community-Based Organizational Coalitions," in Eui-Young Yu and Edward Chang, eds., *Multiethnic Coalition Building in Los Angeles*, 117–147. Claremont, Calif.: Regina Books.

Chubb, John, and Paul Peterson. 1985. *The New Direction in American Politics*. Washington, D.C.: Brookings Institution.

Conlan, Timothy. 1988. *New Federalism: Intergovernmental Reform From Nixon to Reagan*. Washington, D.C.: Brookings Institution.

Culver, Lowell W. 1982. "Changing Settlement Patterns of Black Americans, 1970–1980." *Journal of Urban Affairs* 4 (Fall): 29–48.

Dahl, Robert. 1961. *Who Governs? Democracy and Power in an American City*. New Haven: Yale University Press.

Erie, Stephen. 1988. *Rainbow's End: Irish-Americans and the Dilemmas of Urban Machine Politics, 1840–1984*. Berkeley: University of California Press.

Evans, Peter, Dietrich Reuschemeyer, and Theda Skocpol, eds. 1985. *Bringing the State Back In*. New York: Cambridge University Press.

Farley, John. 1987. "Segregation in 1980: How Segregated Are America's Metropolitan Areas," in Gary A. Tobin, ed., *Divided Neighborhoods: Changing Patterns of Racial Segregation, Urban Affairs Annual Review,* p. 32. Newbury Park, Calif.: Sage.

Frey, William. 1995. "The New Geography of Population Shifts: Trends Toward Balkanization," in Reynolds Farley, ed., *State of the Union: America in the 1990s. Vol. Two: Social Trends,* pp. 271–336. New York: Russell Sage.

Galster, George C. 1991. "Black Suburbanization: Has It Changed the Relative Location of Races?" *Urban Affairs Quarterly* 26 (June): 621–628.

Gosnell, Harold. 1935. *Negro Politicians: The Rise of Negro Politics in Chicago.* Chicago: University of Chicago Press.

Houston, Lawrence O. 1996. "Business Improvement Districts." *Economic Development Commentary* 21:2, 4–9.

Jaret, Charles. 1991. "Recent Structural Changes and U.S. Urban Ethnic Minorities." *Journal of Urban Affairs* 13:3: 307–336.

Johnson, James H., and Melvin Oliver. 1989. "Interethnic Minority Conflict in Urban America: The Effects of Economic and Social Dislocations." *Urban Geography* 10 (September-October): 449–463.

Jennings, Keith, and Clarence Lusane. 1994. "The State and Future of Black/Latino Relations in Washington, D.C.: A Bridge in Need of Repair," in James Jennings, ed., *Blacks, Latinos and Asians in Urban America* pp. 57–68. (Westport, Conn.: Praeger).

Jones-Correa, Michael. 1998. *Between Two Nations: The Political Predicament of Latinos in New York City.* Ithaca: Cornell University Press.

Karnig, Albert, and Susan Welch. 1980. *Black Representation and Urban Policy.* Chicago: University of Chicago Press.

Kasinitz, Philip, and J. Rosenberg. 1994. "Missing the Connection? Social Isolation and Employment on the Brooklyn Waterfront." Working Paper of the Michael Harrington Institute, Queens College, New York.

Kilson, Martin. 1971. "Political Change in the Negro Ghetto, 1900–1940s," in Nathan I. Huggins, Martin Kilson, and Daniel M. Fox, eds., *Key Issues in the Afro-American Experience.* New York: Harcourt Brace Jovanovich.

Kirschenman, Joleen, and Kathryn Neckerman. 1991. "We'd Love to Hire Them But—The Meaning of Race for Employers," in Christopher Jencks and Paul Peterson, eds., *The Urban Underclass.* Washington, D.C.: Brookings Institution.

Lindblom, Charles. 1959. "The 'Science' of Muddling Through." *Public Administration Review* 19: 79–88.

McClain, Paula D. 1993. "The Changing Dynamics of Urban Politics: Black and Hispanic Municipal Employment—Is There Competition?" *Journal of Politics* 55 (May): 399–414.

McClain, Paula, and Albert K. Karnig. 1990. "Black and Hispanic Socioeco-nomic and Political Competition." *American Political Science Review* 84:2 (June): 535–545.

March, James G., and Johan P. Olsen. 1989. *Rediscovering Institutions: The Organizational Basis of Politics.* New York: Free Press.

Martin, Lisa. 1997. "An Institutionalist View: International Institutions and State Strategies." Paper presented at the Conference on International Order in the twenty-first Century, McGill University, Montreal, Canada, May 16–18.

Massey, Douglass, and Nancy Denton. 1993. *American Apartheid: Segregation and the Making of the Underclass.* Cambridge, Mass.: Harvard University Press.

Moreno, Dario. 1996. "Cuban Americans in Miami Politics: Understanding the Cuban Model," in James Jennings, ed., *The Politics of Minority Coalitions: Race, Ethnicity, and Shared Uncertainties,* pp. 145–162. Westport, Conn.: Praeger.

Neckerman, Kathryn, and Joleen Kirschenman. 1991. "Hiring Strategies, Racial Bias, and Inner-City Workers." *Social Problems* 38:4: 433–447.

Nelson, William E. 1978. "Black Mayors as Urban Managers." *Annals of the American Academy of Political and Social Science* 439 (September): 53–67.

Nelson, William E., and Phillip J. Meranto. 1977. *Electing Black Mayors: Political Action in the Black Community.* Columbus: Ohio State University Press.

North, Douglass. 1990. *Institutions, Institutional Change, and Economic Performance.* New York: Cambridge University Press.

Oliver, Melvin L., and James H. Johnson. 1984. "Interethnic Conflict in an Urban Ghetto: The Case of Blacks and Latinos in Los Angeles." *Research in Social Movements, Conflict, and Change* 6:57–94.

Oliver, Melvin L., James H. Johnson, and Walter C. Farrell. 1993. "Anatomy of a Rebellion: A Political-Economic Analysis," in Robert Gooding-Williams, ed., *Reading Rodney King, Reading Urban Uprising,* pp. 117–141. New York: Routledge.

Orfield, Gary. 1986. "Minorities and Suburbanization" in Rachel G. Bratt, Chester Harman, and Ann Myerson, eds., *Critical Perspectives on Housing.* Philadelphia: Temple University Press.

Osofsky, Gilbert. 1966. *Harlem: The Making of a Ghetto: Negro New York, 1890–1930.* New York, Harper & Row.

Palmer, John. 1986. *Perspectives on the Reagan Years.* Washington, D.C.: Urban Institute Press.

Patterson, Ernest. 1974. *Black City Politics.* New York: Dodd, Mead and Company.

Peterson, Paul. 1981. *City Limits.* Chicago: University of Chicago Press.

Pierson, Paul. 1994. *Dismantling the Welfare State? Reagan, Thatcher and the Politics of Retrenchment.* Cambridge: Cambridge University Press.

Pitkin, Hanna. 1969. *The Concept of Representation.* Berkeley: University of California Press.

Porter, Bruce, and Marvin Dunn. 1984. *The Miami Riot of 1980: Crossing the Bounds.* Lexington, Mass.: Lexington Books.

Portes, Alejandro, and Ruben Rumbaut. 1990. *Immigrant America: A Portrait.* Berkeley: University of California Press.

Preston, Michael. 1976. "Limitations of Black Urban Power: The Case of Black Mayors," in Louis Masotti and Robert Lineberry, eds. *The New Urban Politics.* Cambridge, Mass.: Balinger.

Regalado, Jaime. 1994. "Community Coalition Building," in Mark Baldassare, ed., *The Los Angeles Riots,* pp. 205–236. Boulder: Westview Press.

———. 1995. "Creating Multicultural Harmony? A Critical Perspective on Coalition-Building Efforts in Los Angeles," in Eui-Young Yu and Edward Chang, eds., *Multiethnic Coalition Building in Los Angeles,* pp. 35–54. Claremont, Calif.: Regina Books.

Ross, Bernard H., and Myron A. Levine. 1996. *Urban Politics: Power in Metropolitan America* Ithaca, N.Y.: F. E. Peacock.

Rutten, Tim, and Peter Y. Hong. 1997. "Candidates' Complex Views on Race Issues," *Los Angeles Times,* March 30, p. A1.

Skowronek, Stephen. 1982. *Building a New American State: The Expansion of National Administrative Capacities, 1877–1920.* New York: Cambridge University Press.

Smith, James P., and Barry Edmonston, ed. 1997. *The New Americans: Economic, Demographic, and Fiscal Effects of Immigration.* Washington, D.C.: National Academy Press.

Soja, Edward, Rebecca Morales, and Goetz Wolff. 1983. "Urban Restructuring: An Analysis of Social and Spatial Change in Los Angeles." *Economic Geography* 59:2 (April): 195–230.

Tobin, Gary A., ed. 1987. *Divided Neighborhoods: Changing Patterns of Racial Segregation.* Urban Affairs Annual Review 32. Newbury Park, Calif.: Sage.

United States Commission on Civil Rights. 1993. *Racial and Ethnic Tensions in American Communities: Poverty, Inequality, and Discrimination. Vol. 1: The Mount Pleasant Report.* Washington, D.C.: United States Commission on Civil Rights.

———. 1997. *Racial and Ethnic Tensions in American Communities: Poverty, Inequality and Discrimination. Vol. 4: The Miami Report.* Washington, D.C.: United States Commission on Civil Rights.

Waldinger, Roger. 1989. "Immigration and Urban Change." *Annual Review of Sociology* 15: 211–232.

Waldinger, Roger. 1995. "When the Melting Pot Boils Over: The Irish, Jews, Blacks, and Koreans of New York," in Michael Peter Smith and Joe R. Feagin, eds., *The Bubbling Cauldron: Race, Ethnicity, and the Urban Crisis,* pp. 265–281. Minneapolis: University of Minnesota Press.

———. 1996. *Still The Promised City: African Americans and New Immigrants in Post-Industrial New York.* Cambridge: Harvard University Press.

Walker, David. 1995. *The Rebirth of Federalism.* Chatham, N.J.: Chatham House.

Wilson, William Julius. 1987. *The Truly Disadvantaged: The Inner City, The Underclass, and Public Policy* (Chicago: University of Chicago Press).

———. 1997. *When Work Disappears: The World of the New Urban Poor.* New York: Vintage Books.

Chapter 6

The Portrayal of Black America in the Mass Media
Perception and Reality

Brigitte L. Nacos and Natasha Hritzuk

Relatively little research has been devoted to the impact of the mass media on the political condition of African American life. This dearth of empirical work is especially ironic since the media—from the mainstream black press to television—have played a significant role in the modern phase of black liberation and political empowerment.

For centuries before the advent of television, print media were enlisted as a means to undermine American racism and inequality. During the antislavery movement, for example, Whites as well as freed Blacks utilized the power of the pen in newspaper articles to articulate the inhumanity of slavery. After the abolition of the slave trade, Blacks and Whites again joined forces to inform others about the atrocities of lynching and other forms of brutality meted out to racial-minority groups in America. During the world wars, for which Blacks volunteered and in which many fought abroad in the name of freedom that they did not have at home, the contributions of black-owned and operated newspapers underscored how racial discrimination was weakening the American war effort. Most notable, however, was the media coverage of southern violence during the civil rights movement, for it was during this period that America, through the medium of television, came to understand the repression of Jim Crow in the form of Eugene "Bull" Connor's water hoses and attack dogs. Television provided stark evidence, in Selma and throughout the

South, of just how far America had veered from its promises of freedom and justice for all.

And yet the media have hindered black progress. Unflattering images and stereotypes of Blacks have been particularly conspicuous in the television industry. Indeed, since American ethnic and racial groups are often segregated in terms of housing, religious affiliations, and, increasingly, schools, the media often provide the only images that are considered by viewers as "real." Therefore, newspaper and television images of Blacks as criminals and "welfare queens" have fortified negative stereotypes and circumstances of Blacks. The 1968 Kerner Commission Report demonstrated that media portrayal of Blacks was highly problematic, and at least partially responsible for the divide between Blacks and Whites. The Kerner Commission Report forcefully illustrated how the representation of Blacks in newspapers and on television served to validate prejudice in the minds of white viewers and exacerbated racial tensions in American society.

Through a comparative analysis of prominent newspapers and news magazines, Brigitte L. Nacos and Natash Hritzuk assess whether the contemporary media's depiction of black America has improved since the days of the Kerner Commission and whether the media today present more varied images of the black community as a viable part of the larger community. In the face of mounting evidence that news content shapes how racial and ethnic groups view themselves and others, the authors then discuss the implications of their findings.

Introduction

In 1967, following a series of devastating riots in America's inner cities, President Lyndon B. Johnson appointed a National Advisory Commission on Civil Disorders (commonly called Kerner Commission after its chairman, Otto Kerner, who was Governor of Illinois at the time) to investigate the underlying causes of the violent outbursts in predominantly black neighborhoods. The Commission's report warned that America was "moving toward two societies, one black, one white—separate and unequal" (*Report*, 1968, 1). While not blaming the press directly or solely for the societal conditions that led to the riots, the Kerner Commission criticized the mass media's spotty portrayal of black America, concluding that the world of television and newspapers was in appearance and attitude "almost totally white" and portrayed African Americans as if they "do not read the newspapers or watch television, give birth, marry, die, go to PTA meetings" (*Report,* 1968, 383). The Kerner Commission challenged the media to strive to provide comprehensive and authentic reporting on African Americans and thereby to correct the inaccurate perceptions of black America held by both Whites and Blacks (*Report,* 1968, 362–389). In the Commission's words, "[b]y failing to portray the Negro as a matter of routine and in the context of the total society, the news media have, we believe, contributed to the black-white schism in the country" (*Report,* 1968, 383).

When he installed an Advisory Board on Race in the summer of 1997, President Clinton acknowledged the need for a national dialogue on controversial issues surrounding race and cited the nation's most important mission for the twenty-first century as building one America. Thirty years after the Kerner Commission's appeal for "the creation of a true union—a single society and a single American identity" (*Report,* 1968, 23), this goal has not yet been realized. On the contrary, in the 1990s one of two African Americans still believed that they were not simply members of one of many societal groups such as Italian Americans or German Americans but that Blacks formed a nation within the American nation.[1]

Our research examines whether and how the contemporary media's depiction of black America has improved along the lines of the Kerner Commission's recommendations. In the past, most research focused on particular aspects of Blacks in the news such as their portrayal in stories on crime (Gilliam, 1996; Peffley et al., 1996; Iyengar, 1991), poverty (Gilens, 1996; Iyengar, 1991), or in advertising (Humphrey and Schuman, 1984). By establishing the frequency of stories that cover and/or pictures that depict African Americans, several scholars established that the black minority was underrepresented in both the print and the broadcast media (Stempel, 1971; Baran, 1973; Chaudhary, 1980; Lester and Smith, 1990). Still others looked at the overall depiction of Blacks in one particular news medium (Entman, 1992, 1994). In the initial phase of our ongoing research, we were interested in the overall picture of black America in the news, as well as the frequency and the themes of black visuals and how they compared to the depiction of Whites. Most important, we questioned what images and stereotypes of black and white Americans were emphasized and deemphasized. We also wanted to know what individual pieces in the full mosaic of black America were reported or magnified and what features were undercovered or omitted in the visuals the news presented. Although we compared contemporary visuals with those of thirty years ago, our primary focus was on the contemporary media's portrayal of black America. Finally, we wanted to get a sense of how contemporary black Americans evaluate the mainstream media's coverage. In 1968 the Kerner Commission wrote, "our evidence shows that the so-called white press is at best mistrusted and at worst held in contempt by many black Americans" (*Report*, 1968, 383). We wondered, what, if anything, has changed.

There are good reasons why we analyzed the visual news content. Simply on the basis of his observations, Walter Lippmann concluded nearly eighty years ago that "[p]hotographs have the kind of authority over imagination to-day, which the printed word had yesterday, and the spoken word before that. They seem utterly real." More recently, communication researchers have found evidence that news consumers pay more attention to visual images in the news than to the spoken or written word and that they are more engaged by them (Neuman, Just, and Crigler, 1992; Jamieson, 1992; Peffley et al., 1996). In addition, news consumers are far more likely to recall news messages they have seen than those they have heard or read (Graber, 1990); they feel that visuals enhance their understanding of the news (Neuman, Just, and Crigler, 1992). Just as important, "visual images have a great potential for generating powerful emotional responses" (Peffley et al., 1996, 312). This is particularly true with respect to visual images of African Americans, because "the race of people pictured in news stories is a salient aspect of the story for many viewers" (Gilens, 1996, 528).

While most researchers concentrate on television news when they examine the characteristics and influences of visual images, we agree with Gilens's suggestion that pictures in the print media may have greater impact than visuals in TV newscasts. Gilens refers specifically to photographs in news magazines when he suggests that "even those who do not read a story are likely to look at least briefly at the picture as they browse through the magazine."(Gilens, 1996, footnote 13). We believe the same is true for the potency of visuals in daily newspapers—

especially in the context of race. Whereas news stories often do not identify the race of people, photographs provide this information.

Theoretical Foundations

We do not argue that the press has determined in the past or determines today the state of affairs in American race relations. But, in the face of mounting evidence that news content affects how Whites and Blacks view themselves, each other, and a host of public policy issues (Iyengar and Kinder, 1987; Iyengar, 1991; Entman, 1994; Gilens, 1996; Gilliam, 1996; Peffley et al, 1996), the assumption is that the media have a hand in influencing current race relations and related issues in America. In Sig Gissler's words, "Journalism helps shape how racially diverse people think of each other and how public policy on race-related issues is formulated" (Gissler, 1994, 123).

This comes hardly as a surprise. After all, in modern societies citizens depend on the mass media for most basic information about literally all aspects of public life beyond their rather limited personal observations and experiences (Lippmann, [1922] 1965; Robinson and Sheehan, 1983; Ansolabehere et al., 1993; Graber, 1997). People have "virtually nowhere else to turn for information about public affairs and for cues on how to frame and interpret that information" (Neuman, Just, and Crigler, 1992, 11). Because the number of African Americans and Whites who consider a person of the other race a friend has grown significantly over the past few decades, one might assume that contemporary Whites and Blacks know more about each other on the basis of their personal experiences than was the case in 1960.[2] But, since "the interests that enter into the formation of public opinion [on racial policies and issues] are collective rather than personal, group-centered rather than self-centered" (Kinder and Sanders, 1996), personal relationships between individuals may not necessarily override mass-mediated messages about respective group interests.

High on the list of the Kerner Commission's recommendations was the urgent call for racially integrated newsrooms. The idea was that African American reporters, editors, producers, newsroom managers, and publishers would be instrumental in projecting a more complete and authentic picture of black America. In the past three decades, the number of African Americans working in mainstream media organizations increased from virtually zero in the late 1960s to 5.4 percent three decades later (Dates and Barlow, 1993; Campbell, 1995; Stewart, 1997; Shipler, 1998). In 1978 the American Society of Newspaper Editors adopted a "Year 2000" target to increase minority representation in the newsrooms to a level equal to minority representation in the overall population. Several years before the self-imposed deadline, it was obvious that the goal could not be realized. As the turn of the century approached, there was "a widespread sense of diversity fatigue" in news organizations (Barringer, 1998).[3]

Racial and ethnic diversity in the ranks of media personnel is certainly a worthy goal and likely to have some impact on the news. But equitable representation in newsrooms alone is unlikely to change media content in dramatic ways. According to one astute newsman, the problem with the media's lopsided depiction of black America is rooted "as much in our attitudes as in our statistics" (Cose, 1994, 9).

If attitudes figure into news reporting, whose views, preferences, stereotypes, and biases are most influential here? Lippmann recognized an inevitable difference between news and truth and argued that the "function of news is to signalize an event, the function of truth is to bring to light the hidden facts, to set them into relation with each other, and make a picture of reality on which men can act" (Lippmann, [1922] 1965, 226). Empirical evidence has confirmed an inevitable gap between what Lippmann called the environment, meaning truth and reality, and the pseudo-environment, meaning pseudo-reality or media-reality, even when deliberate efforts are made to simply project reality (Donsbach et al., 1993).

However, contemporary media scholars are more concerned with what they perceive as outright bias on the part of the media than with the inherent difference between reality and media-reality. Thus, experts in the field continue to probe whether journalists, editors, and other news personnel are guided in their work by their liberal (Efron, 1971; Lichter et al., 1986) or conservative (Parenti, 1986; Herman and Chomsky, 1988) leanings, rather than by enduring journalistic ideals such as objectivity and accuracy (Gans, 1979) or by organizational structures and bureaucratic procedures (Sigal, 1973; Gitlin, 1980; Epstein, 1974; Gans, 1979; Hess, 1983).

Since the 1960s, when Vice President Spiro Agnew attacked the leading media organizations, namely the television networks, as liberal and out of step with the vast majority of Americans, conservative politicians and some media researchers have portrayed reporters and other news personnel in the most influential media organizations as far more liberal and far more supportive of left-of-center policies than the public at large (Efron, 1971; Lichter et al., 1986). More recently, two researchers wrote,

> The data from our survey of reporters suggests that the journalistic goal of objectivity is more of an ideal than a practice. Evidence from our survey shows that the liberal and Democratic leanings of Washington reporters may, consciously or unconsciously, influence coverage of politics. (Dautrich and Dineen, 1996, 7)

With respect to race, the liberal media paradigm holds that leading anchors, correspondents, reporters, editors, and other media personnel slant their reporting in favor of sources and views supportive of policies, such as affirmative action and social welfare programs, that are thought to benefit the African American minority (Efron, 1971; Lichter et al., 1986).

Others point to the white power elite, its tightening grip on a rapidly growing "media monopoly," and its self-serving influence on the presentation of the news (Mills, 1956; Altschull, 1995; Parenti, 1986; Herman and Chomsky, 1988; Exoo, 1994). For Parenti, the press's major role "is to continually recreate a view of reality supportive of existing social and economic class power (1986, 10). Radical critics, then, see the press as an utterly conservative institution slanted in favor of the sociopolitical status quo. In this view, African Americans and other minorities as well as their fundamental interests are grossly undercovered or not covered at all (Parenti, 1986). Drawing on the thesis of ruling-class dominance (Gramsci, 1971; Marcuse, 1964; Mills, 1956), Exoo argues:

> Hegemony is now so complete it is built into the very foundation of the mass media—into the imperatives, the norms, and the routines of the business—so that perpetrating hegemony is not deliberately benighting the masses. It is merely doing one's job. (1994, 21)

Rejecting the notion of a power elite or a ruling class that uses the media in a domination scheme, we suggest that corporate imperatives, the remnants of the white majority's traditional views and stereotypes about what Lippmann called "the world outside" (Lippmann, [1922]

1965, chapter 1), and the journalistic ideal of a socially responsible press are the influences most likely to enter into the news media's portrayal of black America.

I. Corporate Profit Imperatives

The move toward huge city newspapers and newspaper chains owned by ambitious press lords that began in the late nineteenth century had progressed a great deal by the 1960s. But the situation then was a far cry from the concentration of media power that has occurred more recently. With the demise or takeover of small, medium-size, and large family-owned and public media companies, a small number of mega-corporations dominate the contemporary media market. As cable and satellite television and, more recently, the Internet have escalated the already fierce competition for news consumers, the fight for TV- and radio-audience ratings and print press circulations has intensified. And the most important consideration for the corporate media is the bottom line.

We believe that the imperatives of the large media organizations are informed not by the ideological preferences of a small power elite but rather by large shareholders as well as by company bosses and managers with stock options tied to their employer's fiscal performance. As a result,

> the news product that lands on newsstands, doorsteps, and television screens is indeed hurt by a heightened, unseemly lust at many companies for ever greater profits. In the service of that ambition, many editors are surrendering part of their birthright to marketers and advertising directors, and making news judgments based on criteria that would have been anathema only a few years ago. (Hickey, 1998, 30)

Whether the heads of corporate giants such as GE, Time-Warner, Disney, or Rupert Murdoch's News Corporation get personally involved in the way the news is presented—and some of them do—matters less than their power to put like-minded people in key positions and to have newsroom personnel anticipate what their bosses want (Parenti, 1986; Bagdikian, 1992). Under the pressure to spend money less on reporting and to attract more news consumers, hard news is increasingly giving way to soft news or "new" news that focuses on celebrity, scandal, gossip, lifestyle, and similar so-called human interest stories in efforts to "sweeten the product for easier consumption" (Hickey, 1998, 33). In the past, the best news organizations reported what was important and not simply what was interesting.[4] In the 1990s, even the leading news organizations slant their news in favor of what can be presented as sensational, dramatic, shocking, extraordinary, and user-friendly at the expense of far more important events, developments, and aspects of societal life.

Since audience ratings and circulation determine advertising revenues, one would expect that all large societal groups are targeted and—as far as the news is concerned—covered and pictured in a somewhat evenhanded way. The fact is, however, that corporate advertisers tend to target some demographic groups far more than others—most of all the white middle class. As a result, the mainstream media are said "to ignore the audiences that hold no interest for advertisers" (Campbell, 1995, 32).

Advertisers are increasingly aware of black America's significant and vastly growing buying power and have "changed their policy of totally ignoring African Americans" (Dates and Barlow, 1993, 462); they pay more attention to African-American consumers, but they still spot-target African Americans more often in the major black print and broadcast media than in the mainstream media (Dates and Barlow, 1993). Similarly, when the mainstream news media, especially television, report with black Americans or other minorities in mind, they think more of public service programs, news specials, and documentaries especially devoted to African American, or Latino, or Native American themes.

Moreover, in some corporate circles the idea that it does not pay for advertisers (and presumably news organizations) to target African Americans and other minorities is alive and well. This point was driven home in early 1998, when an internal memo prepared by a New York company that sells national advertising to radio stations was leaked and publicized. The document instructed sales representatives to discourage corporations from placing commercials with black and Hispanic radio stations by saying that "advertisers should want prospects, not suspects" (Pristin, 1998).

II. White Majority Perspectives

While the news judgments of the large media corporations are increasingly and wittingly made with the profit imperative in mind, decisions are also influenced by the prevailing views and stereotypes of the dominant white culture. This does not mean that racism finds its way into the news. On the contrary, today's mainstream media are free of "old-fashioned racism" and "intentional, blatant bigotry" (Campbell, 1995, 37–38). Even in cases of Afro-American protests against a perceived racial offense by the media, black critics tend to assume ignorance and insensitivity rather than outright racism on the part of the white media.[5] Moreover, mainstream news organizations report critically when they become aware of racially motivated bigotry.[6]

Nevertheless, the white elite's experiences, prejudices, and stereotypes, formed over a long time and shaped by prior generations, influence the way the media report on African Americans. Gans found that "the news reflects the white male social order" (Gans, 1979, 61). Lippmann's basic argument that dominant cultural stereotypes do not necessarily relate to the real world but rather reflect the imagined world has been confirmed more recently with respect to the media's portrayal of black America. According to one contemporary observer, "Newsrooms are not hermetically sealed against the [racial] prejudices that play perniciously just beneath the surface of American life" (Shipler, 1998, 28). Dates and Barlow concluded that the white media's "black representations are totally at odds with the reality of African Americans as individual people" (Dates and Barlow, 1993, 5). And Marable has described what can happen when black reality does not correspond to white stereotypes:

> When the reality of blackness contradicts the stereotype of racism, TV producers, directors and corporate executives demand that reality conform to their prejudices. When black film director Kevin Hooks shot a park scene in Harlem, his studio's white executives wanted more trash, filth, and litter dumped on to the set—Harlem was simply "too clean" for white folks to accept for the purposes of the movie. (Marable, 1994, 15)

While this sort of overt prejudice may not affect the presentation of all or most news stories, it is likely to affect overall news judgments—which sources are presented and which left out, what news developments are reported and which not, how people in the news are portrayed.

We have mentioned that the all-white and mostly male newsrooms that still existed in the 1960s have given way to more integrated workplaces. But African American reporters, editors, and even managers do not necessarily change the news portrayal of black America in meaningful ways because "[t]hose who advance often do so by blending in and playing down their blackness, according to some African American journalists; institutional norm tends to sift out iconoclasts" (Shipler, 1998, 30). Moreover, in racially integrated newsrooms the proposals of African Americans are often rejected because "white editors don't always recognize as newsworthy the attitudes and trends in black communities that they would report in white communities" (Shipler, 1998, 30).

III. The Values of a Socially Responsible Press

The values articulated in the canons of journalism and in the tenets of a socially responsible press—both strongly influenced by the ideas of the Progressive era—remain the ideals of most contemporary journalists. While they do not deny that the press is a for-profit business, they recognize that with the unique First Amendment rights of the American media come responsibilities toward the public. Among the high standards they are expected to meet, the news media are expressly charged with projecting "a representative picture of constituent groups in society" and must "accurately portray the social groups, the Chinese and the Negroes, for example, since persons tend to make decisions in terms of favorable and unfavorable images and a false picture can subvert accurate judgment" (Peterson, 1956, 91). And, in fact, a number of news organizations have made systematic efforts to hire and promote African Americans and to expand their source Rolodexes to include more African American experts.

But corporate profit imperatives interfere with journalistic principles. While the values of a socially responsible press have not yet disappeared altogether, according to one newsman, "they've been significantly subordinated to the general ascendancy of market factors, especially the maximization of short-term profits."[7]

Research Methodology

In order to establish how the press pictured black America at the end of the twentieth century compared to thirty years earlier, when the Kerner Commission conducted its investigations, we analyzed photographs published in *Newsweek* over two twelve-month periods (June 1967–May 1968 and June 1997–May 1998) that depicted Blacks. We also reviewed visuals that appeared in the *New York Times* (NYT) over a period of three months (October, November, December) in 1967 and during the same three months in 1997. We also coded the visuals of Whites and of members of other racial groups for comparative purposes. In *Newsweek,* we examined all visuals; in the *Times,* we concentrated on photographs in the sections devoted to international, national, metropolitan, society, and business news. We coded all visuals according to the following categories: advertisements, crime, public officials, professionals, business setting, political/social activists, and wedding/engagements announcements (the latter category in the NYT only). In *Newsweek* we examined a total of 4,138 pictures and, in the *New York Times,* a total of 8,294 visuals.[8]

Additionally, for periods of six months in 1997 and in 1967 (July–December) we coded all visuals in *Newsweek* with respect to two large categories. In the sports/entertainment category we recorded all visuals that depicted domestic figures from sports, entertainment, show business, music, and art; in the politics/other category we registered images from the field of politics/civics, education, health, business, and trends. For this part of our research, we analyzed a total of 2,316 photographs.[9]

We also examined the Black and the White visuals in the *New York Times* (NYT), the *New York Daily News* (DN), the *New York Post* (NYP), and the early-evening broadcast of WABC-TV in New York over a six week period (15 November–30 December 1997) in the sections covering national, regional, and local news; business; sports; and advertising. For this part of our research we examined a total of 4,059 visuals.[10]

For comparative purposes we chose a variety of publications for our analysis. As one of the leadings news weeklies, *Newsweek* is read nationwide. In 1996, 73 percent of the U.S. population was composed of non-Hispanic Whites, and 13 percent was Black.[11] Read nationwide as well—especially by key figures in government, business, entertainment, and sports—and probably the most influential daily newspaper in the United States, the *Times* is at the same time a local and regional newspaper, with readers in the five boroughs of New York City as well as in surrounding cities and counties in the states of New York, New Jersey, and Connecticut. The *Daily News* and the *Post* are tabloids read mostly by people who live and/or work either in or close to the city. Given that an estimated 39 percent of New York City's residents were White and 26 percent Black in the late 1990s, African Americans made up a substantial number of the readers of the city's three daily newspapers. Indeed, according to a 1997 survey of New York city residents, 64 percent of African Americans in New York said that they read the *New York Daily News,* 22 percent the *New York Times,* and 3 percent the *New York Post.*[12] Because most Americans identify television as their number one news source, we also chose one of the local television afternoon/early evening news programs (*Eyewitness News,* aired by WABC-TV) for this part of our analysis.[13]

Finally, we used a survey done in 1997, of adults in New York State to assess how African Americans use and evaluate the mainstream news media and to compare white and black attitudes vis-à-vis the news media.[14]

Findings

Black America in Media Visuals: The Larger Picture

In 1967 nearly 60 percent of all visuals in *Newsweek* that depicted African Americans concerned news from the areas of politics/civics, business, professional life, education, health, crime, and trends (politics/other category), while about 40 percent of the all-black visuals concerned sports, entertainment, show business, or music and the arts. By 1997, these figures had changed drastically; more than two-thirds of the all-black visuals fell into the sports/entertainment category, while fewer than one-third were categorized as related to politics and other areas.

Given the growing influence of the corporate profit imperatives on news reporting and the emphasis on soft or "new" news in recent times, this finding in itself was not surprising. But the all-white visuals in the same publication and over the same time periods did not show such a shift: In 1967 and in 1997 about three-fourths of all photographs depicting Whites fit only the politics/other category, and about one-fourth were in the sports/entertainment area. With respect to all-white visuals, changes in favor of entertainment and sports figures at the expense of

TABLE 6.1
Overall Visuals of Blacks and Whites (Newsweek, 1967/1997) *

| | Sports/Entertainment | | All Other Areas | |
	1967	1997	1967	1997
Whites Only	25.1%	26.2%	74.9%	73.8%
Blacks Only	41.4%	67.3%	58.6%	32.7%

N = 2316
*visuals in advertisements not included

images from politics and other important areas were, in fact, negligible (see Table 6.1).

These results did not change significantly when we compared the proportion of visuals that showed Blacks and Whites alone, with each other, and with members of other racial groups.[15] Thus, the vast majority of the news visuals reflected two of the most common stereotypes of Blacks—the physically superior athlete and the talented entertainer in certain areas of this field. In Andrew Hacker's words, "White America still prefers its black people to be performers" (Hacker, 1992, 34).

Another aspect contributes to the overall picture of black America as projected through the mass media: the images of African Americans as anchors in both local and national newscasts. Rightly or wrongly, anchors are perceived as the stars of newscasts and crucial to the successes and failures of these programs. At the time of our research, Blacks co-anchored the earliest-morning, first-afternoon, and late-night news broadcasts of several local TV stations on weekdays, but the regular anchors in the local newscasts that immediately preceded the major TV networks' evening broadcasts were all white, as were the male-female co-anchor teams of the three TV networks' morning shows and the all-male evening news anchors on ABC, CBS, and NBC. The exception here was CNN, which had a black male/white female team (Judy Woodruff and Bernard Shaw). In short, with the exception of Shaw, white anchors dominated the primary morning and evening national TV newscasts and the local TV news programs seen in the New York metropolitan area during the week.

While two African Americans (Carol Simpson, a regular anchor of ABC's weekend news broadcasts, and Renee Poussaint, a substitute anchor on ABC-TV) were represented on *Media Monitor's* 1997 list of the ten most visible network anchors, they anchored only 5 percent of the news programs, compared to the 95 percent of the broadcasts that the seven white men and one white woman anchors narrated.[16]

The Pieces of the Mosaic

ADVERTISEMENTS/COMMERCIALS

Our expectation that the proportion of Blacks depicted in advertisements had risen significantly in the past three decades was confirmed by our findings. Only 2 percent of all ads published in *Newsweek* in 1967–68 showed either Blacks alone or Blacks with Whites. The few Blacks portrayed in advertisements in the late 1960s were not necessarily African Americans but more often Africans or natives of Caribbean islands that were advertised as ideal vacation spots. By 1997–98 the proportion of advertisements in *Newsweek* that depicted Blacks alone or with members of other racial groups had risen to more than 12 percent (see Table 6.2). An earlier study found that in 1982, close to 10 percent of all advertisements in *Newsweek* included Blacks. Thus, our findings demonstrate a significant increase in the number of black images in advertisements over the past thirty years and a modest rise over the past fifteen years.

In the *New York Times,* the trend was quite similar. Whereas virtually no ads that depicted black persons appeared in 1967, more than 10 percent of the advertisements published in 1997 showed Blacks alone or with members of other racial groups (see Table 6.2).

While our data document meaningful long-term progress in the proportion of Blacks in advertisements, our quantitative and qualitative analyses raise some questions and warnings. Cautioning against the practice of simply counting faces, one media scholar wrote, "Certainly, data verify that there are more black faces, but they get less time, are

TABLE 6.2
*Racial Images in Advertisements (*Newsweek, *1967–1968/1997–1998, and* New York Times, *1967/1997)*

	Whites	Blacks	Whites/ Blacks	Whites/ Others	Blacks/ Others	Whites/Blacks/ Others	Others
Newsweek							
1967/1968	85.9%	0.4%	1.6%	—	—	—	12.1%
1997/1968	80.2%	5%	5.3%	1.2%	0.2%	1.7%	6.4%
New York Times							
1967	99.2%	0.1%	0.2%	—	—	0.002%	0.5%
1997	87%	3.7%	5.5%	1.0%	0.4%	0.8%	1.6%

N *(Newsweek)* = 2600
N *(New York Times)* = 5056

less visible, may be buried in a sea of faces, and rarely interact with Whites" (Greenberg, 1986, 175). To be sure, this was more of a problem in earlier times, but even in 1997 the share of all-white ads in the *New York Times* (87 percent) was higher and that of all-black ads (4 percent) significantly lower than each race's ratio in the population nationwide. In 1997–98 the percentage of all-white advertisements in *Newsweek* (80 percent) was higher than the share of non-Hispanic Whites in the national population, but once again the number of all-black ads (5 percent) was significantly lower than the proportion of African Americans in the U.S. population. In both publications, the percentage of ads depicting both Blacks and Whites was higher than the share of all-black ads. This is an important point, because, in the vast majority of ads showing members of both racial groups, Whites far outnumbered Blacks and were more prominently placed.

Reflecting the high proportion of African Americans who reside in New York City or in the surrounding areas, advertisements in the local news media depicted Blacks more frequently than the ads published in *Newsweek* and in the *New York Times*. Thus, 30 percent of the commercials aired on WABC-TV's *Eyewitness News* program and 23 percent of the ads published in the *New York Daily News* and the *New York Post* either were all-black or showed African Americans with Whites. However, the percentage of all-black commercials and advertisements was very low (2 percent on WABC; 4 percent in the DN; 9 percent in the NYP) and the share of white-black advertisements relatively high. Once again, in almost all ads and commercials we coded as depicting Blacks and Whites, only one or two Black and several White persons were shown. Had we counted each black and white person in those ads, the dominance of white faces would be far greater than is reflected in the numbers we presented earlier.

Several other findings are noteworthy here. Ads that promoted expensive merchandise were more likely to depict Whites only, while ads that offered lower-cost items were more likely to show models of both races or Blacks only. We were especially struck by the relatively small number of Blacks portrayed in the print ads run by those New York City department stores that are frequented by a large number of black customers.

We found that black children, the elderly, and young women were shown far more often than young and middle-aged men. When young and middle-aged men were portrayed, they were often prominent athletes (Michael Jordan, Tiger Woods) or entertainers dead or alive (Louis Armstrong, Stevie Wonder). If not a celebrity, the young and middle-aged black male was depicted in a way that characterized him as worthy, as a good guy—the veteran who lost part of his arm, the physical therapist who worked with a child, the hotel employee who spoke (as the ad revealed) several languages. Wittingly or not, a line was drawn between the advertisement's "good guy" and the stereotypical black male as a negative figure. Advertisers seemed to assume that white males of this age group did not need this sort of legitimation.

Finally, in comparison to Whites, African Americans were disproportionately depicted in advertisements by nonprofit organizations rather than in ads by for-profit businesses. This was more the case in the 1967–68 period but was still in evidence thirty years later.

CRIME: PERPETRATORS AND VICTIMS

Even when crime rates decline significantly as they did in the mid- and late 1990s, the news media seem not to notice. The news, especially local TV news, is said to showcase the most violent crimes (Mifflin, 1997). This is hardly surprising in view of the growing competition for audiences and advertising revenues and of media bosses' belief that news consumers prefer to read, see, and hear reports about shocking tragedies and dramas. Some researchers found that the news media report disproportionately on crimes committed by African Americans. A content analysis of local TV newscasts established that nonwhite Americans were routinely portrayed as criminals (Campbell, 1995). According to Campbell, "Considering the general dearth of minority coverage on the [local] evening news, these [portraits of blacks as aggressors and criminals] may be the most dominant images of nonwhite Americans" (1995, 69). An extensive analysis of crime reports on local TV and the ethnicity of actual criminals in Los Angeles established, however, that "nonwhites in the aggregate were not substantially over-represented in the news coverage of violent crime . . . , white perpetrators were actually overrepresented in the news" (Gilliam, 1996).

Our data show that both *Newsweek* and the *New York Times* devoted far more coverage to crime in 1997-98 than thirty years earlier. But, while *Newsweek* published in 1997–98 far more images of white perpetrators and far fewer visuals of black criminals than it did thirty years earlier, there was a significant decrease in pictures of white criminals and victims and a significant increase in visuals of black perpetrators and victims in the *Times*. The fact that the *Times* covers local and regional news, while *Newsweek* focuses on national news, seems to account for the different trends. This explanation was confirmed by our finding that visual images of Blacks and Whites in the coverage of crime were far more frequently shown in New York's local print media and in local TV newscasts than in the national newsmagazine and in the *Times*. The NYP published slightly more photographs of white than of black criminals, but the DN and WABC's *Eyewitness News* showed slightly more visuals of black than of white perpetrators. A similar picture emerged with respect to black and white victims of crime.

Thus, while the frequency of white and black visuals in the coverage of crime in the local media (DN, NYP, WABC-TV) was different from that in the NYT and, even more so, in *Newsweek,* there was seemingly no evidence for the widely held view that in the mass media criminals are mostly black and victims of crime are mostly white. Why did the crime visuals we examined differ significantly from some earlier findings that established a far greater focus on visuals of African Americans in crime reports? First, during the period of our content analysis the media reported prominently about several major crime cases and trials that involved white perpetrators and mostly white victims (the Unabomber case, the Oklahoma City bombing trial, the Boston nanny case). Second, local newspapers and TV newscasts covered the most dramatic of these national cases regularly and in some length. Third, while many media organizations did not reduce the coverage of individual crime, they were no longer featuring stories about climbing crime rates. In the past, such reports were likely to be illustrated with visuals that perpetuated the Black-as-criminal stereotype. More recent trend stories tended to report falling crime rates and were likely to be illustrated with law-and-order specialists and other public officials, who were typically white.

POLITICS, THE PROFESSIONS, AND BUSINESS

In 1967–68, when far fewer African Americans held elective and appointive public offices than now, *Newsweek* nevertheless published a slightly higher proportion of photographs that depicted black officeholders than it did thirty years later. The *Times* published a higher proportion of pictures showing black public officials in 1997 than it did three decades earlier (see Table 6.3).

TABLE 6.3
*Racial Images of Public Officials and Candidates for
Public Office (*Newsweek, *1967–1968/1997–1998,
and* New York Times, *1967/1997)*

	Whites	Blacks	Whites and Blacks	Other
Newsweek				
1967/1968	95.7%	2.9%	1%	0.5%
1997/1998	97%	2.6%	—	0.4%
New York Times				
1967	86.2%	3.3%	1%	9.5%
1997	82.7%	5.5%	0.9%	10.9%

N *(Newsweek)* = 746
N *(New York Times)* = 878

All in all, even in the late 1990s visuals of black public officials were rare in the national news magazine and not as frequent as one would expect in a newspaper that covers not only international and national affairs but local and regional politics in an area with a substantial number of black citizens and black officials.

In 1967–68 *Newsweek* published slightly more and thirty years later significantly more visuals of black than of white political and social activists. In 1967 readers of the *Times* saw more visuals of white than of black activists, but thirty years later the newspaper published more pictures of black than of white activists. Not surprisingly, at the time of the civil rights and the anti–Vietnam movements in the 1960s, these sorts of visuals were shown far more frequently than they were in 1997–98. Our data reveal that in the late 1990s the leading news media were far more inclined to publish visuals of black activists, whether moderate or radical, than of African Americans who held elective or appointed public offices.

Visuals depicting African Americans alone or with Whites as professionals jumped dramatically, from 6 percent to 19 percent in *Newsweek* and from 5 percent to 15 percent in the *New York Times* between 1967–68 and 1997–98 data. On the other hand, of all visuals depicting people in a business setting that *Newsweek* published in 1967–68 and in 1997–98, the same proportion showed Blacks (6 percent) and Whites (92 percent) in both periods. In the *Times,* the share of Blacks depicted in the business world remained dismally low, increasing from less than 1 percent in 1967 to less than 2 percent three decades later (see Table 6.4).

TABLE 6.4

Racial Images of Individuals in Professional and Business Contexts
(Newsweek, 1967–1968/1997–1998, and New York Times, 1967/1997)

	Whites	Blacks	Whites and Blacks	Whites and Other	Other
Newsweek					
1967–19689	94.1% (P)	4.8% (P)	1.1% (P)	—	—
	2.2% (B)	3.9% (B)	1.1% (B)	—	2.8% (B)
1997–1998	78.1% (P)	17.2% (P)	1.6% (P)	3.1% (P)	—
	92.1% (B)	4.5% (B)	1.1% (B)	2.3% (B)	2.3% (B)
New York Times					
1967	94.4% (P)	3.9% (P)	1.1% (P)	—	0.6% (P)
	96.6% (B)	0.4% (B)	—	—	—
1997	79.4% (P)	13.1% (P)	1.9% (P)	0.5% (P)	5.1% (P)
	93% (B)	1.1% (B)	—	—	2.3% (B)

N *(Newsweek)* = 608
N *(New York Times)* =1096
P = Professional
B = Business Setting

LEADERS, FOLLOWERS, AND ACHIEVERS

In 1997, the visuals of Whites were numerically more dominant when Americans were depicted as leaders in politics, civics, professional life, business, or sports, than they were for any other category we examined. In the NYT 86 percent of visual leadership images were of Whites, in the DN 95 percent, in the NYP 92 percent, and on WABC-TV 89 percent. White leaders were pictured far more often in sports (as coaches and managers) and in all other walks of life than were black leaders. Blacks were frequently pictured as followers and supporters of leaders and prominent personalities in politics, religion, and entertainment, as well as in visuals depicting the public at large. When visuals showed Blacks and Whites together, it was not unusual that the leader was White and the supporting cast fully or partially African American. Taken together, the visuals in New York's three daily newspapers of what we called "supporting cast" depicted Whites in 48 percent, Blacks in 32 percent, and both Blacks and Whites in 20 percent of the relevant photographs. In other words, more than half of these pictures depicted either Blacks or Blacks and Whites together. Readers of the NYP saw the images of Blacks as followers or members of the public far more frequently than those of Whites. Local TV news showed more visuals of white followers alone than of Blacks only and Blacks and Whites together.

At first sight, African Americans were very well represented in visuals that depicted achievements in some area of life. In the daily newspapers, either Whites (NYT, DN) or Blacks (NYP) held a slight advantage here. In local TV news, Whites had the clear advantage. However, a closer look reveals that the bulk of the achievement visuals concerned the world of sports. While this was true for both Whites and Blacks, a far higher percentage of black achievement images compared to those of Whites were taken from sports. In the NYT, for example, 98 percent of all black visuals in the achievement category were of athletes, compared to only 80 percent of white achievement images. In the DN, 97 percent of the black achievement pictures, but only 69 percent of the white photographs, were of people in sports. Because the local TV newscasts did not cover sports as comprehensively as the daily newspapers, they projected overall a higher proportion of Whites in their visuals.

In comparison to the all-white and all-black sports pictures, the number of visuals depicting black and white athletes together was surprisingly low. While this was true as well for visuals in other areas of the news, we had assumed, wrongly as it turned out, that we would not find such a distinct separation in sports between Blacks and Whites, given that many of the sports visuals were drawn from racially integrated team sports.

The small number of black visuals that depicted achievers and leaders in business news was especially striking. Pictures in these sections were either of sports stars who were promoting products, black entrepreneurs in the rap or other "black" music business, or well-known African American activists like Jesse Jackson in campaigns pushing corporations to pay more attention to black America and its buying power. And, yes, when stories about the taxi industry or so-called subprime lenders and risky borrowers needed to be illustrated, pictures of a black taxi driver or a black woman who had defaulted on her mortgage were chosen.

On the other hand, we found some positive examples of Blacks depicted in achievement visuals. Thus, after healthy septuplets were born in Iowa, one news photograph showed two African American physicians who were part of the medical team delivering and caring for the seven babies.[17]

OF WEDDINGS, HEALTH, AND LIFESTYLES

In 1968, when the Kerner Commission pointed out that the white mainstream press acted as if African Americans did not give birth, marry, or die and were not active in all kinds of private and civic activities, there was good reason for such a complaint. We found, for example, that in the fall of 1967 Black faces were virtually absent from the wedding and engagement announcements published by the *New York Times*. Of 841 visuals on these pages, only one photograph showed an African American bride. In the same time period, however, close to 6 percent of all of these visuals were all-black, while an additional 1 percent showed African Americans with members of other racial groups.

But there are still areas of everyday life where African Americans are mostly ignored. According to one recent account, newspapers "rarely write about Blacks' religious faith, for example, or Black women's hair styles" (Shipler, 1998, 30). We found that African Americans were virtually excluded from visuals illustrating health stories, as if this minority had no health problems at all. And when lifestyle and trend stories were devoted exclusively or partly to African Americans, the accompanying visuals almost always depicted stars in sports or entertainment.

How African Americans Use and Evaluate the News Media

A majority of African Americans (60 percent) and a plurality of Whites (47 percent) consider television their major source for political news, while one-fourth of Blacks and more than one-third of Whites look upon newspapers as their most important source for political information. Few Blacks (7 percent) and Whites (6 percent) have "a great deal of trust" in the way the media report the news; 81 percent of African Americans and 68 percent of Whites have "some trust" or "not much trust" in the news media; 11 percent of Blacks and 6 percent of Whites have "no trust" at all in the media as a news source.

More important, nearly three of four Blacks (73 percent) feel that the news media's reporting on African Americans is "too negative," and only 20 percent deem it "fairly balanced." In comparison, only 11 percent of Whites feel that the coverage of white Americans is "too negative," and 60 percent feel that Whites are covered in a "fairly balanced" way. Forty-seven percent of Whites think that the coverage of black America is "fairly balanced," but 40 percent judge news reporting on African Americans to be "too negative." In sharp contrast, few Blacks (6 percent) consider the news coverage of Whites "too negative," and a clear majority (59 percent) consider news reporting on Whites "too positive," with 29 percent deeming it "fairly balanced."[18]

Discussion

In spite of African Americans' critical attitude toward the coverage of Blacks in the mainstream news media, our research revealed improvements in the portrayal of black America in several areas. But our findings established as well that visuals in the contemporary news reflect most of all two of the most common stereotypes: African Americans as talented athletes and entertainers. At first sight, Blacks were less prominent with respect to a third stereotype—visuals depicting Blacks, especially young African American males, as menacing criminals (Campbell, 1995). But were it not for the prominent coverage of a few sensational crime cases and trials that involved Whites only, the enduring stereotype of the male Black as criminal would have been pronounced as well. One way or the other, the seemingly positive stereotypes of Blacks as achievers and stars in sports and in the world of entertainment clearly dominated the pictoral images of African America presented to the nation. While Blacks with accomplishments in these fields certainly deserve news coverage, just as white athletes and entertainers do, the abundance of this sort of coverage and the far smaller amount of news about Blacks in other walks of life contribute to what some critics perceive as a fundamental problem of black America.

Harry Edwards has warned that because of "the high visibility of Black athlete role models, disproportionately high numbers of Black youth are channeled into athletic career aspirations." Edwards argues that "this channeling process" tragically leads millions of Blacks to pursue a goal that is foredoomed to elude all but an insignificant few" (1980, 219). According to Edwards, "the white sports media is a key factor of sustaining traditional definitions of Black realities in sports" (1980, 219). Our findings suggest that the news media as a whole, not simply sports news, perpetuate the uneven portrayal and the stereotyping of black Americans by reporting daily and extensively on African American success stories in athletics without paying similar attention to successful Blacks in business, politics, and other walks of life.

Our research established that black entertainers, too, were allotted far more visuals than African Americans in other areas of life. Seen in this light, the media's tendency to perpetuate day in and day out the seemingly positive stereotype of Blacks as gifted athletes and entertainers points to a lack of balance in the news about black America. When the media devote an average of close to two-thirds of their black visuals to sports and entertainment figures and depict no more than a few thousand African American achievers in those fields while minimizing their coverage of Blacks, or ignoring them altogether, in important areas such as education, health care, welfare, and antipoverty efforts that affect millions of black Americans, the portrayal of the African American minority is lopsided.

To be sure, today African Americans are represented in disproportionately high numbers in many of the most popular professional and amateur athletics, as well as in some areas of the entertainment world. Also, Blacks are still underrepresented in those leadership roles in politics, the sciences, and the world of business that tend to get media attention. Thus, the argument could be made that the media's portrayal of black America reflects more or less the reality of America's contemporary society. Why, then, bother with examining and critically evaluating how the media cover Blacks and how this coverage compares to the media's portrayal of Whites? We have already noted that in one very important aspect news visuals of Blacks were more stereotyped in the late 1990s than they were thirty years earlier, although the reality of black America has certainly not changed in this direction. The shortcomings we found seemed to be the result of dramatic trends toward soft news as dictated by corporate profit imperatives and of lingering institutionalized stereotypes in the newsrooms that still affect which aspects of African American life are emphasized and deemphasized.

If one subscribes to the "social responsibility" ideal and the requirement that the news must report adequately on all relevant groups in society, the mass media's performance remains disappointing. Since journalists, editors, producers, and other news personnel make choices about what to report and how to present the news, they are in a position to present a more complete portrayal of black America (and of other minorities). That would mean, for example, paying more attention to important, not simply interesting, news and making greater efforts to seek out African Americans as sources, especially as experts in fields in which Blacks are chronically undercovered. This would help to counter the predominance of the traditional black stereotypes. We do not suggest quotas in the selection of news sources but urge a greater sensitivity to the need to present a complete and real picture of black America and of other minorities. The recent and growing public journalism movement has reaffirmed the notion of a news media with distinct civic responsibilities (Rosen, 1996), but the largest and most influential media organizations have rejected the ideals of the public or civic press model. Without an increased focus on these sorts of values, the corporate profit imperatives and the remnants of the white majority perspective will continue to prevail in newsroom decisions.

While more and better news coverage of black America is needed, improvements are also required with respect to multiracial images. In advertisements that depict Whites and Blacks together, Whites are generally shown in greater numbers and are placed more prominently. The visuals in the news also reveal a tendency to portray Blacks and Whites as distinctly different groups and individuals. This affirms what one communication researcher found with respect to television: "African Americans and white Americans are not shown as living in an integrated society where they interact as friendly equals, respectful of each other's needs and tolerant of each other's differences" (Corea, 1995, 355).

In 1968 the news media reported extensively and prominently on the Kerner Commission's findings. In 1998, when President Clinton's Advisory Board on Race released its report, "One America for the Twenty-first Century," the media hardly took notice.[19] As a result, even most members of the so-called interested public were unaware of the later report and how it differed in one fundamental way from the Kerner Commission's considerations: In the late 1960s, the debate about race in America concerned Whites and Blacks only, but in the 1990s and beyond, as President Clinton's Advisory Board underlined, discussions about race must not only consider Whites and Blacks but must include other groups, such as Hispanics, American Indians and Alaska Natives, and Asian Pacific Americans, as well.

While this chapter has focused on the news media's portrayal of black America, we suggest that our theoretical premises and our research design can be just as useful in examining and understanding how the American news media picture and stereotype other minorities. Indeed, there are indications that the portrayal of Hispanics, native Americans, and Asian Americans is as incomplete and stereotypical as that of African Americans. Former New Jersey Governor Thomas Kean, a member of President Clinton's Advisory Board on Race, observed, "Almost every [racial] group we've gone to has said that the media is a problem that has to be addressed" (Advisory Board, 1998, 97). And under the head "Media and Stereotyping," the Board noted that "a major problem still remains regarding the representation, coverage, and portrayal of minorities on the news" (Advisory Board, 1998, 97).

One comprehensive study has discovered patterns in the news coverage of Hispanics that are very similar to those we have found for African Americans. When daily newspapers in six southwestern cities where Latinos constitute 20 percent to 65 percent of the population reported on Hispanics, the focus of these stories was mostly on sports. And an astounding 82 percent of all photographs depicting Hispanics concerned soft news and sports (Taylor, 1997).

One expert in the field has concluded that the media's portrayal of minorities "may have significant implications for the capacity of the society to work effectively as a multicultural society based on mutual respect for and understanding of difference" (Jakubowics, 1995, 174). This is a compelling argument. If stereotypes are indeed at the heart of racial divisions and misunderstandings and if dialogue is the best tool for finding common ground, as President Clinton's Advisory Board on Race has suggested, the road to one multicultural America runs through the newsrooms and, even more so, through the boardrooms of corporations that directly and indirectly shape the content of both the news media and the mass media in general.

NOTES

1. According to the 1993–94 Dawson National Black Politics Study, 49 percent of survey respondents held the nation-within-a-nation view, while 46 percent considered Blacks another ethnic group. See "People, Opinions, and Polls: An American Dilemma (Part II)," *Public Perspective* (February/March 1996), p. 42.

2. In 1981, 69 percent of African Americans and 54 percent of Whites knew a member of the other race and considered him or her "a fairly close friend." By 1997, 83 percent of African Americans and 71 percent of Whites spoke of such interracial friendships. See "Ethnicity in Black and White," *Public Perspective* (February/March 1998), p. 64.

3. While African Americans, Hispanics, and Asian Americans constituted about 27 percent of the U.S. population in the late 1990s, newsrooms were only 11.5 percent minority. Recognizing the failure of its "Year 2000" target, the American Society of Newspaper Editors set the more modest goal of 20 percent minority members in the newsrooms by the year 2010.

4. CBS News was one of those organizations that upheld this standard. For example, on the day Elvis Presley died in 1977, this was not the lead story on Walter Cronkite's *CBS Evening News*. For a discussion of this sort of news judgment, see Peter J. Boyer, *Who Killed CBS: The Undoing of America's Number One News Network* (New York: Random House, 1988).

5. In April 1998 *Boston Magazine* came under attack for using the headline "Head Negro in Charge" for an article on Harvard University's Afro-American Studies chairman Henry Louis Gates Jr. The expression "head negro in charge" goes back to slavery and is now commonly used by black scholars to refer to Afro-American individuals who are chosen by the white establishment to speak for their race.

6. Reporting on a baseball game between the Chicago Cubs and the New York Mets, the reporter Jason Diamos wrote, "Imagine then how Butch Huskey [a Black player] must have felt standing in right field at Wrigley Field being subjected to what he called 'racial slurs' from the bleacher bums" (Jason Diamos, "The Rain Must Fall, But Leiter Shines," *New York Times,* 8 April 1998, C1,C3). Describing the pairing of the white golfer Fuzzy Zoeller and the black golfer Tiger Woods at the 1998 Masters one year after Zoeller's racially insensitive remark about tournament winner Woods, Dave Anderson observed critically that "Zoeller inspired much louder reactions from the Masters gallery, which seemed to identify with this good ol' boy from Indiana" (Dave Anderson, "Woods and Zoeller Play a Chilly Round," *New York Times,* 11 April 1998, p. C5).

7. Kurt Anderson, a columnist for *The New Yorker,* is quoted by Neil Hickey, "Money Lust: How Pressure for Profit Is Perverting Journalism," *Columbia Journalism Review* (July/August 1998), p. 30.

8. Because the Kerner Commission began its work in 1967 and published its report the following year, we chose the last six months of 1967 and the first half year of 1968 to examine the visuals published in *Newsweek* during this time. We chose the corresponding time periods in 1997–98 to establish the picture of black America three decades after the Kerner Commission investigated race relations in America. Unlike *Newsweek,* the *New York Times* is published daily. In order to keep our research manageable we had to limit our analysis of this publications to three months each in 1967 and in 1997. The actual coding was very simple in that we counted the number of pictures that showed Blacks and Whites alone, with each other, or with members of other minorities in the easily identifiable categories.

9. Again, we chose these two time periods with the investigation of the Kerner Commission in mind as well as our primary goal of investigating the contemporary media portrayal of black America.

10. In order to manage the analysis of the NYT, DN, NYP, and a local TV-newscast (on WABC) we had to limit our time period to six weeks at the end of 1967 and of 1997.

11. According to Dr. Martha Farnsworth Riche, "A Profile of America's Diversity—The View from the Census Bureau, 1996," *The World Almanac and Book of Facts 1997* (Mahwah, N.J.: World Almanac Books, 1997), pp. 377–378.

12. According to the Columbia-1199 Survey I (1997). The 1997 participation study was conducted by Columbia University/Barnard College Urban

Policy Institute and 1199 Communication Center, a division of the 1199 Health and Human Services in New York City.

13. We content analyzed the "Eyewitness News" broadcast on WABC in New York from 25 November 1997 through 31 December 1997—half the period in the 6:00 P.M.–6:30 P.M. and the other half in the 5:00 P.M.–5:30 P.M. time slot.

14. Columbia-1199 Survey II, conducted in the fall of 1997, polled a total of 1,600 adults, 228 of them Blacks, in the State of New York.

15. We realize that special circumstances, events, or developments during the particular time periods we examined could have affected our results. In an effort to avoid conducting a great deal of additional research at five- or ten-year intervals, we examined all photographs of African Americans in the editorial sections of the *New York Times* and the *New York Daily News* during January 1998. We examined a total of 830 visuals in the sections that reported on international, domestic, regional, and local news, as well as those that provide sports, business, and entertainment/arts coverage. We found that the full mosaic of black America as presented by these two newspapers was quite similar to the portrayal of black America as reflected in *Newsweek* in the second half of 1997: 70 percent of the black images in the NYT and 76 percent in the DN showed African Americans in the context of sports or entertainment and the arts. With respect to Blacks portrayed in the entertainment/arts sections, the numbers do not tell the whole story; the bulk of the pictures showed Blacks who had achieved in jazz or rap music or who were comedians in film and television—just as was the case in *Newsweek* during the summer and fall 1997.

16. We calculated the share of broadcasts narrated by black and white anchors by using information contained in the list of "Most Visible Anchors" in "1997 Year in Review: TV's Leading News Topics, Reporters, and Political Jokes," *Media Monitor* (January/February 1998), p. 4.

17. The photograph of Dr. Paula Mahone and Dr. Karen Drake appeared without headline in the *Daily News* of 20 November 1997, p. 4.

18. The data cited in this section are from the Columbia-1199 Survey II (1997).

19. When the 1998 report was released, the news media were preoccupied with covering the Clinton-Lewinsky scandal and the possible impeachment of the President. Nevertheless, the lack of media attention to the findings of the Advisory Commission on Race was astounding.

REFERENCES

Advisory Board's Report to the President. 1998. *One America in the 21st Century: Forging a New Future.* Prepublication copy issued by the White House, 18 September.

Anderson, Dave. 1998. "Woods and Zoeller Play a Chilly Round." *New York Times,* 11 April 1998, p. C5.

Altschull, Herbert J. 1995. *Agents of Power.* White Plains, N.Y.: Longman.

Ansolabehere, Stephen, Roy Behr, and Shanto Iyengar. 1993. *The Media Game.* New York: Macmillan.

Bagdikian, Ben H. 1992. *The Media Monopoly.* Boston: Beacon Press.

Baran, S. 1973. "Dying Black, Dying White: Coverage of Six Newspapers." *Journalism Quarterly* 50: 761–763.

Barringer, Felicity. 1998. "Editors Debate Realism vs. Diversity." *New York Times,* 6 April, C1, C8.

Bagdikian, Ben H. 1992. *The Media Monopoly.* Boston: Beacon Press.

Boyer, Peter J. 1988. *Who Killed CBS? The Undoing of America's Number One Network.* New York: Random House.

Campbell, Christopher P. 1995. *Race, Myth, and the News.* Thousand Oaks, Calif.: Sage.

Chaudhary, A. 1980. "Press Portrayal of Black Officials." *Journalism Quarterly* 57: 636–641.

Corea, Ash. 1995. "Racism and the American Way of Media," in John Downing et al., eds. *Questioning the Media.* Thousand Oaks, Calif.: Sage.

Cose, Ellis. 1994. "Seething in Silence: The News in Black and White." *Media Studies Journal* 8(3): 1–10.

Dates, Jannette L., and William Barlow. 1993. *Split Image: African Americans in the Mass Media.* Washington, D.C.: Howard University Press.

Dautrich, Kenneth, and Jennifer Necci Dineen. 1996. "Media Bias: What Journalists and the Public Say About It." *Public Perspective,* October/November, pp. 7–10.

Donsbach, Wolfgang, et al. 1993. "How Unique Is the Perspective of Television?" *Political Communication* 18: 37–53.

Edwards, Harry. 1980. *The Struggle That Must Be.* New York: Macmillan.

Efron, Edith. 1971. *The News Twisters.* Los Angeles: Nash.

Entman, Robert M. 1992. "Blacks in the News: Television, Modern Racism, and Cultural Change." *Journalism Quarterly* 69: 341–361.

———. 1994. "African Americans According to TV News." *Media Studies Journal* 8(3): 29–38.

Epstein, Edward Jay. 1974. *News from Nowhere.* New York: Vintage Books.

"Ethnicity in Black and White." 1998. *Public Perspective* (February/March): 64.

Exoo, Calvin F. 1994. *The Politics of the Mass Media.* Minneapolis/St. Paul: West.

Gans, Herbert. 1979. *Deciding What's News.* New York: Vintage Books.

Gilens, Martin. 1996. "Race and Poverty in America: Public Misperceptions and the American News Media." *Public Opinion Quarterly* 60: 515–541.

Gilliam, Franklin D. 1996. "Crime in Black and White." *Press/Politics* 1(3): 6–22.

Gissler, Sig. 1994. "Newspapers' Quest for Racial Candor." *Media Studies Journal* 8(3): 123–132.

Gitlin, Todd. 1980. *The Whole World Is Watching*. Berkeley: University of California Press.

Graber, Doris A. 1990. "Seeing Is Remembering: How Visuals Contribute to Learning from Television News." *Journal of Communication* 40: 134–155.

———. 1997. *Mass Media and American Politics*. Washington, D.C.: Congressional Quarterly Press.

Gramsci, Antonio. 1971. *Selections from the Prison Notebooks*. New York: International.

Greenberg, Bradley S. 1986. "Minorities and the Mass Media," in Jennings Bryant and Dolf Ziman, eds., *Perspectives on Media Effects*. Hillsdale, N.J.: Lawrence Erlbaum.

Hacker, Andrew. 1992. *Two Nations: Black and White, Separate, Hostile, and Unequal*. New York: Scribner.

Herman, Edward E., and Noam Chomsky. 1988. *Manufacturing the News: The Political Economy of the Mass Media*. New York: Pantheon.

Hess, Stephen. 1983. "The Golden Triangle: The Press at the White House, State, and Defense." *Brookings Review* (Summer): 14–19.

Hickey, Neil. 1998. "Money Lust: How Pressure for Profit is Perverting Journalism." *Columbia Journalism Review* (July/August): 28–36.

Humphrey, Ronald, and Howard Schuman. 1984. "The Portrayal of Blacks in Magazine Advertising." *Public Opinion Quarterly* 48(3): 551–563.

Iyengar, Shanto. 1991. *Is Anyone Responsible?* Chicago: University of Chicago Press.

Iyengar, Shanto, and Donald R. Kinder. 1987. *News That Matters*. Chicago: University of Chicago Press.

Jakubowicz, Andrew. 1995. "The Media in Multicultural Nations: Some Comparisons," in John Downing et al., eds., *Questioning the Media*. Thousand Oaks, Calif.: Sage.

Jamieson, Kathleen Hall. 1992. *Dirty Politics*. New York: Oxford University Press.

Kinder, Donald, and Lynn M. Sanders. 1996. *Divided by Color: Racial Politics and Democratic Ideals*. Chicago: University of Chicago Press.

Klite, Paul, et al. 1997. "Local TV News: Getting Away With Murder." *Press/Politics* 2(2): 102–112.

Lester, Paul, and Ron Smith. 1990. "African American Photo Coverage in *Life, Newsweek* and *Time, 1937–1988*." *Journalism Quarterly* 67: 128–136.

Lichter, Robert S., et al. 1986. *The Media Elite*. Bethesda: Adler & Adler.

Lippmann, Walter. [1922] 1965. *Public Opinion*. New York: Free Press.

Marable, Manning. 1994. "Reconciling Race and Reality." *Media Studies Journal* 8(3): 11–18.

Marcuse, Herbert. 1964. *One-Dimensional Man*. Boston: Beacon Press.

Mifflin, Lawrie. 1997. "Crime Falls, but Not on TV." *New York Times,* 6 July, sec. 4, p. 4.

Mills, C. Wright. 1956. *The Power Elite*. New York: Oxford University Press.

Myrdal, Gunnar. [1944] 1972. *An American Dilemma: The Negro Problem and Modern Democracy*. New York: Pantheon.

Neuman, Russell W., Marion R. Just, and Ann N. Crigler. 1992. *Common Knowledge*. Chicago: University of Chicago Press.

Parenti, Michael. 1986. *Inventing Reality: The Politics of the Mass Media*. New York: St. Martin's Press.

Peffley, Mark, et al. 1996. "The Intersection of Race and Crime in Television News Stories." *Political Communication* 13(3): 309–327.

"People, Opinion and Polls: An American Dilemma, Part II." 1996. *Public Perspective* (February/March): 42.

Peterson, Theodore. 1956. "The Social Responsibility Theory," in Fred S. Siebert et al., eds., *Four Theories of the Press*. Urbana: University of Illinois Press.

Pristin, Terry. 1998. "Radio Ad Worker Apologizes for Memo Offending Minorities." *New York Times,* 6 May, p. B3.

Report of the National Commission on Civil Disorder. 1968. New York: Bantam.

Robinson, Michael J., and Margaret A. Sheehan. 1983. *Over the Wire and on TV*. New York: Russell Sage.

Rosen, Jay. 1996. *Getting the Connections Right: Public Journalism and the Troubles in the Press*. New York: Twentieth Century Fund Press.

Shipler, David K. 1998. "Blacks in the Newsroom." *Columbia Journalism Review* (May/June): 26–32.

Sigal, Leon V. 1973. *Reporters and Officials*. Lexington, Mass.: Heath.

Stempel, G. 1971. "Visibility of Blacks in News and News-picture Magazines." *Journalism Quarterly* 60(4): 337–339.

Stewart, Pearl. 1997. "Women of Color as Newspaper Executives," in Pippa Norris, ed., *Politics and the Press*. Boulder: Lynne Rienner.

Taylor, C. R. 1997. "Portrayals of Latinos in Magazine Advertising." *Journalism and Mass Communication Quarterly* 74(2): 285–303.

Part III

Political Behavior

Chapter 7

Who Votes in Multiracial America?
An Analysis of Voting Registration and Turnout by Race and Ethnicity, 1990–1996

Pie-te Lien

For American Blacks the electoral franchise has opened up a world of improvement in social, economic, and political conditions. Not surprisingly then, a great deal of the research on black politics concerns itself with the reasons people vote, the consequences of their decision to register and to vote, and impediments to full participation in the electoral process.

As America confronts its multiethnic future, however, the issue of voting is becoming an increasingly complicated and problematic one, especially as it relates to emerging immigrant groups. While Americans always assume that the de jure factors that have impeded voting by minorities have already been largely dismantled, today's immigrant groups face a host of structural and economic impediments that may preclude them from participation in the electoral process. Residency requirements, language barriers, and difficulties in mobilizing immigrant voters more generally often alienate immigrants and naturalized citizens from the electoral process.

In an effort to understand who votes in multiracial America, Pie-te Lien analyzes data from the Current Population Survey Voter Supplement (CPSVS) files for 1990–1996, to analyzing as two separate phenomena voting registration among voting-age citizens and voting turnout among the registered. The analysis is insightful; it provides a basis for thinking about impediments other than those related to voting rights law violations and geographical boundaries, which may hinder racial and ethnic minorities in their efforts to participate fully in the American political process.

Who votes in America, and who does not? Although the concern over the decline in voter turnout since the 1960 election has inspired a long and distinguished line of research, the question has seldom been addressed from the perspective of nonwhite minorities, even though they represent an increasingly large proportion of the U.S. population and have historically been oppressed in terms of citizenship and related issues regarding immigration, naturalization, suffrage, and political representation. In circumstances where the voting participation of racial and ethnic minorities is researched, attention has been paid mostly to Blacks and/or Latinos[1] (e.g., Verba and Nie 1972; Salamon and Evera 1973; Shingles 1981; Calvo and Rosenstone 1989; Bobo and Gilliam 1990; Hackey 1992; Rosenstone and Hansen 1993; Tate 1993; Verba, Schlozman, and Brady 1995; Arvizu and Garcia 1996; DeSipio 1996; Emig, Hesse, and Fisher 1996; Garcia 1997). When Asian Americans or American Indians are studied, research has been focused on certain localities (e.g., Peterson 1957; McCool 1985; Nakanishi 1986, 1991; Uhlaner, Cain, and Kiewiet 1989; Lien 1994, 1997; Tam 1995; but see Ong and Nakanishi 1996; Lien 1998). Thus, on the verge of the next century, when U.S. Census Bureau estimates show that by 2050 America will be 24.5 percent Latino, 13.6 percent Black, 8.2 percent Asian, and .9 percent American Indian, for a total of 47.2 percent non-White, little research has been done that studies the American electorate from a multiracial and national perspective.

Certainly, research supports the idea that most people vote if they are registered. For years, this thinking has been documented by the empirical observation of the high turnout rates among registered voters and the overlapping determinants of voter registration and turnout *among citizens* (Squire, Wolfinger, and Glass 1987). However, with the increasing number of immigrants, it is important to understand the structural factors that affect registration, the first barrier to voting. In this essay, I assess voting registration among voting-age citizens and voting turnout among the registered as two separate processes that differ not only in time, place, and kind (Timpone 1998) but also in campaign influence (Jackson 1996) and eligibility requirements. This two-stage framework of registration and voting is particularly useful to the study of racial and ethnic differences in voting participation. Whereas the gradual removal of legal barriers to minority enfranchisement in recent decades, including the passage of the National Motor Voter Act of 1993, has been intended to promote equality in voting registration, the practices of strategic mobilization by political parties, interest groups, campaign organizations, and political leaders go a long way in reinforcing inequality in voting participation. In many instances, newly incorporated immigrants and the poor may be systemically undermobilized. A central concern of this essay is to empirically evaluate the significance of race, as compared to other factors, in the two stages of electoral participation in the four major election years of the 1990s— 1990, 1992, 1994, and 1996.

Two questions are assessed in this paper. First, does race matter? More specifically, do race and ethnicity still affect voting turnout even when structural barriers to registration and voting are controlled? Is the difference in turnout just a function of higher average education and income levels among Whites? Second, how should we approach the issue of race in voting research? Is it valid to think of race in terms of Whites and non-Whites, or do we need to consider each racial group independently?

This research answers both questions affirmatively. Race does matter, even when the influence of important factors such as education and income is controlled. Second, race is not a binary variable. Research that deals only with Blacks and Whites, or that aggregates all non-Whites into a single group, may miss important behavior or produce spurious results.

Factors that Influence the Voting Registration and Turnout of Racial Minorities

Although the concept of equality for all in political rights was declared in 1776 and the right to vote regardless of "race, color, or previous condition of servitude" was guaranteed by the Fifteenth Amendment in 1870, the battle to win equal access to the voting ballot for racial and ethnic minorities has proven to be a long and an incomplete one. Throughout history, various citizenship and suffrage restrictions have been imposed upon American Indians, unfree and free Blacks, Latinos, and Asians (McClain and Stewart 1998). Within decades after the Civil

War, a variety of devices, including poll taxes, selective and discriminatory administration of literary tests, periodic registration, residency requirements, grandfather clauses, and white primaries, were adopted in the South to disfranchise Blacks (Key 1949; Kousser 1974). From time to time, some of these disfranchising devices were also used against European immigrants in the North, Asian immigrants in the West, and Mexicans and American Indians in the South and the Mountain West (Crotty 1977; McCool 1985; Kleppner 1987; Rosenstone and Hansen 1993, 205–206). Because the most restrictive disfranchising devices were found almost exclusively in states with significant nonwhite or immigrant population (Alt 1994), a consequence of the widespread adoption of voting registration requirements at the turn of the twentieth century was a sharp decline in the turnout and the curbing of the political influence of Blacks, immigrants, and the poor (Piven and Cloward 1988).

Today, with the enactment of the Voting Rights Act of 1965 and its subsequent amendments, the major legal barriers to the full exercise of the minority franchise have been removed, albeit not the practices of diluting the voting strength of racial minorities (Davidson 1994). In their place has been a slow but liberating trend of registration laws at the national level, evidenced first by the outlawing of poll taxes and literacy tests, then by the abatement of the stringent residency and closing date requirements, and most recently by the passage of the National Motor Voter Act, which attempts to relieve the administrative burdens facing the young, the residentially mobile, and the poor (see Hinghton and Wolfinger 1998). Nevertheless, individual U.S. citizens—and not the government—still bear the responsibility of registering and reregistering following each move across county lines. "The inconvenience of administrative arrangements for voter registration and the frequent need to re-register," Flanigan and Zingale (1994) note, "have offered greater obstacles to voting than has the imposition of other eligibility standards" (p. 28). Clearly, until the burden of self-registration is lifted, a logical first step in answering "who votes?" is to understand "who registers?" And, before asking that, a question important to many nonwhite immigrants is "who is eligible to register to vote?"

Not all voting-age persons who hold a permanent residence in the United States can register to vote. Only native and naturalized citizens are eligible to become registered. Although this is a nonissue for most Americans, this simple gatekeeping measure has kept close to half of adult Asians and nearly 40 percent of adult Latinos in the 1990s from the traditional first stage of voting (Table 7.1). For the foreign-born population, registration cannot take place before naturalization; yet this is often the most difficult aspect of the process, because the acquisition of citizenship for eligible permanent residents who meet the five-year waiting time requirement may still be inhibited by individual factors such as poor English language skills, lack of knowledge about U.S. history and the Constitution, lack of money and time to go through the application process, reluctance to sever emotional ties with the homeland, and lack of trust in the government. Voting is, therefore, in reality more than a two-stage process for many immigrant and refugee Americans. For them, the journey to the polling place begins with the departure from their homelands.

Neither is the satisfaction of the age and citizenship requirements equivalent to receiving a "passport" to vote. In between lies the hurdle of registration, which poses barriers to voting by demanding extra time, skills, and interest. According to the rational-choice argument, the registration requirement may have the most disfranchising effect on those who can least afford to write off its costs. Nonwhite citizens who are either poor or unfamiliar with the system may be among the most affected. Their behavior may be explained by a number of well-established set of factors described in the literature on political participation (e.g., Verba and Nie 1972; Wolfinger and Rosenstone 1980; Conway 1991; Verba, Schlozman, and Brady 1995; Abramson, Aldrich, and Rhode 1998). In general, minority participation can be suppressed by *socioeconomic factors* such as lower levels of education and lower income. Participation can also be inhibited by the degree of *social connectedness* as indicated by residential mobility, nativity, age, employment status, marital status, gender, and union membership. In addition, voting registration and turnout—particularly the latter—can be affected by the amount of campaign stimuli in the *political context,* including media coverage, candidate and party evaluation, significance of office, issue salience, and certainty of outcome (Jackson 1996).

Those who move often or who are foreign-born, very old or young in age, unemployed, or single, unmarried, or married but without the presence of a spouse may have weaker social ties and may be, therefore, less likely to register and vote. Being a member of the labor union may boost participation because of the greater degree of social connection afforded by group affiliation and the opportunity to be exposed to group mobilization efforts. A similar effect may be associated with being female. Although traditional research has suggested that women are less likely than men to participate in political activities, more recent research has shown that being female may enhance participation in voting, if not in other activities (Schlozman, Burns, and Verba 1994; Schlozman, Burns, Verba, and Donahue 1995; Conway, Steuernagel, and Ahern 1997). The extent of influence from social and professional group membership, however, may depend on the success of these movement groups in underwriting the costs and increasing the perceived benefits of participation. In the case of gender, the impact on political attitudes and behavior may vary significantly across racial groups (Lien 1998).

Exposure to campaign stimuli as indicated by the type of election year and resident region is deemed important in this study because of political mobilization (Rosenstone and Hansen 1993), group empowerment (Bobo and Gilliam 1990), and social contagion (Huckfeldt 1995) effects. Individuals are more likely to (re-)register or turn out to vote or do both in presidential election years than in midterm election years because of the higher campaign stimuli associated with the former. According to Rosenstone and Hansen (1993, 178), presidential campaigns are high-stimulus because they engage more resources, activists, and media coverage. However, the effect may be more pronounced on Whites than on non-Whites because of biases in the targeting and timing of mobilization by political parties. Blacks who reside in the southern region of the United States are less likely to participate because of the lingering impact of the disfranchising regional political culture. Minorities who reside in areas outside the South, however, are expected to benefit from greater exposure to group mobilization efforts, which may counter the racially and class-biased effect of strategic mobilization by mainstream political organizations and leaders (Schlichting, Tuckel, and Maisel 1998). Aggressive voter registration and get-out-the-vote drives by community organizations, attractive candidates, and galvanizing issues may also help offset resource and social connection gaps and bridge racial differences by evoke a greater amount of political interest and involvement.

This literature review provides several guiding theoretical frameworks that serve as a foundation for addressing our research question. First, the literature emphasizes a number of nonracial factors that affect political participation, including social networks, education, income, employment status, and region of residence. Second, voting registration and turnout levels for minorities lag behind those for Whites. The existing research on the participation of racial and ethnic minorities is based on a small sample of Blacks and Latinos and virtually no Asians or American Indians. This study breaks new ground by studying large numbers of subjects from all racial groups.

Data and Methods

This study uses information from the Census Bureau's Current Population Survey to examine the impact of race and ethnicity on voting behavior. Data for this research come from the Voter Supplement Files of 1990, 1992, 1994, and 1996. This covers all the election years to date when "Asian or Pacific Islander" and "American Indian or Aleut Eskimo" are added to the response category for the "race" question.

Compared to the American National Election Study (NES), a traditional data source for political research, the census survey (CPS) is well suited for this research. Most important, it has a much larger sample size, which allows even the smaller groups to be well represented. The pooled data set, for instance, includes 13,040 Asians, 28,331 Latinos, 3,891 American Indians, and 38,724 Blacks. This allows a close examination of how race affects each individual racial and ethnic group, something that has not been done in previous research. Second, its less biased representation of low-income and nonwhite minorities in the sample provides a better representation of the American population. Although both data sources are guilty of undersampling minority populations, the problem is much more severe with the National Election Study (NES) surveys (Teixeira 1992). A major CPS revision in 1994, which introduced new population controls based on the 1990 census, adjusted for the estimated population undercount. The differentials in aggregated turnout rates between official records maintained by state officials and the census-based estimates in the 1980s were about seven percentage points, a gap much smaller than the double-digit differentials found when using the NES data. Although higher socioeconomic status and exposure to pre-election polling may largely account for the higher level of reported turnout among NES respondents (Abramson, Aldrich, and Rhode 1994, 1998), the nonpolitical nature of the census survey may reduce respondents' propensity to misreport turnout (Teixeira 1992).

At the same time, there are some costs associated with the use of these data. First, no validation of voting is done for the CPS respondents. Second, only a small number of questions deal with political participation. Third, the special sampling problems of various minorities may result in a substantial undercounting of Latinos, Blacks, and Asians and overcounting of American Indians in urban areas (Passel 1990; Leung and Mar 1991; Harris 1994). Fourth, in addition to miscounting, there can be a lack of consistency in the identification of minorities such as Latinos (Arvizu and Garcia 1996). Fifth, CPS did not collect information on ethnic identity among Asian and Pacific Americans. However, with a major redesign implemented in 1994,[2] new questions on nativity and place of birth permit a limited opportunity for this research to analyze ethnicity by parental lineage. Sixth, changes in questionnaire, data collection, and data management made in 1994 may introduce additional errors when longitudinal data are used. Nevertheless, for this research question, these data are superior to other available data.

Two levels of analysis are used to assess the scope and significance of racial and ethnic differences in registration and voting. In the aggregate, racial and ethnic differences are assessed by several qualifying characteristics. At the individual level, following the three-step procedure in Jackson (1996), each multivariate analysis is presented in three models. The first model (I) adopts the traditional approach by estimating voting among adult citizens. The second model (II) estimates registration among voting-age citizens. The third model (III) estimates turnout among the registered. Separate analyses are conducted for each of the four elections examined using multiracial data, for each of the nonwhite groups using pooled data for 1990–1996, and for Asians using expanded pooled data for 1994–1996.

Because the dependent variables are binary measures, a logistic regression procedure, which bases its estimations using maximum likelihood method, is preferred. Interpretation of the beta coefficients is not straightforward, for the change in the dependent variable is a logarithm of the odds of two probabilities, and the effect size of each variable is dependent on the values of other variables in the model. However, like a linear regression model, larger beta estimates imply larger effects on the dependent variable, and t-scores larger than 1.96 imply significant effects at the $\mu=.05$ level.

The main explanatory variables are race and ethnicity. Each includes a number of collectively exhaustive but mutually exclusive and dichotomous indicators. The five measures of race are: White, Asian, Black, Latino, and American Indian.[3] The four measures of Latino ethnicity are Mexican, Puerto Rican, Cuban, and other (mainly Central and South Americans). The seven measures of Asian ethnicity are Asian Indian, Chinese, Filipino, Japanese, Korean, Vietnamese, and other (mainly South and Southeast Asians from Bangladesh, Burma, Cambodia, Laos, Indonesia, Malaysia, Pakistan, and Thailand). In the multiracial analysis for each election year, white is the comparison group. For the pooled Latino and Asian data, the "other" is the comparison group. As shown in Appendix 7A, the base control variables include gender, age, education, family income, length of residence, marital status, employment status, union membership, and region. The nativity variable is available only for 1994 and 1996. Responses are coded 1 if the respondent is female, is married with spouse present, is unemployed, is employed and belongs to an union or union-like association, is foreign-born, or resides in the South or in the West.[4] Dummy variables are also used in the pooled data for the election years 1990, 1992, and 1994, with the election of 1996 being the comparison year. Age is measured in years. Education is measured in sixteen units ranging from no formal education to Ph.D. degree. Family income is measured in thirteen units, with "annual income in the previous year at or above $75,000" being the highest score. Residential mobility is indicated by the length of time one has been at one's current address and is scored from 1, which means less than one month's stay to 6, which means a stay of five years or more.

Results and Discussion

Before examining the behavior of individual ethnic groups, one can make several broad observations. It is clear that, despite decades of federal enforcement of voting rights legislation, racial inequality in participation persists in the 1990s. As Table 7.1 shows, all the nonwhite groups—Asians and Latinos especially—had much lower registration and voting rates than Whites. Further, the citizenship requirement makes the gap worse. Although promoting registration appears to be a useful strategy for achieving cross-racial equality in voting, the assumption that people will vote if they are registered is shown to be largely false.

TABLE 7.1
Voting and Registration in the Elections of 1990–1996 by Race

	Asian	Latino	Am. Indian	Black	White
November 1990 Election					
Citizenship	51%[a]	59%	96%	93%	96%
Registration	28 (56)[b]	32 (55)	52 (55)	59 (64)	67 (70)
Voting	20(40)[b]	21 (36)	35 (36)	39 (43)	49 (51)
Among Registered	72*	65	66	67	74
Weighted N	2,146	6,492	481	9,469	67,249
November 1992 Election					
Citizenship	53%	58%	99%	95%	98%
Registration	31 (62)	35 (63)	61 (63)	64 (70)	74 (77)
Voting	27 (56)	29 (54)	51 (55)	55 (63)	67 (72)
Among Registered	88	83	84	85	91
Weighted N	2,246	6,506	418	9,204	63,771
November 1994 Election					
Citizenship	55%	59%	99%	96%	98%
Registration	29 (52)	31 (53)	56 (56)	59 (61)	68 (69)
Voting	22 (40)	20 (34)	37 (37)	37 (39)	50 (51)
Among Registered	76*	64	66	64	74
Weighted N	1,958	7,169	392	8,825	59,492
November 1996 Election					
Citizenship	57%	61%	99%	96%	98%
Registration	33 (58)	36 (59)	61 (62)	64 (67)	72 (73)
Voting	26 (46)	27 (44)	45 (46)	51 (53)	60 (61)
Among Registered	79	75	73	80	83
Weighted N	2,482	6,950	522	8,267	54,819

SOURCE: U.S. Department of Commerce, Bureau of the Census. *Current Population Survey: Voter Supplement File*, 1990, 1992, 1994, 1996 (Computer files). ICPSR version. Washington, D.C.: U.S. Department of Commerce, Bureau of the Census (producer), 1990, 1992, 1994, 1996. Ann Arbor, Mich.: Inter-university Consortium for Political and Social Research (distributor), 1992, 1997. All populations are age 18 and over. All tests of significance are conducted with reweighed data calculated by subtracting the mean adult weight from the final adult weight for each case in order to adjust the size of standard errors.

*Chi-square test fails to reject the hypothesis of no racial difference between Whites and Asians. All other white-nonwhite differences are statistically significant at the .05 level or better.

[a] Entries are in percentages. Those reported for citizenship are among valid responses.

[b] Entries in parentheses are those among citizens.

White voting rates exceeded those of all other groups in each of the four elections surveyed from 1990–1996. They ranged from 67 percent in the 1992 presidential election to 50 percent in the two off-year elections. The figures on total voting turnout are listed in the third row for each election in Table 7.1. Among non-Whites, Blacks were the highest group, with off- and on-year averages of 38 percent and 53 percent, respectively. Asians, Latinos, and American Indians voted even less. Off-year participation dipped to 20 percent for Latinos and Asians in 1990, and even in the 1992 presidential election, when all groups were at their peak, only

28 percent of these groups turned out to vote. Eliminating this gap is important because public involvement promotes political equality.

This difference between Whites and other races is partly caused by the citizenship requirement. Many Asians and Latinos are not U.S. citizens and are not eligible to vote even if they want to. As the entries in parentheses in the "Voting" rows in Table 7.1 show, the proportion of Asians and Latino *citizens* who vote is considerably higher than that for the whole population of each racial group. Asian citizen participation reaches 56 percent in 1992 (compared with 27 percent for all Asians); that of Latinos climbs to 54 percent (from 29 percent). Nevertheless, even these higher numbers are smaller than white participation rates, indicating that citizenship is only one part of the problem.

Among citizens who are registered to vote, however, participation rates are relatively similar across the races. These rates are shown in the "among registered" lines of Table 7.1 for each race. Although the percent of Whites who vote is still higher, the gap is much smaller—no more than 10 percent, compared to a peak of 40 percent across the whole population (in the 1994 and 1992 elections, respectively). In 1994, Asians who had registered to vote than voted in higher numbers than Whites did (although the difference in survey responses is not great enough to serve as conclusive evidence about the entire nation).

One interesting result of this study is its finding that people do not always vote if they are registered. The percentage of registered voters who vote is especially low in off-year elections, falling to 66 percent for both Latinos and American Indians. Perhaps some people maintain their registration each year (when they renew their driver's licence, for example), even when they don't particularly intend to vote. More important, though, may be the low-stimulus nature of the off-year elections.

Predicting Registration and Turnout among Multiracial Americans

Looking at the data more closely reveals two key results. First, race matters. Second, the effects of race are complicated. In America's increasingly multiethnic society, it is wrong to think of the impact of race on voting in black/white or white/nonwhite terms. Each different racial group responds to pressures in different ways. A conclusion drawn about Blacks, for example, may not apply to American Indians. To study who votes in America, a scholar must consider the effects of many different colors of race.

The picture is even more complicated for Asians and Latinos. These broad racial categories include many different ethnic groups, each of which maintains its own distinctive identity. This research shows that voting behavior is different for each subgroup within these broad categories. Before unpacking the two groups, however, this research shows that race does matter even after controlling for the influence of other factors.

Racial differences in voting cannot be explained away by differences in resources, social connections, and exposure. The results in Table 7.2 show that even if one controls for education, income, sex, and other variables, the effects of race persist. The coefficients in Table 7.2 are difficult to interpret, but a positive number means that the variable makes people more likely to vote, and a negative one means that they are less likely to vote.

The effects are different for each race. One way of interpreting the coefficients is to find how each factor changes the probability of voting if all the other factors are held constant. Doing this, one finds that Asians are 23 percent less likely to vote than Whites, even if they are the same in all other respects (e.g., education, income). Latinos and American Indians, on the other hand, are similar to Whites who are like them in all the factors studied. Interestingly, Blacks are actually *more* likely to vote than Whites of the same age, income, and so on. This suggests that national efforts to increase black participation have had a positive effect, but social and economic inequalities limit black progress. These differences show the independent effects of race on voting behavior.

Social and economic factors, however, remain important. When race is controlled, other variables in the multiracial data for the four elections studied suggest that, as has been shown in previous research, higher levels of voting and registration may result from having more education, higher family income, being married, getting older, and staying longer in the same residence. The roles of gender, region, unemployment, and union membership are less stable over time. Being female can be associated with greater registration and voting among citizens. However, gender was not significant in predicting voting among the registered in 1990, and the gender advantage in presidential elections turned into a slight disadvantage in turnout among the registered in the midterm election of 1994. Residing in the South is associated with lower levels of participation, but this disadvantage disappeared in the rate of registration for 1996. Being unemployed was related to lower odds of registration only in the early 1990s and to voting turnout in 1996. Being a member of the labor union was not significant in predicting participation in 1992, but it

TABLE 7.2A
Logistic Regression Estimations of Voting Turnout and Registration in
Presidential Elections of 1992 and 1996

	1992			1996		
	(I)	(II)	(III)	(I)	(II)	(III)
Asian	−1.055	−1.066	−.620	−.700	−.670	−.466
	(15.04)	(14.89)	(4.95)	(9.76)	(8.99)	(4.45)
Black	.146	.281	−.138	.368	.327	.321
	(5.10)	(9.16)	(3.09)	(11.81)	(9.70)	(7.48)
Latino	−.181	−.029ᵃ	−.334	−.042ᵃ	.028ᵃ	−.075ᵃ
	(4.54)	(.70)	(5.36)	(1.06)	(.68)	(1.39)
American Indian	−.249	−.124ᵃ	−.390	−.085ᵃ	.048ᵃ	−.230ᵃ
	(2.18)	(1.05)	(2.17)	(.80)	(.44)	(1.67)
Female	.160	.163	.100	.173	.179	.120
	(8.79)	(8.40)	(3.28)	(9.06)	(8.54)	(4.54)
Education (16 = Ph.D)	.257	.265	.167	.246	.253	.173
	(61.34)	(58.88)	(25.24)	(56.05)	(52.59)	(29.11)
Income (13 = $75k+)	.070	.066	.055	.059	.051	.048
	(24.12)	(21.24)	(11.38)	(19.65)	(15.62)	(11.41)
Married	.279	.238	.280	.314	.285	.257
	(13.82)	(11.01)	(8.20)	(14.67)	(12.16)	(8.57)
Age (Raw Score)	.046	.027	.069	.044	.026	.048
	(15.62)	(8.31)	(14.47)	(13.89)	(7.68)	(10.99)
Age Squared	−.000	.000ᵃ	−.001	−.000	.000ᵃ	−.000
	(6.08)	(1.69)	(11.56)	(3.63)	(1.33)	(4.96)
Length (6 = 5 Years+)	.178	.164	.141	.195	.201	.110
	(27.15)	(24.01)	(12.99)	(27.57)	(27.23)	(11.28)
Foreign-born	−.162	−.328	.196			
	(3.47)	(6.65)	(2.81)			
Unemployed	−.078ᵃ	−.109	.041ᵃ	−.132	−.034ᵃ	−.148
	(1.83)	(2.51)	(.56)	(2.50)	(.64)	(2.10)
Union Member	.014ᵃ	.013ᵃ	.051ᵃ	.146	.166	.109ᵃ
	(.22)	(.20)	(.49)	(2.25)	(2.21)	(1.20)
Region (South)	−.222	−.160	−.287	−.149	−.014ᵃ	−.262
	(11.52)	(7.76)	(9.04)	(7.33)	(.63)	(9.52)
Constant	−4.821	−4.032	−2.405	−5.256	−4.153	−2.919
−2 Log Likelihood	86,663	76,891	34,091	77,455	65,446	40,894
At Convergence	73,748	66,088	31,342	65,823	56,474	37,498
% Predicted Correct	73.05	77.21	89.87	70.39	76.52	82.19
% Voted/Registered	67.7	75.2	90.0	58.4	70.9	82.3
Weighted N =	89,341	89,341	68,180	72,386	72,386	54,731

SOURCE AND NOTE: See Table 7.1. Numerical entries are unstandardized logistic coefficients or log odds except where noted. The sizes of t-scores regardless of signs are reported in parentheses. All coefficients are statistically significant at the .05 level or better except those noted with "a"(p > .05). Model (I) estimates turnout among citizens; model (II) estimates registration among citizens; model (III) estimates turnout among the registered.

TABLE 7.2B

Logistic Regression Estimations of Voting Turnout and Registration in Midterm Elections of 1990 and 1994

	1990			1994		
	(I)	(II)	(III)	(I)	(II)	(III)
Asian	−.668	−.832	−.177a	−.609	−.766	−.104ª
	(9.25)	(11.54)	(1.80)	(7.73)	(9.81)	(.92)
Black	.187	.278	.068	.115	.215	.018ª
	(6.73)	(9.60)	(1.96)	(3.91)	(7.15)	(.50)
Latino	−.138	−.113	−.045ª	−.044ª	.070ª	.048ª
	(3.45)	(2.87)	(.87)	(1.09)	(1.77)	(.92)
American Indian	−.143ª	−.103ª	−.062ª	.065ª	.001ª	.114ª
	(1.29)	(.95)	(.44)	(.54)	(.00)	(.73)
Female	.074	.123	−.006ª	.051	.152	−.066
	(4.39)	(6.86)	(.03)	(2.82)	(7.93)	(2.91)
Education (16 = Ph.D)	.189	.212	.120	.230	.224	.174
	(56.81)	(56.93)	(28.97)	(55.99)	(51.21)	(34.01)
Income (13 = $75k+)	.037	.039	.020	.053	.047	.037
	(14.07)	(13.93)	(6.05)	(18.27)	(15.70)	(10.23)
Married	.332	.331	.218	.343	.322	.252
	(17.53)	(6.82)	(9.00)	(16.95)	(15.17)	(9.87)
Age (Raw Score)	.079	.060	.070	.065	.035	.067
	(27.91)	(20.30)	(19.14)	(21.41)	(11.17)	(17.41)
Age Squared	−.001	−.000	−.001	−.000	.000ª	−.000
	(16.63)	(8.73)	(13.03)	(9.87)	(1.30)	(9.62)
Length (6 = 5 Years+)	.282	.296	.143	.280	.291	.142
	(42.93)	(46.50)	(17.07)	(39.94)	(43.01)	(16.06)
Foreign-born				−.271	−.511	.100ª
				(5.81)	(10.72)	(1.56)
Unemployed	−.163	−.152	.048ª	−.078ª	−.056ª	.006ª
	(3.41)	(3.38)	(.78)	(1.48)	(1.13)	(.10)
Union Member	.118	.206	.023ª	.248	.376	.093ª
	(2.18)	(3.35)	(.33)	(4.26)	(5.45)	(1.32)
Region (South)	−.171	−.046	−.221	−.263	−.117	−.303
	(9.51)	(2.41)	(9.81)	(13.64)	(5.78)	(12.69)
Constant	−6.185	−5.197	−3.252	−6.419	−4.670	−4.022
−2 Log Likelihood	99,802	89,764	58,244	89,223	78,810	53,360
At Convergence	84,991	75,847	54,585	74,080	66,957	48,202
% Predicted Correct	68.82	73.33	72.89	70.08	74.00	73.50
% Voted/Registered	49.3	68.2	72.4	48.4	67.1	72.0
Weighted N =	91,792	91,792	63,804	84,454	84,454	59,937

SOURCE AND NOTE: See Table 7.2A.

boosted voter registration in the three other elections. These fluctuations may reflect changes in registration laws, campaign context, and group mobilization efforts. Last, although being foreign-born was sometimes associated with lower rates of registration and voting among citizens, those foreign-born who were registered were actually more likely to turn out in both 1994 and 1996, when the place-of-birth question was asked.

Predicting Registration and Turnout within Each Nonwhite Race

These socioeconomic factors have different effects on each racial group. Tables 7.3A and 7.3B show the results from a logistic regression of socioeconomic factors on the propensity to register and to vote for each race. The four nonwhite groups differ in the roles of gender, marital status, union membership, region, and age in determining registration and turnout. Specifically, being female and a citizen can be associated with greater likelihood of registering for all groups except Asians. Being female and registered, however, is associated with a greater probability of voting, except among Blacks. Being married may increase the odds of registration for all groups; it is not useful in predicting turnout among the registered except for Blacks. Belonging to a labor union may increase the likelihood of registration except for Asians and Blacks; it does not have an independent influence on voting either among citizens or among the registered. Being very old may deter participation for Latinos and Blacks, but this effect may not apply to Asians and American Indians. Last but not least, the relationship between residence in the South and lower rates of turnout can be observed only among Latino and black registrants. Although residing in the West is linked to higher rates of registration for Asians but lower rates for Blacks and American Indians, residence in the West is tied to increased turnout among the registered for Asians, Latinos, and American Indians.

These results invite prudence when making cross-racial generalizations about the predictors of voting. The effects of race are different for each group of people in American society. This study shows that when we study voting behavior, we must consider each group independently, instead of setting up a binary black/white situation.

Predicting Registration and Turnout among Multiethnic Latinos and Asians

A study of race and turnout cannot be complete without recognizing that fact that both Latinos and Asians are composed of multiple ethnic groups with diverse histories and experiences in the United States. Each group may possess a participation pattern that may differ significantly from the pan-ethnic group norm. Appendixes 7.B and 7.C show turn-out rates for different Latino and Asian subgroups.

Among Latinos, Cuban Americans have been the most politically active. In fact, comparing Appendix 7.B to Table 7.1, we find that Cuban

TABLE 7.3A
Logistic Regression Estimations of Voting Turnout and Registration among Non-Whites, 1990–1996

	Asian			Latino		
	(I)	(II)	(III)	(I)	(II)	(III)
Mexican				−.086[a]	.070[a]	−.234
				(1.79)	(1.46)	(3.36)
Puerto Rican				−.089[a]	.048[a]	−.225
				(1.45)	(.79)	(2.55)
Cuban				.214	.177[a]	.219[a]
				(2.42)	(1.88)	(1.75)
Female	.051[a]	.099[a]	−.071[a]	.157	.198	.036[a]
	(.95)	(1.84)	(.85)	(4.36)	(5.58)	(.71)
Education (16 = Ph.D)	.151	.168	.058	.167	.166	.109
	(14.53)	(15.92)	(3.57)	(23.41)	(23.39)	(11.03)
Income (13 = $75k+)	.048	.037	.047	.046	.038	.036
	(6.00)	(4.49)	(3.59)	(8.32)	(7.01)	(4.64)
Married	.154	.147	.066[a]	.126	.101	.105[a]
	(2.43)	(2.29)	(.65)	(3.19)	(2.60)	(1.90)
Age (Raw Score)	.039	.025	.044	.055	.044	.050
	(3.90)	(2.56)	(2.73)	(8.96)	(7.17)	(5.77)
Age Squared	−.000[a]	−.000[a]	−.000[a]	−.000	−.000[a]	−.000
	(1.08)	(.02)	(1.39)	(3.31)	(1.80)	(2.72)
Length (6 = 5 Years+)	.155	.162	.064[a]	.213	.189	.140
	(7.38)	(7.92)	(1.91)	(16.43)	(15.68)	(7.89)
Unemployed	−.002[a]	.048[a]	−.104[a]	−.040[a]	−.107[a]	.125[a]
	(.00)	(.31)	(.44)	(.48)	(1.41)	(1.05)
Union Member	.309[a]	.335[a]	.162[a]	.185[a]	.357	−.034[a]
	(1.86)	(1.98)	(.64)	(1.62)	(2.91)	(.23)
Region (South)	−.001[a]	−.030[a]	.050[a]	−.126	.025[a]	−.282
	(.00)	(.29)	(.32)	(2.35)	(.48)	(3.81)
Region (West)	.453	.264	.590	.150	−.055[a]	.311
	(7.11)	(4.14)	(6.15)	(2.86)	(1.05)	(4.12)
1990	−.173	−.148[a]	−.169[a]	−.470	−.311	−.481
	(2.25)	(1.89)	(1.47)	(9.22)	(6.21)	(6.94)
1992	.319	.045[a]	.753	.344	.102	.593
	(4.31)	(.60)	(6.01)	(6.86)	(2.00)	(7.93)
1994	−.329	−.345	−.216[a]	−.495	−.341	−.495
	(4.39)	(4.55)	(1.91)	(9.75)	(6.84)	(7.18)
Constant	−4.695	−3.759	−1.855	−4.857	−3.720	−2.339
−2 Log Likelihood	9,053	8,772	3,8602	1,195	21,634	10,723
At Convergence	8,175	8,015	3,6221	8,322	18,937	9,695
% Predicted Correct	65.36	65.80	80.88	68.23	67.39	74.06
% Voted/Registered	46.5	57.7	80.7	41.4	57.0	72.7
Unweighted N =	6,532	6,532	3,944	15,528	15,528	9,133

SOURCE AND NOTE: See Table 7.2A.

TABLE 7.3B
Logistic Regression Estimations of Voting Turnout and Registration
among Non-Whites, 1990–1996

	Black (I)	(II)	(III)	Indian (I)	(II)	(III)
Female	.229	.290	.094	.176	.309	−.042[a]
	(8.87)	(10.81)	(2.72)	(2.35)	(4.10)	(.41)
Education (16 = Ph.D)	.190	.179	.147	.128	.124	.086
	(33.61)	(29.57)	(19.67)	(8.21)	(7.71)	(4.17)
Income (13 = $75k+)	.048	.040	.036	.081	.066	.070
	(12.11)	(9.60)	(6.75)	(7.30)	(5.87)	(4.61)
Married	.180	.199	.129	.293	.336	.126[a]
	(6.27)	(6.43)	(3.35)	(3.66)	(4.16)	(1.15)
Age (Raw Score)	.073	.062	.063	.066	.050	.052
	(18.50)	(15.19)	(11.77)	(5.21)	(3.98)	(3.00)
Age Squared	−.000	−.000	−.000	−.000	−.000[a]	−.000[a]
	(10.74)	(7.72)	(7.50)	(2.66)	(1.56)	(1.63)
Length (6 = 5 Years+)	.237	.200	.181	.220	.164	.198
	(25.66)	(22.17)	(14.90)	(8.33)	(6.60)	(5.58)
Unemployed	.004[a]	.024[a]	.026[a]	.102[a]	.019[a]	.237[a]
	(.09)	(.50)	(.39)	(.75)	(.15)	(1.25)
Union Member	.028[a]	.113[a]	−.034[a]	.223[a]	.785	−.189[a]
	(.34)	(1.33)	(.34)	(.69)	(1.98)	(.49)
Region (South)	−.114	−.052[a]	−.170	−.030[a]	−.443	.317
	(4.35)	(1.89)	(4.89)	(.28)	(4.13)	(2.23)
Region (West)	−.069[a]	−.181	.057[a]	.340	−.169	.742
	(1.36)	(3.45)	(.81)	(3.86)	(1.95)	(6.54)
1990	−.596	−.349	−.791	−.368	−.456	−.151[a]
	(16.38)	(9.07)	(14.29)	(3.42)	(4.22)	(1.05)
1992	.180	−.015[a]	.371	.228	−.114[a]	.591
	(4.90)	(.38)	(7.04)	(2.18)	(.29)	(4.01)
1994	−.700	−.355	−.846	−.275	−.232	−.256[a]
	(19.18)	(9.17)	(17.62)	(2.63)	(2.16)	(1.88)
Constant	−5.127	−3.843	−2.903	−5.164	−3.227	−3.267
−2 Log Likelihood	44,218	39,590	24,975	4,886	4,684	2,638
At Convergence	38,091	35,390	22,467	4,238	4,180	2,380
% Predicted Correct	67.61	71.57	75.34	67.59	68.43	73.88
% Voted/Registered	49.5	66.3	74.7	44.0	60.9	72.2
Unweighted N =	31,911	31,911	21,970	3,548	3,548	2,228

SOURCE AND NOTE: See Table 7.2A.

American citizens vote as often as Whites do, or more. This finding is supported by the data in Table 7.3A, which show that Cuban Americans are more likely to vote than are equivalent Whites. This finding may be the result of their background as political refugees and their long opposition to the Castro government in Cuba. Puerto Ricans tend to vote more than other Latinos, but this finding may result their being U.S. citizens from birth.

The role of Asian ethnicity in voting participation is shown in Table

TABLE 7.4
*Logistic Regression Estimations of Voting Turnout and
Registration among Asians, 1994–1996*

	(I)	(II)	(III)
Chinese	−.086[a]	−.252[a]	.167[a]
	(.58)	(1.75)	(.78)
Japanese	.148[a]	−.153[a]	.596
	(.75)	(.75)	(1.98)
Korean	−.124[a]	−.092[a]	−.011[a]
	(.62)	(.49)	(.00)
Filipino	.305	.148[a]	.403
	(2.09)	(1.02)	(1.97)
Asian Indian	.306[a]	−.028[a]	.698
	(1.58)	(.14)	(2.44)
Vietnamese	.356	−.076[a]	1.061
	(1.97)	(.44)	(3.50)
Female	−.099[a]	−.052[a]	−.125[a]
	(1.12)	(.57)	(.93)
Education (16 = Ph.D)	.156	.158	.074
	(9.12)	(9.42)	(2.95)
Income (13 = $75k+)	.051	.040	.053
	(3.66)	(2.98)	(2.53)
Married	.105[a]	.009[a]	.159[a]
	(1.03)	(.10)	(1.03)
Age (Raw Score)	.032	.030	.024
	(9.48)	(8.72)	(4.76)
Length (6 = 5 Years+)	.073	.085	.012[a]
	(2.10)	(2.51)	(.22)
Foreign-born	−.483	−.536	−.176[a]
	(4.09)	(4.42)	(1.01)
Unemployed	.060[a]	−.193[a]	.345[a]
	(.22)	(.75)	(.78)
Union Member	.209[a]	.563[a]	−.303[a]
	(.73)	(1.79)	(.42)
Region (South)	.175[a]	−.094[a]	.182[a]
	(1.15)	(.63)	(.83)
Region (West)	.355	.123[a]	.568
	(3.36)	(1.17)	(3.74)
1994	−.390	−.399	−.266
	(4.43)	(4.51)	(2.00)
Constant	−3.982	−2.827	−1.784
−2 Log Likelihood	3,343	3,282	1,536
At Convergence	3,004	2,987	1,434
% Predicted Correct	65.90	65.03	77.16
% Voted/Registered	41.8	54.4	77.0
Unweighted N =	2,425	2,425	1,432

SOURCE AND NOTE: See Table 7.2A and Appendix 7.C.

7.4. The results indicate that ethnic origin may make little difference in the likelihood of voting (I) and registration (II) among citizens. When differences in socioeconomic resources, social connections, and political context are controlled among citizens, only Asians of Filipino and Vietnamese origin may be more likely to vote—but not more likely to register—than other Asians from South and Southeast Asia. In fact, the insignificant logistic coefficients for all ethnic groups in the registration model demonstrate that ethnic differences can be fully accounted for by the control variables.

Nevertheless, the significant and positive-slope coefficients that predict the odds of turnout *among the registered* indicate otherwise. Compared to other Asian registrants from South and Southeast Asia, Vietnamese Americans are the most likely to vote, followed, in descending order of effect size, by Asian Indian Americans, Japanese Americans, and Filipino Americans. This ethnic edge in voting may reflect in part leadership and organizational strength in mobilizing beyond voter registration within these communities. The turnout rates may be affected as well by the unique immigration history of each Asian subgroup.

In short, ethnic identity within the Asian and the Latino communities can be important at both stages of the voting process—the decision to register and the decision to vote.

Conclusion

This research revisits the often-studied relationship between race and voting turnout but adds an expanded conception of race and yields an unprecedented and more reliable set of data. Although the findings affirm a continuing and troubling aspect of the U.S. democracy regarding racial inequality in electoral participation, the analysis, which controls for structural constraints, offers more detailed information about the achievement of and opportunities for mobilization at the individual level. Results from the multiracial data for the elections of 1990, 1992, 1994, and 1996 indicate that, when factors such as socioeconomic resources, connection to social network, and exposure to environmental stimuli are controlled for, the significance of race in rates of registration and voting may decline for Latinos and American Indians. Under equal conditions, the turnout deficit among Asians may not be overcome unless they first conquer the registration hurdle *and* unless it is a midterm election in which the effect of community mobilization may have a greater impact than in a stimulant-rich presidential election in which strategic campaign mobilization heavily favors the mainstream electorate. For Blacks, although they enjoy a net advantage in voting registration, this advantage may not be sustained in the polls without aggressive voter mobilization to get out the vote.

Race has a different meaning for the turnout of each group, and this significance may be conditioned not only by individual resources in class and connections but also by institutional constraints and the context of political mobilization. For Asians and Latinos, the relationship between race and turnout is further complicated by ethnic group differences that may not be fully explained away by controls that are sufficient only to account for cross-racial differences. This suggests the need for future research to explore determinants of participation within each ethnic group. For the purpose of this research, results from the analysis by race do identify education, age, length of residence, and income as the most consistent predictors of participation. More research is needed to interpret the different meanings of gender, region, marital status, union membership, and aging in the registration and voting patterns of each racial group.

In the final analysis, this research suggests that the quest for racial equality in participation needs to be tackled not only from the social and political levels but also from the institutional level, beginning at the bottom layer of the incorporation process. Although the focus of this research is on what Davidson and Grofman (1994) label first-generation research questions, the issue of political equality cannot be addressed before the hurdle to minority enfranchisement is fully understood and resolved. Only then can we comprehend other challenging issues of political representation and coalition building across races.

Appendix 7A: Descriptions and Coding Schemes of Control Variables

Gender: Female = 1, Male = 0.

Education: 0 = none, 1 = less than 1st grade, 2 = 1st to 4th grade, 3 = 5th to 6th grade, 4 = 7th to 8th grade, 5 = 9th grade, 6 = 10th grade, 7 = 11th grade, 8 = 12th grade—no diploma, 9 = high school diploma,

10 = some college but no degree, 11 = Associate degree in occupational/ vocational program, 12 = Associate degree in academic program, 13 = Bachelor's degree, 14 = Master's degree, 15 = Professional school degree, 16 = Doctorate degree.

Family Income: 0 = less than $5,000, 1 = $5,000 to $7,499, 2 = $7,500 to $9,999, 3 = $10,000 to $12,499, 4 = $12,500 to $14,999, 5 = $15,000 to $19,999, 6 = $20,000 to $24,999, 7 = $25,000 to $29,999, 8 = $30,000 to $34,999, 9 = $35,000 to $39,999, 10 = $40,000 to $49,999, 11 = $50,000 to $59,999, 12 = $60,000 to $74,999, 13 = $75,000 and over

Marital Status: Married with spouse present = 1, Other = 0

Age: Actual age in each increment year; those older than 90 were coded as 90.

Age squared: Squared product of actual age to account for the decreasing level of activity at the tail end of the life span.

Length of Residence at Current Address: 1 = less than 1 month, 2 = 1 to 6 months, 3 = 7 to 11 months, 4 = 1 to 2 years, 5 = 3 to 4 years, 6 = 5 years or more

Foreign-born: Country of birth not in the United States, Puerto Rico, or U.S. outlying area = 1, Other = 0

Employment Status: Unemployed, looking for work or on layoff = 1, Other = 0

Union Membership: Member of a labor union or of an employee association similar to a union = 1, Other = 0

Region (South): The fourteen states of Alabama, Arkansas, Florida, Georgia, Kentucky, Louisiana, Mississippi, North Carolina, Oklahoma, South Carolina, Tennessee, Texas, Virginia, and West Virginia

Region (West): The thirteen states of Montana, Idaho, Wyoming, Colorado, New Mexico, Arizona, Utah, Nevada, California, Oregon, Washington, Alaska, and Hawaii

Election Year: Dummy variables for each election year of 1990, 1992, 1994, and 1996

Appendix 7B: Voting and Registration among Latinos, 1990–1996

	Mexican	Puerto Rican	Cuban	Other
November 1990 Election				
Citizenship	57%[a]	92%	56%	47%
Registration	31(54)[b]	49(53)	42(76)	27(57)
Voting	19(33)[b]	29(32)	30(54)	20(43)
Among registered	62	60	71	76
November 1992 Election				
Citizenship	54%	93%	55%	43%
Registration	33(60)	56(60)	42(76)	30(70)
Voting	26(49)	45(48)	38(70)	26(60)
Among registered	81	80	92	86
November 1994 Election				
Citizenship	58%	99%	58%	45%
Registration	31(53)	50(50)	38(66)	23(51)
Voting	19(33)	28(29)	30(52)	17(37)
Among registered	63	57	78	73
November 1996 Election				
Citizenship	58%	100%	60%	50%
Registration	33(58)	54(55)	42(70)	32(63)
Voting	24(42)	38(39)	35(59)	26(51)
Among registered	73	71	84	82

SOURCE AND NOTE: See Table 7.1.

Appendix 7C: Voting and Registration among Asians, 1994–1996

	Chinese	Japanese	Filipino	Korean	Indian	Vietnamese	Other
November 1994 Election							
Citizenship	50%[a]	54%	65%	43%	43%	42%	33%
Registration	23(46)[b]	40(73)	34(52)	20(45)	24(56)	17(40)	14(42)
Voting	16(32)[b]	36(65)	25(39)	12(27)	19(45)	13(31)	9(26)
Among Registered	70	88	75	59	81	79	64
November 1996 Election							
Citizenship	53%	54%	68%	47%	42%	59%	33%
Registration	30(56)	30(55)	44(64)	25(53)	27(64)	30(49)	20(59)
Voting	23(43)	26(48)	35(52)	17(36)	22(52)	26(45)	14(42)
Among Registered	76	88	81	68	79	89	70

SOURCE AND NOTE: See Table 7.1.
   Only those who are of the first or second generation, which covers 88 percent of Asians surveyed in 1994 and 90 percent of those surveyed in 1996, are included. Major countries of origin for the "Other" group include Bangladesh, Burma, Cambodia, Indonesia, Laos, Malaysia, Pakistan, Singapore, and Thailand.

NOTES

1. The usage of "race" in this essay refers to the traditional categories of African Americans or Blacks and Anglos or (non-Hispanic) Whites. It also refers to multiethnic groups, such as Asian and Pacific Islander Americans or Asians, Hispanic Americans or Latinos, and American Indians, that have been lumped together in the political arena over time through the processes of racialization (Omi and Winant 1994) and panethnicization (Lopez and Espiritu 1990). Together, they make up the multiracial America studied here. The term "ethnicity," by contrast, refers only to national or cultural groups within each race, such as Mexican Americans, Cuban Americans, Chinese Americans, Asian Indian Americans, and so on. Scholars from different disciplines and origins may disagree on the usage of these terms.

2. Major components of the redesign include a new questionnaire, a computer-assisted method of data collection, and new population controls based on the 1990 census. See CPS-94 Technical Documentation, Attachment 5, "Revisions to the CPS" for details.

3. Unlike figures previously released by the Census Bureau, those reported here fall into mutually exclusive racial categories. Thus, "white" refers to "non-Hispanic white," "Black" refers to "non-Hispanic Black," and "Asian" refers to "non-Hispanic Asian or Pacific Islanders." This change in racial categorization results in an increase of about two percentage points in white registration and turnout.

4. Residence in the West region is controlled only in the single-race models.

REFERENCES

Abramson, Paul, John Aldrich, and David Rhode. 1994. *Change and Continuity in the 1992 Elections.* Washington, D.C.: Congressional Quarterly.

———. 1998. *Change and Continuity in the 1996 Elections.* Washington, D.C.: Congressional Quarterly.

Abramson, Paul, and William Claggett. 1991. "Racial Differences in Self-Reported and Validated Turnout in the 1988 Presidential Election." *Journal of Politics* 53: 186–197.

Alt, James E. 1994. "The Impact of the Voting Rights Act on Black and White Voter Registration in the South." In *Quiet Revolution in the South: The Impact of the Voting Rights Act, 1965–1990,* ed. Chandler Davidson and Bernard Grofman. Princeton: Princeton University Press.

Arvizu, John, and F. Chris Garcia. 1996. "Latino Voting Participation: Explaining and Differentiating Latino Voting Turnout." *Hispanic Journal of Behavioral Sciences* 18: 104–128.

Bobo, Lawrence, and Franklin D. Gilliam, Jr. 1990. "Race, Sociopolitical Participation, and Black Empowerment." *American Political Science Review* 84: 377–393.

Calvo, Maria A., and Steven J. Rosenstone. 1989. *Hispanic Political Participation*. San Antonio: Southwest Voter Research Institute.

Conway, M. Margaret. 1991. *Political Participation in the United States*, 2nd ed. Washington, D.C.: Congressional Quarterly.

Conway, M. Margaret, Gertrude Steuernagel, and David Ahern. 1997. *Women and Political Participation*. Washington, D.C.: Congressional Quarterly.

Crotty, William J. 1977. *Political Reform and the American Experience*. New York: Thomas Crowell.

Davidson, Chandler. 1994. "The Recent Evolution of Voting Rights Law Affecting Racial and Language Minorities." In *Quiet Revolution in the South: The Impact of the Voting Rights Act, 1965–1990,* ed. Chandler Davidson and Bernard Grofman. Princeton: Princeton University Press.

Davidson, Chandler, and Bernard Grofman, eds. 1994. *Quiet Revolution in the South: The Impact of the Voting Rights Act, 1965–1990*. Princeton: Princeton University Press.

DeSipio, Louis. 1996. *Counting on the Latino Vote: Latinos as a New Electorate*. Charlottesville: University Press of Virginia.

Emig, Arthur, Michael Hesse, and Samuel Fisher III. 1996. "Black-White Differences in Political Efficacy, Trust, and Sociopolitical Participation: A Critique of the Empowerment Hypothesis." *Urban Affairs Review* 32: 264–276.

Flanigan, William H., and Nancy H. Zingale. 1994. *Political Behavior of the American Electorate*, 8th ed. Washington, D.C.: Congressional Quarterly.

Garcia, John A. 1997. "Political Participation: Resources and Involvement among Latinos in the American Political System." In *Pursuing Power*, ed. F. Chris Garcia. Notre Dame: University of Notre Dame Press.

Hackey, Robert B. 1992. "Competing Explanations of Voter Turnout among American Blacks." *Social Science Quarterly* 73: 71–89.

Harris, Davis. 1994. "The 1990 Census Count of American Indians: What Do the Numbers Really Mean?" *Social Science Quarterly* 75: 580–593.

Hinghton, Benjamin, and Raymond E. Wolfinger. 1998. "Estimating the Effects of the National Voter Registration Act of 1993." *Political Behavior* 20: 79–104.

Huckfeldt, R. Robert. 1995. *Citizens, Politics, and Social Communication: Information and Influence in an Election Campaign*. New York: Cambridge University Press.

Jackson, Robert A. 1996. "A Reassessment of Voter Mobilization." *Political Research Quarterly* 49: 331–349.

Kelly, Stanley, Jr., Richard E. Ayres, and William G. Brown. 1967. "Registration and Voting: Putting First Things First." *American Political Science Review* 61: 359–379.

Key, V. O., Jr. 1949. *Southern Politics in State and Nation.* New York: Vintage.

Kleppner, Paul. 1987. *Continuity and Change in Electoral Politics, 1893–1928.* Westport, Conn.: Greenwood Press.

Kousser, J. Morgan. 1974. *The Shaping of Southern Politics: Suffrage Restriction and the Establishment of the One-Party South, 1880–1910.* New Haven: Yale University Press.

Leung, Vitus, and Don Mar. 1991. "1990 Census Outreach to Asian and Pacific Americans in the San Francisco Metropolitan Area." *Asian American Policy Review* II: 3–15.

Lien, Pie-te. 1994. "Ethnicity and Political Participation: A Comparison between Asian and Mexican Americans." *Political Behavior* 16: 237–264.

———. 1997. *The Political Participation of Asian Americans: Voting Behavior in Southern California.* New York: Garland.

———. 1998. "Does the Gender Gap in Political Attitudes and Behavior Vary across Racial Groups? Comparing Asians to Whites, Blacks, and Latinos." *Political Research Quarterly* 51: 869–894.

Lopez, David, and Yen Espiritu. 1990. "Panethnicity in the United States: A Theoretical Framework." *Ethnic and Racial Studies* 13: 198–224.

McClain, Paula D., and Joseph Stewart Jr. 1998. *"Can We All Get Along?" Racial and Ethnic Minorities in American Politics,* 2nd ed. Boulder: Westview Press.

McCool, Dan. 1985. Indian Voting. In *American Indian Policy in the Twentieth Century,* ed. Vine Deloria Jr. Norman: University of Oklahoma Press.

Nakanishi, Don T. 1986. "Asian American Politics: An Agenda for Research." *Amerasia Journal* 12(2): 1–27.

———. 1991. "The Next Swing Vote? Asian Pacific Americans and California Politics." In *Racial and Ethnic Politics in California,* ed. Byran O. Jackson and Michael B. Preston. Berkeley: IGS Press.

Omi, Michael, and Howard Winant. 1994. *Racial Formation in the United States,* 2nd ed. New York: Routledge.

Ong, Paul, and Don Nakanishi. 1996. "Becoming Citizens, Becoming Voters: The Naturalization and Political Participation of Asian Pacific Immigrants." In *Reframing the Immigration Debate,* ed. Bill Ong Hing and Ronald Lee. Los Angeles: LEAP Asian Pacific American Public Policy Institute and UCLA Asian American Studies Center.

Passel, Jeffrey. 1990. "Effects of Population Estimates on Voter Participation Rates." In *Studies in the Measurement of Voter Turnout,* U.S. Bureau of the Census. Current Population Reports, Population Characteristics Series P-23 No. 168. Washington, D.C.: U.S. Government Printing Office.

Peterson, Helen L. 1957. "American Indian Political Participation." *Annals of the American Academy of Political and Social Science,* 31: 116–126.

Piven, Frances Fox, and Richard A. Cloward. 1988. *Why Americans Don't Vote*. New York: Pantheon.

Rosenstone, Steven J., and John M. Hansen. 1993. *Mobilization, Participation, and Democracy in America*. New York: Macmillan.

Salamon, Lester, and Stephen Evera. 1973. "Fear, Apathy, and Discrimination: A Test of Three Explanations of Political Participation." *American Political Science Review* 67: 1288–1306.

Schlichting, Kurt, Peter Tuckel, and Richard Maisel. 1998. "Racial Segregation and Voter Turnout in Urban America." *American Politics Quarterly* 26: 218–236.

Schlozman, Kay, Nancy Burns, and Sidney Verba. 1994. "Gender and the Pathways to Participation: The Role of Resources." *Journal of Politics* 56: 963–987.

Schlozman, Kay, Nancy Burns, Sidney Verba, and Jesse Donahue. 1995. "Gender and Citizen Participation: Is There a Different Voice?" *American Journal of Political Science* 39: 267–293.

Shingles, Richard D. 1981. "Black Consciousness and Political Participation: The Missing Link." *American Political Science Review* 75: 76–91.

Silver, Brian D., Barbara A. Anderson, and Paul R. Abramson. 1986. "Who Overreports Voting?" *American Political Science Review* 80: 613–624.

Squire, Peverill, Raymond Wolfinger, and David Glass. 1987. "Residential Mobility and Voter Turnout." *American Political Science Review* 81: 45–65.

Tam, Wendy. 1995. "Asians—A Monolithic Voting Bloc?" *Political Behavior* 17: 223–249.

Tate, Katherine. 1993. *From Protest to Politics: The New Black Voters in American Elections*. Cambridge: Harvard University Press.

Teixeira, Ruy A. 1992. *The Disappearing American Voter*. Washington, D.C.: Brookings Institution.

Timpone, Richard. 1998. "Structure, Behavior, and Voter Turnout in the United States." *American Political Science Review* 92: 145–158.

Uhlaner, Carole J., Bruce E. Cain, and D. Roderick Kiewiet. 1989. "Political Participation of Ethnic Minorities in the 1980s." *Political Behavior* 11: 195–232.

Verba, Sidney, and Norman H. Nie. 1972. *Participation in America*. New York: Harper & Row.

Verba, Sidney, Kay Schlozman, and Henry Brady. 1995. *Voice and Equality: Civic Volunteerism in American Politics*. Cambridge, Mass.: Harvard University Press.

Wolfinger, Raymond E., and Steven J. Rosenstone. 1980. *Who Votes?* New Haven: Yale University Press.

Chapter 8

Congress, Race, and Anticrime Policy

Marion Orr

To the extent that the literature on black politics has assessed the substantive focus of congressional legislation, it has concerned itself primarily with civil rights and with social welfare policy. These issues have often been regarded as a litmus test of sorts by which to gauge an individual congressperson's racial sentiments and support of policies beneficial to the black community. Very recently, scholars have also devoted attention to foreign policy legislation as a measure of racial sentiment and progressiveness. In comparison, however, very little attention has been devoted to anti-crime legislation, although its disproportionate impact on Blacks has been known since the beginning of the twentieth century.

At the national level, the important link between race and anticrime legislation was recently illuminated by two public policy flareups, the first involving a concern of a section of the black political leadership that the U.S. government might be involved in the inner-city drug trade, the second regarding racial disparities in criminal sentencing for drug-related crimes. These two episodes have underscored the inextricable link between race and anticrime legislation.

Anticrime policy has implications for urban politics as well. As mayors deal with the challenges of the urban drug trade, interethnic conflict, and gang wars, they often rely on various anticrime laws in their efforts to make their cities safer. They are, however, caught between the proverbial rock and a hard place. On the one hand, mayors are pressured by citizens and business interests alike to ensure safer streets and communities. Thus, they need anticrime legislation to provide them with the necessary funding

and policy framework to expand the police force, support com-
munity policing initiatives and, above all, wage an all-out war
against drugs and gangs.

On the other hand, however, mayors must also ensure that in
protecting citizens they do not endanger the rights of the accused
through the use of unnecessary or unreasonable force or of un-
lawful searches and seizures. Anticrime policy not only has an in-
extricable link to racial issues but also involves an extraordinarily
complex set of issues.

The following essay provides an insightful historical-political
overview of the ways in which crime, race, and anticrime policy
intersect and clash, as well as an empirical analysis of almost
three decades of roll-call data.

On no other issue is the dividing line so clear, on no
other issue is my opponent's philosophy so completely
at odds with mine, and I would say the common sense
attitudes of the American people, than on the issue
of crime.

—George Bush, October 7, 1988[1]

Crime and crime policy have traditionally been a subtheme in racial politics. In the 1930s, African American leaders lobbied President Franklin D. Roosevelt to support federal antilynching legislation. Roosevelt refused, fearing such a law would alienate southern white voters. That the antilynching legislation was designed to protect African Americans from white mob violence made Roosevelt's support too risky. Roosevelt doubted the political wisdom of challenging the widespread southern belief that states' rights doctrine precluded Congress from punishing civil rights violations by private individuals. In the 1960s and 1970s, Richard Nixon used the "law and order" theme to energize a white backlash in opposition to African American political mobilization. "Combatting violence on the street" became widely used as a codephrase for Nixon's racial conservatism. Race was at the bottom of Nixon's message. In the 1980s and 1990s, crime became a central concern of African American leaders as they resisted the increase in violent crime in inner-city communities.

Since the 1960s, the national political parties have consistently disagreed over what to do about crime. Democrats have traditionally approached crime control by emphasizing treatment and rehabilitation, prevention measures, and due-process rights. Republicans, on the other hand, have tried to make it easier for law enforcement agencies to catch and punish criminals. Republicans have sought to reduce crime by catching more criminals, convicting more of those caught, and subjecting those convicted to more severe punishment.

This essay explores empirically the question of partisan support for anticrime laws. I analyze congressional roll call voting to determine the scope and nature of the congressional enacting coalitions that adopted major anticrime legislation. I also address several related questions: How solidly grounded in the empirical realities of the adoption of anticrime legislation is the conventional wisdom about Democrats and Republicans? What is the partisan nature of the enacting coalitions? Which political parties have been key partners in the legislative coalitions that forge major anticrime laws? Finally, in what way does race influences the political parties' stance on anticrime policy?

The Politics of Enacting Policy

A useful framework for studying the enactment of anticrime legislation is provided by the work of Tatalovich and Daynes on "social regulatory" policy.[2] According to Tatalovich and Daynes, social regulation "involves the use of authority to modify or replace social values, institutional practices and norms of interpersonal behavior with new modes of conduct based upon legal proscriptions."[3] Social regulatory policy differs from economic regulation in that it is less concerned with narrow economic questions and more concerned with broad issues of public safety, health, or morals. Social regulation focuses on social relationships, rather than economic and business activities. Examples of social issues cited by Tatalovich and Daynes include abortion, gun control, women's rights, pornography, affirmative action, gay rights, school prayer, and crime control. As this list suggests, these issues are among the most controversial facing American society. "Because they impinge on our private lives and define our social positions, social regulations have at their core a moral and normative debate about the place of the individual in the community."[4]

As compared to the politics of economic regulation, political policy in the social regulatory arena is more ideological, more intense, more polarized, and less open to compromise. Social regulatory issues provoke moral conflict. The normative underpinnings of social regulatory policy are such that the politics of such policy cannot be understood except in terms of the liberal-conservative cleavage.

There is a distinct partisan dimension to "social regulatory" policy. Republicans, according to Tatalovich and Daynes, "exploit social regulatory policy to mobilize conservative voters."[5] Because Democrats held the edge in partisan identification among voters for many years, Republicans needed issues that could attract Democrats and Independents. Social regulatory issues are such magnets. "Focusing on social regulatory policy gives the GOP an opportunity to attract working-class, southern, and Catholic voters from the Democratic party because these groups often are more conservative on social regulatory questions."[6]

The key political actors in social regulatory policy-making are the president and Congress. Tatalovich and Daynes hypothesize that the president provides only "modest" leadership on social regulatory policy. They suggest that political considerations constrain strong presidential leadership on social regulatory issues. Whenever presidents enter the social regulatory arena, their actions carry a strong partisan motivation. Congress, however, is likely to respond more directly to respond electoral pressure whenever social regulatory policy leads to conflict among the citizenry. Congress is expected to take a more assertive role in enacting social regulatory policy.

The Politics of Anticrime Policy

Social regulatory policy provides a useful context through which to view the politics of how anticrime legislation is enacted. The ideological divisions inherent in social regulatory policy are present in the crime issue. Liberals have seen crime itself as a function of failed social arrangements. Crime, it is suggested, occurs when people live in conditions of poverty and have experienced all of its side effects. Factors often cited include poverty, lack of education, and high unemployment. In this view, crime is merely one part of the pathology of poverty, the equivalent of a socially induced illness. The blame for crime rests with the social conditions in which it is bred. The appropriate response to crime is to recognize that these conditions need to be changed and to expect that changing them will cause crime to be reduced or eliminated. If sufficient social welfare programs were available, the disadvantaged would not turn to criminal behavior.

The conservative ideological approach to the nature of crime assumes that criminals express rational calculation rather than pathological behavior.[7] Crime is seen as the result of deliberate calculations of costs and benefits; people commit crimes when there is more to be gained from criminal activity than from obeying the law. The criminal is assumed to be motivated like everyone else. According to this view, because the individual has chosen to commit a crime, that individual is responsible for the criminal behavior. This view underlies conservative thought and explains why conservatives favor severe penalties (such as capital punishment) thought to deter individuals from making the wrong choices.

If we examine the politics of enacting anticrime legislation, it is evident that Republicans and other conservative candidates have indeed used crime to mobilize conservative voters, especially Whites in the Deep South.[8] And, because Republicans are interested in mobilizing white southerners, racial politics are part of the partisan dimension that help shape anticrime enacting coalitions.

Presidents from Franklin Roosevelt through Dwight Eisenhower saw no need to make crime a national or partisan issue.[9] By the mid-1960s, however, crime began to occupy a significant place in national politics. Both major parties began to address crime as a national concern. This is reflected in the data presented in Figure 8.1, which shows the result of a content analysis of the two parties' platforms from 1960 to 1992.[10] The data show that in 1960, except for a cursory reference in the Democratic party's platform to rising crime rates, crime was not discussed. Neither party mentioned crime in its platform in 1964. However, beginning in 1968 both parties began to devote more attention to crime control in their party platforms. Statements about crime have become permanent features of the two major parties' platforms.

Crime became a concern of the national parties in the 1960s for several reasons. First, there was a rise in reported crime. FBI statistics released in the mid-1960s showed a growing incidence of reported street crime—muggings, assaults, and robberies.[11] Public unease about street crime was exacerbated by a series of highly controversial Supreme Court decisions that favored the rights of criminal defendants. Another reason

FIGURE 8.1
Party Platform and Crime: 1960-1992

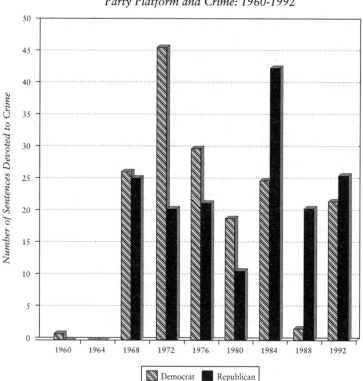

crime became a national issue in the 1960s was the development of a counterreaction to the perceived tactics of the civil rights movement; although they were nonviolent, civil rights demonstrations were nonetheless perceived by many as disruptive. Finally, beginning in the summer of 1964, serious racial disturbances that led to riots occurred in a number of American cities, including New York (in Harlem and in Brooklyn), Chicago, Philadelphia, Rochester, and Jersey City. The following summer, rioting erupted in the Watts section of Los Angeles. Predictably, public opinion polls reported that, by 1968, the American people considered crime among the most serious of our national problems. Such a context provided an opportunity for conservative politicians to employ crime as a "code word" to mobilize conservative voters.

The racial subtext of anticrime policy and politics has played a significant role in most presidential elections since 1964. For example, in his abortive campaign for the Democratic nomination for president in 1964, George Wallace, Alabama's segregationist governor, embraced "crime in the streets" as a major theme. Because of his national ambitions, Wallace found it expedient to downplay southern and racial themes per se, replacing them with code words like "law and order" and "crime in the streets."[12] In his 1968 presidential bid, Wallace returned to his law and order theme. The 1964 Republican presidential nominee, Barry Goldwater, spoke often and emotionally about the erosion of respect for law and order. Richard Nixon's 1968 campaign, however, was the first Republican presidential effort to use "law and order" successfully as a main component of the GOP's well-known "southern strategy."[13] Jules Witcover observed that Nixon's "emphasis on the crime rate, civil disobedience and restlessness among minority groups had, obviously, two purposes: to tap the general discontent among Whites and to counter George Wallace."[14] In sum, in the 1960s, when crime became a national issue, race quickly became linked to it. Those who demanded "law and order" played on the fears and unease of conservative Whites. The text may have been crime; the subtext was race. "The demand for 'order' came loudest from those most resolutely set against black demands—reactionary southern Democratic and Republican senators and congressmen. . . . For many, the call to restore law and order was only a publicly acceptable way of expressing racist attitudes."[15]

During the mid- to late 1970s, the nation was concerned with the Watergate scandal and the restoration of faith in the U.S. government. Street crime took a back seat as a national issue. By the 1980s, however, crime again became an issue of widespread public concern. Of particular concern was the growth in the number of violent crimes—murders, rapes, carjackings, drive-by shootings. Many analysts attributed the rise in violent crime to the growing trafficking in and use of illegal drugs. Widespread media coverage of violence fueled Americans' concern about crime. "There was a sense that society itself was in danger of being swamped by a rising tide of drug-related crime. From negligence in the workplace by casual users, through street muggings by addicts, to internecine turf wars among dealers, drugs seemed a root cause of the appreciable increase in crime and violence."[16] The arrival in 1984 of crack, a cheap form of cocaine that proved highly addictive, strengthened the perceived link between drug abuse and urban violence.[17] While the national debate focused on controlling violent crime, the fact that a disproportionate share of reported crime took place in large urban centers added a racial subtext to the crime issue.

In 1980 and again in 1984, Ronald Reagan used the crime issue to help mobilize conservative voters in support of his presidential bid. Winning the support of conservative Whites was a critical part of Reagan's election and reelection campaign strategies.

The 1988 presidential contest between the Republican nominee, George Bush, and Massachusetts Governor Michael Dukakis, the Democratic candidate, brought the issues of crime, race, and partisan politics to a new level. The Bush campaign used advertisements about a Massachusetts prison inmate, Willie Horton, to move white voters to the GOP camp. Horton, a black felon, raped a white woman while he was on furlough from a Massachusetts prison. Bush's campaign used the Horton incident to attack Dukakis for being "soft on crime" but was then attacked as racist because of the way it used the incident.[18]

By the 1980s, then, crime had reemerged as a national issue. During this second period, illegal drugs and violent crime provided the context for debate about anticrime policy. Crime, however, remained linked to race and racial politics. By the early 1990s, "Crime became a shorthand signal, to crucial numbers of white voters, of broader issues of social disorder, tapping powerful ideas about authority, status, morality, self-control, and race."[19]

According to the social regulatory policy-making framework and the conventional wisdom concerning crime and politics, the process of enacting anticrime legislation has ideological, partisan, and racial dimensions. Hence, we can propose the following statements: (1) Conservative members of Congress are likely to be strong partners in the coalitions that enact anticrime legislation; (2) because they are largely conservative, we can expect Republicans to be the strongest partners in these enacting coalitions; and (3) black members of Congress are not likely to be strong anchors in coalitions that enact anticrime laws.

The literature does not provide much in the way of academic analyses and/or empirically based studies of the political parties' support for anticrime laws. Students of Congress and public policy have not paid much attention to the Republican and Democratic parties and anticrime laws.[20] Indeed, some of the major textbooks on Congress include separate chapters on civil rights, education, social spending, and other domestic issues but largely ignore the issue of anticrime legislation. This analysis attempts to fill this void.

Data and Methodology

To examine congressional support of anticrime laws, I have chosen to analyze the roll call vote for six major anticrime laws enacted during the period 1967–1994: (1) the 1967 District of Columbia Crime Bill; (2) the 1968 Omnibus Crime Control and Safe Streets Act; (3) the District of Columbia Court Reform and Criminal Procedure Act of 1970; (4) the 1984 Anticrime Package; (5) the Crime Control Act of 1990; and (6) the Violent Crime Control and Law Enforcement Act of 1994.[21]

The methodological technique I apply is proportional percentages or party support ratios. In this approach, I calculate the proportion of Democratic and Republican party support for anticrime laws. Party support ratios reveal the precise support that each party gave to anticrime legislation. The party support ratio also has the advantage of revealing the proportion of support *within each party* and captures the different level of support *between the two parties*. Using proportional percentages, I can determine which party and which groups were part of the enacting coalitions that adopted major anticrime laws. In this study, I chose to focus only on the House of Representatives because it provides a larger and varied number of observations.

In an insightful essay, Brady and Buckley highlight the important role of coalitions in congressional policy-making.[22] They note that in the United States "factions within the two major parties sometimes form cross-party coalitions to set party policy; at other times cross-party coalitions are formed on the basis of common interests."[23] The present study shows that coalitions continue to be critical in congressional policy-making, especially when it comes to anti-crime legislation.

Anticrime Legislation: 1960s and 1970s

Of the three major pieces of anticrime legislation enacted during the 1960s and 1970s, two affected only the District of Columbia. The third bill, the 1968 Omnibus Crime and Safe Streets Act, was the first sweeping anticrime law. The D.C. laws are considered here because they were the first federal anticrime laws to be enacted by Congress. Moreover, as the only city in which the federal government had direct responsibility for street crime, Washington, D.C., is the one place where presidents and members of Congress can directly address crime at the local level.[24]

1967 District of Columbia Crime Bill

The first major anticrime law was a congressional initiative. Originally passed by Congress in 1965 but vetoed by President Lyndon Johnson, the 1967 D.C. crime bill "was largely the work of the southern-dominated House Committee on District Affairs."[25] The bill was introduced in the House by Basil Whitener, a conservative Democrat from North Carolina and chairman of Subcommittee No. 5 of the Committee on the District of Columbia.[26]

Whitener's D.C. crime bill was controversial. It authorized police officers to question a person they had probable cause to believe had committed or was committing a crime. If unsatisfied, police could detain the person for up to four hours, after which the subject had to be either charged or released without record of arrest. The bill also permitted investigators to apprehend and detain material witnesses for up to six hours. Another controversial provision increased minimum mandatory penalties for certain crimes; for example, the minimum penalty for robbery was raised from six months to five years. The bill also made it a crime to willfully to engage in or urge others to engage in a riot.

Race quickly became an issue in the debate. Opponents pointed out that the harsh legislation was being forced on the heavily African American city by white southern congressmen.[27] Representative Whitener, however, denied that he had "fashioned this bill so that it will do injury to certain people."[28]

Critics of the D.C. crime bill also argued that the legislation violated civil liberties protections. A minority report signed by a bipartisan group of members of Whitener's subcommittee concluded that the legislation "poses a danger to liberty and freedom and good government, not only in the narrow confines of the District of Columbia, but also throughout the United States."[29]

Despite these criticisms, the bill passed the House on March 22, 1965, and an amended version passed the Senate on August 31, 1965. Because of its controversial provisions, the bill languished in conference for nearly a year. The final version contained most of the major provisions of Whitener's original bill with only superficial changes. It cleared Congress in October 1966, a few weeks before the congressional elections. President Johnson, however, vetoed the legislation, asserting that it raised serious constitutional questions and would provoke years of litigation.

Representative Whitener reintroduced the D.C. crime bill conference report in the next Congress. It cleared both houses and by December 1967 was again sent to Johnson for his signature. By this time, the context had changed. President Johnson was politically vulnerable; he was preoccupied with Vietnam, and his popularity had plummeted. This was also the year before the 1968 presidential election, and Republicans, who had made significant advances in the 1966 elections, were insisting that federal officials "do something" about the "breakdown of law and order." Facing a potentially tough reelection campaign, Johnson signed the bill into law.

1968 Omnibus Crime Control and Safe Streets Act

The next major anticrime law, the Omnibus Crime Control and Safe Streets Act of 1968, was a presidential initiative. It was unveiled by President Johnson early in February 1967. Introduced during a time of major social upheaval, the bill changed as the political context transformed. President Johnson was still on the defensive. The war in Vietnam, and the protest surrounding it, had escalated. As the President's proposal made its way through the legislative maze, deliberations took place against a backdrop of a national wave of violence. Forty-three people died rioting in Detroit on July 22, 1967; elsewhere, many others were killed or injured in the worst series of violent civil disturbances in the country's history. Indeed, final passage of the Act came one day after the assassination of Senator Robert F. Kennedy.

As proposed, Johnson's grant-in-aid program empowered the attorney general, acting through a Director of Law Enforcement and Criminal Justice Assistance, to underwrite the costs of preparing plans for dealing with local crime problems, to make grants pursuant to such plans for innovative projects, to finance capital construction projects, and to finance research and demonstration projects. Johnson's proposal called for direct grants to local governments. In addition, it provided for the creation of a federally supported institute to undertake research on crime and a program to support education and training for criminal justice system personnel.

The Democratic chairman of the House Judiciary Committee, Emanuel Cellar (N.Y.), was able to report out a bill that provided for direct grants to local law enforcement agencies and was in accord with most of the provisions of the Administration's bill. However, twelve of the fifteen

Republicans on the committee strongly disagreed with the committee's bill and took their case to the full House. The Republicans mobilized the rest of their party colleagues and many southern Democrats against the Administration's bill.

The coalition of Republicans and southern Democrats opposed the President's proposal for several reasons. Many viewed the Administration's crime bill as a threat to state's rights. Republican leaders wanted to give control of the federal funds to states, rather than directly to the cities. Others objected to the new authority granted to the attorney general to dictate policies to local law enforcement officials. Attorney General Ramsey Clark had been widely criticized by conservative leaders for being, as they put it, "soft on crime," arguing that he had been excessively lenient in handling the racial disturbances plaguing the nation's cities.

All these factors together contributed to the defeat of the Administration's version of the bill on the House floor and promoted the adoption of a bill that provided that the grants were to be distributed in block grants, whereby funds were given to the states to be allocated to the communities. The new anticrime proposal passed the House on August 8, 1967.

In the Senate, Republicans worked to "toughen" the bill. The version passed by the Senate included two essentially unrelated titles that made confessions admissible at trial and that expanded the use of electronic wiretapping. The White House strongly opposed both items. As in the House, Senate Republicans and southern Democrats were able to form a majority coalition to defeat the President's bill and to substitute their own version. In conference, the Administration's most prestigious supporter, House Judiciary Chairman Cellar, found himself overwhelmed and was unable to do anything to salvage the bill. The final boost for the Act came from the assassination of Senator Robert F. Kennedy, the House voted for the Senate version of the bill on June 6, a day after Kennedy was shot. President Johnson found objectionable much of the omnibus bill, which differed drastically from what the Administration had proposed. Eventually, it was signed by a reluctant President who could comment only that he was signing the bill because on balance it contained "more good than bad."

1970 District of Columbia Crime Control Act

The political context had again changed dramatically by the time Congress enacted the next major federal anticrime law, the 1970 D.C.

Crime Control Act. Richard M. Nixon was now in the White House. As a presidential candidate in 1968, Nixon promised a "get tough" approach to crime. He singled out Washington, D.C., as "one of the crime capitals in the nation."[30]

> From the beginning of his first term, President Nixon showed a personal interest in lowering the crime rate in Washington, D.C. The District crime rate was strategically important: as the only city in which the federal government had direct responsibility for street crime, the District would certainly be read in 1972 as Nixon's record of accomplishment or failure in the war on crime; as a convenient showcase for his personal commitment to law and order, the District could be used to highlight the hard-line image of the administration.[31]

President Nixon's D.C. crime initiative was controversial, in particular two provisions of the bill that concerned pretrial detention and the so-called no-knock provision. The pretrial detention provision authorized federal courts to detain before trial any defendant deemed to be too dangerous to be allowed to go free. A judge could order such a person detained for sixty days before trial. The no-knock provision authorized police to enter premises without notice to serve search and arrest warrants if the officer had "probable cause to believe" that prior notice was likely to result in either the destruction of evidence or danger to the life or safety of the policemen or another person.

Nixon's D.C. crime control bill was introduced in the Senate by Roman Hruska, a conservative senator from Nebraska, early in July 1969. Final passage in the Senate came by a voice vote in September. On the House side, the Administration's proposal was introduced by John L. McMillan (S.C.), a conservative Democrat who chaired the House D.C. committee.

Opponents attacked the bill as unconstitutional. Abner J. Mikva (D-Illinois) stated that he was "appalled at the way in which the Administration is relying on ignorance, prejudice and outright deception to support the passage of preventive detention."[32] Editorials around the country denounced the bill as "dangerous." The *Baltimore Afro-American* observed that the no-knock provision "could create large-scale disorders."[33]

Nixon's spokesmen and their congressional allies declared the bill "a model anticrime program." House Minority Leader Gerald Ford maintained that the legislation was "a sound, constitutional bill of great depth and dimension that will make history as one of the most progressive crime control measures ever enacted by the Congress." Final passage of the D.C. crime bill came on a vote of 332-64. On July 29, 1970, President Nixon signed into law the District of Columbia Court Reform and Criminal Procedure Act of 1970.

The Enacting Coalitions: 1960s and 1970s

Having reviewed each of the three pieces of major anticrime legislation passed in the 1960s and 1970s, I now explore the congressional roll call voting data to determine the scope and nature of the enacting coalitions that pushed the laws through the House of Representatives.

Table 8.1 shows the party support ratios for the three major anticrime laws of the 1960s and 1970s. The data show that during the 1960s and 1970s, all major anticrime laws were enacted by a *bipartisan* coalition of Republicans and Democrats.

As depicted in Table 8.1, the 1967 District of Columbia Crime Bill was supported by 96 percent of the members of the House of Representatives. The Republicans' and Democrats' party support ratio were nearly identical (97 percent and 96 percent, respectively). One advantage of examining roll call voting using the proportional percentage approach is that it allows for a closer analysis of voting patterns *within* the parties. For example, Table 8.1 shows that southern Democrats were the strongest supporters of the 1967 D.C. crime bill. All southern Democrats voting supported the first D.C. crime law. This finding is consistent with the literature on southern Democrats, which argues that they are ideologically distinctive from the rest of their fellow Democrats (Rae, 1994). Northern Democrats, on the other hand, are often characterized as representing the liberal wing of the Democratic party. It might be expected that their level of support for anticrime laws would be lower than that of the more conservative southern Democrats and Republicans. However, the data reveal that northern Democrats were strong supporters of the first D.C. crime bill; 93 percent of those voting cast a yes vote. Northern and southern Democrats were joined by Republicans and forged the enacting coalition that adopted the 1967 D.C. crime bill.

Given the racial dynamics concerning crime issues, I further disaggregated the Democrats' party support ratios by examining the support

TABLE 8.1
Party Support Ratios for Anticrime Laws, 1960s and 1970s

Total Party	Proportion Voting Yes	Total No. of Votes
1967 D.C. Crime Law		
Total vote	96	369
Republican vote	97	162
Democratic vote	96	207
Northern Democrats	93	128
Southern Democrats	100	79
Black Democrats	40	6
1968 Omnibus Safe Streets Law		
Total vote	96	386
Republican vote	99	173
Democratic vote	92	213
Northern Democrats	89	133
Southern Democrats	99	80
Black Democrats	25	4
1970 D.C. Crime Law		
Total vote	84	396
Republican vote	97	173
Democratic vote	74	223
Northern Democrats	60	142
Southern Democrats	98	81
Black Democrats	0	9

SOURCE: Compiled from data in *The Congressional Quarterly Almanac* (Washington, D.C.: Congressional Quarterly).

of black Democrats.[34] The data reveal that African American Democrats provided the smallest support ratio for the D.C. crime bill in the House. Only 40 percent of black Democrats voting supported the 1967 D.C. crime bill. The gap between black Democrats and other Democratic House members was 56 percent. Thus, African Americans were not significant partners in the enacting coalition for 1967 D.C. crime bill.

The bipartisan coalition of Democrats and Republicans held together to enact the 1968 Omnibus Crime Control and Safe Streets Act. Ninety-six percent of the all House members voting on the omnibus crime bill voted yes. Again, the Republicans and the southern Democrats anchored the enacting coalition. Their party support ratios were identical: 99 percent. Table 8.1 also shows the party support ratios within the Democratic party. Among the Democrats, southern Democrats were the strongest supporters of the 1968 omnibus anticrime bill. Northern Democrats remained strong members of the enacting coalition; 89 percent of them cast yes votes. Black Democrats, as Table 8.1 shows, were not part of the enacting coalition for the 1968 omnibus anticrime law. The support ratio for African Americans was only 25 percent.

Of all the anticrime laws, the 1970 D.C. Crime Control Act was the most controversial. Thus, while it too received strong bipartisan support, the support was not as strong as that given the two previous bills. Table 8.1 shows that 84 percent of the House members voting supported the D.C. Crime Control Act (down from 96 percent for the previous bills). The enacting coalition was led by southern Democrats and by Republicans, who had support ratios of 98 percent and 97 percent respectively. Hence, the enacting coalition for yet another anticrime law was forged by the "conservative coalition" of southern Democrats and Republicans.

Table 8.1 also shows the party support ratio for Northern Democrats and black Democrats. Northern Democrats' support for the 1970 D.C. Crime Control law dropped to 60 percent. Clearly, liberal Democrats from the North found it difficult to support a bill that included a no-knock provision and other measures that many argued infringed on citizens' rights and civil liberties. Black Democrats, as the data in Table 8.1 show, strongly opposed the 1970 D.C. Crime Control law. No African American member supported the D.C. crime law.

In summary, the data reveal that during the 1960s and 1970s, the enacting coalitions for the major anticrime laws were *bipartisan*. The data also show that among Democrats, southern legislators were the strongest anchor in the enacting coalition for all three anticrime laws. The southern Democratic vote exceeded the party support ratios for all other Democrats. The principal enacting coalition for anticrime laws in the House of Representatives was forged by the "conservative coalition" of southern Democrats and Republicans. Northern Democrats were also significant partners in the enacting coalition of all three anticrime laws. For the most part, African Americans were not part of the congressional enacting coalitions of the major anticrime laws; black Democrats provided the smallest level of support for crime legislation in the House during the first period of anticrime legislation.

Anticrime Laws: 1980s and 1990s

Congress enacted no major anticrime legislation during the mid- and late 1970s. The Watergate scandal dominated the congressional agenda. The public seemed more concerned about crooked public officials than about crime on the street, and public concern with crime diminished during this period.[35]

In the early 1980s, crime again became an issue of widespread public concern. Particularly troubling was the growth in violent crime generated primarily by increased trafficking in and use of illegal drugs. Three major anticrime laws were enacted in the 1980s and 1990s: the 1984 Anticrime Package, the Crime Control Act of 1990, and the Violent Crime Control and Law Enforcement Act of 1994.

1984 Anticrime Package

President Reagan "believed that much of the nation's crime was the result, either directly or indirectly, of drug and narcotic use. . . . Controlling drug use and availability in the United States, in Reagan's opinion, would solve many other social problems, including increased crime."[36]

The 1984 Anticrime Package was a presidential initiative. And Reagan's anticrime proposal embodied much of the Administration's concern about drugs and crime. The Administration's proposal was introduced in March 1983, in a Republican-controlled Senate, by Strom Thurmond, chairman of the Judiciary Committee. In less than a month the bill passed the Senate, with only one member voting against it.

The bill made it more difficult for a defendant to be released on bail pending trial. It standardized federal sentencing guidelines to reduce disparities in punishment for convicted defendants who had committed similar crimes. It weakened the exclusionary rule by allowing evidence seized in "good faith" to be introduced in criminal cases and strengthened the use of criminal forfeitures by allowing federal prosecutors to confiscate the assets and profits of criminal enterprises. The bill also limited the insanity defense to only those persons who were unable to understand the nature and wrongfulness of their criminal acts and increased penalties for trafficking in drugs.[37]

In the House, Hamilton Fish (R-N.Y.), the ranking Republican on the Judiciary Committee, introduced the Administration's proposal. The House, however, moved slowly. The House Judiciary Committee approved several elements of the Senate bill as separate pieces of legislation, and the full House passed those bills. However, action on sentencing reform and pretrial detention lagged behind action on others of the bill's provisions. In the summer of 1984 President Reagan made the crime bill a campaign issue and "regularly castigated the Democratic-led House for bottling up" the anticrime package that had been passed by the Republican-controlled Senate.[38]

On September 25, 1984, House Republicans employed what the *Congressional Quarterly* called "an end run to get the Senate crime bill passed." Republicans successfully moved to send the fiscal 1985 continuing appropriations resolution back to the Appropriations Committee with instructions to attach a House bill identical to the Senate crime package and return the measure to the full House. The Republican motion passed by a vote of 243-166. The funding bill, with the crime package attached, promptly returned to the House floor and was passed on the same day. When the funding bill got to the Senate, members decided to retain the crime provisions. The Senate action ensured that major crime legislation would be enacted in 1984. In October 1984, Reagan signed the 1984 Anticrime Package into law.

Crime Control Act of 1990

The next major anticrime law, the Crime Control Act of 1990, was another presidential initiative. As a candidate for president, George Bush made crime a significant theme in his campaign. Once elected, Bush continued Reagan's emphasis on illegal drugs and its association with violent crime. Bush outlined his major anticrime proposal in a speech to the National Peace Officers Memorial Day Service in May 1989. This proposal called for new laws banning some semiautomatic and assault weapons, the doubling of mandatory minimum penalties for the use of semiautomatic weapons in crimes involving violence or drugs, the end of plea bargaining for those accused of violent federal firearms offenses, and the imposition of the death penalty for those who kill."[39]

Senator Thurmond introduced Bush's anticrime in the Senate. However, at around the same time, Joseph Biden, the Democratic chairman of the Senate Judiciary Committee, introduced a crime bill of his own. Biden's bill touched on six controversial areas, including the federal death penalty, revisions of habeus corpus appeals and in the exclusionary rule, a reorganization of the Justice department, regulation of firearms, and proposals to combat international money laundering. Biden's bill passed the Judiciary Committee, but when it reached the Senate floor a ban on semiautomatic weapons was attached. A threatened Republican filibuster against the weapons ban basically killed the Biden proposal.

Eventually, since neither Senate Democrats nor Republicans wanted to take the blame for blocking an election-year crime bill, a compromise was reached, and this compromise passed the Senate on July 11, 1990. Many of the provisions endorsed by Biden remained in the final Senate version of the bill; most notable of these was the ban on nine foreign and domestic semiautomatic weapons. But the bill also included a Republican-supported provision that expanded the use of the federal death penalty so that it would apply to a total of thirty more crimes.

On the House side, Hamilton Fish (R-NY), the ranking member on the Judiciary Committee, and other GOP members introduced an array of bills containing many of the Senate Republicans' anticrime proposals. Many of these Republican-backed proposals, however, languished in the House Judiciary Committee. Not wanting to be outdone in an election year, Democrats drafted and passed their own anticrime proposal.

The House bill differed from the Senate proposal. For example, while the Senate expanded the number of federal capital punishment offenses to thirty, the House committee allowed for only ten. The House bill also included a provision (pushed by John Conyers, a senior black Democrat on the Judiciary Committee) that allowed defendants to challenge their death sentences on grounds of racial discrimination. Missing from the House bill was a strong gun-control provision. Judiciary Committee Chairman Jack Brooks (D-TX) was not a strong gun-control supporter; neither was House Speaker Thomas Foley of Washington.

Facing two different bills, House and Senate conferees met to iron out their differences. With congressional elections not far away, compromise was likely. In the end, the controversial death penalty, gun, and racial justice provisions were removed. The stripped-down bill went first to the Senate and then to the House and passed both chambers overwhelmingly. On November 29, 1990, while expressing frustration with the bill's limitations, President Bush signed the new Crime Control Act of 1990.

Violent Crime Control and Law Enforcement Act of 1994

The final major anticrime law enacted during the period under study was the Violent Crime Control and Law Enforcement Act of 1994. The political context that helped shape the congressional enacting coalition had changed completely since 1990. A Democrat was in the White

House. Elected as a centrist Democrat, Bill Clinton was able to avoid the charge of being "soft on crime." With polls showing that most Americans viewed Republicans as better able to handle crime than Democrats, candidate Clinton convinced voters that as a "new Democrat" he could be trusted to reduce crime.[40]

The 1994 Violent Crime Act was a presidential initiative. In August 1993 Clinton announced a broad anticrime package, central components of which were proposals to put more police officers on the streets, make it harder for inmates to appeal their death sentences, and require a waiting period for handgun purchases. In November 1993 the Senate passed an omnibus anticrime bill, crafted by Judiciary Committee Chairman Joseph Biden.

The Biden bill embraced many of Clinton's proposals and more. It included gun control measures and rehabilitation programs; it provided for more jails and more jail time for convicted criminals. It allocated money for new federal prisons, state boot camps, shelters and services for battered women, one hundred thousand new police officers, prison drug treatment centers, and youth crime prevention projects. It also included harsh penalties against perpetrators of hate crimes, mandatory minimum sentences, stiffer penalties for juveniles who committed serious federal crimes, and criminals who used weapons in the course of committing a crime. The federal death penalty was extended to about fifty additional crimes. The Senate legislation also included an amendment banning the sale, manufacture, and possession of nineteen assault weapons. In November 1993 an omnibus anticrime bill passed the Senate on a vote of 94-4.

In the House, Judiciary Chairman Jack Brooks was unable to persuade his committee to support the omnibus anticrime bill, which many liberals found too harsh. Brooks broke out the more popular pieces of the Senate-passed proposal into a series of separate bills. Late in 1993 the House adopted several measures, including a bill that authorized a new grant program to hire about fifty thousand additional police officers; a measure to provide funding to help states provide drug treatment; a proposal to help states fight juvenile gangs and drug trafficking; a grant program to support local initiatives for preventing school violence; and a bill that provides grants to states to develop alternative sentencing for youthful offenders. Brooks's strategy assured that no omnibus anticrime bill would be enacted in 1993.

When Congress returned in January 1994, the future of the Senate-passed omnibus crime bill was a top agenda item. The kidnaping and death of twelve-year Polly Klaus in California by a twice-convicted felon and the shooting of passengers on the Long Island Rail Road helped shaped the context for enacting the 1994 anticrime law. By April the House had approved a bill that authorized federal grants to pay for the hiring of about fifty thousand new police officers, construct new prisons, support prevention programs that targeted youths, and develop a police corps program. The bill included so-called get tough measures, including an expansion of the death penalty to apply to dozens of federal crimes; mandatory life imprisonment for anyone convicted of a third violent felony; and trial as adults for juveniles thirteen or older charged with certain violent crimes.

The House-passed bill, however, was different from the bill adopted by the Senate. At the insistence of the Congressional Black Caucus, the House bill had included a provision that allowed a defendant to challenge a death sentence as racially discriminatory by using sentencing statistics. Furthermore, the House bill did not include an assault weapons ban. The two bills also differed in cost. The Senate crime bill authorized $22.3 billion over five years; the House authorized about $28 billion over six years.

In conference, the racial justice provision was dropped, and House conferees accepted the Senate's assault weapons ban and approved spending $33 billion for the anticrime package. However, on August 11 an unlikely coalition of black lawmakers and gun rights advocates held up final House action on the massive anticrime bill. Conservative House members who opposed the assault weapons ban joined with black members who objected to the death penalty provisions to defeat a procedural vote that would have brought the conference bill to the floor. On August 21 the House passed a bipartisan compromise negotiated by President Clinton and other Democratic leaders with moderate Republicans. The compromise bill costs $3.3 bill less than the original conference report, with the major share of the cut coming from social programs that Clinton and Congressional Democrats had favored. President Clinton succeeded, however, in keeping the controversial ban on certain assault weapons. In September 1994, amid great fanfare, Clinton signed into law the Violent Crime and Law Enforcement Act.

The Enacting Coalitions: 1980s and 1990s

Having reviewed each of the three major anticrime laws of the 1980s and 1990s, I now explore the nature of the enacting coalitions for these laws during this second period. Table 8.2 displays the party support ratios for the three major anticrime laws enacted during the 1980s and 1990s. The data reveal some changes in the enacting coalition for crime laws in the contemporary era.

Clearly, the enacting coalition for the 1984 legislation was different from that for the earlier legislation. Table 8.2 shows a considerable decline in Republican support for the 1984 anticrime package. Only 69 percent of the Republicans voting supported it. Part of the explanation for this drop in support perhaps lies in the fact that the anticrime package was attached to a spending measure.

The other significant change occurred with the black Democrats; their party support ratio for the 1984 law climbed to 63 percent. Significantly, the 1984 anticrime package was the first major law under study that did not include new death penalty provisions. A coalition of black House members in the early 1980s and 1990s—led by John Conyers and Ronald Dellums—has consistently opposed any anticrime law that included capital punishment. Southern Democrats' party support ratio for the 1984 law was 88 percent. They remained strong participants in enacting anticrime laws, in which they were joined by northern Democrats; 80 percent of the northern Democrats voting supported the 1984 anticrime package. Hence, the enacting coalition for the 1984 anticrime package consisted of southern, northern, and black Democrats.

With the Crime Control Act of 1990, the bipartisan enacting coalition forged in the earlier era reemerged. This election-year legislation was supported by 87 percent of all House members. Many of the most controversial provisions—gun control and revision of habeus corpus—were removed from the bill before final passage. However, the Republicans continued to have a higher party support ratio (99 percent) than the Democrats (79 percent). Southern and northern Democrats had party support ratios of 91 percent and 99 percent, respectively. For the 1990 Crime Control Act, however, black Democrats' party support ratio returned to a level reminiscent of that of the 1960s and 1970s—32 percent.

TABLE 8.2
Party Support Ratios for Anticrime Laws, 1980s and 1990s

Total Party	Proportion Voting Yes	Total No. of Votes
1984 Anticrime Package		
Total vote	78	407
Republican vote	69	155
Democratic vote	83	252
Northern Democrats	80	169
Southern Democrats	88	83
Black Democrats	63	19
1990 Crime Control Act		
Total vote	87	423
Republican vote	99	171
Democratic vote	79	252
Northern Democrats	99	166
Southern Democrats	91	80
Black Democrats	32	22
1994 Violent Crime Act		
Total vote	55	430
Republican vote	26	177
Democratic vote	75	252
Northern Democrats	82	172
Southern Democrats	59	80
Black Democrats	66	35

SOURCE: Compiled from data in *The Congressional Quarterly Almanac* (Washington, D.C.: Congressional Quarterly, 1984, 1990, 1994).

The most dramatic change in the enacting coalition for anticrime laws during this period occurred with the 1994 Violent Crime and Law Enforcement Act. The 1994 anticrime law was the first major crime bill in which House Republicans were not part of the enacting coalition. The Republican party support ratio was only 26 percent. For the first time, the Democrats' party support ratios were higher than the Republicans'. Seventy-five percent of congressional Democrats supported the 1994 law. The principal partners in the enacting coalition for the law were Democrats. Northern Democrats had the highest party support ratio—82 percent. They were joined by black Democrats; a record 66 percent of the black Democrats supported the crime bill. Only 59 percent of the southern Democrats voting supported the 1994 omnibus crime law.

In sum, the enacting coalition for anticrime laws in the 1980s and 1990s diverged from the pattern of the 1960s and 1970s. By the 1980s and early 1990s, Republican House members were not part of the coalition that passed comprehensive anticrime legislation. By 1994, Republican support ratio had fallen to 26 percent.

The other striking change in the second period occurred within the Democratic party. Black Democrats displayed a dramatic divergence from the pattern of support for anticrime laws displayed in the 1960s and 1970s. Black House members were important components of the enacting coalition that adopted the 1984 and 1994 anticrime laws. However, it is important to emphasize that black Democrats' voting patterns continued to differ from those of other Democrats. Their party support ratios were consistently lower than those of Democrats as a whole. In 1980s and 1990s, black Democrats remained less likely to be strong anchors in coalitions enacting anticrime laws.

A Summary of Enacting Coalitions and Partisan Support

Figure 8.2 depicts the party support ratios (the proportion of Democrats and Republicans voting yes in the House of Representatives) for the six major anticrime laws enacted from the 1960s through the 1990s. It reveals that the enacting coalitions for the anticrime laws in the 1960s and 1970s were bipartisan. While Republican support was higher than Democratic support in the House, the difference was not significant. During the turbulent years of the decade of the 1960s, both parties responded to the public's concern about crime. Bipartisan support for fighting crime was clearly evident in the 1960s and 1970s.

Clearly, the 1984 and 1994 anticrime legislation received support from different parts of Congress compared to that for earlier legislation. Earlier, public officials had been concerned with street crimes (purse snatchings, muggings, burglaries). But crime became much more violent in the 1980s and 1990s, and, as the nature of crime changed, legislative efforts to address crime increasingly incorporated both liberal (preventive) and conservative (punishment) perspectives. Significantly, in the 1960s and 1970s, conservative southern Democrats controlled the key committees that drafted the major anticrime legislation of the era (Rae, 1994); in the majority of cases, these laws reflected the philosophy of the conservative-leaning committees (Rae, 1994, p. 83).

By the 1980s, the House Judiciary Committee, the committee that handled the major anticrime bills, was controlled by liberal Democrats.[41] As Rae observed, "The Judiciary Committee became much more

FIGURE 8.2
Party Support Ratios

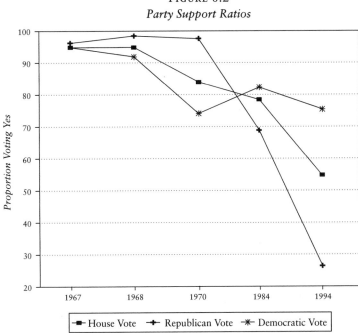

liberal because of the civil rights revolution."[42] During the 1980s and 1990s, liberal Democrats—Peter Rodino, Barney Frank, Don Edwards, John Conyers, and William Kastenmeir, for example—were in a position to ensure that major anticrime laws included "liberal" approaches to fighting crime.

As the liberal Democrats pushed their approach to crime, the nature and composition of the enacting coalitions changed. The 1994 Violent Crime and Law Enforcement Act is a prime example. Republican opposition to the 1994 crime bill centered around the "prevention" provisions. Conservatives, both Republican and Democratic, ridiculed prevention programs as of coddling criminals or fiscal profligacy. While Republicans were successful in reducing spending for the prevention measures, the prevention proposals remained key components of the new law. Mainly because of their opposition to the spending on prevention (and because of partisan politics), Republicans were not part of the enacting coalition for the 1994 crime law. A Republican convergence against anticrime laws—especially those laws that incorporate crime "prevention" provision—appears to be occurring. One of the most troubling findings of this research concerns what may be an emerging pattern of partisan divergence, a divergence that precludes the ability to forge bipartisan enacting coalitions.

Race and Anticrime Policy

In Figure 8.3 the Democratic party is separated into two sectional groups and one racial group and the proportion of congressional representatives from these sectors of the party who supported anticrime legislation are compared. Overall, House Democrats have been key components of the coalitions that have enacted anticrime coalitions. Southern Democrats have exhibited a consistently high and linear level of support for anticrime legislation and have been central in forging enacting coalitions in support of all major anticrime laws. This finding confirms Tatalovich and Daynes's (1988) hypothesis concerning support of anticrime laws by conservative politicians. Only recently has this level of support declined. Among northern Democrats there is an uneven but steady support for anticrime laws.

The most obvious outliers among Democrats are African American members of the House. Black Democrats have not been incorporated into the enacting coalitions that adopted anticrime laws. During the 1960s and 1970s, Blacks were reluctant to join enacting coalitions, believing that laws often incorporated measures that gave law enforcement too much leeway. Given the history of the relationship between Blacks and local law enforcement agencies, one should not be surprised that African American representatives were reluctant to support laws like the 1970 D.C. crime bill.

In the 1980s and 1990s, black Democrats have shown an uneven but steady increase in their support for anticrime legislation. Why is this so? By the 1980s and 1990s, the situation had changed. African Americans were disproportionately victims of crime. Part of the explanation for black Democrats' convergence with their Democratic colleagues is the growing incidence of, and fear of, violent crime in the African American community. Cooper notes that during the debate on the 1994 anticrime bill, black Democrats received calls and letters in favor of the crime bill from black homeowners' groups, black mayors, black county officials, and black police chiefs.[43]

FIGURE 8.3
Democratic Support Ratios

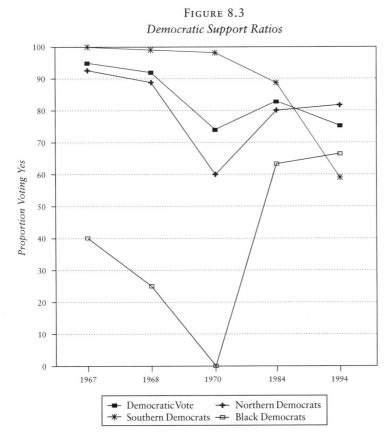

However, it is important to emphasize that throughout the entire thirty-year period covered in this analysis, there is a considerable and persistent gap between the position of black Democrats and that of the rest of their Democratic colleagues. I have already suggested why this was the case in the earlier period. The explanation for the voting behavior of contemporary black legislators is a little more complicated. First, while it is true that Blacks are disproportionately victims of crime, they are often disproportionately victims of the criminal justice system. Racial disparities between Blacks and Whites in rates of arrests, jailing, and imprisonment steadily worsened after 1980. Moreover, racial discrimination in the use of the death penalty makes Blacks wary of broadening its use.

Finally, the low level of black support for anticrime laws may be linked to partisan politics and crime policy. Conservative Republicans in national elections have "played the race card" by using anticrime positions (Willie Horton, for example) as a way to appeal to antiblack sentiments of white voters. Given the political milieu of the crime issue, black legislators may be reluctant to forcefully embrace anticrime laws.

Conclusion

What hypotheses concerning anticrime enacting coalitions are supported by my analysis of support ratios for anticrime laws? I return to the three proposition proffered earlier. First, the data confirm that conservative House members are more likely to be strong partners in coalitions that enact anticrime legislation. Both conservative southern Democrats and Republicans were the strongest anchors in the coalitions that adopted major crime bills during the 1960s, 1970s, and 1980s. Republican support ratios were almost uniformly higher than those for all other groups in the House. Their support did not begin to taper off until well into the 1990s. Moreover, southern Democrats, the most conservative and distinctive bloc in the Democratic party, were both principal initiators and supporters of anticrime bills in the House. Southern conservatives have traditionally been associated with reactionary positions across the entire spectrum of issues, especially those that touch on race relations. In the contemporary House, southern Democrats remain ideologically distinctive from their fellow Democrats, although perhaps less so than in the recent past. It will be interesting to see how southern Democrats continue to handle the crime issue, which has historically carried a subtext of race. How will southern Democrats react as the movement of southern black voters into the electorate continues to have a transforming effect on the Democratic party?

The data presented also support the proposition that Republican members of the House are likely to be the strongest partners in the coalitions that enact anticrime laws. An interesting finding, however, is the dramatic decline of Republican support for the 1994 Crime Control Act. As noted earlier, Republican support for the 1994 crime bill weakened as more "prevention" provisions were incorporated into the final version of the legislation. However, given the partisan shift in control of the House following the 1994 election, this pattern of declining GOP support is not likely to continue.

Finally, the data confirm that black members of Congress are not likely to be strong anchors in coalitions that enact anticrime laws. The biggest change among Blacks occurred in the vote for the 1994 anticrime law, when black support increased significantly. This law included potentially important provisions that could help prevent the causes of crime. As the Republican-controlled House, uses a more conservative approach to anticrime laws, it is expected that black members will return to being only junior partners in the congressional coalitions that enact anticrime laws.

NOTES

1. Quoted in Thomas Edsall and Mary Edsall, *Chain Reaction* (New York: Norton, 1991), p. 225.

2. Raymond Tatalovich and Byron W. Daynes, eds. *Social Regulatory Policy: Moral Controversies in American Politics* (Boulder: Westview Press, 1988), pp. 74–110.

3. Ibid., p. 26.

4. Ibid, p. 210.

5. Ibid., p. 218.

6. Ibid., p. 216. See also Earl Black and Merle Black, *The Vital South: How Presidents Are Elected* (Cambridge, Mass.: Harvard University Press, 1992); James M. Glaser, *Race, Campaign Politics, and the Realignment in the South* (New Haven: Yale University Press, 1996).

7. James Q. Wilson, *Crime* (Princeton: Princeton University Press, 1984).

8. Black and Black, *The Vital South*; Edsall and Edsall, *Chain Reaction*; Jules Witcover, *The Resurrection of Richard Nixon* (New York: Putnam, 1971).

9. James Calder, "Presidents and Crime Control: Kennedy, Johnson, and Nixon and the Influence of Ideology," *Presidential Studies Quarterly* 12 (1982): 574–589; Gregory Caplan, "Reflections on the Nationalization of Crime, 1964–1968," *Law and the Social Order* 583 (1973): 582–635.

10. Previous research used a similar technique to gauge the two parties' position on civil rights. See Edward G. Carmines and James A. Stimson, *Issue Evolution* (Princeton: Princeton University Press, 1989).

11. Nancy Marion, *A History of Federal Crime Control Initiatives, 1960–1993* (Westport, Conn.: Praeger, 1993).

12. Black and Black, *The Vital South*, pp. 162–63.

13. Witcover, *The Resurrection of Richard Nixon*.

14. Ibid., p. 364.

15. Thomas E. Cronin, Tania Z. Cronin, and Michael E. Milakovich, *U.S. vs. Crime in the Streets* (Bloomington: Indiana University Press, 1981), pp. 14–15.

16. Anthony King and Giles Alston, "Good Government and the Politics of High Exposure," in Colin Campbell and Bert A. Rockman, eds., *The Bush Presidency: First Appraisals* (Chatham, N.J.: Chatham House, 1991), p. 270.

17. B. D. Johnson, T. Williams, K. A. Dei, and H. Sanabria, "Drug Abuse in the Inner City: Impact of Hard-drug Users and the Community," in Michael Tonry and James Q. Wilson, eds., *Drugs and Crime* (Chicago: University of Chicago Press, 1990), pp. 9–67.

18. Katherine Tate, *From Protest to Politics* (Cambridge, Mass.: Harvard University Press, 1994), p. 76.

19. Edsall and Edsall, *Chain Reaction,* p. 224.

20. See, for example, Aage Clausen, *How Congressmen Decide: A Policy Focus* (New York: St. Martin's Press, 1973); and John Kingdon, *Congressmen's Voting Decisions* (New York: Harper and Row, 1981).

21. I acknowledge the limitation of relying exclusively on this particular form of legislative participation. For example, the roll call votes that arise on the floor and are observable by the analyst are nonrandom. An institutionally complex set of processes that precedes floor action censors some proposals for floor consideration and not others.

22. Henry Brady and Kara Buckley, "Coalitions and Policy in the U.S. Congress," in L. Sandy Maisel, ed., *The Parties Respond: Changes in American Parties and Campaigns,* 2d ed. (Boulder: Westview Press, 1994), pp. 319–341.

23. Ibid.

24. Before Congress granted the residents of Washington, D.C., limited home rule in 1973, the District of Columbia was under the complete control of the federal government.

25. Cronin et al., *U.S. vs. Crime in the Streets,* p. 38.

26. Congressman Whitener opposed the 1964 Civil Rights Act and the 1965 Voting Rights Act. Rae's study of southern Democrats points out that the District of Columbia Committee was "dominated" by conservative southerners in the 1960s "owing to fear that the capital, with its heavily black population, might be the thin end to the wedge on desegregation if allowed self-government." See Nicol C. Rae, *Southern Democrats* (New York: Oxford University Press, 1994), p. 85.

27. *Washington Post,* 22 March 1965, p. A16.

28. *Congressional Record,* 22 March 1965, p. 5585.

29. *Congressional Record,* 22 March 1965, p. 5579.

30. *Washington Post,* 23 June 1968, p. A1.

31. Cronin et al., *U.S. vs. Crime in the Streets,* p. 93.

32. *CQ Almanac,* 1970, p. 215.

33. "Bad Crime Bill," *Baltimore Afro-American,* editorial, 20 June 1970, p. A1.

34. While cautioned should be exercised in drawing too firm a conclusion about black Democrats, because their numbers were so small, the data show a consistent pattern across the entire period under study.

35. Marion, *A History of Federal Crime Control Initiatives,* p. 117.

36. Ibid., p. 152.

37. The insanity provision was largely an outgrowth of concern over the acquittal of John Hinckley Jr., who shot President Reagan, along with three other people, in an assassination attempt in 1981.

38. Marion, *A History of Federal Crime Control Initiatives,* p. 144.

39. Ibid., p. 193.

40. The Democratic party's political advertisements were carefully tailored to remind voters that Governor Bill Clinton had executed people. The candidate even flew back to Arkansas to oversee the execution of an African American convict. See Monte Piliawsky, "The Clinton Administration and African Americans," *Black Scholar* 24 (Spring 1994): 3–6.

41. For example, in 1986 the House Judiciary Committee was chaired by Peter Rodino, a New Jersey Democrat whose by the Americans for Democratic Action rating for 1986 was 100. Liberal Democrats such as Barney Frank (D-Massachusetts), John Conyers (D-Michigan), William Kastenmeir (D-Wisconsin), and Don Edwards (D-California) chaired subcommittees. Each of these subcommittee chairmen had ADA ratings of 100 in 1986.

42. Rae, *Southern Democrats,* p. 86.

43. Kenneth Cooper, "Crime and Punishment," *Emerge* (November 1994): 42–51.

REFERENCES

Black, Earl, and Merle Black. *The Vital South: How Presidents Are Elected.* Cambridge, Mass.: Harvard University Press, 1992.

Brady, Henry, and Kara Buckley. "Coalitions and Policy in the U.S. Congress," in *The Parties Respond: Changes in American Parties and Campaigns,* ed. L. Sandy Maisel. Boulder: Westview Press, 1994.

Calder, James. "Presidents and Crime Control: Kennedy, Johnson, and Nixon and the Influence of Ideology." *Presidential Studies Quarterly* 12 (1982): 574–589.

Caplan, Gregory. "Reflections on the Nationalization of Crime, 1964–1968." *Law and the Social Order* 583 (1973): 582–635.

Carmines, Edward G. and James K. Stimson. *Issue Evolution.* Princeton: Princeton University Press, 1989.

Clausen, Aage. *How Congressmen Decide: A Policy Focus.* New York: St. Martin's Press, 1973.

Congressional Record, March 22, 1965.

Cooper, Kenneth. "Crime and Punishment," *Emerge* (November 1994): 42–51.

Cronin, Thomas E., Tania Z. Cronin, and Michael E. Milakovich. *U.S. vs. Crime in the Streets.* Bloomington: Indiana University Press, 1981.

Edsall, Thomas, and Mary Edsall. *Chain Reaction.* New York: Norton Books, 1991.

Glaser, Thomas M. *Race, Campaign Politics, and the Realignment of the South.* New Haven: Yale University Press, 1996.

Johnson, B. D., T. Williams, K. A. Dei, and H. Sanabria. "Drug Abuse in the Inner City: Impact of Hard-drug Users and the Community," in *Drugs and Crime,* ed. Michael Tonry and James Q. Wilson. Chicago: University of Chicago Press, 1990.

King, Anthony, and Giles Alston. "Good Government and the Politics of High Exposure," in *The Bush Presidency: First Appraisals,* ed. Colin Campbell and Bert A. Rockman. Chatham, N.J.: Chatham House, 1991.

Kingdon, John. *Congressmen's Voting Decision.* New York: Harper and Row, 1981.

Lin, Ann Chin. "The Troubled Success of Crime Policy," in *The Social Divide,* ed. Margaret Weir. Washington, D.C.: Brookings Institution, 1998.

Marion, Nancy. *A History of Crime Control Initiatives, 1960–1993.* Westport, Conn.:Praeger, 1993.

Piliawsky, Monte. "The Clinton Administration and African Americans." *Black Scholar* 24 (Spring 1994): 3–6.

Rae, Nicol C. *Southern Democrats.* New York: Oxford University Press, 1994.

Tatalovich, Raymond, and Byron W. Daynes, eds. *Social Regulatory Policy: Moral Controversies in American Politics.* (Boulder: Westview Press, 1988.

Tate, Katherine. *From Protest to Politics* Cambridge, Mass.: Harvard University Press, 1994.

Washington Post, March 22, 1965; June 23, 1968.

Wilson, James Q. *Crime.* Princeton: Princeton University Press, 1984.

Witcover, Jules. *The Resurrection of Richard Nixon.* New York: Putnam, 1971).

Chapter 9

Representation, Ethnicity, and Congress
Black and Hispanic Representatives and Constituencies

James W. Endersby and Charles E. Menifield

Representation lies at the root of American politics, dating back to that moment when colonists decided that they would no longer stand for the ordeal of taxation without representation. On this basis, they began the process of establishing their independence from the British, and the United States of America was born.

Representation is an issue that is umbilically connected to the process and practice of black politics. Recall that slaves were counted as three-fifths of a person and that the Fourteenth Amendment, by extending citizenship to Blacks, transformed them, for representational purposes, into whole persons for the first time. Yet concerns about representation among Blacks did not end with that amendment. The issue of representation continually rears its head in the guise of voting rights legislation, redistricting, congressional voting behavior, and municipal elections. Of recurring importance to scholars of black politics is the extent to which black elected officials have demonstrated substantive representation by working to pass legislation that is beneficial to community interests.

It is only fitting that this volume include some discussion of the extent to which the multiethnic landscape of American society poses problems for representation among Blacks and other minority groups. Toward that end, James Endersby and Charles Menifield examine the role of the racial characteristics of individual representatives and of certain districts and weigh a host of

257

other demographic factors to assess what influences substantive representation. Particularly exciting is the extent to which their chapter goes beyond the traditional black-white framework to assess substantive representation among Hispanics.

Introduction

The number of African American and Hispanic representatives increased dramatically following the 1992 congressional elections. Many attributed this change to the legislative redistricting that followed the 1990 census. Scholars immediately began to assess the effects of this election on representation of these minority ethnic groups in the United States. While the literature on congressional representation is vast, however, it frequently omits key variables, such as the ethnic and racial composition of districts and the gender and ethnicity of their representatives (Hill, 1995; Bullock, 1996). The main thrust of this chapter is to determine whether ethnic similarity between members of Congress and their constituents is necessary or sufficient for substantive representation of black and Hispanic communities within congressional districts. In examining this thesis, the following questions come to the fore: (1) Do black and Hispanic communities need minority representatives in order to receive adequate representation? (2) Do policy preferences of minority communities vary by policy type? (3) Can models that seek to explain congressional behavior be improved by considering the gender, ethnicity, race of the members of Congress, and the ethnic composition of the congressional district?

In this chapter, we propose a model of congressional voting behavior that incorporates variables for the ethnicity of the representatives themselves and their constituencies and for the interaction of the two. Through empirical testing of the model, we attempt to evaluate the relative influence of these three components of ethnicity.

Representation and Minority Representation

Chief among the several functions served by legislative institutions is the representation of constituents. Yet representation can take many forms. No consensus on what is meant by representation can be found in the relevant literature. Rather, scholars have identified several categories of representation. For the purposes of this study, a group or community achieves representation if the policy preferences of its members are reflected in the actions of its elected officials. We define representation operationally through an analysis of congressional roll calls.

Pitkin (1967) succinctly divides representation into two types. Descriptive representation occurs when demographic characteristics of the constituents correspond to those of the composition of the legislature. Substantive representation, however, demands that the policy preferences of constituents be translated into legislative behavior. Policy responsiveness is necessary for substantive representation. Although descriptive forms of representation can be critical for the expression of minority viewpoints and agenda control, policy responsiveness is at the center of what is meant by the representation function. In her landmark study of black representation in Congress, Swain (1995) concurs. She concludes that "descriptive representation of blacks guarantees only black faces and is, at best, an intangible good; substantive representation is by definition real and color blind" (211).

Through successful responsiveness, the chances of conflict between the representatives and their constituents is kept a minimum. Eulau and Karps (1977) expanded the definition of representation by emphasizing that legislators have four areas of concern. First, they argue that a legislator has a service responsibility to particular constituents, including the pursuit and securing of legislation that brings benefits to these constituents. Second, legislators have an allocation responsibility to their entire district. In this case, legislators are responsible for securing legislation that will benefit their entire district. The third area is policy responsiveness. Legislators are expected to mingle with their constituents and to learn about constituents' policy preferences. The final area emphasized by Eulau and Karps (1977) is symbolic responsiveness, which builds trust and confidence and convinces constituents that policymakers represent them effectively.

Miller and Stokes (1963) provide seminal piece of early research on legislative voting behavior. In their analysis of the 1958 House of Representatives, they found that representatives' voting behavior is strongly influenced both by personal policy preferences and by perceptions of what the constituents want. When Miller and Stokes categorize votes into a typology, however, the relative influence of these factors varies. For example, on foreign policy issues, they found that legislators adopt the role of trustee, whereas on social and welfare issues they are more likely to function as delegates who act in accordance with constituent opinions. However, Miller and Stokes do acknowledge that no one configuration explains how all members of Congress decide to vote. Subsequent research, based on their work, further refines their typologies; such work includes Cherryholmes and Shapiro (1969) and their predisposition model; Matthews and Stimson (1970, 1975) and their cue-taking model; Kingdon (1973) with his consensus model; Fiorina (1974) and his electoral incentive model; and Asher and Weisberg (1978) and their voting history model. This research tradition, however, pays little attention to the interests of minority communities.

Whitby (1987), following in this tradition, examined congressional responsiveness to black constituents in the South and found that an increase in the number of black constituents in a district affected both parties. The Democrats were more supportive of programs or legislation that would benefit black constituents then were Republicans. This was especially true in large urban black districts (see also Keech 1968; Singh 1998).

In a broader study of African Americans in the United States, Whitby (1997) found that African Americans are more cohesive than other groups in their views on social policies. They support the establishment of education quotas for minority participants, preferences for Blacks in hiring and promotion, more government spending on social services, and more government intervention in securing jobs and improving the standard of living for African Americans. Whitby found that African American members of Congress agree with these liberal policies, as do white representatives from the South who represent large black constituencies (see also Whitby and Gilliam 1991; Vega 1993; Menifield 1998; Menifield and Julian 1998). He found that party identification and the desire for reelection are important intervening variables that, combined, lead white representatives to become more responsive to the needs of their black constituents. Last, he found that Democrats tend to be much more supportive of social programs that benefit minorities than are the more conservative Republicans.

Measuring Minority Representation in Congress

This research aims to uncover relationships between congressional behavior and member and constituency characteristics, in particular, indicators of ethnicity.[1] Our focus is the U.S. House of Representatives (in part because few members of minority groups have been elected to the Senate, so there is little ethnic variance among incumbents).[2] The data for the dependent variable sample the first sessions of the 101st through the 104th Congresses. We chose these Congresses to test for the effects of ethnicity on legislative behavior both before and after the redistricting that was done subsequent to the 1990 census and the intentional creation of majority minority districts. During this time also there was an increase in diversity among representatives. Minority groups considered here include Blacks and Latinos; we necessarily omit other ethnic minorities such as Asian and Native Americans. While other minority groups may have pockets of population concentration, their proportions of the total population and of the House membership are too low to permit a meaningful statistical analysis.

To be consistent with most of the previous literature, we used an index of congressional roll call votes as the operational definition of legislative behavior. The particular measure for the dependent variable differs somewhat from that used in earlier work, however. Rather than rely on a single measure of ideology, we used as dependent variables in this study vote scores that fall into three different categories: economic, foreign, and social policies. It seems reasonable, for instance, that the legislative force of ethnicity may vary by the policy field.[3] All of these scores were obtained from reports of the *National Journal*. To calculate each member's scores, a panel first selects key legislative votes. The *National Journal* then calculates, for each policy area—economic, social, and foreign—a percentile that represents how often the member voted for the liberal or conservative side on each of these key roll calls. Thus, the data are bound by zero and 100, where zero indicates the member of Congress never voted with the perceived liberal (or conservative) bloc and the upper boundary indicates consistent support of that bloc. Using separate models, we tested the data using both the liberal and the conservative scores. Our findings were similar for both blocs. We therefore decided arbitrarily to provide the results using the liberal scores for each of the three policy areas.

Legislative behavior is modeled through ordinary least squares regression. Voting scores are a function of three phenomena: descriptive characteristics of a particular member of Congress, the composition and preferences of the constituents who live in the member's district, and the interaction between these two influences. The OLS regression model used in this research is:

$$y=b_0+b_1x_1+b_2x_2+b_3x_3+b_4x_4+b_5x_5+b_6x_6+b_7x_7+b_8x_8+b_9x_9+e$$

where

y = Congressional Voting Score (economic, social, or foreign policy; support for the liberal agenda measured as a percentile, 0–100)

x_1 = Representative's party identification (1 = Democrat,[4] 0 = republican)

x_2 = Representative's gender (1 = Female, 0 = Male)

x_3 = Black (Representative's ethnicity: 1 = Black, 0 = other)

x_4 = Latino (Representative's ethnicity: 1 = Latino, 0 = other)

x_5 = Percentage of voting-age African Americans in the district (0–100)

x_6 = Percentage of voting-age Hispanic Americans in the district (0–100)

x_7 = Percentage of the district's two party vote for the Democratic presidential candidate (0–100)

x_8 = African American Interaction term (x_3x_5)

x_9 = Hispanic American Interaction term (x_4x_6)

The data for individual members of Congress and for the two-party presidential vote were compiled from biannual editions of the *Almanac of American Politics*. Demographic data for the 1980s also come from the *Almanac of American Politics*. Data for votes that took place after redistricting are taken from *Congressional Districts in the 1990s*. The interaction variable was created by multiplying the interval variable that measures the ethnic composition of the constituency and the categorical variable for the ethnicity of the member of Congress.

Also included were a number of other socioeconomic characteristics of constituencies that are omitted from the report of our findings that follows. The original models incorporated variables designed to capture the effects of the average education level and income of a district's residents. However, the models revealed no independent relationships between these socioecoonomic variables and its representative's behavior. For parsimony, these socioeconomic variables were excluded from the model in favor of emphasizing more theoretically relevant data. Earlier efforts also included the Liberalism Quotient compiled by the

Americans for Democratic Action as a measure of members' political ideology.

We add one final word of caution regarding the use of secondary data. Following the well-traveled path of earlier scholars using secondary, aggregate data, we took presidential election results from the *Almanac of American Politics*. Few resources identify actual votes cast for presidential candidates on the congressional district level. While we encountered only one typographical error in the *Almanac* for the data for 1992, there were errors in the voting data reported for several states and districts for the 1988 presidential elections. For instance, if the district votes for Bush and Dukakis are aggregated for the state of Illinois, the total vote indicates that Dukakis won Illinois and its twenty-four electoral votes.[5] The actual vote total for Illinois, however, reveals that Bush defeated Dukakis. Inaccurate election totals are reported for several other states, as well. Without better information, data for the 1988 presidential election should be viewed as estimates. Of course, our difficulties point toward broader problems with data collection and secondary data analysis. Nevertheless, we remain confident that our findings are good approximations of the parameters for which we search.

Indicators of Roll Call Voting Behavior

Results from the regression models produce mixed results regarding whether ethnicity of a member or ethnic composition of the district influence legislative behavior. Partisanship, both of the representative and of the district, provides a much better measure of House roll call votes. The influence of ethnicity on substantive representation in the Congress seems weak, but its influence is felt within certain policy areas.

Tables 9.1, 9.2, and 9.3 present the estimated parameters and summary statistics for the regression model outlined earlier. Table 9.1 reports the results for the model fitting the liberal scores for roll call votes on economic policy to the independent variables. Table 9.2 does this for social policy votes, and Table 9.3 does the same for foreign policy votes. Each column in the tables represents a model for the first session of each Congress from 1989 to 1993. Parameter estimates that are significantly different from zero provide evidence that the variable is

TABLE 9.1
Factors Related to Economic Policy Roll Call Votes, U.S. House
of Representatives, 101st–104th Congresses

	1989	1991	1993	1995
Characteristics of Representative				
Democrat	39.98***	37.91***	37.64***	43.73***
	(1.57)	(1.52)	(1.70)	(2.02)
Woman	2.34	7.61***	6.08***	1.39
	(2.92)	(2.80)	(2.25)	(2.51)
Black	12.57	5.36	1.89	−7.45
	(9.77)	(7.30)	(9.58)	(9.94)
Latino	33.48	35.74	−6.21	−8.65
	(28.87)	(29.05)	(18.43)	(20.78)
Characteristics of Constituency				
African Americans (%)	−0.55***	−0.30***	−0.25**	−0.04
	(0.08)	(0.07)	(0.10)	(0.11)
Hispanic Americans (%)	−0.04	−0.14**	−0.14*	−0.23***
	(0.10)	(0.04)	(0.08)	(0.09)
Democratic Presidential Vote (%)	0.94***	0.92***	0.78***	0.83***
	(0.08)	(0.08)	(0.09)	(0.10)
Interaction between Characteristics				
African Americans	0.14	0.05	0.16	0.14
	(0.19)	(0.14)	(0.20)	(0.21)
Hispanic Americans	−0.74	−0.50	0.26	0.47
	(0.56)	(0.47)	(0.32)	(0.36)
Intercept	−15.14***	−14.48***	−14.92***	−17.58***
	(3.30)	(3.31)	(3.95)	(4.69)
F	168.39***	151.68***	147.53***	161.58***
R^2	.78	.77	.76	.77
(Adjusted R^2)	(.78)	(.76)	(.75)	(.77)

Table reports unstandardized coefficients with standard errors in parentheses.
*Significant at the .10 level.
**Significant at the .05 level.
***Significant at the .01 level.

associated with changes in the voting score, when other variables are controlled. The overall models are uniformly strong and typically explain more than 70 percent of the variance in the voting scores.

We first consider the findings for the economic policy vote models. Table 9.1 indicates that partisanship, of both the representative and of the constituency as measured by the percentage of the two-party presidential vote, are significant indicators of economic roll call votes for all four sessions of Congress. In fact, these relationships hold for social and foreign policy votes, as well. As expected, partisanship of incumbents and voters is closely related to economic policy roll call votes.

Moreover, the African American constituency variable reaches significance at the .01 level (rounded off) for three of the sessions: 1989,

1991, and 1993. The direction of this strong relationship, however, is counterintuitive. Once we control for partisanship, the model provides strong evidence that constituencies with larger than average numbers of African Americans are associated with a somewhat more *conservative* agenda for economic policy. Similar results link Hispanic Americans to economic policy votes. The percentage of Hispanics in the congressional district is significantly but negatively related to roll calls for 1991, 1993, and 1995.

This finding seems to go against expectations,[6] but the changes in this coefficient across time seem to suggest alternatives more in line with our intuition. For 1989 and 1991, the negative relationship between the relative size of the African American constituency and a liberal record on roll calls is quite strong. This relationship weakens substantially by 1993 (p = .0148) and disappears altogether by 1995. At least two alternatives can explain this counterintuitive result. First, this pattern suggests a dynamic relationship, perhaps the result of the growing electoral power of African Americans and the election of more Blacks to Congress. Another reasonable explanation is that this disparity may be a result of the disproportionate electoral support of African Americans for the Democratic party, which also may overestimate the support of a liberal economic agenda.

The trend for Hispanic constituencies, on the other hand, seems to be going in the opposite direction; it shows no significance in 1989, weak relationships in 1991 and 1993, and a strong negative relationship for 1995. The two alternative explanations just suggested may apply here as well. Although the numbers of Latino representatives elected to Congress increased during these years, so did the size of the Hispanic population, leaving in place a large, continuing disparity between the proportion of the general population that is Hispanic and the proportion of congressional representatives who are Hispanic. Many Hispanic groups, particularly Mexican Americans, vote disproportionately in favor of the Democratic party, which again may overestimate their liberalism.

This second objection is of an econometric nature. Although several tests for multicollinearity in the models failed to reveal it as a critical problem, contemporary data on representation still remain mired in the trap of indeterminate cause and effect. Minority populations and minority representatives overwhelmingly tend to support liberal and Democratic party agendas, to the extent that we cannot separate ideological preferences from group and partisan pressures.

Of these two explanations, the first alternative proposes a link between substantive representation and symbolic representation. As political issues isolate a minority community from the majority, partisan or ideological preferences become increasingly identified with one agenda (here, the Democratic and/or liberal agenda). As symbolic disparities wane, the minority's influence becomes more mainstream and the level of support for one party or ideology recedes to a level commensurate with that of the rest of the population. Unfortunately, the data available are insufficient to test either of these two proposed alternatives. We are left with an unusual finding that deserves further investigation.

For 1991 and 1993, the gender variable also reaches significance; women representatives in these sessions of Congress were more likely to cast votes in accordance with their more liberal colleagues. Gender, however, is the only characteristic of an incumbent that approaches statistical significance in any of the regression models. Congressional votes on economic policy appear unrelated to a representative's own ethnic background, once partisanship and constituency are controlled.

Similarly, the interaction variables that link minority ethnic composition of a district to minority representation reveal no statistical significance. The values for these variables are zero for most constituencies, those with White/Anglo representatives. When the incumbent is from a minority group, the variables take on a value equal to that minority group's percentage of the district population. Should substantive representation for minority populations demand a representative from that ethnic group, the estimated coefficient should be significantly different from zero. However, the regression models find little support for the notion that substantive representation depends on election of representatives from within an ethnic minority. There is no evidence of such a relationship on economic policy votes in Congress.

The second set of models presented in Table 9.2 provides the results of the regression analysis for the social policy roll calls. Again, we find the strong, omnipresent influence of representative and constituency partisanship on voting behavior. The African American district composition variables also reach levels of significance for each session except 1995. The proportion of Hispanics in a constituency weakly relates to roll call votes on social policy only in 1989; thereafter, the size of the Hispanic population is unrelated to votes on social issues. The direction of the relationship between district minority size and representatives' votes remains paradoxical and is absorbed into larger issues of

TABLE 9.2
Factors Related to Social Policy Roll Call Votes, U.S. House
of Representatives, 101st–104th Congresses

	1989	1991	1993	1995
Characteristics of Representative				
Democrat	32.32***	34.16***	32.29***	36.03***
	(1.99)	(1.84)	(1.87)	(2.29)
Woman	6.39*	10.87***	13.15***	8.67***
	(3.68)	(3.41)	(2.49)	(2.84)
Black	17.05	7.22	8.29	9.72
	(12.63)	(8.85)	(10.59)	(11.31)
Latino	49.40	7.58	7.01	5.32
	(36.88)	(35.32)	(20.37)	(23.52)
Characteristics of Constituency				
African Americans (%)	−0.35***	−0.27***	−0.19*	−0.19
	(0.10)	(0.09)	(0.11)	(0.13)
Hispanic Americans (%)	0.25*	0.07	−0.03	−0.03
	(0.13)	(0.08)	(0.09)	(0.10)
Democratic Presidential Vote (%)	0.99***	1.01***	0.88***	0.77***
	(0.10)	(0.10)	(0.09)	(0.11)
Interaction between Characteristics				
African Americans	−0.13	0.04	0.01	−0.04
	(0.25)	(0.17)	(0.22)	(0.24)
Hispanic Americans	−1.23*	−0.21	−0.09	−0.07
	(0.72)	(0.58)	(0.36)	(0.41)
Intercept	−15.21***	−19.66***	−18.82***	−10.61**
	(4.25)	(4.02)	(4.35)	(5.32)
F	86.39***	102.03***	115.03***	92.67***
R^2	.65	.69	.71	.66
(Adjusted R^2)	(.64)	(.68)	(.70)	(.66)

Table reports unstandardized coefficients with standard errors in parentheses.
* Significant at the .10 level.
**Significant at the .05 level.
***Significant at the .01 level.

partisanship and ideological orientation; larger minority populations often correlate with more conservative representation on social issues when other factors are controlled.

It is noteworthy that the ethnicity of the representative plays no important role in any of these models, but the gender variable stands out. Recorded votes imply that women representatives are far more likely to support a liberal social agenda. The interaction terms between representative and constituency ethnicity show a weak relationship for Latinos for 1989 only. Our results on the interactive effect of minority groups and representatives are subsumed by other indicators.

Table 9.3 reports the results for foreign policy votes. Initially, foreign policy issues resemble the relationships found among the independent

TABLE 9.3
Factors Related to Foreign Policy Roll Call Votes, U.S. House
of Representatives, 101st–104th Congresses

	1989	1991	1993	1995
Characteristics of Representative				
Democrat	36.80***	39.50***	39.14***	40.49***
	(1.78)	(1.63)	(1.87)	(1.89)
Woman	5.08	11.12***	6.79***	0.74
	(3.37)	(2.99)	(2.49)	(2.36)
Black	18.39*	3.76	−7.59	−1.89
	(11.02)	(7.79)	(10.65)	(9.35)
Latino	25.66	−0.04	−5.43	−8.09
	(32.56)	(30.99)	(20.38)	(19.45)
Characteristics of Constituency				
African Americans (%)	−0.61***	−0.43***	−0.32***	−0.17*
	(0.09)	(0.08)	(0.11)	(0.10)
Hispanic Americans (%)	−0.30***	−0.12	−0.20**	−0.23***
	(0.11)	(0.07)	(0.09)	(0.08)
Democratic Presidential Vote (%)	1.14***	0.92***	0.74***	0.84***
	(0.09)	(0.08)	(0.09)	(0.09)
Interaction between Characteristics				
African Americans	0.03	0.25*	0.38*	0.12
	(0.22)	(0.09)	(0.22)	(0.20)
Hispanic Americans	−0.44	0.02	0.16	0.26
	(0.64)	(0.51)	(0.35)	(0.34)
Intercept	−21.13***	−15.12***	−12.08***	−13.72***
	(3.75)	(3.55)	(4.36)	(4.39)
F	130.13***	145.39***	121.02***	156.74***
R²	.74	.76	.72	.77
(Adjusted R²)	(.73)	(.75)	(.71)	(.76)

Table reports unstandardized coefficients with standard errors in parentheses.
* Significant at the .10 level.
**Significant at the .05 level.
***Significant at the .01 level.

variables in economic and social policy votes. The party identification and Democratic presidential vote variables are significant in each of the four models. In the case of foreign policy issues, the African American constituency variable also remains consistently and strongly related to roll call votes (though still in a counterintuitive direction). In 1991 and 1993, the African American interaction term is also weakly significant.

In the case of foreign policy, another variable rises to significance; a congressional district's proportion of Hispanics shows strong (though negative) relationships to roll call behavior for three of the four congressional sessions. However, no association with the interaction for Latino representatives and constituencies is found. Nevertheless, some evidence suggests that Hispanics may serve as an attentive issue public for elements of foreign policy. Although they encompass a wide diversity of interests, districts with a large concentration of Hispanic Americans are associated with distinct legislative representation on foreign policy votes.

Characteristics of individual representatives are linked inconsistently to legislative behavior. Being female is correlated with having more liberal foreign policy positions in 1991 and 1993 but the relationship is insignificant in 1989 and 1995. Black members of Congress have a more liberal record in 1989, but no statistical relationships exist between a representative's ethnicity and foreign policy roll calls in other years. For foreign policy votes, as with economic and social policy, partisanship and constituency measures serve as better indicators of legislative decision making than do personal characteristics (with the possible exception of sex) and multiplicative relationships.

Ethnicity and Substantive Representation

As indicated in the introduction, the purpose of this research is to investigate whether African American and Hispanic citizens are affected by the election or loss of minority members of Congress. To address this question, we examined variables pertaining to ideology, partisanship, and ethnicity and applied them to data on ideological scores derived from roll call votes in three policy areas over four congressional sessions. Our findings confirm relationships among partisanship and ideology, but the link to minority representation is comparatively much weaker. We conclude that black and Hispanic citizens do not necessarily benefit from the election of a minority member of Congress in terms of substantive or policy representation. Quite the contrary, we found that the ethnicity of the representative is of secondary importance. The ethnic composition of the district is more strongly correlated with roll call voting behavior, depending on the type of policy votes considered (foreign, economic, or social).

Despite the increase in the number of African American and Hispanic legislators between 1989 and 1995, we did not find incumbent characteristics to be an important factor in determining policy votes. As expected, party identification appears to be the major factor influencing legislative behavior. However, a representative's gender does appear to be an important intervening variable, particularly in the area of social policy.

The interaction between the proportion of minority members of a district and minority incumbency made no significant contribution to our efforts to explain patterns of roll call votes. In fact, the inclusion of the interactive variables masked underlying relationships between an individual representative's ethnicity and liberalism.[7] Rather than supporting the anecdotal evidence that majority minority districts should produce better representation of minority groups, the findings presented here suggest that such districts are no more effective in providing *substantive* representation.

Nevertheless, our results suggest that models that seek to explain congressional voting behavior should consider not only the gender and ethnicity of the representatives, and the demographic makeup of the district but also how these factors affect policy choices when different type of votes are considered. Generally speaking, race and ethnicity have been overlooked in traditional models of voting behavior in Congress and are considered only in research on ethnic minorities. Some studies include an indicator variable for black members of Congress, but the underlying theoretical relationship goes beyond any particular minority group. According the Census Bureau, the number and proportion of Hispanics in the United States, for example, is growing rapidly and will continue to do so. In fact, it is estimated that the numbers of Latinos will surpass that of African Americans within the next ten years. Given this prediction, it is clear that the impact of policy of the growing Hispanic and other minority communities (such as Asian Americans) could be tremendous. As a result, congressional scholars should include variables for minority groups when developing models of legislative behavior.

NOTES

1. By emphasizing policy responsiveness, we neglect issues of race and ethnicity in election campaigns. Reeves (1997), for instance, notes the pervasiveness of ethnicity as an electoral issues that may disadvantage some minority candidates. On the other hand, a few minority candidates, such as Gary Franks (R-CT) and J. C. Watts (R-OK), were elected from predominantly white districts. Our research avoids the admittedly important subject of what occurs before and during elections and analyzes what occurs in Congress after the election.

2. The actual sample size varies slightly from 435 because of vacancies and

because some representatives (such as the Speaker of the House) cast a few roll call votes.

3. This is, in fact, what we find. Ethnic indicators are poorly related to overall ideological orientations (such as liberalism as defined by ADA scores), but they do correlate to roll call votes within certain policy sectors.

4. Partisanship for Vermont's independent representative Bernard Sanders is coded as 1 with the Democrats.

5. The popular vote in Illinois, summed across congressional districts, is 2,295,969 for Dukakis and 2,230,910 for Bush. The actual vote total in Illinois was 2,310,939 for Bush and 2,215,940 for Dukakis.

6. Bivariate correlations of the percentage of African Americans and Hispanics in a constituency and their district's representative's scores on economic, social, and foreign policy votes are all positive. The unusual relationships detected here exist only after controls are included in the multivariate models.

7. That is, at least in the case of black members of Congress. The Latino variable still produces no significant consistent relationship with roll call votes. Black members of Congress exhibit weakly more liberal records on all policy issues in the years of a Democratic majority (when the interaction terms are omitted).

REFERENCES

Almanac of American Politics. 1989, 1991, 1993, 1995. Boston: Gambit.

Asher, Herbert B., and Herbert F. Weisberg. 1978. "Voting Change in Congress: Some Dynamic Perspectives on an Evolutionary Process." *American Journal of Political Science* 22: 391–425.

Bullock III, Charles S. 1996. "Racial Composition of District Population and the Election of African American Legislators." *Southeastern Political Review* 24: 611–628.

Cherryholmes, Cleo H., and Michael J. Shapiro. 1969. *Representatives and Roll Calls: A Computer Simulation of Voting in the Eighty-eighth Congress.* Indianapolis: Bobbs-Merrill.

Congressional Districts in the 1990s: A Portrait of America. 1993. Washington, D.C.: Congressional Quarterly.

Eulau, Heinz, and Paul D. Karps. 1977. "The Puzzle of Representation: Specifying Components of Responsiveness." *Legislative Studies Quarterly* 2: 233–254.

Fiorina, Morris P. 1974. *Representatives, Roll Calls, and Constituencies.* Lexington, Mass.: Heath.

Hill, Kevin A. 1995. "Does the Creation of Majority Black Districts Aid Republicans? An Analysis of the 1992 Congressional Elections in Eight Southern States." *Journal of Politics* 57: 384–401.

Keech, William R. 1968. *The Impact of Negro Voting: The Role of the Vote in the Quest for Equality.* Chicago: Rand-McNally.

Kingdon, John W. 1973. *Congressmen's Voting Decisions.* New York: Harper & Row.

Matthews, Donald R., and James A. Stimson. 1970. "Decision Making by U.S. Representatives: A Preliminary Model." In S. Sidney Ulmer, ed., *Political Decision Making.* New York: Litton.

———. 1975. *Yeas and Nays: Normal Decision Making in the U.S. House of Representatives.* New York: Wiley.

Menifield, Charles E. 1998. "A Loose Coalition or a United Front: Voting Behavior within the Congressional Hispanic Caucus." *Latino Studies Journal* 9: 26–44.

Menifield, Charles E., and Frank Julian. 1998. "Changing the Face of Congress: African Americans in the Twenty-first Century." *Western Journal of Black Studies* 29: 32–50.

Miller, Warren, and Donald Stokes. 1963. "Constituency Influence in Congress." *American Political Science Review* 57: 45–56.

National Journal (various issues).

Pitkin, Hanna F. 1967. *The Concept of Representation.* Berkeley: University of California Press.

Reeves, Keith. 1997. *Voting Hopes or Fears? White Voters, Black Candidates, and Racial Politics in America.* New York: Oxford University Press.

Singh, Robert. 1998. *The Congressional Black Caucus: Racial Politics in the U.S. Congress.* Thousand Oaks, Calif.: Sage.

Swain, Carol M. 1995. *Black Faces, Black Interests: The Representation of African Americans in Congress,* 2d ed. Cambridge, Mass.: Harvard University Press.

Vega, Arturo. 1993. "Variations and Sources of Group Cohesiveness in the Black and Hispanic Congressional Caucuses." *Latino Studies Journal* 14: 79–92.

Whitby, Kenny J. 1987. "Measuring Congressional Responsiveness to the Policy Interest of Black Constituents." *Social Science Quarterly* 68: 367–377.

———. 1997. *The Color of Representation: Congressional Behavior and Black Interests.* Ann Arbor: University of Michigan Press.

Whitby, Kenny J., and Franklin D. Gilliam Jr. 1991. "A Longitudinal Analysis of Competing Explanations for the Transformation of Southern Congressional Politics." *Journal of Politics* 53: 504–518.

Chapter 10

Pride and Pragmatism
Two Arguments for the Diversification of Party Interests

Lawrence J. Hanks

Since the War on Poverty of the 1960s and its component Great Society programs, Blacks have for the most part resided comfortably within the Democratic party. Blacks' positions on key political issues, research shows, tend to be closely aligned with those of the Democrats. The Democratic party is therefore considered by many to represent black interests; southern white Democrats have thus frequently sided with the Republican party.

At the same time, Democrats, realizing that they cannot win elections solely with the liberal white vote and that of liberal racial minorities, implicitly court a wider, politically more diverse range of Democrats in an effort to expand their base. In the most recent presidential campaigns, Democratic presidential aspirants have avoided the use of racial terms and have also stayed away from urban issues, as these are often associated with Blacks. This has often left Blacks feeling taken for granted.

At the same time, even as Republicans try to reach out to the center to expand their constituency, party leaders have in the last quarter century clearly not had Blacks' racial interests at heart. The Willie Horton advertising campaign used by George Bush during the 1988 presidential campaigns and the more recent Contract with America, in which Congress, backed by the full weight of the Republican party, undermined many of the programs connected to black interests, did little to endear Republicans to Blacks. And so, in important ways, Blacks seem out of place in

either party: overlooked by the Democrats because they are con-
sidered to have nowhere else to go and disregarded by many Re-
publicans who don't expect to win their votes in any event.

   At a time when both parties are making bids to incorporate
newer immigrant groups into their fold, this chapter presents an
impassioned argument for party diversification.

African Americans joined Franklin Roosevelt's New Deal Coalition in
1936. Since that time, the majority of the African American electorate
has voted for the Democratic nominee for the presidency. Additionally,
since 1960, an overwhelming majority of the African American electorate has supported the entire Democratic slate (Walters 1998; Bartels
1998, 63–69). Despite the call for loyalty from the Democratically
aligned African American leadership, the African American electorate
needs to seriously reconsider its relationship with the Democratic party
and to orchestrate a calculated redistribution of its support. The call
for this redistribution is informed by the guiding principles:

1. Political power is limited in its ability to transform the socioeconomic status of African Americans. Thus, neither political party
   is going to eradicate, from without, the problems within the
   African America community that can be impacted by internal
   strategies.
2. Politicians like to say that they serve the public interest and the
   greater good. However, the realism of politics dictates that "you
   reward your friends and punish your enemies."
3. Political support is a necessary condition if one's public preferences are to be implemented. However, it is not sufficient to ensure this implementation.
4. The further development of African American political power has
   a prominent place in the quest for political, social, and economic
   parity. However, the development of a healthy economic infra-
   structure within the framework of American capitalism appears
   to be a viable and pragmatic strategy to alleviate the problem of
   inequality in the African American community.
5. Loyalty and fidelity are ideal foundations for personal and romantic relationships. However, these ideals should play a far
   smaller role, if any, in political relationships. Political relation-

ships should be based on self-interest. To the extent that they are not, the results have the potential to be disastrous.

6. Primarily because of the way people are socialized and the values, perspectives, and ideologies they acquire, reasonable persons can differ with respect to the merit of any given strategy within a spirit of civility and good faith.

My rationale for urging this reconsideration and defection by African Americans is based on two elements—pride and pragmatism.

The Pragmatic Argument for Diversification

An unstable electorate, regardless of is race, gender, creed, socioeconomic status, ability, sexual orientation, or other distinguishing characteristic, demands special attention. The unstable electorate is courted as parties and politicians attempt to add it to their list of supporters. If the electorate's behavior is consistent and therefore predictable, its support is taken for granted, its power to bargain for concessions is weakened, and the time, energy, and other resources of the party are directed toward capturing the vote of other, unstable, potential constituencies.

Because of its extreme loyalty to the Democratic party since 1960, the African American electorate finds itself on the receiving end of two negative actions: It is taken for granted by the Democrats, and it is ignored by the Republicans. Like a battered wife, the African American electorate stays with the Democratic party because it feels that it has nowhere else to go. So, it stays and hopes that things will get better. Abusive husbands do not usually get better until the battered wife chooses to exercise an option other than staying in the abusive relationship. Similarly, the Democratic party will not treat African Americans better until they choose an option other than voting as a virtual monolith for the Democratic ticket.

The abused wife has at least four options: (1) She may leave and forsake all romantic and platonic relationships; (2) she may stay in the relationship, demand a cessation of the abuse, lessen her emotional investment in the relationship, and choose to develop relationships outside her marriage; (3) she may seek to find happiness with another man, or (4) she may choose to lead a life of independence, a life without the liabilities and benefits of a permanent relationship with any one man. Her relationships should be based on her own self-interest. If her interests are being met, she continues the relationship. If they are not being met, she takes whatever actions are most reasonable and appropriate to change the situation.

The national African American electorate has at least four options: (1) It can become apolitical, that is, simply not have a life of overt political participation; (2) it can remain in the party, reduce its level of support for the party, demand more respect, and choose to develop political relationships outside the Democratic party; (3) it can choose to shift most of its support to the Republican party, or (4) it can choose to become a highly registered, mobilized, and unstable electorate with a political life characterized by the lack of a strong attachment to any political party, distributing its vote and other resources as each occasion presents itself. The goal of this strategy is the attainment of ends based on the ability of the relationship to produce progress toward a stated goal. Option 4, hereafter referred to as the "synthetic equal opportunity posture," with a stable and dynamic component, is a long-term goal. However, any combination of options 1–3 would lay the groundwork for the eventual implementation of option 4.

The traditional civil rights establishment is quick to point out that the African American collective does not generally fare well under Republican administrations. Nonetheless, the African American collective has survived the Middle Passage, slavery, segregation, Nixon, Reagan, and Bush. Regardless of who is in the White House, African Americans will continue to survive, although the pace of group self-actualization may be impeded. Despite the record of Republican administrations on civil rights issues and the apparent philosophical incompatibility between most African Americans and most Republicans, it is in the long-term best interest of the African American collective to provide a moderate degree of support for the Republican party, since support provides the basis for laying claim to public policy benefits. Other forms of defections from the Democratic party, such as staying home or voting for candidates of minor parties, would send a message to the Republican party that this electorate is available for courtship. Moreover, the diversification strategy does not demand diversification in all national elections. Defecting from the Democratic party at the presidential level while simultaneously working to ensure Democratic party control of the House and Senate would provide ideological comfort for some without threatening the benefits of the national diversification strategy. The national election of 1956 provides an example.

The strategy of decreasing African American support for the Democratic party is not a novel idea. The African American electorate defected in 1956 and reaped the benefits of being an unpredictable and unstable electorate. After having grown tired of the Democrats' kowtowing to the South on the issue of civil rights, black northerners decreased their support for the Democratic ticket and aided Eisenhower in his quest for reelection to the White House. The defections took two major forms: (1) A portion of the electorate stayed home; and (2) another portion of the electorate voted for the Republican ticket. The Democratic leadership, after having been shown that African American voters would defect (O'Reilly 1995, 177; Walters 1988, 28), decided to court African American voters, since they were concentrated in the electorally rich industrial states.

The battered wife mustered the courage to run away, and the abusive husband wanted her back. He recognized that her contributions were pivotal if he was to achieve his goals. Having expressed an interest in another man, the abused wife found herself the object of a struggle. Both the Democrats and the Republicans courted the black vote between 1956 and 1960. This courtship provided the groundwork for the Civil Rights Act of 1957, the first piece of civil rights legislation since the Reconstruction era, the Civil Rights Act of 1960, and the pragmatic courtship of the black electorate by John F. Kennedy in 1960 (Hanks 1987, 29–31).

Politics is a struggle over the allocation of scarce resources. The aim of any political activity is to ultimately have resources allocated according to your interest. In order to optimize the probability of a favorable distribution of resources, most individuals and groups endeavor to spread their influence by providing some measure of support to all of the actors who may possibly have influence over the formation of public policy. To give all of one's support to one actor, especially when that actor is experiencing a series of losses, is an unwise use of political power at best and politically naive at worse. Most advocates of the theory of black political empowerment now realize that political power does not necessarily increase group economic power. Nonetheless, the economic uplift component of political power, already marginal, is further undermined by the lack of a diversified vote on the part of the African American electorate.

Neither political party is going to save the African American collective from the internal problems that plague it—problems of individual judgment such as drug usage, pregnancy, crime, and low levels of academic achievement (Howard and Hammond 1985). The most that can be done is to solicit the help of the government as the battle is fought from within. Because of the large amount of financial resources that may be necessary to adequately address these problems, governmental involvement is crucial. Thus, the importance of a diversified African American electorate becomes even clearer: African Americans can ill afford a denial of governmental resources as Republicans follow their own agenda, which is unsympathetic to the needs of African Americans. A diversified African American electorate would optimize the resource base for group advancement efforts.

The Argument for Diversification Based on Pride

Jesse Jackson's presidential candidacy, in 1988, illustrates how poorly the Democratic party treats the African American electorate. Virtually every African American with a sense of group consciousness, indeed, every individual who values decency and equal opportunity, can easily find cause for discomfort with the manner in which the Jackson candidacy was handled. The conventional Democratic party wisdom held the following: (1) The nation was not ready for an African American president (and certainly not Jackson); (2) the nation was not ready for an African American vice president (and certainly not Jackson); and (3) the nation was not ready for a candidate who was too heavily influenced by an African American (especially if that African American was Jesse Jackson.)

The party establishment was content with the Jackson candidacy as long as its success was deemed impossible. When Jackson stunned America and the Democratic party with his two-to-one drubbing of Massachusetts Governor Michael Dukakis in the Michigan caucus, Democrats' despair was documented across America. Newspaper headlines were most telling: "Democratic leaders' worries mount as Jackson campaign rolls up victories" (Painton (a) 1988); "Jackson's growing strength stirs concern in Democratic hierarchy" (Painton (b) 1988); "Jackson candidacy posing dilemma for black mayors, other office holders" (Straus 1988).

Even the late Lewis Grizzard, who was a humorist for the *Atlanta Constitution* and whose column usually had a humorous bent, assumed a deadly serious posture as he wrote a column that could have been appropriately titled, "The Case against the Jackson Candidacy" (Grizzard 1988).

The *New York Times* reported that a Jackson nomination was conceivable. At this point in the primary season, Jackson, with 460.55 delegates, and Dukakis, with 464.50 delegates, were virtually tied, with half of the delegates left to be chosen. The Democrats had the opportunity to make or break the Jackson candidacy. A moderate number of endorsements by established White Democratic politicos might have provided the necessary push from within to give Jackson a real chance at the nomination. A strong call to take the high road would have breathed crucial life into the Jackson candidacy.

The shoe was now on the other foot. Whereas Jackson had always been asked to deliver African American votes for Caucasian candidates, it was Whites' turn to deliver the votes for an African American candidate who had already shown an ability to secure a moderate amount of crossover support on his own. Not only did they not rise to the occasion; they started a de facto "Stop Jesse Movement" (Raspberry 1988). In essence, Jackson was told that he was not wanted on the Democratic team but that he could stay if he accepted a new designated position. His position on the team, at least for 1988, would have to be beneath his perceived abilities: He could not be the manager, the coach, the starting quarterback, or the second-string quarterback. The only position available to him was that of a cheerleader with severe limitations: He could lead the cheers of the African American community only and would have to stay away from the white fans.

Such a position takes gall, in this case on outgrowth of the deeply held belief that African American voters would not be offended to the point of defecting. A defection was viewed as not feasible because of the poor relations between the African American electorate and the Republican party. Thus, Democrats reasoned that, regardless of how Jackson was treated, the black electorate would be in the Democratic column in November. A defection would have caused the Democratic party strategists to rethink their game plan. In the end, the African American electorate registered 88 percent of its vote for Dukakis (Walters 1998).

Many well-meaning Caucasians in general and Caucasian Democrats in particular are offended by the charge that many Caucasians refused to vote for Jackson primarily because of his race. They maintain that it was Jackson's ideology, not his race, that prevented his widespread acceptance within the party. This position loses a good deal of its merit when one realizes that the Democratic delegates were much closer to Jackson than to Dukakis on a number of issues. Although one might accept as fact that Democratic delegates are not representative of the more moderate party regulars, the present and past role of race in American sociocultural life makes it difficult for even the most optimistic African Americans to believe that racism exerted only a mild impact on the Jackson candidacy. Insult is added to injury when widespread acceptance is bestowed on Caucasian ethnics and Caucasian women while it appears that African Americans continue to be shunned.

Most political observers concurred that the Democratic nomination in 1988 was Mario Cuomo's (an Italian American), for the asking; Dukakis, a Greek American, received the nomination. In 1984 Walter Mondale chose Geraldine Ferraro, an Italian American, as his running mate. After the initial historical impact of her candidacy was absorbed, it was business as usual, with only passing mention of Ferraro's gender. It is noteworthy that Dukakis did not choose an African American female. If someone of the late Barbara Jordan's stature had still been in the House, would Mondale have had the courage to choose her? Probably not. Blacks in general are still considered liabilities and are shunned when the stakes are high. This is the same behavior that characterized the "Stop Jesse Movement."

In his moving speech to the 1988 Democratic convention, Jackson spoke metaphorically of sailing his little boat within the confines of the harbor bar. He spoke also of his need to go out in the deep with the larger ships. The metaphor was most appropriate.

In the collective mind of African Americans, the "harbor bar" is racism, and it will not let Jackson or other aspiring black politicians out. Those who hold this view do not necessarily claim that Caucasian Democratic party members are themselves racist. However, they do often believe that the Democrats acquiesce in the racism of other groups as they plan their political strategy. As is the case in American society in general, it appears that everyone has fused in the Democratic melting pot except African Americans. Although the Democratic party may not be responsible for the residual racism that still permeates American culture, it can certainly be held responsible for acquiescing in it. Defections by African Americans may help the Democratic party to understand that it must move from acquiescing to racism to wholeheartedly embracing the candidacies of qualified African American political aspirants.

African American pride should also be offended when African Americans are treated like the proverbial "ugly admirer." An "ugly admirer" is perceived as riddled with liabilities yet is welcome at times when its resources can be utilized with public acknowledgment. Although the black electorate has been the most loyal and faithful voting bloc to support the Democratic party, it is like an ugly admirer—the Democrats are reluctant to be seen with it during the day, especially at social gatherings where they wish to create a favorable impression. Democrats want to exploit this group's available resources even while failing to publicly acknowledge and validate its interests lest they offend the sensibilities of another would-be suitor, the conservative White voter. Thus, there is a need for Democratic nominees to perform a balancing act: respecting the African American electorate while also respecting the large sector of white moderate-to-conservative voter. Like a love interest that is dogged out in public, the African American electorate is told that it must understand the slight because it is the only way that its suitor will be in a position to take care of its needs. In other words, the African American electorate is the other woman, while the moderate and conservative Caucasian vote is the wife. The African American electorate deserves better treatment, but it will not receive it until it demands respect by diversifying its vote.

Jesse Jackson, like most of the leadership in the African American community, is a team player within the Democratic party. Despite the treatment Jackson received as a candidate, it was not surprising that he was not a disruptive force at the 1988 Democratic Convention, given his new status as a team player. Jackson did not have a choice; he had to endorse the Democratic ticket or jeopardize his bright political future. One should not expect Jackson, or any of the African American politicians in the Democratic party, to preach the virtues of a diversified African American vote. Although African American Democrats undoubtedly understand the logic of the strategy, their standing in the party blurs their vision. While respect is due to African American politicians in the Democratic party, African Americans should not blindly follow their leadership. A diversified African American vote will mark a major step toward maximizing the political effectiveness of the African American collective.

The Synthetic Equal Opportunity Posture—
Dynamic and Stable

The synthetic equal opportunity strategy—stable and dynamic—is clearly a rational approach to optimizing the political influence of the African American electorate. This posture posits an African American electorate with three major components: (1) a 40 percent yellow-dog Republican base; (2) a 40 percent yellow-dog Democratic base; and (3) a 20 percent independent base that is activated to support the candidate from the major parties whose views and values are most like those of the African American community. The best possible scenario is one in which 60 percent of the African American electorate, the 40 percent yellow-dog base and the 20 percent independent base, combine to support the winning candidate.

This posture has many strengths: (1) The African American vote is no longer taken for granted; (2) both parties actively court the African American vote; (3) there is a greater chance that public policy preferences will be honored; (4) there is a strong claim for patronage; and (5) perhaps most important, with this posture, even in the worst-case scenario, in which the independent component votes for the losing candidate, a 40 percent level of support still provides a solid claim to patronage and to support for African Americans' public policy preferences. This position is ideal for optimizing the political influence of the African American electorate. The major problem with this posture lies in charting the course by which the African American electorate arrives at this point.

Given that the African American electorate has given only up to 12 percent of its vote to the Republican party between 1980 and 1996, there is a huge gap between the proposed ideal and the current situation. What can be done to increase African American support for the Republican party? In order to develop prescriptive strategies, an understanding of the challenges must be attained. Arguably, the two main barriers to diversification of the African American electorate are the perceptions on the part of the African American electorate that the Republican party is racist and that it is not supportive of the quest for African American equity.

The charges of racism and nonsupport are mutually reinforced. Given the southern white defection to the Republican party after the Democrats embraced the goals of the post–World War II civil rights movements, there is arguably a basis for this perception. This perception is exacerbated by a schism regarding the best way to attain equity for African Americans. While the African American electorate favors strong enforcement of civil rights laws, affirmative action programs, and programs to help the poor, Republicans argue that they support the ends of these efforts but not the means. From the Republican perspective, optimal utilization of resources dictate that they not be used to court a nonsupportive constituency.

This schism can be bridged in at least three ways: (1) The African American electorate can convince the GOP to adopt its means; (2) the GOP can convince the African American electorate to adopt its means; or (3) the two parties can agree to compromise. While the feasibility of the first two options are at best questionable, the compromise option holds promise.

While the African American electorate is indeed overwhelmingly Democratic and liberal, except on most social issues, African American conservatives are putting forth an effort to compete for the loyalty of the African American electorate. A major level of prominence was attained by black conservatives during the Reagan administration; their visibility has continued to be enhanced with the appointment of Clarence Thomas to the Supreme Court, the emergence of J. C. Watt, and the visibility of various Republican-affiliated African American organization such as the Center for New Black Leadership, the Center for Equal Opportunity, and the Black Americans' Political Action Committee.

Conservative African American leaders argue that the Republican party is a viable option for the African American electorate. While they tend to de-emphasize the role of race as an impediment to African American progress, they do acknowledge racism in the culture and the need to fight against it. Given the tremendous gap between the policy preferences of the African American electorate and those of the Republican party, African American conservatives seem to offer the most promising course for diversification. Perhaps some middle course can be devised that will advance the cause of both groups.

While they are often derided as pariahs in the African American community, black conservatives are still African Americans and have a shared experience, even though their perspective differs from that of the traditional African American leadership. Moreover, they are connected philosophically to the mainstream of the Republican party. Thus, they represent a bridge.

The African American electorate and the GOP are trapped in a vicious cycle: The African American electorate does not support the GOP because the party does not assume the proper posture on issues of importance to the black community; in turn, the GOP refuses to support a constituency that does not vote for it, especially since it has won three of the five presidential elections held from 1980 to 1996 without substantial African American support. Both the African American electorate and the GOP stand to gain from a compromise; the Democratic party would no longer take the African American vote for granted, racial demagoguery would lose its viability as a campaign strategy, and the GOP could shed its racist image. The GOP should decide to work with African American conservative leaders to facilitate bipartisanship among the African American electorate. This effort would mark a major milestone for American politics in general and for African American politics in particular.

BIBLIOGRAPHY

Bartels, Larry. "Where the Ducks Are: Voting Power in a Party System," in *Politicians and Party Politics,* ed. John Geer. Baltimore: John Hopkins University Press, 1998.

Bivens, Larry. "Jackson, Key Democrats Meet." *Newsday,* 31 March 1988, 4.

Grizzard, Lewis. "It's Time to Ask Jesse Jackson Tough Questions." *Atlanta Constitution,* 1 April 1988, A-13.

Hanks, Lawrence J. *Black Political Empowerment in Three Georgia Counties.* Knoxville: The University of Tennessee Press, 1987.

———. "Compromise between Black Voters and GOP Would Benefit Both." *Atlanta Constitution,* 22 December 1988, A-18.

Howard, Jeff, and Ray Hammond. "Rumors of Inferiority." *New Republic* 193(11) (1985): 17–21.

Jackson, Jesse L. Speech given before the 1988 Democratic National Convention, Atlanta, Ga., July 19, 1988.

O'Reilly, Kenneth. *Presidents and Racial Politics from Washington to Clinton.* New York: Free Press, 1995.

Painton, Priscilla (a). "Democratic Leaders' Worries Mount as Jackson Rolls Up Victories." *Atlanta Constitution,* 29 March 1988, A-1.

——— (b). "The Presidential Campaign: Jackson's Growing Strength Stirs Concerns in Democratic Hierarchy." *Atlanta Constitution,* 17 March 1988, A-8.

Raspberry, William. "No-Stop Jackson Movement? Take Another Look." *Atlanta Constitution,* 12 April 1988, A-19.

Straus, Hal. "Jackson Candidacy Posing Dilemma for Black Mayors, Other Office Holders." *Atlanta Constitution,* 24 March 1988, A-7.

Walters, Ron. *Black Presidential Politics in America: A Strategic Approach.* Albany: SUNY Press, 1988.

———. "Is the Party Over?: African American's Romance with Democrats Is Fading." *Emerge* 10(2) (1998): 56.

Chapter 11

Comparing Support for Affirmative Action among Four Racial Groups

Pie-te Lien and M. Margaret Conway

Research on public attitudes about affirmative action have tradi-
tionally focused on the two major racial groups in American soci-
ety, Blacks and Whites. Over the years, Whites have expressed
less and less support for affirmative action policies, believing that
such policies are tantamount to reverse discrimination. In con-
trast, Blacks in overwhelming numbers support affirmative action
as a necessary governmental campaign to "make up" for the in-
justices of the past.

Yet, the debate over affirmative action has been complicated,
indeed completely altered, by the influx of Asians, Latinos, and
Blacks from the Caribbean and Africa. Affirmative action, often
cast as a policy devised for Blacks, is increasingly beneficial to
Latinos and some members of Asian ethnic groups, as well.

This chapter provides a realistic look at affirmative action pol-
icy and the extent to which Americans of different ethnic and
racial backgrounds support it. Stressing the importance of racial
attitudes, political principles, and conflicts of interest, Pie-te Lien
and M. Margaret Conway help us understand how well these ex-
planations account for support of affirmative action policies
among very recent American immigrants.

The Research Problem

The issue of affirmative action has become a central part of political and
public debate in recent years because of the emergence of several ballot

initiatives in California and in other states that threatened to remove basic social services and equal protection from immigrants and minorities. This threat was underlined by California Governor Pete Wilson's 1996 presidential campaign, which emphasized the elimination of affirmative action. Nationwide, the issue has garnered attention because of President Clinton's review of federal affirmative action programs, the formation and conduct of his panel on race, and the Senate Judiciary Committee's reluctance to confirm the nomination of Bill Lann Lee, a well-qualified but pro-affirmative action candidate, for the nation's top civil rights position in the Department of Justice. Perhaps fundamental to the increasing or renewed interest in the concept and implementation of affirmative action, however, is the nation's rapidly changing racial demography and the challenges it presents to a political regime dominated by Whites as well as to our ability to get along as a nation.

What are the roles of long-standing principles, interests, and attitudes in structuring American public opinion on affirmative action? How do they differ across racial groups? And how does education matter? Prior research in the United States has focused primarily on Whites' attitudes toward Blacks and on policies that create preferences in school admission and employment for minorities; Blacks are usually seen as the principal beneficiaries of such policies, although in fact other racial minority groups, as well as women of all races, benefit as well from the thirty-year-old policies.[1] In the research reported here, we attempt to expand the parameter of debate from a biracial to a multiracial one. We first discuss alternative theories about support for and opposition to race-targeted policies. Then, we analyze a national survey of four racial groups to explore the underlying pattern of affirmative action opinion. This is followed by a series of ordinary least-squared regression procedures to test the ability of alternative theories to explain public support for affirmative action in the multiracial sample as well as in the same population grouped by race and by education. We conclude by summarizing our research findings and discussing their implications.

Three Theoretical Approaches

Several theories have guided research on racial attitudes and attitudes toward government policies designed to fight discrimination. These theories rely on different explanatory concepts: biologically based racial prejudice and group stereotypes; symbolic racism;[2] political principles; self-interest; and group interest. Three of these are the focus of our research. Symbolic racism theory suggests that for some individuals early socialization processes that foster racial antagonism combined with support for traditional values such as self-reliance and individualism result in opposition to government policies, such as affirmative action, perceived as targeted toward racial minorities (Kinder and Sears 1981; Kinder 1986).[3] A second set of theories emphasizes group identity and support for or concern about a privileged group's position. Among the alternative formulations of this approach are social group dominance (Sidanius, Pratto, and Bobo 1996), group position theory (Bobo and Hutchings 1996), group conflict theory (Bobo 1988), and social identity theory (Tajfel and Turner 1986). A third approach is based on research into reasoning processes and belief consistency. Sniderman, Brody, and Tetlock (1991) argue that ideology influences patterns of consistency, with conservatives who prefer a minimal federal government opposing affirmative action policies. A more general theory of public opinion incorporates all three theories, suggesting that attitudes on public issues are a function of perceived self- and group interests, the political principles supported by individuals, and their attitudes toward social groups. Its proponents have applied this general approach to the study of Whites' attitudes on social policies and support for or opposition to federal government activity in those policy areas (Kinder and Sanders 1996).

Symbolic Racial Attitudes

As Sears (1988) discusses in a summary of symbolic racism theory, this perspective was originally introduced to explain the political role of Whites' attitudes. White backlash against busing, support for political candidates who spout rhetoric perceived as racist, opposition to affirmative action policies in employment—all represent opposition among Whites that Sears and his research colleagues argue is different from the old form of blatant racism, with its antagonisms toward Blacks per se. Symbolic racism is viewed as replacing blatant or "old-fashioned" racism. Kinder and Sears (1981) describe symbolic racism as consisting of a blend of antiblack affect and traditional moral values such as individualism and self-reliance. It is the "conjunction of traditional values and anti-black affect that produce symbolic racism, which in turn produces opposition to pro-black policies and black candidates" (Sears 1988).[4]

Theoretically, symbolic racism may structure not just the attitudes of Whites toward Blacks but the attitudes of any one group toward another that is perceived as different and thus inferior or threatening or both. Latinos and Asians are two nonwhite groups whose numbers have matched or surpassed the number of Blacks in many localities in the nation. Therefore, symbolic racism may also explain the antagonistic attitudes of Whites toward Latinos and Asians, as well as the attitudes nonwhite groups hold about each other. In the initial stage of this research we focus on the effects of symbolic racism's racial attitudes component on support for affirmative action. In the combined model we can examine the relative effects of attitudes and political principles on support for affirmative action.

Self versus Group Interest

Rational choice theory suggests that individual self-interest plays a significant if not determining role in structuring both opinions and actions. Examining White opposition to policies perceived as targeted to benefit racial minorities, Tuch and Hughes (1996a, 1996b) conclude that attitudes about race-targeted policies are in part based on interest, but they argue that it is impossible to disentangle self-interest from group interest. Sears and Jessor (1996) disagree, arguing that self-interest can be separated from group interest and has different effects, with self-interest having no effect on opposition to race-targeted policies, while group interest does. Davis (1996) argues that, in evaluating the role of group interest, one must use measures that accurately portray a credible and perceived threat to the group being studied. Furthermore, individuals may pursue self-interest, then cloak it in the mantle of group interest or political principles.[5]

Research on either group or self-interest confronts problems of both conceptual definition and operational measurement. Some research has focused on self-interest defined as direct tangible benefit or loss (Sears, Hensler, and Speer 1979). An alternative approach is to focus on group interest, justifying that strategy with the argument that political decisions are collective action decisions, with benefits and costs allocated on the basis of some type of group characteristic (Sniderman and Tetlock 1986a). Reasoning about how to respond to controversial issues such as referenda on race- and gender-based higher education admissions might be based on group interest for all members of a racial/ethnic group but also on self-interest for some members of the group. For example, an Asian American denied admission to a university because the "quota" for Asians was filled would have both a self-oriented and a group-oriented interest in having such a quota abolished.

However, the impact of either self-interest or group interest can be expected to be conditional, occurring under some conditions but not others. The competing frames provided by policy proponents and opponents and conveyed by interest group leaders and the mass media may present alternative stimuli that influence whether interest will be defined as group interest or self-interest or both. (Nelson and Kinder 1996; Stoker 1996; Kuklinski et al. 1997; Peffley, Hurwitz, and Sniderman 1997).

Political Principles

A substantial body of research emphasizes the role played by individuals' values, expressed through support for political principles such as individualism, egalitarianism, social responsibility, and limited government (Davis 1996; Gilens 1995, 1996; Kinder and Sanders 1996; Sears and Jessor 1996) as well as through self-identified party identification and political ideology. How individuals resolve conflicts between seemingly divergent principles such as individualism and social responsibility or egalitarianism and limited government influences patterns of public opinion. Those who place greater value on individualism and limited government may be less likely to support policies such as affirmative action, while those who are more supportive of the role of government in aiding the disadvantaged and more supportive of the general principle of equality tend to have more favorable attitudes toward such policies (Sniderman and Hagen 1985; Sears 1988; Sniderman, Tetlock, and Carmines 1993; Kinder and Sanders 1996).[6] Support for the principle of egalitarianism may be limited to equal opportunity or may take the more extreme position of support for equal outcomes.[7]

Possible Effects of Educational Attainment and Social Context

Scholars differ over the impact of educational attainment on support for or opposition to affirmative action policies. The effects of educational attainment have been assessed in two ways. One approach includes a measure of educational attainment in multivariate analyses (Bobo and Kluegel 1993). An alternative is to estimate the same model for respondents grouped by level of educational attainment (Sniderman, Brody, and Tetlock 1991; Sidanius, Pratto, and Bobo 1996; Sears et al. 1997). An analysis of models of support for government action on behalf of social equality that uses the latter approach finds that different explanatory models are appropriate for various levels of educational attainment. Those with higher levels of educational attainment bring more considerations into the reasoning process (referred to as higher levels of differentiation) and display a greater degree of integration of those considerations (higher levels of integration) (Sniderman, Brody, and Tetlock 1991, ch. 4). Sniderman and his colleagues provide evidence that in reasoning about social policy alternatives, attitudes about racial equality are affect driven among those with lower levels of education (ch. 5). The conclusion that antiblack affect is an important determinant of attitudes toward policies on racial equality is supported by other research (cf. Bobo and Kluegel 1993; Sears et al. 1997). However, some other scholars argue that antiblack affect should not be the only indicator of racism and that increased sophistication through education does not erode but rather fortifies opposition to affirmative action (Sidanius, Pratto, and Bobo 1996).

A variety of contextual factors may influence patterns of public opinion. Measures of personal experiences such as contacts with members of other racial or ethnic groups, attentiveness to the media's political content, and both "chronic" and domain knowledge about politics and policies have been incorporated into examinations of the effects of political principles, self- and group interests, and attitudes toward groups in structuring policy preferences and the expressions of those preferences in public opinion.

The focus of most of the research we have reviewed here has been on explaining Whites' support for or opposition to black-targeted policies. In our research, we examine support for or opposition to a range of affirmative action opinions among four American racial or ethnic groups:

Whites, African Americans, Latinos, and Asian Americans. We examine the ability of indicators derived from the racial attitudes component of the symbolic racism, political principles, and self-versus-group interest approaches, as well as a combined model, to account for patterns of support for and opposition to a composite measure of affirmation action policies.

Data and Patterns of Attitudes toward Affirmative Action

The data for the analysis are from a national survey conducted by Chilton Research Services for the *Washington Post,* Kaiser Foundation, and Harvard University in 1995. Adults residing in the forty-eight contiguous states were interviewed by phone between July 20 and August 9, 1995, as part of an Omnibus, which is a national survey using random-digit-dialing sampling conducted weekly on a variety of topics. In the course of this interview, a race demographic (Black, White, and other) was collected. The "other" respondents originally identified in the Omnibus were then oversampled to ensure sufficiently large samples of ethnic and racial minorities.[8] The resulting sample has a total of 1,970 respondents, including 451 Blacks, 251 Latinos, and 352 Asians.

Thirty years after President Johnson's Howard University speech on affirmative action, and months after President Clinton ordered a sweeping review of federal affirmative action programs in 1995, the issue of "affirmative action" was in the consciousness of most of the respondents. Seven out of ten respondents professed to understand the term "affirmative action" very or fairly well (71 percent). About three-fifths of respondents reported paying close or very close attention to news stories and other information on race relations and affirmative action (62 percent). However, Table 11.1 shows that the survey respondents in the aggregate hold contradictory forms of opinions about affirmative action. Although more than half of the sample believe affirmative action is a good thing for the country (56 percent), an equal percentage of respondents favors congressional action limiting affirmative action. Similarly, although three-fourths of the respondents perceive discrimination against minorities as a bigger national problem than discrimination against Whites (76 percent), an equally large percentage of respondents prefers to base hiring, promotion, and college admissions strictly on merit and qualifications. Further, although seven out of ten (69 percent) respondents support enacting tougher antidiscrimination laws to govern the workplace, more than half of the sample favor getting rid of affirmative action despite the negative consequences on diversity in education and workplace of doing so. In the end, only about one out of ten (13 percent) respondents is a hard-core supporter of a race-targeted solution to redistributive policies regardless of the potential consequence of discrimination against "more qualified" Whites.

Significant variations in opinions do exist across race. Of the four groups, Blacks exhibit the strongest concern over the problem of racial discrimination and show an overwhelming support for tougher government action against discrimination. Blacks also appear to appreciate most the value of affirmative action and strongly oppose any legislative proposal that would limit existing programs. Nonetheless, a large majority of Blacks endorse merit-based rather than race-based criteria for college admission and employment. A similar but less lopsided opinion pattern exists among other nonwhite groups. Although support for the reform proposal to limit affirmative action is stronger among Asians and Latinos, none matches the degree of support among Whites. Generally, there is an opinion gap between Whites and non-Whites with Whites expressing much less concern about racial discrimination and less sympathy for race-based remedies.

Some consistency in affirmative action opinions and common patterns across racial groups can also be identified. For instance, results from cross-tabulating the five questions in Table 11.1 indicate that those who favor limiting affirmative action programs tend to be less likely to perceive affirmative action and diversity as desirable values, to consider discrimination against minorities as a bigger national problem than discrimination against Whites, and to endorse more government intervention to remove racial discrimination in the workplace. Further, similar to what Schuman and Steeh (1996) report in their examination of racial attitudes over the past fifty years, the distribution of affirmative action opinion patterns reveals a wide gap between principles and implementation among Whites and nonwhite groups. In each group, the percentage who support race-conscious policy is much lower than the percentage who support affirmative action as a good societal value, which, in turn, is lower than the percentage who recognize discrimination as a national problem.

Measures and Models

The opinion patterns we have described suggest that contemporary public opinion on the future of affirmative action may be closely related to public perception of diversity as a value, to public concern over racial discrimination as a problem, and to the public's attitudes toward other government intervention efforts. The dependent variable is measured by a five-item summed index of the five survey items in Table 11.1 (alpha reliability = .65).[9] A confirmatory factor analysis supports the inclusion of these five items in the index measuring attitudes on affirmative action.[10] Because of the continuous nature of the dependent variable, a multivariate regression procedure based on ordinary least-squares is adopted.

On the basis of the research reviewed earlier and the survey items available for analysis, we test four models in this research: racial attitudes, conflict of interest, political principle, and a combined model. Measures used in the racial attitudes model are part of the racial attitudes measures encompassed within the symbolic racism theory delineated in Sears et al. (1997). They include indicators of the denial of continuing racial discrimination (Blacks no problem), the absence of positive evaluation of nonwhite minorities (bad impact), and the perception of Blacks and other minorities as lacking in work ethic (no special help). The Cronbach's alpha (.34) is too low for creating a valid index using these three measures. Therefore, we include all three measures in subsequent analyses. (A detailed list of independent and control variables used and their coding can be found in the Appendix.)

A second model tests the explanatory power of self- and group-based interests. The self-interest measure is a four-item index composed of retrospective assessments of perceived changes in the opportunities for self and family in employment, housing, and health care and in staying together. These items share an underlying construct of concern over infringed self-interest and have a marginal inter-item alpha of .55. A number of variables can be used to gauge competitive racial group-based interest. One set is based on perceived group discrimination, while the other is based on individual experience of discrimination. As is the case with racial attitudes measures, we consider the alpha for the three measures of perceived group interest (.43) too low for further computation. Only the highest loading measure of the infringed group interest construct (perceived group discrimination) is used in the multi-

TABLE 11.1

Frequency Distribution of Affirmative Action Opinions by Race

	Whites	Blacks	Latinos	Asians	All
Base N	802	451	251	352	1856

Q72. *Generally speaking, do you think affirmative action is a good thing or a bad thing for the country, or doesn't it affect the country much?*

	Whites	Blacks	Latinos	Asians	All
A bad thing	38%	7%	16%	18%	23%
Doesn't do much	20	17	25	25	21
A good thing	43	76	59	57	56

Q2. *Should Congress limit affirmative action?*

	Whites	Blacks	Latinos	Asians	All
Yes, strongly favor	46	27	34	32	37
Not strongly favor	22	11	16	26	19
Not strongly oppose	15	9	18	14	14
No, strongly oppose	17	52	33	27	30

Q79. *Which do you see as the bigger national problem: Whites losing out to minorities in the workplace due to unfair preferences in hiring or promotion, OR minorities facing discrimination and lack of opportunity for advancement?*

	Whites	Blacks	Latinos	Asians	All
Minorities facing discrimination	60	96	84	79	76

Q42.5. *The federal government should enact tougher antidiscrimination laws to reduce racial discrimination in the workplace.*

	Whites	Blacks	Latinos	Asians	All
Agree	48	90	83	77	69

Q64. *Which of these statements comes closer to the way you feel? A. Diversity benefits our country economically and socially, so race or ethnicity should be a factor when deciding who is hired, promoted, or admitted to college. B. Hiring, promotions, and college admissions should be based strictly on merit and qualifications other than race or ethnicity. [If supporting statement A] Q67. Would you still feel that way if it meant that more qualified Whites sometimes lost out to less qualified minorities for jobs, promotions, or college admissions? [If supporting statement B] Q68. Would you still feel that way if it meant that minorities were underrepresented in some types of jobs, or that few or no minorities were hired by some companies or admitted to certain colleges?*

	Whites	Blacks	Latinos	Asians	All
Support A	13	30	23	25	21
Even if Whites lose	8	18	11	16	13
Support B	87	70	77	75	79
Even if alienating minorities	62	41	45	56	56

SOURCE: *Washington Post* Poll, July-August, September 1995 (#95-5742) released by Roper Center. Chi-square tests of racial differences for all the variables are significant at .0001 level or better.

variate analysis. The measure of personal experience of discrimination is a three-item summed index based on the respondent's and the respondent's primary group's experience with racial or ethnic discrimination (alpha = .80).

The third model tests the efficacy of political principles to explain public support for affirmative action. It consists of measures of four normative beliefs, as well as measures of political ideology and partisanship. The measure of belief in limited government is a six-item index created by summing the respondent's ranking of a list of reasons for supporting a smaller government (alpha = .93). The belief in social responsibility measure is a four-item index consisting of summed scores of public opinion items on the future of America and the perceived responsibility of society to aid low-income minorities (alpha = .60). We rely on a measure of economic individualism to gauge the traditional belief in individualism. Last but not least, a respondent is considered as subscribing to the egalitarian belief if he or she values equal opportunity more than racial integration.[11]

A number of contextual variables are included as controls in the regression analyses. These include income, education, racial makeup of the residential neighborhood, age, region (South/non-South), degree of urbanity by place of residence, and frequency of information seeking by following news stories about racial relations and affirmative action.[12] In the combined model, dummy measures of racial or ethnic identity are included, with Whites being the omitted category.

Tests of Alternative Models

We first examine public support for affirmative action with four alternative models in the multiracial sample. Table 11.2 shows that, when analyzed separately, all the indicators of racial attitudes, group-based interest, and political principles are significant predictors of opinion on affirmative action. When combined into one model, all the measures remain significant except the one gauging economic individualism. Thus, the identified racial attitudes tend to deter support for affirmative action; so does concern about infringed group interest. Having the experience of discrimination against oneself or significant others may induce support, but being concerned about individual self-interest lacks any significant impact. Holding certain normative beliefs such as support for limited government and individual egalitarianism impairs support for affirmative action, as does being Republican in partisanship and conservative in political ideology, but belief in economic individualism does not. Believing in the principle of social responsibility, on the

TABLE 11.2
OLS Models Predicting Support for Race-Based Affirmative Action

	Racial Attitude	Self- vs. Group Interest	Political Principle	All
No Special Help	−.318***			−.197***
	(.024)			(.023)
Blacks No Problem	−.111***			−.066*
	(.024)			(.022)
Bad Impact	−.108**			−.051*
	(.028)			(.026)
Self Interest		.038		.010
		(.027)		(.024)
Perceived Group Discrimination		−.135***		−.053*
		(.025)		(.022)
Experience of Discrimination		.117***		.055*
		(.033)		(.028)
Limited Government			−.010***	−.074***
			(.015)	(.015)
Social Responsibility			.454***	.323***
			(.048)	(.048)
Individualism			−.129**	−.070
			(.039)	(.039)
Egalitarianism			−.056*	−.054*
			(.021)	(.021)
Ideology			−.059***	−.051***
			(.012)	(.012)
Party ID			−.044***	−.037***
			(.008)	(.008)
Black	.339***	.468***	.304***	.247***
	(.030)	(.032)	(.030)	(.031)
Latino	.251***	.291***	.211***	.190***
	(.037)	(.040)	(.036)	(.035)
Asian	.156***	.151***	.152***	.133***
	(.032)	(.036)	(.031)	(.031)
Female	.037*	.050*	.000	.002
	(.023)	(.025)	(.022)	(.021)
Income	−.009	−.005	.004	.000
	(.005)	(.006)	(.005)	(.005)
Education	.000	.015	.011	−.001
	(.010)	(.011)	(.010)	(.009)
Age	−.015	−.006	−.017	−.014
	(.011)	(.012)	(.011)	(.011)
South	−.073*	−.092**	−.064*	−.056*
	(.024)	(.026)	(.023)	(.022)
Urbanity	−.008	.019	−.007	−.001
	(.011)	(.012)	(.010)	(.010)
Racial Makeup	.015	.003	.004	.017
	(.023)	(.025)	(.022)	(.021)
Information Seeking	.011	.027	.020	.011
	(.013)	(.014)	(.012)	(.012)
Adjusted R² (%)	32.4	21.3	37.9	42.5
N = 1275				

SOURCE: See Table 11.1.
NOTE: Entries are unstandardized ordinary least-square based regression coefficients; standard errors are in parentheses. Constant is included in each model. * $p \leq .05$, ** $p \leq .001$, *** $p \leq .0001$

other hand, can be associated with greater support for affirmative action policies and their continued implementation.

Other conditions being equal, the size of explained variance (adjusted R-square) indicates that political principles best explain support for affirmative action, followed by racial attitudes and competitive group interest. When political principles are divided into normative beliefs and political predispositions, a greater percentage of explained variance is provided by normative beliefs (34.2 percent) than by partisanship and ideology (28.8 percent).

With few exceptions, the significance of variables in single-theory models is maintained in the combined model. The exceptions include individualism, which becomes insignificant when racial attitude and interest are taken into account, and gender, which loses its predictive value after differences in political principles are controlled. The model that combines the measures from the three single-theory models performs best, explaining about 43 percent of the variation in support for affirmative action. Across models, the control variables for race and region are significant in predicting support, whereas measures of income, education, age, urbanity, neighborhood racial makeup, and information seeking are not.[13] Being a member of any of the three nonwhite groups suggests support for affirmative action. Other conditions being equal, those residing in the South are more likely to express opposition to affirmative action.

When public support for affirmative action is analyzed by racial groups, the results in Table 11.3 show that groups vary greatly in terms of the relative effects of racial attitudes, self- and group interest, and political principles. Each theoretical approach receives some support in predicting the opinions of Whites. As in the combined model described in Table 11.2, Whites' support for affirmative action can be influenced by their racial attitudes, by perceived conflict of group interest, and by political principles. Whites' support for affirmative action is not significantly affected by a perceived negative impact arising from the increase in the proportion of non-Whites in the country, by personal experience of discrimination, or by residence in the South. Among Blacks, only one indicator in each theory attains statistical significance, and the signs are not all the same as those for Whites. Black support for affirmative action can be lowered by the denial of differences in the adaptation experiences between European and non-European immigrants. Their support can be increased by perceptions of group discrimination

TABLE 11.3
OLS Models Predicting Support for Race-Based Affirmative Action by Race

	Whites	Blacks	Latinos	Asians
No Special Help	−.172***	−.220***	−.211*	−.124*
	(.036)	(.047)	(.067)	(.056)
Blacks No Problem	−.091*	−.031	.020	−.019
	(.031)	(.048)	(.065)	(.056)
Bad Impact	−.013	−.017	−.110	−.062
	(.034)	(.054)	(.080)	(.094)
Self-Interest	.003	−.009	.026	−.036
	(.036)	(.043)	(.069)	(.061)
Perceived Group	−.239***	.080*	.010	.098
Discrimination	(.033)	(.041)	(.063)	(.059)
Experience of	−.006	.091	.018	.051
Discrimination	(.048)	(.051)	(.075)	(.066)
Limited Government	−.098***	.011	−.065	−.086*
	(.022)	(.030)	(.048)	(.038)
Social Responsibility	.157*	.312*	.612**	.394**
	(.060)	(.146)	(.186)	(.117)
Individualism	−.108	−.087	.034	.005
	(.067)	(.065)	(.119)	(.087)
Egalitarianism	−.063*	−.011	−.063	−.035
	(.029)	(.040)	(.061)	(.053)
Ideology	−.062**	−.020	−.033	−.070*
	(.018)	(.021)	(.031)	(.034)
Party ID	−.038**	−.018	−.065**	−.012
	(.011)	(.020)	(.020)	(.019)
Female	.038	−.000	−.005	−.065
	(.030)	(.042)	(.070)	(.055)
Income	−.003	.002	.007	.000
	(.007)	(.010)	(.015)	(.013)
Education	−.019	.026	.014	−.028
	(.014)	(.019)	(.024)	(.026)
Age	−.018	−.010	−.003	−.003
	(.015)	(.022)	(.033)	(.027)
South	−.027	−.115*	.070	.010
	(.031)	(.042)	(.065)	(.066)
Urbanity	.017	.033	.004	.005
	(.014)	(.021)	(.030)	(.030)
Racial Makeup	−.014	−.013	.080	.045
	(.031)	(.041)	(.063)	(.062)
Information Seeking	.003	.055*	.079*	−.049
	(.019)	(.024)	(.036)	(.032)
Adjusted R² (%)	46.7	23.5	29.4	14.9
N	561	318	157	239

SOURCE AND NOTE: See Table 11.2.

and by a sense of social responsibility for aiding lower income Americans. African Americans who reside outside the South and those who score higher on the information-seeking measure also tend to express more support for affirmative action. Latinos' and Asians' opinions on affirmative action can be influenced by the same measures of racial attitudes and political principles that influence Blacks' opinions, but not by any of the interest measures or by residence in the South. Among Latinos, political partisanship and news attentiveness are additional factors that influence support. In contrast, Asian support or nonsupport is better predicted by political ideology and by beliefs about the optimal size of government. An examination of the sizes of standardized coefficients (not shown) indicates that white opinion is most influenced by group conflict, black opinion by a racial attitudes measure, and both Latino and Asian opinions by a measure of political principles—social responsibility. Across the four groups, only indicators of racial attitudes and of political principles are significant in shaping support for affirmative action, whereas the measures of self-interest and of sociodemographic characteristics, except for region, are not. The combination of the three theories is able to account for 47 percent of the variation in Whites' opinions, but only 15 percent of the variation in Asians' opinions. This wide discrepancy in the percentage of explained variance, along with the observations on the various efficacy of the three theories, implies that alternative models more sensitive to race-specific characteristics may need to be developed in future studies.

Does higher education reduce the impact of racial attitudes and increase that of ideology? Results in Table 11.4 seem to indicate no, contrary to Sniderman and Piazza's (1993) findings. The slope coefficients for the top indicator of racial attitudes remain negative in sign but increase significantly in size with college education. This is particularly true among Whites, but is also true for Blacks as well as for the four-group sample. Ideology and partisanship, in contrast, cease to be significant with increased education among Whites. A similar decrease in statistical significance occurs with increased education among the multiracial group sample. Education changes little the role of ideology and partisan identification among Blacks. However, it enhances the roles of social responsibility, urbanity, and information seeking among that group. It also enhances the roles of political principles among Whites and in the multiracial sample of respondents. In addition, it reduces the impact of perceived group discrimination among the four-group sample. Last, college education appears to boost the fitness of the complete model by significantly increasing the percentage of explained variance across the three sets of respondents.[14]

Table 11.4

OLS Models Predicting Support for Race-Based Affirmative Action by Education

	All		Whites		Blacks	
	No College	College Grads	No College	College Grads	No College	College Grads
No Special Help	−.18***	−.23***	−.12*	−.25***	−.21***	−.37**
	(.03)	(.04)	(.04)	(.06)	(.05)	(.11)
Blacks No Problem	−.04	−.09*	−.08*	−.07	.01	−.13
	(.03)	(.04)	(.04)	(.06)	(.06)	(.10)
Bad Impact	−.03	−.10	.01	−.05	.01	−.09
	(.05)	(.05)	(.04)	(.07)	(.06)	(.12)
Self-Interest	.05	−.05	.02	−.07	.01	−.03
	(.03)	(.04)	(.04)	(.07)	(.05)	(.09)
Perceived Group Discrimination	−.06*	−.05	−.24***	−.24***	.07	.06
	(.03)	(.04)	(.04)	(.06)	(.05)	(.08)
Experience of Discrimination	.05	.05	−.05	.10	.11	−.03
	(.03)	(.05)	(.06)	(.08)	(.06)	(.11)
Limited Government	−.05*	−.13***	−.07*	−.18***	−.01	.05
	(.02)	(.03)	(.03)	(.04)	(.04)	(.06)
Social Responsibility	.26***	.40***	.13	.22*	.09	.57*
	(.06)	(.08)	(.07)	(.11)	(.19)	(.24)
Individualism	−.02	−.13*	−.01	−.15*	−.06	−.16
	(.05)	(.06)	(.08)	(.05)	(.08)	(.11)
Egalitarianism	−.03	−.08*	−.01	−.15*	−.01	.00
	(.02)	(.04)	(.03)	(.05)	(.05)	(.08)
Ideology	−.04**	−.06*	−.08**	−.03	−.04	.07
	(.01)	(.02)	(.02)	(.04)	(.02)	(.04)
Party ID	−.03**	−.04*	−.04**	−.03	−.01	−.04
	(.01)	(.01)	(.01)	(.02)	(.03)	(.03)
Black	.27***	.23***				
	(.04)	(.06)				
Latino	.18***	.27***				
	(.04)	(.07)				
Asian	.15**	.13*				
	(.04)	(.05)				
Female	−.02	.02	.01	.05	.01	−.05
	(.03)	(.04)	(.04)	(.06)	(.05)	(.08)
Income	−.00	.00	−.01	.00	.00	.03
	(.01)	(.01)	(.01)	(.01)	(.01)	(.02)
Age	−.01	−.02	−.02	−.02	.00	−.06
	(.01)	(.02)	(.02)	(.03)	(.03)	(.04)
South	−.05	−.07	−.01	−.06	−.13*	−.07
	(.03)	(.04)	(.04)	(.06)	(.05)	(.08)
Urbanity	.00	−.01	.01	.03	−.01	−.16**
	(.01)	(.02)	(.02)	(.03)	(.02)	(.05)
Racial Makeup	.01	.02	.02	−.03	−.08	.14
	(.02)	(.04)	(.04)	(.06)	(.05)	(.08)
Information Seeking	.01	.02	.02	−.02	.05	.16*
	(.01)	(.02)	(.02)	(.04)	(.03)	(.05)
Adjusted R² (%)	39.1	48.3	40.9	57.1	18.4	35.4
N	781	494	358	203	220	98

NOTE: See Table 11.2

Conclusions

Despite recent developments that threaten to eliminate or overhaul existing affirmative action programs, Americans of all racial origins are still more concerned about minorities facing discrimination than about reverse discrimination against Whites. However, significant differences exist between Whites and non-Whites on these issues. When we examine the multiracial sample, the evidence suggests that being Black, Latino, or Asian is associated with stronger support for affirmative action. The multiple regression results also support the independent roles of racial attitudes, group interest, and political principles in structuring supportive attitudes. However, the analysis by race indicates that the efficacy of these explanations is not the same for each group. The two exceptions are the symbolic racism measure of "no special help" and the sense of social responsibility, which are statistically and substantively significant in explaining support for affirmative action across the four races (see Tables 11.2 and 11.3).

Political principles contribute significantly to explaining patterns of support for affirmative action among the total sample both when modeled separately in a political principles model and when studied in a model that combines all explanatory variables. However, when the analysis is run by race, the measures of political principles that contribute significantly to explaining supportive opinion vary substantially in their effects for each of the four groups. Individualism is significant in none of the groups. The belief in limited government and ideology are useful predictors only for Whites and for Asians. Partisan identification is significant only among Whites and Latinos. And egalitarianism is useful only to predict Whites' opinions.

The self- and group interest variables also differ significantly in their effects within the multiracial sample and for each specific racial group. In the multiracial sample, those who have personal or family experience of discrimination are more likely to support the federal remedy. In contrast, those who score higher on the group conflict measure are less likely to support affirmative action that targets certain races. If we turn to the separate analyses for each racial group, only among Blacks and Whites is perceived group discrimination significant. Furthermore, the personal experience of discrimination is not significant for any of the four groups. One explanation for this lack of significance might be that the within-group experience of discrimination is so similar that there is insufficient variation in the independent variable within each group, but an examination of the variable's distribution within each group leads us to reject that hypothesis. Individuals' personal experience of discrimination, like self-interest and economic individualism, appears to play a relatively insignificant role in shaping public policy opinions on group-based policies such as affirmative action.

Our findings on the effect of higher education, though different from those obtained in some previous studies, are in line with other recent research results (e.g., Sidanius, Pratto, and Bobo 1996; Sears et al. 1997). They imply that the affirmative action opinions of better-educated Whites and Blacks are shaped more by racial attitudes and normative beliefs than by other long-standing political values. We do note that living in a particular residential context and following the news are uniquely important for black college graduates.

The multiracial analysis suggests that Whites and non-Whites differ greatly in their opinions on affirmative action. The analysis by racial group membership leads to the conclusion that different factors influence support for affirmative action across races. The combined model best explains white support and is least successful in explaining Asian American support. Although we find that both white and nonwhite support for affirmative action can be influenced by racial attitudes and social responsibility, we also find that white opinion is most influenced by perceived group conflict of interest, black opinion by symbolic racial attitudes, and both Latino and Asian opinions by certain political principles. More attention should be devoted to examining patterns of multiracial differences in public opinion and the causes of those differences. Future studies may also want to develop a theoretical approach that can better account for patterns of attitudes toward race-related government policies among both white and nonwhite groups.

Appendix: Question Wording and Coding Schemes of Independent and Control Variables

Racial Attitudes

1. *No Special Help.* Q58. The Irish, Italians and many other groups overcame prejudice and worked their way up. African Americans

and other minorities should do the same without any special help from government. (agree)

2. *Blacks No Problem.* Q20.5. With the exception of a small number of African Americans who have severe economic and social problems, most African Americans have the same standard of living and opportunities as Whites. (agree).

3. *Bad Impact.* Q16. If the number of minorities increases a lot/a little, do you think that would be a good thing or a bad thing for the country, or wouldn't it make much difference? (1 = bad thing, 0 = otherwise).

Self- versus Group Interest

A. *Self-Interest.* Q6,Q7,Q8. During the past ten years, has it become easier or harder for [people/families] like you to [get good jobs/find decent, affordable housing/stay together], or hasn't that changed? (3 = harder, 2 = no change, 1 = easier) Q9. During the past ten years, has health care for families like yours gotten better, worse, or stayed about the same? (3 = worse, 2 = no change, 1 = better).

B. *Group Interest*

Perceived Group Discrimination. Q47. Thinking about [African Americans/Hispanics Americans/Asian Americans], do you think discrimination against them because of their racial or ethnic background has increased, decreased, or stayed about the same during the past ten years? (Among each racial group, 1 = increased, 0 = otherwise; among Whites, 1 = seeing Whites losing out to minorities as the bigger national problem in Q79, 0 = otherwise).[15]

Racism. Q44. How big a problem is racism in our society today? (4 = a big problem, 3 = somewhat of a problem, 2 = a small problem, 1 = not a problem at all)

Racial Tension (Raceten). Q53. During the last ten years, do you think tensions between racial and ethnic groups in this country have increased, decreased, or stayed the same? (3 = increased, 2 = stay the same, 1 = decreased)

C. *Experience of Discrimination.* Q49. During the last ten years, have/has [you/a family member/a close friend] experienced discrimination because of your/their racial or ethnic background, or not? (1 = yes, 0 = otherwise).

Political Principles

1. *Limited Government.* Q33. Reasons some people have given for why they would rather have the federal government cost less in taxes and provide fewer services: A. The federal government is too big and is doing too much already. B. The federal government is inefficient and does not do a good job providing services. C. I would rather have lower taxes. D. We need to balance the budget. E. The federal government is spending too much on low-income minorities. F. The services provided by the federal government do not help people like me. (2 = major reason, 1 = minor reason)
2. *Social Responsibility.* Q60. R's opinion on statements regarding the future of America and the role of low-income minorities in it: A. We need to invest in helping low-income people become better prepared for the workforce because America needs as many well-trained people as possible to be competitive and strong economically. (agree) C. We should not have programs aimed at helping low-income minorities because they are not effective. (disagree) D. We should invest in the education and health of low-income minority children to make sure that they have a chance for a good future and a higher standard of living. (agree) E. We need to help low-income minorities because it is the right thing to do. (agree)
3. *Individualism.* Q60B. Low-income minorities need to take more individual responsibility and become less dependent on government. (agree)
4. *Egalitarianism.* Q20. Which statement comes closer to the way you feel? A. It's important that people of different races and ethnic groups live, go to school, and work more closely with each other. B. It's not important that people of different races and ethnic groups live, go to school, and work more closely with each other—as long as everyone is treated fairly and has the same opportunities in life. (2 = equal opportunity is more important, 1 = racial integration is more important)
5. *Ideology.* (5 = very conservative, 4 = conservative, 3 = moderate, 2 = liberal, 1 = very liberal)

6. *Party identification.* (5 = Republican, 4 = leaning Republican, 3 = independent, 2 = leaning Democrat, 1 = Democrat)

Sociodemographic Variables

Income. Household income for 1994. (9 = more than $75k, 8 = $50k to $74,999, 7 = $40k to $49,999, 6 = $30k to $39,999, 5 = $25k to $29,999, 4 = $20k to $24,999, 3 = $12k to $19,999, 2 = $8k to $11,999, 1 = less than $8k)

Education. Last grade of school completed. (6 = Post graduate, 5 = graduated college, 4 = some college, 3 = graduated high school or some trade school, 2 = some high school, 1 = 8th grade or less)

Age. (4 = over 60, 3 = 45 to 60, 2 = 31 to 44, 1 = 18 to 30)

South. The fourteen states of Alabama, Arkansas, Florida, Georgia, Kentucky, Louisiana, Mississippi, North Carolina, Oklahoma, South Carolina, Tennessee, Texas, Virginia, and West Virginia.

Urbanity. R's self-described area of residence. (1 = rural area, 2 = small town, 3 = suburb of a large city, 4 = large city)

Racial Makeup. R's self-described neighborhood racial makeup. (1 = segregated, 0 = integrated)

Information Seeking. Q92. R's closeness of following news stories and other information about racial relations and affirmative action. (4 = very closely, 3 = fairly closely, 2 = not too closely, 1 = not at all closely)

NOTES

1. The issue of deciding program beneficiaries is a complex one. For some issue areas such as higher education admissions and academic scholarships, certain ethnic groups such as Chinese and Asian Indian Americans may perceive themselves as being discriminated against by the application of affirmative action policies. For the purpose of this study and to simplify the discussion, we focus our analysis on broad, racialized groupings and do not differentiate among issue areas. Readers should bear in mind that these umbrella terms may disguise great variations in ethnic origin, ideology, socioeconomic status, and specific program impacts.

2. A variant is labeled modern racism. See Alvarez and Brehm (1997). Although we invoke these different labels of racial attitudes, we don't intend, nor are we prepared, to engage ourselves in the debate over whether there is a fun-

damental transformation of American racial attitudes in the South or elsewhere (cf. Kuklinski, Cobb, and Gilens 1997; Sears et al. 1997). In fact, a study of Dutch students reveals that separate forms of racism may be treated as steps on a cumulative attitude dimension (Kleinpenning and Hagendoorn 1993).

3. The dominant theoretical approach prior to the development of the symbolic racism model, blatant racism, cannot be tested, since no measures of blatant racism were included in the data set. That alternative theoretical approach suggests that blatant racial prejudice among some Whites still structures their attitudes toward social problems and policy areas such as crime, social welfare, and affirmative action (Kuklinski et al. 1997; Peffley, Hurwitz, and Sniderman 1997).

4. In a more recent discussion, Sears et al. (1997) state that symbolic racism can be viewed in three ways. First, they suggest, its symbolic nature derives from its statement in terms that are abstract and symbolic, reflecting prescriptive views about appropriate moral codes for society. Second, they argue, the cognitive content of symbolic racism applies to Blacks as a group and to individuals. Third, the origins of symbolic racism are assumed to be a combination of antiblack affect and the perception that Blacks violate traditional American values such as the work ethic, respect for authority, and traditional morality.

5. Group interest may be structured by a perceived social construction differential between an individual's identity group and other groups (Link and Oldendick 1996). One implication is that the larger the differential, the more likely policies that aid the other group will be opposed.

6. The definition, application, and measurement of equality are far from coherent or uncontroversial. Kinder and Sanders (1996) caution that arguments and statements about equality often "betray views about politics and political actors" (p. 327). Depending on how the issue is framed, equality may facilitate affirmative action because of its potential benefits to bring true equality of opportunity to life, or it may evoke opposition because of the perceived violation of equal opportunity for individuals (p. 277).

7. However, Jackman (1996) asserts that Whites' endorsement of equality may be limited and may not extend to support for racial equality. She argues that the wording of some public opinion survey items may lead individuals to confuse support for individual rights with support for racial equality.

8. The RDD national sample and the "other" augment failed to locate enough cooperative Asian females to inspect that group separately. An additional 100 Asian females were surveyed on September 18–28, 1995, using a list source of Asian females. We are aware that this may introduce some bias to the representativeness of the survey. However, we don't know of any other multigroup national survey that has come close to including a sufficient number of respondents for each nonwhite group to permit separate analyses of each group of that has come up with a reasonable way to overcome the multitude of difficulties that arise

in surveying opinions across the four major racial/ethnic groups. A preliminary examination of the distribution within our sample of sociodemographic characteristics by race shows general compatibility to the results of the 1990 Census (U.S. Bureau of the Census 1993).

9. We rely on Cronbach's alpha technique throughout to estimate reliability. According to Bollen (1989, pp. 202–222), although Cronbach's alpha coefficient makes relatively few assumptions, it may underestimate the reliability of congeneric measures.

10. The factor scores for the five questions that appear in Table 11.1 are .732, .613, .679, .660, and .547.

11. The measure may be a more stringent test of public belief about equality per se than is found in previous studies, which often equate egalitarianism with racial integration. We would prefer to have separate questions and not to have to assume the existence of a direct conflict between support for equality for each racial or ethnic group and support for equal opportunity for each individual. However, this assumption regarding the role of competing conceptions of equality in forming affirmative action opinions may be appropriate and finds strong support in recent research involving survey-based experiments (e.g., Sniderman, Tetlock, and Carmines 1993; Sniderman and Carmines 1997).

12. A number of analyses were completed with income removed. In every instance, education continues to be insignificant.

13. In analyses with race and gender interactions, none of the interactive terms reached a .05 level of significance. This lack of significance of gender across racial groups may reflect the prevalence of race in the debate on the future of affirmative action.

14. The analyses of opinions by educational category for Latinos and Asians are not reported because of the limited number of cases in certain categories; however, preliminary results indicate that college education has a similar effect within each of these groups.

15. Because Q47 does not refer to discrimination against Whites, we are forced to rely on two separate questions to gauge the extent of perceived discrimination against group interest for each of the four groups.

REFERENCES

Alvarez, R. Michael, and John Brehm. 1997. "Are Americans Ambivalent towards Racial Policies?" *American Journal of Political Science* 41: 345–374.

Bobo, Lawrence. 1988. "Group Conflict, Prejudice, and the Paradox of Contemporary Racial Attitudes," in *Eliminating Racism: Profiles in Controversy,* ed. Phyllis Katz and Dalmas Taylor. New York: Plenum.

Bobo, Lawrence, and V. L. Hutchings. 1996. "Perceptions of Racial Group

Competition: Extending Blumer's Theory of Group Position to a Multi-Racial Social Context." *American Sociological Review* 61: 951–973.

Bobo, Lawrence, and James R. Kluegel. 1993. "Opposition to Race-Targeting: Self-Interest, Stratification Ideology, or Racial Attitudes?" *American Sociological Review* 58: 443–464.

Bollen, Kenneth A. 1989. *Structural Equations with Latent Variables.* New York: Wiley.

Davis, Darren. 1996. "White Americans' Opposition to Racial Policies: Where Are the Political Expectations?" *Social Science Quarterly* 77: 746–749.

Gilens, Martin. 1995. "Racial Attitudes and Opposition to Welfare." *Journal of Politics* 57: 994–1014.

———. 1996. "'Race Coding' and White Opposition to Welfare." *American Political Science Review* 90: 593–604.

Jacoby, William G. 1994. "Public Attitudes toward Government Spending." *American Journal of Political Science* 38: 336–361.

Jackman, Mary R. 1996. "Individualism, Self-Interest, and White Racism." *Social Science Quarterly* 77: 760–767.

Kinder, Donald R. 1986. "The Continuing American Dilemma: White Resistance to Racial Change Forty Years after Myrdal." *Journal of Social Issues* 42(3): 151–171.

Kinder, Donald R., and Tali Mendelberg. 1995. "Cracks in American Apartheid: The Political Impact of Prejudice among Desegregated Whites." *Journal of Politics* 57: 402–424.

Kinder, Donald R., and Lynn Sanders. 1996. *Divided by Color.* Chicago: University of Chicago Press.

Kinder, Donald R., and David O. Sears. 1981. "Prejudice and Politics: Symbolic Racism versus Racial Threats to the Good Life." *Journal of Personality and Social Psychology* 40: 414–431.

Kleinpenning, Gerard, and Louk Hagendoorn. 1993. "Forms of Racism and the Cumulative Dimension of Ethnic Attitudes." *Social Psychology Quarterly* 56: 21–36.

Kuklinski, James H., Michael D. Cobb, and Martin Gilens. 1997. "Racial Attitudes and the New South." *Journal of Politics* 59: 323–349.

Kuklinski, James H., Paul M. Sniderman, Kathleen Knight, Thomas Piazza, Philip E. Tetlock, Gordon R. Lawrence, and Barbara Mellers. 1997. "Racial Prejudice and Attitudes toward Affirmative Action." *American Journal of Political Science* 41: 402–419.

Link, Michael W., and Robert W. Oldendick. 1996. "Social Construction and White Attitudes toward Equal Opportunity and Multiculturalism." *Journal of Politics* 58: 149–158.

Nelson, Thomas F., and Donald R. Kinder. 1996. "Issue Frames and Group-Centrism in American Public Opinion." *Journal of Politics* 58: 1055–1078.

Peffley, Mark, John Hurwitz, and Paul M. Sniderman. 1997. "Racial Stereotypes and Whites' Political Views of Blacks in the Context of Welfare and Crime." *American Journal of Political Science* 41: 30–60.

Schuman, Howard, and Charlotte Steeh. 1996. "The Complexity of Racial Attitudes in America," in *Origins and Destinies: Immigration, Race, and Ethnicity in America,* ed. Silvia Pedraza and Ruben Rumbaut. Belmont, Calif.: Wadsworth.

Sears, David O. 1988. "Symbolic Racism," in *Eliminating Racism: Profiles in Controversy,* ed. Phyllis A. Katz and Dalmas A. Taylor. New York: Plenum Press.

Sears, David O., C. P. Hensler, and L. K. Speer. 1979. "Whites' Opposition to 'Busing': Self-Interest or Symbolic Politics?" *American Political Science Review* 73: 369–384.

Sears, David O., and Tom Jessor. 1996. "Whites' Racial Policy Attitudes: The Role of White Racism." *Social Science Quarterly* 77: 751–759.

Sears, David O., Colette Van Laar, Mary Carrillo, and Rick Kosterman. 1997. "Is It Really Racism? The Origins of White Americans' Opposition to Race-Targeted Policies." *Public Opinion Quarterly* 61: 16–53.

Sidanius, Jim, Felicia Pratto, and Lawrence Bobo. 1996. Racism, Conservatism, Affirmative Action, and Intellectual Sophistication: A Matter of Principled Conservatism or Group Dominance? *Journal of Personality and Social Psychology* 70: 476–490.

Sniderman, Paul M., Richard A. Brody, and Philip E. Tetlock. 1991. *Reasoning and Choice Explorations in Political Psychology.* Cambridge: Cambridge University Press.

Sniderman, Paul M., and Edward G. Carmines. 1997. *Reaching Beyond Race.* Cambridge, Mass.: Harvard University Press.

Sniderman, Paul M., Edward G. Carmines, Geoffrey C. Layman, and Michael Carter. 1996. "Beyond Race: Social Justice as a Race Neutral Idea." *American Journal of Political Science* 40: 33–55.

Sniderman, Paul M., and Michael Gary Hagen. 1985. *Race and Inequality.* Chatham, N.J.: Chatham House.

Sniderman, Paul M., and Thomas Piazza. 1993. *The Scar of Race.* Cambridge, Mass.: Harvard University Press.

Sniderman, Paul M., and Philip E. Tetlock. 1986a. "Symbolic Racism: Problems of Motive Attribution in Political Analysis." *Journal of Social Issues* 42(2): 129–150.

———. 1986b. "Reflections on American Racism." *Journal of Social Issues* 42(2): 173–187.

Sniderman, Paul M., Philip E. Tetlock, and Edward G. Carmines. eds. 1993. *Prejudice, Politics, and the American Dilemma.* Stanford: Stanford University Press.

Stoker, Laura. 1996. "Understanding Differences in Whites' Opinions across Racial Policies." *Social Science Quarterly* 77: 768–777.

Tajfel, H., and J. C. Turner. 1986. "The Social Identity Theory of Intergroup Behavior," in *Psychology of Intergroup Relations,* ed. S. Worchel and W. G. Austin, 2d ed. Chicago: Nelson-Hall.

Tuch, Steven A., and Michael Hughes. 1996a. "Whites' Opposition to Race-Targeted Policies: One Cause or Many?" *Social Science Quarterly* 77: 778–788.

———. 1996b. "Whites' Racial Policy Attitudes." *Social Science Quarterly* 77: 723–745.

U.S. Bureau of the Census. 1993. *1990 Census of Population: Social and Economic Characteristics.* Washington, D.C.: U.S. Government Printing Office.

Part IV

Race Consciousness and Gender

Chapter 12

Expressions of Racial Consciousness in the African American Community
Data from the Million Man March

Joseph McCormick 2d and Sekou Franklin

Marches and demonstrations are forms of political action generally associated with marginalized segments of the population, groups that do not have the resources within the normal political channels and institutions to demand change and redress. There was thus a certain irony to the timing of the Million Man March in Washington, D.C., in October 1995. Two years earlier, the largest number of elected black representatives in the country's history had been sworn in as members of Congress. And black men, in greater numbers than ever before, were present in prominent political offices and state legislatures and in the offices of corporate America. Compared to the climate a quarter century earlier, when Dr. Martin Luther King Jr. led the March on Washington, in 1963, the incorporation of Blacks into the political and economic mainstream had improved dramatically.

What, then, was, and is, the utility of such a march, and marches like it? According to Joseph McCormick 2d and Sekou Franklin, the Million Man March was not aimed merely at getting the attention of political officials; it was also reassertion of racial consciousness. Using survey data gathered on the day of the March, the authors offer a detailed understanding of the political orientation and policy disposition of participants in general. The authors discuss the findings of the survey as well as the implications of racial consciousness in multiracial America.

Introduction

In September 1998 the President's Initiative on Race issued its final report.[1] This advisory panel had been authorized fifteen months earlier, in June 1997, by President Clinton when he issued Executive Order 13050. The panel was created by the President to advise him "on how to build one America for the twenty-first century." More specifically, it was charged "with examining race, racism, and the potential for racial reconciliation in America using a process of study, constructive dialogue, and action."

One of the themes in the report focused on what was called "the changing face of America." The report noted that the "discussion of race in this country is no longer a discussion between and about blacks and whites. Increasingly," the report went on to say, "conversations about race must include all Americans, including, but not limited to, Hispanics, American Indians and Alaskan Natives, and Asian Pacific Americans" (Advisory Board to the President's Initiative on Race, 1998: 3). With regard to the changing racial and ethnic composition that is envisioned to occur over the course of the next five decades, the Advisory Board noted that:

> by the year 2050, the population of the United States will be approximately 53 percent white, 25 percent Hispanic, 14 percent black, 8 percent Asian Pacific American, and 1 percent American Indian and Alaska Native. This represents a significant shift from our current demographics of 73 percent white, 12 percent black, 11 percent Hispanic, 4 percent Asian Pacific American, and 1 percent Indian and Alaska Native. (p. 3)

The demographic reality varies significantly from Miami, Florida (where Cuban Americans are now dominant but where Haitian Americans have become organized politically), to Washington, D.C. (where the fastest-growing ethnic group is immigrants from Central America), to Los Angeles, California (statewide, the Mexican American population is already three and one-half times the size of the African American population; U.S. Bureau of the Census, 1998). As these data suggest, America of the twenty-first century will clearly be a very different place from what it is now.

These demographic changes are likely to have an impact on two traditional streams of black politics: inclusionary politics and noninclusionary or nationalist politics.[2] In this chapter, we examine these two streams of political ideology and the behaviors that attend them in the context of the historic Million Man March. The Million Man March, a mass-based expression of racial solidarity held in Washington, D.C., in October 1995, was the largest gathering of African Americans[3] that had ever come together anywhere in the United States.[4] This event provides students of public opinion research with a unique opportunity to examine the positions held by African American men on a range of race-specific issues and to gauge the levels of racial consciousness among those who attended this event. As we shall see, there is reason to believe that racial consciousness within the African American community will remain high despite the demographic changes that are now occurring in the larger society. Notwithstanding the emerging multiracialism of America, and perhaps in part because of it, expressions of racial consciousness among African Americans will continue well into the early part of the twenty-first century.

In order to gain a better understanding of these two traditions in black politics and their relationship to the demographic changes we have described, we answer two questions in this chapter: (1) How did marchers' reasons for attending the Million Man March differ by self-selected ideology (nationalist versus nonnationalist)?, and (2) given the high levels of racial consciousness exhibited by the marchers, how did their positions on selected strategies for addressing the multifaceted black predicament in America differ by self-selected ideology (i.e., nationalists versus nonnationalists)?

Before answering our research questions, we think it appropriate to situate our analysis in the context of what we call the "inclusionary dilemma." Such a discussion will clarify the concept of racial consciousness and the two traditional streams of African American politics: inclusion and noninclusion (or black nationalism). We will follow this discussion with a description of our data set, the statistical models that we used to answer our research questions, and a discussion of the findings that emerged from our statistical analyses. We end this chapter with a discussion of the likely impact of demographic change on these two traditional streams of black politics.

Racial Consciousness and the Inclusionary Dilemma

Bracey, Meier, and Rudwick (1970) offer one of the more useful discussions of what can be seen as points along a continuum of racial consciousness, with *racial solidarity* at one end and *black nationalism* at the other. They observe:

> The simplest expression of racial feeling that can be called a form of black nationalism is *racial solidarity*. It generally has no ideological or programmatic implications beyond the desire that black people organize themselves on the basis of their common color and oppressed condition to move in some way to alleviate their condition. The concept racial solidarity is essential to all forms of black nationalism. (xxvi)

Racial consciousness in its most fundamental sense refers to how a race of people sees itself vis-à-vis other races.[5] The notion of racial consciousness allows a group of people to position itself in a stream of historical events and to locate itself in terms of a place of origin. As a socially derived construct, racial consciousness among a group of people who share certain physical characteristics and a common history can be said to be most pervasive when that group qua racial group sees itself threatened by forces outside the racial group (see Brown, 1931; Verba and Nie, 1972; Shingles, 1981; Miller et al., 1981; Allen, Dawson, and Brown, 1989; Morris, 1992; Durant and Sparrow, 1997; and Thornton, Tran, and Taylor, 1997).

Much of the historical and contemporary experience of African Americans in America points to efforts to gain access to an opportunity structure free of racial impediments. In effect, much of the history of African Americans has involved various efforts to be included within the larger opportunity structure (Franklin and Moss, 1988; Barker, Jones, and Tate, 1999). On the other hand, there have been numerous instances when the inclusionary drive has come under attack, principally from forces outside the African American community, whether in the form of Ku Klux Klan terrorism (as was seen during the era of Reconstruction; Foner, 1990; Rable, 1984), repressive race-specific public policies and practices regarding housing, schools, and employment (which was the case until 1964; see Graham, 1990), or more recent, racially conservative court decisions, such as *City of Richmond, Va. v. J. A. Croson Co., Shaw v. Reno,* or *Miller v. Johnson,* and *Adarand Constructors, Inc. v. Pena,* in the late 1980s and the mid-1990s. For much of their existence in the United States, African Americans have organized themselves to withdraw from these sources of racial animus and/or to create and reinforce those institutions that they controlled and to which they could turn for economic, political, and social opportunities. *Black nationalism* is the term that has been typically used to describe one set of responses by African Americans to sources of racial animus external to the African American community.

As African Americans have attempted to take advantage of economic, political, and social opportunity, both as individuals and as a group, and to be included within the larger opportunity structure of American society, they have encountered racial *and* economic opposition (Lewinson, 1932; Cox, 1948, Wilson, 1980). This has given rise to what we call the "inclusionary dilemma." Those who have chosen to take the inclusionary route find themselves in a dilemma (hence the term) because, as they attempt to make their way through the opportunity structure in America, an opportunity structure legally free of racial impediments, they not only encounter racially hostile institutional barriers, both in the private sector (racial discrimination at Denny's and Texaco) and in the public sector (the conservative Supreme Court decisions that we have cited) but also confront far more vicious acts at the individual level (e.g., the heinous murder of James Byrd Jr. in Jasper, Texas, and the roadside murder of Ennis Cosby in Los Angeles, California, both in the late 1990s, two high-profile examples that have been covered by the media). These acts of institutional and individual racism tend to reinforce the position of the black separatists who believe that, fundamentally, there is little chance of a rapprochement between Blacks and Whites in America, leaving African Americans with little choice but to pursue some form of self-imposed racial autonomy or territorial, tactical, or value withdrawal (Holden, 1973).

By November 1994, eleven months before the Million Man March, the fiscal and social conservatism that had gained momentum during the Reagan-Bush years achieved another major electoral victory: In the mid-term elections, Republicans captured the majority of the seats in the U.S. Senate, the U.S. House of Representatives (thus controlling that chamber of Congress for the first time in forty years), and in seventeen of the fifty state legislatures (see Bositis, 1995: 1). Upon taking office in January 1995, this Republican majority in the 104th Congress constructed a collection of anti–"big-government" legislative proposals, dubbed the Contract with America,[6] and severely crippled or eliminated scores of revenue transfer programs enacted between the Roosevelt years (1933–1945) and the first Nixon administration (1969–1973). Here again, we place major emphasis on the nature of the larger political context. As the first session

of the 104th Congress came to an end, the *Washington Post* columnist
David Broder observed:

> Whatever happens in the final weeks of this session, it is now a certainty
> that the 104th Congress will go in to the history books as one of the most
> significant in the last half-century. It marks as fundamental a rightward
> turn in domestic policy as the Great Society of the 89th Congress [domi-
> nated by the Democratic Party] of 1965–66 did a turn to the left.(1995: A9)

This conservative legislative agenda was complemented by conservative
decisions handed down by the U.S. Supreme Court. The appointment
of conservative jurists to the Court during the Reagan and Bush administrations contributed mightily to a string of judicial decisions that had
chilling effects on affirmative action in minority contracting (*City of
Richmond, Va., 1989 v. J. A. Croson Co.* and *Adarand Constructors,
Inc. v. Pena*, in June 1995) and in the maintenance of majority minority
congressional districts that had been made possible by the Voting
Rights Act of 1965, as amended (*Shaw v. Reno*, in 1993, and *Miller v.
Johnson*, in June 1995).

It was in this political context that many African American men responded to Minister Louis Farrakhan's call for the Million Man
March, which he referred to as "A Holy Day of Atonement and Reconciliation."[7] One month after the November 1994 mid-term elections,
Farrakhan called for the Million Man March in the *Final Call*, the
newspaper of the Nation of Islam. In an article dated December 14,
1994 (Farrakhan, 1994), Farrakhan claimed that it had been the Hon-
orable Elijah Muhammed, the founder of the Nation of Islam, who had
inspired the Million Man March and who had suggested such a march
after the 1963 March on Washington. With this background in mind,
we now describe the data set on which the remainder of the analysis in
this chapter rests.

Data and Methodology

The data from the Million Man March examined in this chapter were
collected on October 16, 1995, by a team from Howard University that
included members of the political science faculty, graduate students,
undergraduate students, and private researchers.[8] Our interviewers ad-
ministered a thirty-seven-item instrument whose questions allowed for

dichotomous, continuous, and Likert-scale type responses. Topically, our survey instrument covered questions on the reasons the participants attended the March, race relations, strategies for black empowerment, electoral politics, assessment of black leadership and selected black organizations, and speculations about the future of the country. A standard array of demographic questions (focused on age, education, household income, religious preference, occupation, income, and marital status) was also in included. While approximately 1,200 actual interviews of randomly selected persons were conducted on the day of the March, the database on which this chapter is based consists of 1,070 completed interviews.

To answer our first research question, we employed cross-tabular analysis to determine whether there were any differences between those who called themselves "nationalists" and those who did not use this label in terms of the reasons that were selected for attending the March. We also used ordinary least squares regression to further examine the relationship between three specific reasons that were given for attending the March on the one hand and a set of relevant independent variables on the other.

We conducted statistical analysis at two levels to answer the second research question. First, we ran a frequency distribution to determine how the marchers endorsed various strategic options. To examine the possible validity of statistically significant relationships between these strategic options and the ideological positions of the marchers, we constructed two models, using ordinary least squares regression. One of these models is built around a set of options that the avowed nationalist would be most likely to select (we call this the noninclusionary model). The other model consists of a set of options that the literature suggests would be most likely to be associated with those who do not claim to be nationalists (the inclusionary model). The fundamental theoretical difference between these two models has to do with the type of strategies that each entails. Our analysis of the data not only allows us to gauge the level of racial consciousness among those who attended the Million Man March (hereafter MMM) but also permits us to develop an empirical sense of how the strategic positions of nationalists and nonnationalists differ regarding the best way to resolve the multifaceted black predicament. Before turning to the research questions, however, we take a look at a demographic profile of those who attended the MMM.

Who Attended the March?

The data indicate (see Table 12.1) that men who attended the MMM were older (mean age: 34) and better educated (almost 23 percent reported having completed four years of college) than African American men generally.[9] The respondents in the MMM sample also reported extraordinarily high household incomes (est. median, $43,000, compared to $19,333 for all black households nationally; see Bennett, 1995). While not presented in Table 12.1, the data suggest that almost 17 percent of those surveyed indicated that they held blue-collar unskilled jobs (e.g., security guard or construction worker); almost 40 percent said that they held blue-collar skilled jobs (e.g., fireman, policeman, or production foreman); about 15 percent held white-collar nonprofessional jobs (salesperson, office worker, or government employee), and approximately 29 percent said that they held white-collar professional

TABLE 12.1

Selected Demographic Characteristics of Participants in the Million Man March Compared with U.S. Census Data

	MMM Sample	U.S. Census Data for African American Men
Age		
18–29	4.3%	NA
30–44	43.2	23.6
+45	22.5	20.9
Median	34.0	26.4
Education		
Less Than High School	3.7%	28.2%
Completed High School	19.1	36.9
Some College or Technical School	38.3	22.1
Complete 4 years of Collage	22.7	12.8
Some Graduate School	6.1	NA
Income		
Under $15K	7.4%	50.6%
$15–24,999	11.7	21.8
$25–49,999	36.7	22.3
$50k+	41.1	5.3
Refused	3.1	NA
Median	$42,499 (est.)	$19,333
Employment Status		
Employed Full/Part-Time	87.6%	86.1%
Unemployed	10.3	14.0

SOURCES: *Final Results: Million Man March Poll* (Wellington Group and Howard University Political Science Faculty and Students), October 16, 1995, selected tables; see Bennett (1995), selected tables, for census data.

TABLE 12.2
Self-Identified Ideology of the Marchers

Ideology	Frequency
Liberal	38.4% (326)
Moderate	26.8% (228)
Conservative	15.9% (135)
Socialist	5.3% (45)
Nationalist	10.8% (116)

SOURCE: HU-Wellington MMM Survey, October 25, 1995.
The numbers in parentheses are the absolute frequencies.

jobs (e.g., teacher, doctor, attorney, or consultant). Compared to the national averages for African American men, the men who attended the MMM disproportionately held managerial and professional jobs.[10] The socioeconomic diversity seen in this sample suggests a widespread interest in this event among African American men that crosses class lines. However, the disproportionate number of older, better educated, and comparatively well-off African American men with white-collar jobs leads us to speculate that (1) members of the black middle class were better able to bear the costs of attending this event (October 16 fell on a Monday, not on a weekend, which may have been less of a constraint for members of the managerial and professional class), and (2) those who were less well off may not have been as able to attend the March and therefore may be underrepresented in our sample.

The Findings

How did the reasons for attending the March differ by self-selected ideology (i.e., nationalist vs. nonnationalist)? In order to effectively answer this question, we must first look at how those who attended the March classified themselves ideologically. Marchers were asked this question: "Thinking about your basic position on most issues, would you say you are more of a liberal, moderate, conservative, socialist, nationalist, or something else?" As Table 12.2 points out, 10.8 percent of the marchers identified themselves as nationalists. The remaining respondents identified themselves as liberals (38.4 percent), moderates (26.8 percent), conservatives (15.9 percent), and socialists (5.3 percent).

With these data in mind, we examined the reasons given by our respondents for attending the March and classified them by ideology.[11]

TABLE 12.3
Reasons for Attending the March by Self-Declared Ideology
(Percentage of Respondents Who Said "Very Important")

	CHRISMIN	BCON	BLKUNITY	ATONE&RECONCIL
Nationalists	39.7%	87.8%	90.5%	85.3%
Nonnationalists	36.3	74.5	85.5	76.0
	p < .475	p < .002	p < .139	p < .024

	SELF-DETER	BLKVALUE	FARRAKHAN	JESSE JACKSON
Nationalists	91.4%	90.5%	43.1%	13.8%
Nonnationalists	85.1	88.5	30.8	17.7
	p < .067	p < .517	p < .007	p < .292

SOURCE: HU-Wellington MMM Survey, October 25, 1995.

The data indicate that of the eight reasons given by the marchers for attending this event, three reasons were statistically significant: The
March "supports independent black economic programs" and "calls
for atonement and reconciliation among Blacks" (we call these message
reasons) and the March "was initiated by Minister Louis Farrakhan"
(we call this a messenger reason).[12] Interestingly, these messages were
most closely associated with Louis Farrakhan. The data show that
those who called themselves nationalists were more likely than nonnationalists to have given these reasons for attending the March (see
Table 12.3).

In order to get a more refined idea of the differences that existed
among the marchers regarding the reasons for their attendance, we
constructed three regression models that used each of the three statistically significant reasons just identified as the dependent variables. For
each model, the independent variables were: self-identified ideological
position (nationalist vs. nonnationalist); socioeconomic status,[13] optimism about the future,[14] and age (over 30 vs. under 30).[15] We present
these three models in Table 12.4.

Our first model focuses on the relationship between the identified
independent variables and the message reason "supports independent
black economic programs" (the dependent variable). The regression
model indicates that three independent variables were found to be statistically significant: education, employment status, and ideology. Better-educated respondents, those employed full time, and nationalists
were more likely to indicate that they attended the March because they
thought this event supported independent black economic programs.

The dependent variable in the second model in Table 12.4 is the message reason "calls for atonement and reconciliation among blacks." In this model, the only independent variable that was found to be statistically significant was household income. Respondents who came from lower-income households were most likely to state that this message reason was "very important" in their decision to attend the March.

Our third model looks at the relationship between the independent variables and the message reason "[the March] was initiated by Minister Louis Farrakhan." Strongest support for this reason was shown by those with lower levels of education, those who came from lower-income households, and those who identified themselves as nationalists. Interestingly, even though Farrakhan seemingly has greater appeal among younger black men (see Shaw et al., 1998; Dyson 1995), our results revealed that black men over the age of thirty said that they were more likely to attend the March because it was initiated by Farrakhan. While other independent variables were found to be important, these three models indicate that self-identification as a nationalist was the

TABLE 12.4
Explanatory Variables Associated with Reasons for Attending the March

Independent Variables	Model One Black Econ. Programs	Model Two Atonement/ Reconciliation	Model Three Initiated by Farrakhan
Education	5.002*	3.002	–.198*
	(.026)	(.026)	(.050)
Household Income	–1.0052	–4.003*	–.119*
	(.021)	(.021)	(.040)
Employment			
(Full-Time = 1)	–.168*	.148	–4.001
(Other = 0)	(.081)	(.082)	(.155)
Nationalist Self-Identification	.216*	.137	.630*
(Yes = 1)	(.098)	(.099)	(.187)
Age			
(Over 30 = 1)	8.004	4.002	.437*
(Under 30 = 0)	(.070)	(.071)	(.134)
Optimism			
(Improved Conditions = 1)	–1.001	–2.006	–.127
(Worsening Conditions = 0)	(.063)	(.063)	(.120)
N	1070	1070	1070
Adjusted R-square	.008	.004	.043
Standard error of the estimate	.99	1.00	1.88

Each dependent variable utilizes a scale that ranges from 1 to 6 where 6 is very important and 1 is not important at all.

*Indicates variables that are significant at $p < .05$. The numbers in parentheses are the standard errors.

most consistent variable in explaining why African American men selected the three reasons we have discussed.

Given the high levels of racial consciousness exhibited by the marchers, how did their positions on selected strategies for addressing the multifaceted black predicament in America differ by self-selected ideology (i.e., nationalist versus nonnationalists)? We attempted to answer this question by looking at two types of strategies that the marchers endorsed, "inclusionary" and "noninclusionary" strategies. Inclusionary strategies have been historically used by African Americans to gain access to the socioeconomic opportunity structure of the larger society. As early as 1900, in an attempt to halt Jim Crow practices in streetcars in at least twenty-five cities in the South, African Americans instituted economic boycotts (Meier and Rudwick, 1967). Aldon Morris (1984: 48), for example, tells us that "in 1955–56, in Orangeburg, South Carolina, white businessmen began to use severe economic reprisals against blacks fighting for school desegregation. Blacks 'replied with the only weapon known to them—the boycott.'" In the upper portion of Table 12.5 we provide data on the proportion of those who attended the March who said that they were "very likely" to donate their money and time to support what we call inclusionary strategies, such as various forms of economic boycotts and unspecified pressure directed at banks to encourage them to invest in black business and home ownership. Of these strategies, about 70 percent of the marchers endorsed pressure on banks, while only about half of those surveyed said that they were very likely to donate time or money to boycott major retailers who move out of the inner city.

Noninclusionary strategies are more nationalistic in character and reflect a sense of racial autonomy or racial solidarity; African Americans who support noninclusionary strategies rely on themselves to create socioeconomic and political opportunities. A long-standing point of emphasis among what Harold Cruse (1967: 4–5) would call the "rejected, or nationality strain" has been the idea of self-determination. This thematic emphasis was seen in the efforts of the economic nationalist Booker T. Washington in Tuskegee (Harlan, 1972), the territorial nationalist Marcus Garvey, and the religious-territorial nationalist Elijah Muhammad (Bracey, Meier, and Rudwick, 1970). Each of the six noninclusionary (or nationalistic) strategies that we include in Table 12.5 reflects this idea of self-determination. The data in the lower part of Table 12.5 focus on those nationalistic strategies that those who attended the Million Man March said that they were "very likely" to

TABLE 12.5
Strategies Endorsed by the Marchers (Rank Ordered)

Strategy	Percentage Who Indicated "Very Likely"*
Inclusionary	
Pressure more banks to invest in black businesses and home (PRESSURE)	71.9
Boycott companies that don't appropriate a fair share of their economic resources to the black community (BOYCOMP)	67.3
Boycott corporations that don't comply with affirmative action requirements (BOYCORP)	61.7
Boycott major retailers that move out of the inner city (BOYRET)	51.9
Noninclusionary	
Pool financial resources in Black-owned bank** (POOLFIN)	91.9
Develop more Black-owned business (DEVBLK)	86.2
Buy more goods and services from Black-owned businesses (BUYBLK)	78.8
Elect responsible black politicians (BLKPOL)	59.4
Form an independent black political party (BLKPARTY)	51.9
Pressure the U.S. government to pay reparations to Blacks for the crime of slavery (REPARA)	51.9

SOURCE: HU-Wellington MMM Survey, October 25, 1995.
*This question asked: "How likely are you to donate your money and time to support the following strategies?" Note: Only the "very likely" responses are reported.
**This question asked: "In order for black people to pool their financial resources, are you willing to establish an account in a Black owned bank and put 50 percent or more of your resources there?" Note: Only the yes responses are reported.

support with time and money. The data show that higher percentages of respondents endorsed at least half of these nationalistic strategies—pooling financial resources in a Black-owned bank, developing more Black-owned businesses, and buying more goods and services from Black-owned businesses—than any of the strategies identified as inclusionary. Interestingly, however, the two strategies that had the least support among the marchers were the ideas of forming an independent black political party and pressuring the U.S. government to pay reparations to African Americans for the crime of slavery. Slightly more than half of those surveyed indicated that they were "very likely" to support these options with their time and money. Notwithstanding this finding, the generally high percentages of support for noninclusionary or nationalist strategies suggest a deeply rooted nationalist sentiment among those who attended this event.

Finally, we utilize ordinary least squares regression to examine differences between nationalists and nonnationalists when other variables are controlled. In order to take a closer look at the levels of support for both the inclusionary and the noninclusionary strategies, we constructed two regression models. For each model, the independent variables were self-identified ideological position (nationalist vs. nonnationalist); socioeconomic status;[16] optimism about the future; and age (over age thirty vs. under age thirty). The dependent variable in the first model consists of an additive index that groups the responses by the marchers to the four questions that look at the inclusionary strategies. A high or positive score represents strong support for these strategies by the respondents.

The dependent variable for the second model also consists of an additive index that groups the responses by the marchers to the six questions that look at the noninclusionary strategies. A high or positive score represents strong support for these strategies. We present the two models in Table 12.6.

According to the first model, nationalists were, surprisingly, more likely to endorse the inclusionary strategies than were nonnationalists (e.g., liberals, conservatives, socialists). Also, stronger support for the inclusionary model was expressed by those black men over thirty years of age and those black men employed full time. The respondents' education, household income, and optimism about the future were found to have no effect on whether they endorsed inclusionary strategies.[17]

The dependent variable in the second model refers to the noninclusionary strategies presented in Table 12.6. The only statistically significant independent variable found in this model was ideological self-identification. As expected, nationalists were more likely than nonnationalists to endorse noninclusionary strategies. When we controlled for education, household income, employment status, age, and optimism, we found the nationalists showed almost twice as much support for noninclusionary strategies as for inclusionary strategies. The stronger support among nationalists at the Million Man March for noninclusionary strategies demonstrates that those who called themselves nationalists associated their ideological self-identification with similar or comparable expressions and strategies. One of the methodological problems that has faced previous attitudinal analyses on ideological self-identification was the difficulty that respondents had in associating their own ideological self-identification with analogous explanations and definitions (Tate, 1993: 31).[18] Our findings indicate that, among those who called themselves "nationalists," there was a

TABLE 12.6
Explanatory Variables Associated with Inclusionary and
Noninclusionary Strategies

Independent Variables	Model One* Inclusionary Strategies	Model Two** Noninclusionary Strategies
Education	1.0001	1.005
	(.037)	(.041)
Household Income	2.007	1.0004
	(.030)	(.033)
Employment		
(Full-Time = 1)	.288***	.182
(Other = 0)	(.116)	(.127)
Nationalist Self-Identification		
(Yes = 1)	.427***	.833***
(Other = 0)	(.140)	(.153)
Age		
(Over 30 = 1)	.365***	5.007
(Under 30 = 0)	(.100)	(.110)
Optimism		
(Improved Conditions = 1)	−8.007	−4.005
(Worsening Conditions = 0)	(.089)	(.098)
N	1070	1070
Adjusted R-square	.034	.026
Standard error of the estimate	1.4070	1.5419

*This dependent variable consists of an index composed of the four questions on inclusionary race consciousness strategies. A positive number or high score indicates strong support for these strategies.

**This dependent variable consists of an index composed of six questions on noninclusionary race consciousness strategies. A positive number or high score indicates strong support for these strategies.

***Indicates those variables that are significant at $p < .05$. The numbers in parentheses are the standard errors.

consistency between what these people call themselves and what the literature tells us such people claim to believe.

Black Politics at the Close of the Twentieth Century

What do the ideological positions and attendant strategies of those who attended the March tell us about the nature of what we call the "inclusionary dilemma" faced by African Americans at the end of the twentieth century? As we have indicated, much of the historical and contemporary experience of African Americans in America revolves around efforts to gain access to an opportunity structure free of racial impediments. Ongoing efforts by African Americans to gain access to the social, economic, and political opportunity structure of this nation have been so vigorous and so continuous as to be characterized as an inclusionary imperative. Yet, as we have also pointed out, there have been numerous instances when the inclusionary drive has come under attack, principally from forces outside the African American community. It is these attacks that have contributed to a rise in racial consciousness in the African American community. In effect therefore, the inclusionary dilemma is a dialectical process wherein emergent racial consciousness on the part of African Americans can be seen as a response to the racial impediments that African Americans encounter as they attempt to gain access to the economic, social, and political opportunity structure of the larger society.

It is no small wonder, therefore, that racial consciousness, as a response to hostile forces external to the African American community, is evident in the data that we have discussed in this chapter. As we have pointed out, racial consciousness among a group of people who share racial characteristics can be said to be most pervasive when that group qua racial group sees itself threatened by outside forces. Notwithstanding these hostile attacks at both the institutional and the individual levels, which contribute to what we call the inclusionary dilemma, what we call the inclusionary imperative within the African American community remains dominant in the face of most variations of black separatism. How do we account for this paradox? In spite of the opposition from forces of racial retrogression and backlash, African Americans have continued their march forward to challenge the values and institutions that would seek to reestablish the racial discrimination that prevailed before the Supreme Court's ruling in *Brown v. Board of Education of Topeka Kansas,* in 1954. With the exception of the black urban underclass, which appears to be trapped at the bottom of the opportunity structure and whose situation has worsened with the advent of so-called welfare reform (see Edelman, 1997; Wilson, 1997), many African Americans have made material progress since the end of, and because of, the civil rights movement (Landry, 1987). The inclusionary imperative has produced material gains for many African Americans. However, many of these same African Americans feel that progress can occur only so long as the protective regulatory apparatus of the federal government charged with protecting voting rights and the compensatory policies associated with various forms of affirmative action remain in place. Inclusion has been productive *because of* interventions by the government and its ameliorative public policy efforts (Carnoy,

1994), not in spite of them, as some conservatives on race-specific public policies have recently argued (Thernstrom and Thernstrom, 1997).

The fundamental difference between the inclusion-oriented African Americans of today and their ideological predecessors—the integrationist stratum, in Cruse's scheme of things—is that the inclusion-oriented African Americans of today are far more race-conscious than were the integrationists of the pre-1965 era. Those who belong to this stratum are far more concerned with reforming the economic, political, and social order and removing racial impediments to their progress than with mere racial integration per se. Hence, they are more appropriately called "race reformers" (in the tradition of W. E. B. Du Bois from 1910 to 1934; see also Marable, 1998: 41–55).

For those in the inclusionary stream of black politics, the emerging demographic reality discussed at the outset of this chapter is likely to produce coalition building, as well as intense competition, depending on the realities of local politics in this nation. For those in the noninclusionary or nationalist stream, the increasing racial and ethnic diversification of America is likely to more deeply entrench their nationalistic tendencies as other racial and ethnic groups competitively expand their efforts to acquire scarce goods and resources, thus exacerbating the sense of external threat, traditionally associated with white institutional racism, that has fueled African American racial consciousness.

While discussion of more specific impacts that these demographic changes are likely to have on black politics would be premature, it is clear that this emerging reality will force both students and practitioners of black politics to reexamine the core assumptions of the black-white paradigm that has been at the core of American race relations since the eighteenth century and to take into account the new realities of a multiracial, multiethnic America.[19]

NOTES

1. A complete copy of this report, *One American in the Twenty-first Century: Forging a New Future,* can be accessed at: http://www.Whitehouse.gov/Initiatives/OneAmerica/cevent.html.

2. The theoretical underpinning of these two streams of black politics can be found in the work of Harold Cruse (1967). In this seminal work, Cruse associated the highest level of "Afro-American ethnic group consciousness," that

is, racial consciousness, with those he called the "separatist" or "nationalist" stratum, while those whom he saw as considerably less race conscious were called the "integrationist" stratum. There is little difference, in our descriptive model, between the notion of noninclusionary (or black nationalist) African Americans and what Cruse called "separatists." However, as our empirical analysis reveals, inclusion-oriented African Americans are the more racially conscious descendants of what Cruse once called "integrationists."

3. We use the terms "African American" and "Black" interchangeably throughout this chapter.

4. Faculty and students at Howard University also conducted a survey at the Million Woman March, on October 25, 1997. The sample for that event was 456 women eighteen years of age and older. See J. P. McCormick 2d and S. Franklin, eds., *A Report on the Findings of the Million Woman March,* unpublished paper, August 1998. This was the second largest mass-based demonstration of African Americans to be held in the late 1990s.

5. The issue of what is meant by the use of the term "race" is fraught with controversy in the social and behavioral sciences. We accept the position taken by Omi and Winant (1986: 60) and other scholars, who maintain that "race" is a sociohistorical concept. They write: "Racial categories and the meaning of race are given concrete expression by the specific social relations and the historical context in which they are embedded."

6. The Contract with America has been described by one black member of Congress as a document "overburdened with inflammatory, coded messages designed to arouse the over-taxed, underpaid, financially insecure White middle-class to revive racist policies of the past."

7. Elsewhere McCormick (1997) has found that African American men who attended the Million Man March were more likely to have indicated that they attended the March for reasons other than the fact that this event was initiated by Minister Louis Farrakhan. See also note 13.

8. This was one of two comprehensive surveys that was conducted on the day of the March. The other was conducted by Ronald Lester and Associates for the *Washington Post.* The *Post* survey contains 1,047 randomly selected participants, compared to 1,070 randomly selected participants in the Howard-Wellington survey. The margin of sampling error for both samples is plus or minus 3 percentage points. The demographic profiles of both samples have been found to be remarkably similar.

9. U.S. Census Bureau data indicate that in 1993 the proportion of African American men who had earned at least a bachelor's degree or more was almost 12 percent. See Bennett (1995), Table 7, p. 45.

10. About 18 percent of African American men nationally held managerial or professional jobs in 1993 (see Bennett, 1995).

11. The responses to our ideological question were recoded into two cate-

gories: nationalists and nonnationalists, the latter category being a composite of the other choices.

12. The five message-related reasons were: calls for improving and affirming moral values in the black community (BVAL); encourages building broad-based black unity (BUNITY); calls for self-determination by the black community (SELF-DETER); supports independent black economic programs (BECON); and calls for atonement and reconciliation (ATONE&RECON). The three messenger-related reasons were [that the March] involved various Christian ministers (CHRISMIN); [the March was] initiated by Minister Louis Farrakhan (FAR-RAK); and [the March was] endorsed by the Reverend Jesse Jackson (JJACK). These reasons are examined in Table 12.3.

13. Three variables were chosen to highlight the respondents' social class and socioeconomic position: education, household income, and employment status. Given the high number of respondents who claimed to be employed full-time (See McCormick, 1997), we chose to recode our dummy variable on employment as full-time = 1, other = 0. The "other" category represents those respondents who are working part-time or seasonally or who are unemployed.

14. We measured this variable via this question: "Overall, in the next ten years do you expect conditions in America to be (1) better (2) worse or (3) same as now?" This variable was recoded, with 1 = better and 0 = worse or same as now.

15. Previous research on racial group identification (Thornton, Tran, and Taylor, 1997), and work on black nationalist and feminist tendencies in the African American community (Shaw et al., 1998) indicate that age is an important predictor variable in understanding various indicators of racial consciousness.

16. As indicated in the first three regression models, education, income, and employment status are the independent variables that highlight the socioeconomic status of the marchers.

17. In this chapter we are interested primarily in the relationship between self-identified ideologies and the strategic options for resolution of the multifaceted black predicament endorsed by those who attended the Million Man March. We are not necessarily concerned with the socioeconomic correlates of the two ideological tendencies examined herein. Tate (1993) and Dawson (1994), who use data from the National Black Election Panel Study (1984–1988), found that support for certain nationalist strategies was greatest among younger African Americans and among those from a lower socioeconomic background. In a preliminary study that utilized data from the 1993–1994 National Black Political Study (NBPS), Dawson (1994) offers a rather ambiguous discussion on the relationship between what he calls "black autonomy" and "class." On the one hand he tells us, "Unlike earlier research, income was not a strong predictor of black autonomy." In a footnote from the source of this quote, however, he observes: "Preliminary comparison of the support for indicators of black autonomy and black

nationalism in the NBPS and the 1983–84 [NBES] suggests that the increase in support comes primarily from a shift among affluent blacks" (Dawson, 1994: 30). This quotation suggests that the greatest support for what Dawson calls black autonomy came from Blacks with higher incomes. We think that Dawson's notion of black autonomy is conceptually equivalent to our notion of a noninclusionary or nationalist strategy. In fact, Dawson writes, "Black autonomy has strong links to black nationalism" (33).

18. In other words, previous analyses have indicated that self-identified liberals, conservatives, nationalists, and so on had difficulty in associating strategies, programs, and expressions with their own ideological self-identification. From this analysis of the Million Man March participants, we discovered the exact opposite.

19. A recent article by the demographer William Frey (1998), however, argues that much of this multiethnic, multiracial growth is concentrated in only twenty-one of the nation's 271 major metropolitan areas.

REFERENCES

Advisory Board to the President's Initiative on Race. 1998. *One America in the Twenty-first Century: Forging a New Future—The President's Initiative on Race*. Washington, D.C.: U.S. Government Printing Office.

Allen, R. L, M. C. Dawson, and R. E. Brown. 1989. "A Schema-Based Approach to Modeling and African American Racial Belief System." *American Political Science Review*, 83, no. 3 (June): 421–441.

Barker, L. J., Jones, M., and K. Tate. 1999. *African Americans and the American Political System*. Upper Saddle River, N.J.: Prentice-Hall.

Bennett, C. E. 1995. *The Black Population in the United States: March 1994 and 1993*, Current Population Reports, P20–480. Washington, D.C.: U.S. Government Printing Office.

Bositis, D. 1995. *African Americans and the 1994 Midterms: What Happened?* Washington, D.C.: Joint Center for Political and Economic Studies.

———. 1997. *National Opinion Poll—Politics* Washington, D.C. : Joint Center for Political and Economic Studies.

Bracey, J. A., A. Meier, and E. Rudwick. 1970. *Black Nationalism in America*. Indianapolis: Bobbs-Merrill.

Broder, D. 1995. "A Rout of Historic Proportions." *Washington Post*, September 20, A9.

Brown, W. O. 1931. "The Nature of Race Consciousness." *Social Forces* 10: 90–97.

Carnoy, M. 1994. *Faded Dreams: The Politics of Race and Economics of Race in America*. New York: Cambridge University Press.

Cox, O. C. 1948. *Caste, Class and Race: A Study in Social Dynamics*. Garden City, N.Y.: Doubleday.

Cruse, H. 1967. *The Crisis of the Negro Intellectual*. New York: Morrow.

Dawson, Michael. 1994. *Behind the Mule: Race and Class in African-American Politics*. Princeton: Princeton University Press.

Durant, T. J. and K. H. Sparrow. 1997. "Race and Class Consciousness among Lower and Middle Class Blacks." *Journal of Black Studies* 27, no. 3 (January): 334–351.

Dyson, Michael Eric. 1995. *Making Malcolm: The Myth and Meaning of Malcolm X*. New York: Oxford University Press.

Edelman, P. 1997. "The Worst Thing Bill Clinton Has Done." *Atlantic Monthly* 279, no. 3 (March): 120–142.

Farrakhan, L. 1994. "Minister Louis Farrakhan Calls for a One Million Man March." *Final Call* 14, no. 4 (December 14), accessed at: http://www.afrinet.net/~islam?March/march.html.

Foner, E. 1990. *A Short History of Reconstruction, 1863–1877*. New York: Harper & Row.

Franklin, J. H. and A. A. Moss Jr. 1988. *From Slavery to Freedom*. 6th ed. New York: Knopf.

Frey, W. 1998. "The Diversity Myth." *American Demographics* (June); 10pgs. accessed at: http://www.demographics.com/publications/ad/98_ad/9806_ad/ad980626.htm.

Graham, H. D. 1990. *The Civil Rights Era*. New York: Oxford University Press.

Harlan, Louis R. 1972. *Booker T. Washington: The Making of a Black Leader, 1856–1901*. New York: Oxford University Press.

Holden, M. 1973. *The Politics of the Black "Nation."* New York: Chandler.

Landry, B. 1987. *The New Black Middle Class*. Berkeley: University of California Press.

Lewinson, P. 1932. *Race, Class, and Party: A History of Negro Suffrage and White Politics in the South*. New York: Russell & Russell.

Marable, M. 1985. *Black American Politics: From the Washington Marches to Jesse Jackson*. London: Verso Books.

———. 1991. *Race, Reform and Rebellion: The Second Reconstruction in Black America: 1945–1990*. Jackson: University Press of Mississippi.

———. 1998. *Black Leadership*. New York: Columbia University Press.

McCormick, J. P. 1997. "The Messages and the Messengers: Opinions from the Million Men Who Marched." *National Political Science Review* 6: 142–164.

McCormick, J. P., and Sekou Franklin, eds. 1998. *A Report on the Findings of the Million Woman March*. August. Unpublished.

Meier, A., and E. Rudwick. 1967. "The Boycott Movement against Jim Crow

Streetcars in the South, 1900–1906." *Journal of American History* 51 (March): 35–52.

Miller, Arthur H., Patricia Gurin, Gerald Gurin, and Oksana Malanchuk. 1981. "Group Consciousness and Political Participation." *American Journal of Political Science* 25, no. 3 (August): 494–511.

Morris, A. M. 1984. *The Origins of the Civil Rights Movement: Black Communities Organizing for Change.* New York: Free Press, 1984.

———. 1992. "Political Consciousness and Collective Action," in A. D. Morris and C. M. Mueller, eds., *Frontiers in Social Movement Theory* (pp. 351–373). New Haven: Yale University Press.

Omi, M., and H. Winant. 1986. *Racial Formation in the United States: From the 1960s to the 1980s.* New York: Routledge & Kegan Paul.

Rable, G. C. 1984. *But There Was No Peace: The Role of Violence in the Politics of Reconstruction.* Athens: University of Georgia Press.

Shaw, Todd, et al. 1998. "Lessons Learned?: Black Gender and Intergenerational Differences on Attitudes toward Black Nationalism and Black Feminism." Paper presented at the Mid-Western Political Science Association, Chicago, Illinois, April.

Shingles, R. D. 1981. "Black Consciousness and Political Participation." *American Political Science Review* 75: 76–91.

Tate, K. 1993. *From Protest to Politics: The Black Voters in American Elections.* New York: Russell Sage.

Thernstrom, S., and A. Thernstrom. 1997. *America in Black and White: One Nation, Indivisible.* New York: Simon & Schuster.

Thornton, M. C., T. V. Tran, and R. J. Taylor. 1997. "Multiple Dimensions of Racial Group Identification among Adult Black Americans." *Journal of Black Psychology* 23, no. 3. (August): 293–309.

U.S. Bureau of the Census. 1998. *States Ranked by Black Population in 1997,* accessed at: http://www.census.gov/population/estimates/state/rank/sorb97.txt; and *States Ranked by Hispanic Population in 1997,* accessed at: http://www.census.gov/population/estimates/state/rank/sorh97.txt.

Verba, Sidney, and Norman H. Nie. 1972. *Participation in America: Political Democracy and Social Equality.* New York: Harper & Row.

White, J. 1990. *Black Leadership in America: From Booker T. Washington to Jesse Jackson.* 2d ed. New York: Longman.

Wilson, W. J. 1980. *The Declining Significance of Race: Blacks and Changing American Institutions.* Chicago: University of Chicago Press.

———. 1997. *When Work Disappears: The World of the New Urban Poor.* New York: Knopf.

Chapter 13

War, Political Cycles, and the Pendulum Thesis

Explaining the Rise of Black Nationalism, 1840–1996

Errol A. Henderson

Nationalism has always been a part of the American psyche. It was a nascent form of nationalism that led the American colonist to rebel against the British, declare their independence, and form their own government. The bitterness of the anticolonial nationalists stemmed from various acts of injustice to which they had been subjected, including taxation without representation.

In the 1920s, it was nationalism that spurred the Jamaica-born leader Marcus Garvey to create his "Back to Africa" movement. In the late 1960s, nationalism served as a framework for Stokely Carmichael (later Kwame Ture) and others to call for an end to black subjugation and for what they described as "Black Power." More recently, a particularly virulent strain of nationalism has reared its ugly head among American white extremist groups. While there exists a vast literature on the subject of nationalism, only recently have scholars focused their attention on the rise and decline of black nationalism.

Enlisting a series of logistic regression models, Errol Henderson here assesses the role of war, a backlash against black civil rights, economic factors, and the effect of political cycles on the rise of black nationalism from 1840 to 1996. Placing his findings in the current sociopolitical context, as defined by various threads of white nationalism, black nationalism, and a recurring Latino nationalism, the author predicts that the American political land-scape will be a volatile one in the time ahead.

In his seminal work, *The Crisis of the Negro Intellectual* (1968), Harold Cruse noted that "American Negro history is basically a history of the conflict between integrationist and nationalist forces in politics, economics, and culture, no matter what leaders are involved and what slogans are used. The pendulum swings back and forth, but the men who swing with it always fail to synthesize composite trends" (p. 564). While Cruse relies on historical anecdote to make his point, it is important for scholars to systematically examine the correlates of the putative shifts that Cruse describes. The most challenging aspect of Cruse's thesis is that it requires an explication of the correlates of black nationalism. While quite a few studies have been devoted to analyses of integration, few scholars have devoted much time to the analysis of black nationalism. This intellectual myopia has led Walton (1985: 29) to conclude that black nationalism is among the most misunderstood concepts in American politics. In this study, I examine some of the factors associated with the rise of black nationalism in order to account for the pendulum shifts in black leadership strategies suggested by Cruse. First, I review Cruse's thesis and delineate the black leadership phases suggested by his analysis. Second, I provide a theoretical rationale for Cruse's pendulum shifts and devolve testable propositions on the factors that give rise to black nationalism. Third, I evaluate the propositions through logistic regression analysis for the period 1840–1996. Fourth, I examine the findings from the data analyses and briefly discuss their implications for policy and further research.

Cruse's Pendulum Thesis

In its simplest form, Cruse's pendulum thesis suggests that since the mid-1800s national black leadership has vacillated between advocacy of nationalism and of integration.[1] Nationalism is the belief that the cultural and political unit should be congruent (Gellner 1983). Black nationalists insist that African Americans as a distinct people should pursue collective political action rooted in their common history and their ostensibly common interests. Politically, black nationalists largely pursue racially exclusive political organizations; economically, they advocate for black economic self-sufficiency; and culturally, they emphasize their black and primarily pan-Africanist identity. Black integrationists, on the other hand, emphasize the "Americanness" of their identity and they largely embrace the melting pot notion of U.S. society. They view their political interests and objectives as consistent with, if not identical to, those of Americans in general and European Americans in particular. Therefore, "black" organizations, economic self-sufficiency, and political ends that suggest racial exclusivity are eschewed for interracial organizations, noneconomic liberalism,[2] and cultural assimilation—primarily with respect to Whites.

Cruse's pendulum thesis implies an ambivalence among black leadership toward a unified strategy for liberation and social justice. This ambivalence may be rooted, on the individual level, in Duboisian double consciousness (Du Bois [1903] 1961: 16–17). For Cruse (1968: 7–8) the impetus for ideological vacillation is rooted in black leaders' failure to appreciate the culture group basis of American politics. Cruse argues that, notwithstanding the celebration of individualism, culture group power is the template for individual power in the United States, which is dominated by one group—white Anglos (p. 456). America, for him, is the result of a "badly-bungled process of inter-group cultural fusion" where white skin privilege provides the glue that binds ruling groups (pp. 7–8). This white supremacy is stitched into the fabric of the American tapestry, leaving the black patchwork, in particular, threadbare.

The failure to appreciate the culture group orientation of American society has been particular debilitating to the black community because even as individual Blacks ascend America's social ladder, Blacks as a group remain outcast and denigrated, consistently ranking below Whites across any meaningful standard of quality of life and equality of opportunity. If Cruse is correct that power derives from one's group standing, then the melting pot notion that is embedded in American popular culture is exposed as myth. In its place is the reality of not only a group-based democracy but, under white supremacy, a Herrenvolk democracy. Under such conditions, one would expect that black leadership would eschew integrationism in order to pursue group-focused strategies such as nationalism. However, since the mid-1800s, black leadership has been dominated by integrationists. It would be an oversimplification to assume that this is simply the result of the fact that the leadership, often consisting of the more privileged classes, has pursued its class interests at the expense of mass interests. Nonetheless, it is difficult to deny Du Bois' ([1940] 1991: 305) observation that "[t]he upper class Negro has almost never been nationalistic," while nationalism "has always been a thought up-surging from the masses." Actually, the interplay of several forces within and outside the black community works to denude nationalist initiatives and promote integrationist ones.

To my mind, the prevalence of nationalist sentiments among Blacks is largely the result of the separation of the vast majority of Blacks from Whites, both historically and in the present. Even today, the majority of Blacks live a day-to-day existence as political, economic, and cultural outcasts in White-dominated American society. Nationalists mobilize on the basis of these caste—more than class—interests while, integrationists proffer assimilationist strategies for black uplift. Integrationists have often made their way by navigating the landscape of the mainstream system, but for the black masses, many of them poor, the integrationist dream is not representative of their daily—and very separate—reality. It also appears that, while internal circumstances might promote nationalist sentiment, external factors militate against it. However, it is unfair to label integrationists as simply puppets of external forces, since their ascendancy results in a large part from the fact that they dominate the central political institution in the black community—the black church—which is ironic, since, at their inception, the black churches were highly nationalistic. Nevertheless, through domination of the black church, integrationists have greater access to the internal resources in the black community. Further, by embracing the "American dream," they are more likely to secure greater external support compared to nationalists (especially in the twentieth century).[3] In fact, external support is more likely to be aimed at undermining nationalist initiatives.

While intuitively plausible, Cruse's thesis has not been systematically examined, nor did he provide a clear theoretical rationale for the alternation of black leadership ideologies and strategies. Part of the difficulty is that systematic analyses of black nationalism—a chief component of the Crusian thesis—have not been forthcoming for several reasons, not least among them (as noted earlier) the fact that black nationalism is among the most misunderstood concepts in American politics (Walton 1985: 29). This misunderstanding is, in part, a result of the failure of analysts to differentiate between Eurocentric and Afrocentric perspectives of nationalism (Henderson 1995). The former suggests that nations aspire to possess a state, and advocates of this view tend to reject the nationalist claims of African Americans as both marginal and untenable. However, Afrocentric perspectives of black nationalism suggest a pan-Africanist criterion for nationhood wherein historically polyglot black cultural groups are wedded to a common political purpose that suggests group autonomy, though not necessarily statehood. In the latter conceptualization, nationalists may aspire to self-determination within a culturally plural state (see Cruse 1987) as opposed to secession. Too often, scholars equate black nationalism (if they consider it seriously at all) with separation, instead of viewing it as a political ideology rooted in the legitimate national self-determination claims of African Americans. Since the nation status of African Americans has been historically denied by European Americans, it stands to reason that the political philosophy of black nationalism would be denigrated, ignored, or treated as an anomaly in Eurocentric approaches. Nonetheless, the view that Blacks constitute a nation persists throughout black communities in the United States. Where there is often disagreement among Blacks is over what such an identification entails for their political, economic, and cultural interaction with European Americans and other citizens in the multicultural (or multinational) republic.

Phases of Black Leadership

Cruse (1968) suggests that black nationalist leadership in the United States begins with Martin Delany, followed by Washington, Garvey, and Malcolm X, while integrationist leadership begins with Frederick Douglass, followed by Du Bois and King. I extend Cruse's original list to include (1) a nascent period of nationalist dominance in the 1840s; (2) prominent organizational leadership;[4] and (3) national leaders who emerged after publication of Cruse's work, such as black elected officials (BEOs), Jesse Jackson, and Louis Farrakhan.

Because some national leaders have shifted their positions over the years, their categorization is problematic. For example, although Du Bois was not a nationalist, he resigned from the NAACP in 1934 over his advocacy of independent black economic development (Du Bois [1940] 1991: 197–220). There were also "elements of assimilationist thought in the philosophies of pioneering Black nationalists . . . just as

TABLE 13.1
Shifts in Black Leadership Strategies, 1840–1996

Pendulum Shift	Phase	Leadership Type
	1840–1845	Nationalism
1845	1846–1850	Integrationism
1850	1851–1868	Nationalism
1868	1869–1895	Integrationism
1895	1896–1915	Nationalism
1915	1916–1919	Integrationism
1919	1920–1925	Nationalism
1925	1926–1967	Integrationism
1967	1968–1975	Nationalism
1975	1976–1995	Integrationism
1995	1996–	Nationalism

there were elements of black nationalism in the philosophies of such as-similationists as Frederick Douglass" (Moses 1978: 43). For example, though hailed as a black nationalist, David Walker opposed coloniza-tion, emigration, racial separatism, and laws prohibiting intermarriage (p. 39). Similarly, Moses (pp. 38, 41) contends that Douglass, Cruse's prototypal integrationist, belonged to "that tradition of *black national-ists* who militantly asserted their right to American citizenship [empha-sis added]," espousing the "nation" status of black America but to-ward an integrationist end. Additionally, Delany's nationalism was muted during his post–Civil War advocacy of "a union of the two races," and his sharing of a gubernatorial slate with a white Democra-tic supporter of the planter class in 1876, for which he was vilified as a "nigger Democrat" (Painter 1988: 167–169). He eventually reaffirmed his pre–Civil War advocacy of black emigration (pp. 170–171).

Although problematic, it is possible to outline the black leadership phases since the mid-1800s (Table 13.1); moreover, because Cruse's thesis requires that one identify not so much the leaders themselves but only the dominant political strategy or ideology among the leadership, it is not necessary to capture every subtle distinction in individual lead-ers' perspective(s). That is, the shifts occur between the competing strategies and not necessarily among the personalities; therefore, the shifting of individual perspectives does not necessarily suggest the shift-ing of dominant national strategies. For example, although during the Depression Du Bois appears to have shifted toward a more nationalis-tic perspective, the dominant strategy among national black leadership as a whole remained integrationist.

Although Cruse does not suggest a temporal origin for the pendulum shifts, it appears that black leadership cycles from the mid-1800s begin with a nationalist phase marked by Richard Allen's personal leadership and the organizational leadership of the earliest independent black churches. Extending Cruse, the black leadership list includes the nationalists—Allen, Delany, Washington, Garvey, and Farrakhan—and the integrationists—Douglass, Du Bois, the NAACP, King, the BEOs, and Jesse Jackson. The pendulum shifts took place in 1845, 1850, 1868, 1895, 1915, 1919, 1925, 1967, 1975, and 1995.[5] A discussion of the time periods and the cyclical shifts in strategy is provided in the Appendix.

Toward a Theoretical Rationale for Cruse's Pendulum Shifts

While Cruse is correct that black leadership has vacillated between nationalism and integration, he does not provide a theoretical argument to account for the shifts. This absence reflects the dearth of systematic research on the correlates of black nationalism. While several authors have examined the factors that give rise to black nationalism (Essien-Udom 1964; Walton 1985; Van Deburg 1992), these analyses are largely descriptive. Although clearly opposed to black nationalism, Marable (1985) nevertheless outlines three factors that can lead to the rise of black nationalism in the United States: (1) economic expansion in which black workers' wages and job opportunities lag behind those of their white counterparts; (2) attacks by the white ruling class on civil rights and the promotion of racist vigilantism; and (3) the failure of black leadership to articulate the demands of the black masses through new policies and programs (p. 57). For Marable, all three conditions existed in the 1850s: economic expansion; the Compromise of 1850 and the Kansas-Nebraska Act of 1854, which both strengthened and extended slavery; and the failure of Douglass and other integrationists to successfully counter the nationalist political appeal of Delany and H. Ford Douglas. He maintains that the coincidence of these factors was again evident seven decades later in "the 'Red Summer' of 1919, the mushrooming of the Ku Klux Klan, the retreat of both capitalist parties from the principle of biracial democracy, and the inability of Du Bois, James Weldon Johnson and other NAACP leaders to express the aspirations of the Black urban working class and farmers" (pp. 57–58).

What resulted was the largest mass organization of Blacks in the history of the United States—Garvey's nationalist Universal Negro Improvement Association and African Communities League (UNIA & ACL). In all, Marable viewed black nationalist "hegemony" as emerging in the 1850s, 1880s, 1920s, and 1960s.[6]

While Marable's third factor is discussed more fully later, his first two factors suggest the following propositions:

(P1) Economic expansion is positively associated with the rise of black nationalism.

(P2) A repressive national political climate is associated with the rise of black nationalism.

While Marable's thesis is tenable, it is incomplete. Specifically, it fails to adequately capture the larger macropolitical factors—to which Cruse (1968) calls our attention—that give rise to black nationalism, including war. For example, even a cursory review of Marable's periods of nationalist hegemony reveals a striking coincidence between the emergence of nationalism and U.S. involvement in war. That is, while the expansionism of the 1850s was certainly highlighted by the controversy surrounding the Kansas-Nebraska Act, one might note that the United States had also just ended the Mexican-American War (1848) and that the Civil War would commence a little over a decade later. The subsequent rise of nationalism under Booker T. Washington (1896) corresponds with America's imperialist wars of 1898–1902 (the Spanish-American War, the Second Philippines War, and the Boxer Rebellion). Similarly, the rise of Garvey (1920) is signaled as much by the Great Migration as by the end of fighting in World War I (1918). The nationalism of the Black Power movement was ushered in by the apotheosis of conflict in Vietnam (1968) and was closely bounded by the end of U.S. involvement in that conflict (1973). Finally, the rise of Farrakhan (1996) closely followed the end of the Gulf War (1991).

While the absence of nationalist ascendance during World War II and the Korean War cautions against assuming too direct a relationship between war and black nationalism, we are reminded that Myrdal (1944) also posited a similar relationship.[7] He thought that wars provided the opportunity for a redefinition of the status of Blacks (p. 997) inasmuch as their wartime sacrifice in defense of democracy called into question the basis of the racial caste system while exposing the huge disjuncture between the American creed of liberty, equality, and justice and the persistence of white racism, lynch-law, Jim Crow, and black privation. Following Myrdal, Kryder (1997: 5) points out that war has a tremendous impact on domestic politics, in general, and on race relations in the United States, in particular, because "war [i]s arguably the most powerful mechanism by which the American Creed and the American Dilemma [a]re communicated to the black and white masses." Kryder posits that "war mobilization and prosecution drove the state to routinize and consolidate its relationships to social groups through quasi-corporatist arrangements as state officials bargain[ed] more openly and directly with peak organizations in an effort to secure services or resources for national defense" (p. 22). Further, he maintains that "the American war mobilizations of the first half of this century and [the] ideological contradictions they entailed stimulated black advocacy and race conflict in the US" (p. 17). This pattern of promise and disappointment, Kryder argues, not only showed "the fraud of the American Creed for black Americans" but also stimulated black mobilization, intensified black resistance, and "fueled the militancy with which Blacks expressed their grievances" (p. 17).

White supremacism "contradicted core ideals of the American polity and of American foreign policy," and this was especially evident as the United States evolved to the status of a major power (p. 5). Kryder notes that, in many of the country's wars, Blacks "continually pointed to the contradiction between the ideals of the war and the practices of the administration" (p. 6). This was apparent during World War I, when black troops faced the hypocrisy of fighting a war abroad to "make the world safe for democracy" when they did not enjoy democratic rights at home. Similar sentiments were echoed during World War II in the popular "Double V" campaign among Blacks to signify the struggle for victory "over enemies from without [and] over enemies from within" (p. 5). This incongruity was also apparent during the Vietnam War when the popular sports hero and draft recusant Muhammad Ali echoed a dominant theme among many Blacks that "no Vietnamese ever called me nigger."

While Myrdal assumed that European Americans faced with the hypocrisy of the philosophical ideals of the American republic and the practice of white supremacism that became increasingly apparent during times of war would seek to change their attitudes and support black citizenship rights, Kryder took a less sanguine view of the prospects for changing white attitudes to provide for black liberation. He correctly pointed out that the civil rights movement demonstrated that black liberation would emerge from Blacks' own "sustained social movement activity" and not primarily from a change in white attitudes, as Myrdal had suggested. Nonetheless, both Myrdal and Kryder agree that war provides an impetus for black militancy, and I maintain that a similar logic is at work in the relationship between war and black nationalism.

For instance, war requires not only the mobilization of a state's military resources but also domestic support in the form of patriotic or even jingoistic endorsement of the war effort, the mobilization of human resources, and, at times, the imposition of restrictions on some types of expression if not outright intolerance of popular dissent. During wartime, minorities may be viewed as a "fifth column" within the state. On the other hand, to the extent that a minority group represents a "strategic resource," its importance is magnified. The significance of such groups largely results from their capacity to deliver electoral victory to candidates for elective office. Therefore, where minority groups are integrated into the body politic, there is an increased likelihood that policymakers will make clientelistic overtures to them. The marginal black electorate has not played such a role in national politics, though the increased probability of their holding a strategic electoral "balance of power" has been noted since Moon (1948). With respect to Blacks, then, policymakers may select either of two options: (1) They may discourage protest among dissident black groups and encourage their leadership to shelve their demands and "close ranks" around the war effort, as Du Bois ([1918] 1983: 184) advocated during World War I, or (2) they may pursue internal repression of black groups, rationalizing such policies in the name of "national security" (Churchill and Vander Wall 1989), as did the FBI under J. Edgar Hoover, who branded King's nonviolent protesters "communist agents" and threats to "national security" during the Vietnam War (Garrow 1981; Churchill and Vander Wall 1989) and characterized the fledgling Nation of Islam (NOI) as a front for Japanese-sponsored subversion during World War II (Evanzz 1992: 24–26, 138–140). Such rationalizations serve to justify the repression of these groups, especially during wartime.[8]

As they face wartime repression, it becomes evident to Blacks that they are viewed as a foreign caste or a sort of domestic alien population within the United States. In such a context, they are put upon by Whites encouraged by the jingoism of war mobilization, who turn outwardly focused racist attitudes inward toward Blacks and other domestic groups for which there is historic and ongoing racial antipathy (such as Japanese Americans during World War II). This was evident during both the Civil War, and the expansionist wars at the turn of the century, in the years that followed World War I, and during World War II (Hunt 1987). These periods witnessed some of the worst instances of white supremacist violence against Blacks, such as the New York draft riots of 1863, the Wilmington "coup d'etat" of 1898 (Prather 1984), the Red Summer of 1919 (see Bennett 1965), the Tulsa riot of 1921 (Ellsworth 1982), and the Detroit riot of 1943. These relationships are consistent with Stohl's (1975) finding that in the United States from 1890–1970 there was a significant correlation between war and domestic violence. Such increasingly repressive environments bind and reaffirm African Americans in their common subjugation, common fate, and common identity. Increasingly faced with their caste condition, Blacks reject integrationists' assimilationist arguments, and nationalist assertions become increasingly compelling. Therefore, shortly after U.S. involvement in a war, nationalist leadership becomes ascendant.

If war helps to generate Black nationalism, then why is there an absence of nationalist ascendancy during the World War II and Korean War eras? This absence seems to derive from what Kryder (1996: 166–167) describes as an increased sophistication among "state officials" who "managed to turn the [insurgent] challenge aside, in part by inventing new techniques by which to control the disruptions." He points out that during World War II "[e]fficiency concerns first drove the state to employ a familiar set of regime 'tools': a variety of symbolic concessions and appointments, including high visibility black officers and 'black cabinet' officials; small steps toward reform . . . and most often, harsh repression and punishment" until "over time, new techniques helped stabilize and pacify the races" (pp. 166–167).

During World War II, a shift toward nationalism was prevented by "concessions" by the Roosevelt Administration to demands by integrationists who were threatening a march on Washington in 1941. Among these concessions was Executive Order 8802, which outlawed discrimination in both the defense industry and the federal government. Roosevelt also appointed William Hastie as a civilian aide to the War Department, and he awarded B. O. Davis his general's star. Roosevelt's "acquiescence" was viewed as a vindication of the integrationists, and it strengthened their leadership position.[9] Similarly, the Korean War period did not result in a shift largely because of the success of the

NAACP's legal strategy to destroy de jure segregation, as evidenced in the Supreme Court's decision in *Brown v. Board of Education of Topeka, Kansas,* in 1954, and in Eisenhower's use of federal troops to challenge segregation in Little Rock's Central High School. The success of the highly publicized Montgomery bus boycott further solidified the integrationist position and militated against the rise of nationalism following the Korean War. Nevertheless, notwithstanding the two exceptions of World War II and the Korean War, it appears that the rise of Black nationalism is associated with U.S. war involvement. Therefore I posit that:

(P3) War is positively associated with the rise of black nationalism.

Appreciating the impact of war on the rise of black nationalism allows us to account for Marable's third factor in the rise of nationalism: the failure of black leadership to articulate the demands of the black masses through new policies and programs. Moreover, the impact of war on black political change suggests that factors external to the black community have a profound impact on black politics. That being the case, external factors other than war that help shape black political ideology should be analyzed for their impact on pendulum shifts, as well. Of these factors, political cycles are among the most important, as is discussed in the next section.

On Political Cycles and Black Leadership Shifts

Since the pendulum thesis, as I've extended it thus far, suggests an interplay between domestic politics and war, the cycles in which we are interested should suggest a nexus between these two policy domains. Consistent with such an orientation, Klingberg (1979: 38) observed several cycles of introversion and extroversion in U.S. foreign policy (See Table 13.2). Klingberg's cycles are based on his analysis of U.S. naval spending, events data on U.S. territorial annexations, military expeditions, the use of diplomatic pressure, popular support for foreign policy, and content analysis of annual presidential messages, inaugural addresses, and major party platforms. In periods of introversion, there is a declining use of the military abroad; restraint on the use of the military by Congress, supported by the media, interests groups, and the

TABLE 13.2
The U.S. Foreign Policy Cycle

Period	Phase	Dates
I	Introvert	1776–1798
	Extrovert	1798–1824
II	Introvert	1824–1844
	Extrovert	1844–1871
III	Introvert	1871–1891
	Extrovert	1891–1918
IV	Introvert	1918–1940
	Extrovert	1940–1966
V	Introvert	1966–1988
	Extrovert	1988–2014

SOURCE: Originally from Klingberg (1979: 43); revised by Schweller, Pollins, and Hannon (1995)

public; an increasing significance of domestic problems; mutual criticism between allies; closer ties with former enemies; promotion of peace abroad; and decreased international tension levels. On the other hand, periods of extroversion are characterized by a greater emphasis on power projection (measured as by the average rate of increase in the naval budget), an increased number of territorial annexations and armed expeditions, and a greater stress on foreign affairs in public pronouncements of both political parties (pp. 51–52).

The focus on foreign policy moods in the analysis of pendulum shifts is justified, given the contention that, within the United States, a domestic diversionary use of force relationship emerges during wartime between the white leadership and the black minority. In addition, the ideals trumpeted to rationalize U.S. involvement in war abroad—such as "making the world safe for democracy"—are often in clear contradiction to the practice of white supremacism at home. These influences increase the salience of nationalist arguments, which focus on the caste status of Blacks, over integrationist appeals, which reductively conflate caste and class.

Pendulum shifts, then, are to some extent rooted in the interaction of macropolitical factors that affect the salience of group-based mobilization among Blacks. Where group-based mobilization is mitigated by the absence of war and the presence of a period of introversion, integrationist arguments become increasingly salient, and integrationist leadership becomes dominant. However, where group salience is heightened, such as in times of extroversion and war, nationalism becomes ascendant. Under such circumstances the integrationist focus on assimilation appears quixotic. It follows that:

> (P4) Extrovert periods are positively associated with the rise of black nationalism.

To summarize, pendulum shifts in black leadership strategies appear to be more irregular oscillations than the "backing and forthing" suggested by the term "pendulum." As foreign policy moods turn toward extroversion, the likelihood of war is increased. War and its aftermath create socioeconomic dislocations and engender rationalizations for resultant economic downturns, which often result in the scapegoating of Blacks. As their second-class citizenship persists in spite of their wartime sacrifices, Blacks' frustration is heightened. An environment of increased political repression results as attacks from the white community bind and reaffirm African Americans' common subjugation, common fate, and common identity. In this context, Marable's third inducement for nationalist hegemony—the failure of black leadership to articulate the demands of the black masses through new polices and programs—becomes apparent. Increasingly aware of their caste condition, Blacks reject integrationists' assimilationist arguments, and nationalist assertions become increasingly compelling. In time, a nationalist leadership becomes ascendant.

Eventually, however, nationalists are stymied by their failure to build substantial coalitions prior to the relaxation of more overt forms of repression as the jingoism of the war period wanes and the political cycle begins to shift toward introversion. The shorter duration of nationalist dominance (see Table 13.1) is also a function of nationalists' relatively restricted resource base. In addition, integrationists usurp the more practical aspects of the nationalist agenda and graft it onto their own. Moreover, nationalist organizations are often isolated from the major institutions of the community that are dominated by black elites, who, according to Du Bois, are more likely to have integrationist leanings. For example, in the post–World War II era, integrationists received greater external funding, less negative media, and less intense attacks from government agencies and police.[10] Drawing on their greater institutional support, especially through churches and mutual aid institutions, and the perquisites they derive from their interracial organizations, integrationists offer tangible rewards to their black (and non-black) constituents. At the same time, integrationists exploit nationalists' myopia and the latter's apparent unwillingness to mobilize non-black interests.

During peacetime, nationalists cannot rely on the glaring contradictions between the American creed and American racism to provide the impetus for black mobilization in the way that it does during wartime; instead, they must articulate meaningful programs that arise from Blacks' legitimate claims to national self-determination. Historically, nationalists have been largely ineffective in providing such programs, and in this century, especially, their attempts have too often been tied to ill-conceived "emigrationist" programs, nebulous community control initiatives, or abortive insurgency strategies. These types of initiatives largely fail to address the pluralistic politics to which Blacks appear most responsive (see Cruse 1987). One result is that nationalists during peacetime, like integrationists during wartime, are often unable to promote policies and programs that reflect the overarching group interests of Blacks. Interestingly, during wartime, integrationists often fail to capture the "black" aspect of black American (a) oppression, (b) resistance, and (c) opportunity—especially (a) and (b)—while during peacetime, nationalists often fail to capture the "American" aspect of black American (a) oppression, (b) resistance, and (c) opportunity—especially (b) and (c). Therefore, in the postwar era, integrationists reemerge and largely pursue juridical concessions from the ruling white caste elite. These concessions, while at times meaningful and lasting, are limited in that they fail to ultimately address the caste basis of black marginalization—a reality that is rejected by the white ruling caste itself. Nonetheless, by effectively eschewing group-based political mobilization, integrationists reduce the amount of coercive pressure that the black community can exert on an increasingly recalcitrant white-dominated society. Concessions to black interests ultimately engender white revanchism that serves to alter the dominant policy mood of the country, helping to drive the next political cycle and thus starting the pendulum process over again.

In short, it appears that black political leadership strategies are intertwined in a matrix of cycles and phases born of a nexus of domestic and international factors. Black leaders' attempts to respond to these interdependent processes result in the oscillation of strategies between nationalism and integration. This is to argue not that black social movements are not affected by internal factors (see Morris 1984), but only that black ideological shifts, in particular, are strongly influenced by macropolitical factors. Cruse (1968) was correct in that in order to understand black political behavior one had to study it within a broader macropolitical context. What remains, then, is to empirically analyze the impact of these macro-level factors on the rise of black nationalism.

Research Design

The spatial-temporal domain of this study includes annual observations of the dominant Black leadership strategies from 1840 to 1996. The outcome variable, the ascendance of Black nationalist leadership (*Nationalism*), is a dichotomous measure that takes the value of (1) for those years where the prominent leadership is nationalist and (0) for those years where the leadership is integrationist (see Table 13.1). Predictor variables include *War*, which is coded (1) for the years of U.S. war involvement and (0) for nonwar years. War data are from the Correlates of War (COW) project (Singer and Small 1994), which records that the United States has been involved in ten wars since the mid-1800s: the Mexican-American War, the U.S. Civil War, the Spanish-American War, the Second Philippines War, the Boxer Rebellion, World War I, World War II, the Korean War, the Vietnam War, and the Gulf War. The political cycle variable, *Extroversion,* is coded as (1) for extroversion phases and (0) for introversion phases (see Table 13.2). Economic growth (*Growth*) is measured as the annual percentage change in the gross national product (GNP) and takes the value of (1) for non-negative- and (0) for negative-growth years. Data on economic growth are from Mitchell (1993) and from the U.S. Department of Commerce (1975, 1996). The presence of a repressive political climate (*Poli-Climate*) is measured as $(1 - p_i\, p_2)$ where p_i is coded (1) for those years where the political party favorable to the black electorate occupies the presidency (Republicans until the 1932 election and Democrats thereafter) and (0) otherwise; and p_2 takes the value of (1) for those years of black protest, whether under nationalist or integrationist auspices, and (0) for the years of more accommodationist policies (see Appendix).

Actually, such protests are prevalent throughout most of the years covered in this study, with three exceptions: the accommodationist period of Booker T. Washington, the short BEO-inspired period of accommodation from 1976 to 1980, and the present accommodationist nationalist period. During periods when either protest is low (an accommodationist period) or the presidency is occupied by a party hostile to Blacks, one would expect a greater degree of black repression, and in such cases the variable takes the value of one. For example, the earlier accommodationist period of Washington (1896–1915) was one of high levels of political and physical attacks on the civil rights of Blacks as Reconstruction legislation was rolled back and separate but equal became the law of the land with the decision of the Supreme Court in *Plessy v. Ferguson,* in 1896. Moreover, on average, more than one hundred Blacks were lynched annually in the decade of the 1890s.[11] The mid- to late 1970s was also a period of white backlash against affirmative action, and it was the fading years of the FBI's Counter-Intelligence Program (COINTELPRO). Finally, the present period is one of black church burnings, further incursions into civil rights gains, and the proliferation of white supremacist militias.

Only in periods marked by protest (the dominant form of black political activity) and a favorable political party in the White House do I expect that repression is relatively tempered, and in these cases the variable takes a value of 0. This may seem counterintuitive in that protest is often viewed as a symptom of repression. However, to my mind, repression is a function not only of government action but of the ability of targeted groups to mobilize opposition. Such mobilization, it appears, is possible only where there are fissures in the political opportunity structures of the society (McCarthy and Zald 1977). Where oppressed groups are accommodative, I contend that repression is high, a view that is supported by empirical studies that have long held that severe repression decreases collective action (e.g., Gurr 1970). Therefore, absent a direct measure of the presence of a repressive antiblack climate covering the entire timespan of the study, accommodationist periods of black leadership are utilized as part the larger proxy (i.e., *Poli-Climate*) of the phenomenon.[12]

In addition, use of a time variable (*Year*) allows us to control for any secular trends in the data, since it is clear that over time the likelihood of nationalist ascendance has declined as Blacks have become further integrated into U.S. society. This variable takes the value of the year of the observation.

A multivariate logistic regression model is specified to evaluate the propositions. Logistic regression is similar to linear regression except that it utilizes a maximum likelihood estimator of the logistic function and suggests the relationship between the predictor variables and the log-odds of the probability of one of two outcomes (Menard 1995). The logistic regression model takes the form: $Pr(Nationalism) = 1 / (1 + e^{-Zi})$, where $Pr(Nationalism)$ is the probability that the outcome variable *Nationalism* equals 1 and Zi is the sum of the product of the coefficient values (bi) across all observations of the predictor variables (Xik), that is:

$$\alpha + \beta_1 \ War + \beta_2 \ Extroversion + \beta_3 \ Poli\text{-}Climate + \beta_4 \ Growth + \beta_5 \ Year$$

As noted earlier, the focus on the role of the wartime scapegoating of Blacks in the rise of black nationalism approximates a sort of domestic "diversionary use of force" model, and Levy (1993) insists that such models should be estimated using a time lag; therefore, I expect that the pendulum relationship operates through a time lag sufficient to account for the time necessary for nationalist mobilization to emerge from changes in our predictors. As for the specific lag to be used, Russett (1990: 131) found that the impact of economic downturns on U.S. participation in interstate disputes from 1853–1976 operates with a two-year time lag. I expect that, at minimum, an additional year is necessary for the impact of a state's response to international conflict to generate the scapegoating of Blacks and the subsequent shift in black leadership strategy toward nationalism. Therefore, a three-year time lag on *War, Poli-Climate,* and *Growth* is used to capture these delayed effects.

I also bifurcate the temporal domain across the pre– and post–World War II periods in order to determine whether in the years after World War II the government's inclination to redress African American civil rights claims increased as the United States abandoned its historic isolationist foreign policy stance and attempted to promote an image of itself as the leader of the "free world." If foreign policy orientations help drive the pendulum process, then one should control for potential epochal impacts on the pendulum relationship, and the bifurcation of the temporal domain allows us to account for such effects.

Findings

The original pendulum model *(Eqn 1)* does quite well; it successfully accounts for 83 percent of the outcomes (128/154), including 73 percent of the cases of nationalist leadership, and the X2 value of the dif-

TABLE 13.3
*Logistic Regression of Factors Associated with
Black Nationalism, 1840–1996*

Variable	Eqn 1 1840–1996	Eqn 2 1840–1945	Eqn 3 1946–1996
War	1.50***	.65	6.51***
	(.50)	(.72)	(2.04)
Extroversion	1.08**	2.13***	−1.09
	(.44)	(.59)	(1.41)
Poli-Climate	1.20***	.99*	−2.50
	(.44)	(.54)	(1.69)
Growth.27	.55	2.64	
	(.51)	(.56)	(54.70)
Year	−.02***	−.01	.16**
	(.01)	(.01)	(.06)
Constant	38.24***	16.39	−319.22**
	(9.93)	(16.89)	(135.75)
X2	52.80***	43.17***	26.10***

NOTE: Standard errors are in parentheses; * $p < .10$, ** $p < .05$ level; *** $p < .01$ level

ference between its log likelihood score and that of the null model is statistically significant below the .01 level (see Table 13.3).[13] Three of the four propositions are supported. There is a positive and significant relationship between *Poli-Climate, War,* and *Extroversion,* on the one hand, and *Nationalism,* on the other, which supports P2, P3, and P4, respectively. The negative and significant coefficient for *Year* verifies our assumption of a decline in the probability of nationalism over time. Interestingly, the relationship between *Growth* and *Nationalism* (P1) is not significant, which undermines Marable's thesis that economic factors are important in the rise of Black nationalism; however, it provides some support for McAdam's (1982) view that black political mobilization is rooted mainly in noneconomic factors.

In bifurcating the model across the pre– and post–World War II time periods, it is clear that the results of the original model are largely driven by relationships in the prewar era. *Eqn 2,* which focuses on the pre–World War II era, accurately predicts 82 percent of the outcomes and 83 percent of the episodes of nationalism. Although the coefficient for *War* is not significant in this era (probably because of the impact of the ascendancy of integrationists during World War II, as noted earlier), the directions of the coefficients for the variables in *Eqn 2* are consistent with those of *Eqn 1.* Turning our attention to the post–World War II era, we find only partial support for the view of an epochal impact on black leadership strategies. That is, while *Eqn 3* accurately predicts 91 percent of the outcomes and 67 percent of the episodes of nationalism, the direction of *Poli-Climate, Extroversion,* and *Year* are inverted in the post–World War II period. Nevertheless, *War* has a consistently positive impact on the probability of nationalist ascendance in the post–World War II era; in fact, the coefficient for *War* is the most significant of all the variables in the post–World War II model.

In its entirety, *Eqn 3* suggests that in the post–World War II era *Extroversion* and *Poli-Climate* are associated with an increased likelihood of *integrationist* rather than *nationalist* leadership. This is consistent with the earlier point that integrationists were in a better organizational position, at least up to the time of the assassination of King—to take advantage of the changes in the domestic and foreign policies of the United States in the post–World War II era. However, the relationship between *War* and *Nationalism* is not consistent with the thesis of an epochal impact on black leadership strategies, since *War* remained positively and significantly associated with *Nationalism* in the post–World War II era, as well.

Unlike in *Eqn 1* and *Eqn 2*, there is a potential multicollinearity problem in *Eqn 3*, since the correlation between *War* and *Year* in *Eqn 3* is $r = .77$. When we examine the bivariate relationships among each of these variables and *Nationalism* over the entire period, we find a significant positive correlation between *War* and *Nationalism* ($r = .26$) and a significant negative correlation between *Year* and *Nationalism* ($r = -.36$), while *Nationalism* and *Year* are not significantly correlated with each other. When we alternately drop either variable from *Eqn 3*, we find that the model that includes *War* but excludes *Year* still predicts more than 90 percent of the outcomes and more than half of the instances of nationalist ascendance (5/9), with *War* remaining significant in the model. On the other hand, the model that excludes *War* but includes *Year* fails to correctly predict any of the cases of nationalism, and the coefficient for *Year* is highly insignificant. Clearly, in the post–World War II period the positive association between *War* and *Nationalism* is not an artifact of the collinearity between *Nationalism* and *Year* but a result of the actual independent impact of *War* on *Nationalism*.

While these findings are instructive, it is also important to determine the relative impact of the predictors on the outcome. Kaufman's (1996) technique allows us to estimate the independent impact of each predictor variable on the probability of the outcome and therefore to determine the relative strength of each predictor variable's effect, which is reflected in its Kaufman's Coefficient (KC) value; the greater the value of KC, the greater the predictor variable's effect. Utilizing this procedure, I find that, ceteris paribus, *War* has the greatest relative impact on the rise of black nationalism (KC = .61), followed by *Poli-Climate* (KC = .60), *Extroversion* (KC = .54), and, last *Growth* (KC = .12). These results provide additional support for the centerpiece of my theoretical argument that war, inter alia, is a powerful factor giving rise to black nationalism in the United States. In addition, it further refutes Marable's view—and a persistent view of Marxists, socialists, and many integrationists—that economic factors are the most important correlates of Black political activity. In sum, it appears that war, political cycles, and a repressive political climate are important correlates of black nationalism.

Conclusion

In this study, I have attempted to determine the correlates of the alternations of black leadership strategies since the mid-1800s. Specifically, I have examined the relationship among war, political cycles, the presence of a repressive political climate, and economic growth on the emergence of black nationalism in the United States. One may quarrel with the designation of the leadership phases, but considering the novelty of this enterprise there is little alternative but to glean—in an impressionistic but nonetheless informed fashion—from the historical record of the past century and a half a reasonable categorization of the respective leadership phases and the political strategies that characterized them. These tentative findings push the analysis of black nationalism in a more systematic direction, and in that effort alone they are a contribution to the study of black politics and, therefore, American politics. The findings indicate that, ceteris paribus, within three years of U.S. war involvement there is an increased likelihood of the ascendance of black nationalist leadership. Further, the findings suggest that war, political cycles, and a repressive political climate, more than economic factors, account for the rise of black nationalism. In sum, it appears that Cruse (1968) was correct in stating that changes in black leadership are strongly linked to macropolitical factors.

It is also important that we not fail to more fully consider the utility of the rival approaches to black progress. To be sure, integrationist and nationalist strategies both have strengths and weaknesses. For example, the former appreciates the "American" nature of black oppression but too often rejects the significant culture group basis of black mobilization, while the latter appreciates the culture group basis of political mobilization but often fails to attend to the "American" nature of interest group and coalition politics. Although the perspectives are complementary, instead of seeking a synthesis of the two, adherents of both camps remain in continued conflict as they seek to mobilize the black community. Interestingly, the ideological standoff does not preclude the usurpation by one side of the successful programs of its rivals. One result is that *nationalists* today "March on Washington" to "atone" in a manner that was nearly laughable for nationalists thirty years ago (the Black nationalist Malcolm X labeled the 1963 march that was led by integrationists "The Farce on Washington"). By the same token, *integrationists* celebrate racial self-help initiatives, "buy-black" campaigns, and Black Studies programs that at least superficially reflect the Black Power perspective that integrationists eschewed in the 1960s.

Even as both camps borrow from each other, their ideological rift is maintained almost as a matter of identity. The consequence of this is that although both strategies have contributed to great improvements in the quality of life of African Americans—and Americans in general—a useful synthesis of the two approaches has not been forthcoming. One logical synthesis of the two strategies would wed the juridical focus of integrationist approaches to the community control initiatives of nationalists. One focal point of such a strategy could be a project to both defend and expand affirmative action initiatives through a focus on legal challenges that draw on arguments related to the eradication of "badges of slavery" implied by the Thirteenth Amendment as opposed to arguments that rely on the Fourteenth Amendment's ambiguous "equal protection clause," which is, ironically, being used by opponents of affirmative action to dismantle such programs. This strategy may provide, inter alia, a legal foundation for black reparations and a more persuasive basis for black mobilization with regard to affirmative action than "diversity" arguments (see Henderson 1998). In addition, such a focus could provide a template for independent black political mobilization, which may take the form of an independent black political party or a multicultural third party. Notwithstanding such developments, the suggestion of a synthesis of integrationist and nationalist approaches is not meant to imply that a diverse group of 40 million black people should be unified in a single political strategy. What is clear is that, as black leadership wavers between nationalism and integrationism, black marginalization remains constant; a continuation of such a condition is unconscionable, and black intellectuals and political leaders especially—though not exclusively—should do their best to both comprehend and provide remedies for this situation.

Finally, if the relationships uncovered in this study persist, they suggest that African American leadership will be dominated by nationalists into the first decades of the twenty-first century. The interplay of black nationalism, white nationalism, and emergent Latino, as well as Asian nationalism, suggests a potentially volatile cultural mix for U.S. domestic politics in the next millennium. The major source of volatility is the white nationalist agenda, which has historically (and in the present) been largely aimed at insuring white hegemony in the United States. The attacks on black access to affirmative action are only the most prominent of the white nationalist movement's offensives for mobilizing its adherents and supporters. Nevertheless, the challenge of demands for multiculturalism at home and for a foreign policy that responds to popular perceptions of "clashing civilizations" abroad (Huntington 1996; for a critique, see Henderson 1999), suggests that cultural issues are likely to dominate the political landscape in the upcoming century. These developments remind us that Du Bois was quite prescient in his view that the problem of the twentieth century would be the problem of the *color line*. They also remind us that Cruse was no less prescient; his pendulum thesis suggests that the challenge of the twenty-first century will be the challenge of the *culture line*—at home and abroad.

Appendix

In this Appendix, I provide a brief outline and discussion of the periodization of the black leadership phases used in this study.

1840–1845, Protest Nationalism: Independent Black Churches and National Leadership

Arguably, the first dominant black political leader of national stature was Richard Allen, leader of the African Methodist Episcopal

(AME) Church. Established in 1794 as the African Church of Philadelphia, by 1816 it had become the AME Church, with Allen as its first bishop. The annual AME conference had a membership of 6,784 in 1818 and by 1826 had 10,937 members in the North and the South (Raboteau 1988: 11). Though Allen died in 1831, his independent black church organization and the black convention movement that emerged from it continued to dominate black politics. However, the convention movement defies the simple categorization suggested by Cruse. McCartney (1992) views it as integrationist, Obadele (1989) suggests its nationalist foundation, while Pease and Pease (1971: 205) maintain that through the 1850s it advocated individual assimilation, communal integrative action, and separatism. Nonetheless, following the criteria I have outlined, it appears that during this time the foci of national black leadership appeared to have been nationalist.

1846–1850, Protest Integration: The Abolitionists and the Emergence of Douglass

Frederick Douglass emerged out of the abolitionist movement, and his rise signals the beginning of a clear period of national black leadership. An author and publisher, he became an international spokesperson for black liberation. Douglass's emergence was evident by 1843 as he moved the Negro Convention of that year to defy Henry Highland Garnet's call for enslaved Blacks to revolt against their captors. The publication of his autobiography in 1845 established his national status. A Garrisonian abolitionist at that time, he did not declare his support for political action beyond moral suasion to bring about the liberation of enslaved Africans until the 1850s and the passage of the infamous Fugitive Slave Act. Prior to that time he accepted the integrationist focus of a significant part of the larger abolitionist movement.

1851–1868, Protest Nationalism: Delany, Separatism, and Emigration

Black insurgency increased during this period (Harding 1983: 196), and by 1850 the nationalists led by Delany had become prominent. After the publication in 1852, of his book *The Condition, Elevation, Emigration, and Destiny of the Colored People of the United States,* Delany claimed leadership of the emigrationist arm of the black nationalists (Bracey, Meier, and Rudwick 1971: 184). By as early as 1830, 1,420 Blacks had emigrated to Africa (McCartney 1992: 17). The resurgent black nationalism of the 1850s suggested greater emigration options, including Haiti. To his consternation, Douglass acknowledged that in the 1850s "no less than one quarter of the black population of the North appeared open to the possibilities of emigration" (Harding 1983: 184). Further, Delany's 1854 National Convention in Cleveland pulled in 1,600 delegates from across the country (p. 186). By comparison, Douglass's 1853 Rochester Convention had faired poorly and had been indecisive (p. 182). Until passage of the Fourteenth Amendment, in 1868, the nationalist variant of political leadership was dominant. During this period, Douglass also began to couch his rhetoric in nationalist terms, though he rejected emigrationism.

1869–1895, Protest Integrationism: Douglass and the Failure of Reconstruction

Frederick Douglass's integrationist leadership was clearly dominant during this period. He was hardly alone as a leader, with contemporaries such as Langston, Bruce, Revels, Price, Fortune, Turner, and Truth. During this time, Delany became an advocate for the Freedman's Bureau and accepted some of the basic integrationist economic goals of Reconstruction before returning to the advocacy of emigration (p. 54). Following the passage of the Fourteenth Amendment, Douglass reemerged as the dominant black leader, and his leadership rested firmly on his integrationist philosophy. Although at times Douglass used nationalism for integrationist ends, scholars generally agree that he was not a nationalist (Moses 1978: 41, 84), and he even married a white woman, Helen Pitts, in 1884. Douglass's integrationism remained preeminent until his death in 1895.

1896–1915, Accommodationist Nationalism: The Era of Washington

Washington's Atlanta Exposition speech of September 1895 signaled his ascendancy to national leadership, which largely derived from his organizational strength as head of Tuskegee and his unmatched white support—he was financed by multimillionaires such as Carnegie, Rosenwald, Huntington, and Schiff (Aptheker 1971: 128). Most historians, and even

Washington's ideological nemesis, W. E. B. Du Bois ([1940] 1991), agreed that the era from Douglass's death to 1915 was the era of Washington. Washington's was also the first era of accommodationism. Not only did Washington dominate the Tuskegee machine, but he also organized the powerful National Negro Business League (NNBL) in 1900. In 1906, 1,200 delegates attended its Atlanta meeting (Meier 1991: 124), and some six hundred branches of the NNBL were in existence by 1915 (Quarles 1968: 169). Washington took over the prominent newspaper *New York Age* from T. Thomas Fortune in 1907.

However, there were powerful counters to Washington, such as the Niagara Movement, which, though it never exceeded four hundred members before passing off the scene in 1910 (Quarles 1968: 173–174; Meier 1991: 179), provided a power base for his eventual successors. Washington's decline was evident with his ouster from control of the Afro-American Council in 1907 (Meier 1991: 180–181). His critics attacked his failure to condemn Roosevelt's handling of the Brownsville Incident and the continued lynching of Blacks. Moreover, Washington failed to appreciate the progressive tide among Whites, including supporters such as Milholland and Villard, who abandoned him in favor of the emergent protest integrationist forces in the Constitution League (pp. 181–182). After the Springfield, Illinois, riot of 1908, his critics organized a national conference on the Negro question, and by 1910 the NAACP had emerged with its legalistic brand of integrationism, though it would be several years before Washington was supplanted as the nation's preeminent black leader.

1916–1919, Protest Integrationism: War, Urbanization, and the rise of the NAACP

In 1914, the NAACP had six thousand members in fifty branches, and its publication, *Crisis,* edited by Du Bois, had a circulation of 31,540. A year before, NAACP members had organized a petition drive and obtained twenty thousand signatures against federal Jim Crow. Monroe Trotter delivered the petitions to President Wilson in person on November 6, 1913 (Quarles 1968: 177). A few months before Washington's death, the NAACP scored its first legal victory, having an Oklahoma grandfather clause declared unconstitutional. Washington's death in 1915 provided a bigger platform for fledgling protest integrationists led by Du Bois's NAACP and, to a lesser extent, to the mutual-aid-oriented Urban League. The Amenia Conference, in 1916, brought NAACP and Tuskegee leaders together under the dominance of the NAACP (Peeks 1971: 168). The Amenia Conference was hailed as the birth of a new spirit of unified purpose and effort. Actually, it signaled the growing black commitment to public agitation and litigation for civil rights in place of the accommodationism of the Washington period (p. 171). By 1917, the NAACP had eighty branches and 9,200 members; by 1918 these had increased to 165 branches with forty-five thousand members, twelve thousand in the South. The average monthly circulation of *Crisis* magazine was 41,289 in 1917 and 74,187 in 1918 (Aptheker 1971: 170). Although civil rights issues were salient during this era, there was a concurrent need for housing, employment, and mutual aid as millions of Blacks migrated from the South to prospective jobs in the North. This need was answered, in large part, by the Urban League, which was founded in 1911. However, neither the NAACP nor the Urban League seemed to capture the growing militancy of increasingly urbanized Blacks, nor did their political orientations excite the imagination and the loyalty of the grass roots. This vacuum was filled by the admixture of self-help, race consciousness, and grass-roots organizing of Garvey.

1920–1925, Protest Nationalism: The Garvey Era

By 1919, Garvey and his UNIA & ACL emerged with a brand of protest nationalism and mass organization that dwarfed and overshadowed the NAACP, the UL, and, later, Randolph's Sleeping Car Porters. By 1918, there were several thousand members in the UNIA & ACL, and they held a rally in 1919 in Madison Square Garden that was attended by thousands. By the early 1920s there were more than eight hundred chapters in forty countries on four continents, with reportedly over a million members (Vincent 1971: 13). Their paper, *The Negro World,* which was published from 1918 to 1933, was staffed entirely by Blacks and boasted a circulation of nearly two hundred thousand with editions in English, Spanish, and French (p. 127). Garvey's convention of 1920 was attended by five thousand supporters, including two thousand official delegates organized into two hundred voting units (p. 113). Garvey ushered in a movement of black nationalism similar to that which emerged in the 1850s. An external propellant was provided by the atrocities of the Red Summer (1919), the rare but notable accommodationism of Du Bois, who encouraged Blacks to "close ranks" with Whites to fight World War I, and the increasing failure of integrationist organizations to provide programs to deal with the day-to-day reality of the grass-roots community. Garvey seemed to take the best of Washington and wedded it to the best of the emergent pan-Africanist movement (which was largely indebted to Du Bois) and synthesized them in a mass organization. But Garvey also amassed enemies, prominent among them Du Bois and the NAACP, A. Philip Randolph and other socialists, and the black bourgeoisie exemplified in *The Chicago Defender*'s head, Robert S. Abbott. Abbott, along with other prominent Blacks, petitioned the federal government to investigate Garvey. By 1925 Garvey had been convicted of fraud in a contrived case and subsequently deported to his native Jamaica (Churchill and Vander Wall 1989).

1926–1967, Protest Integrationism: From Legalism to Nonviolent Activism

This period was dominated by the leadership of the NAACP, and its protest integrationist focus was shared by diverse organizations from the Sleeping Car Porters, the NACW, the National Negro Congress, and CORE. Individual leaders and spokespersons also emerged in Mary McCleod Bethune, Adam Clayton Powell, Paul Robeson, Ralph Bunche, the artists of the Harlem Renaissance, and arguably even sports figures such as Joe Louis, Jesse Owens, and Jackie Robinson. Nationalist organizations consisted mainly of scattered remnants of Garvey's organization and marginal groups such as the Moorish Science Temple (MST) and the NOI. NOI founder Fard Muhammad and the organization's subsequent leader Elijah Muhammad were both associated with Detroit's MST and with the UNIA & ACL. This period also witnessed the rise of Father Divine's Peace Missions and Daddy Grace's United House of Prayer.

While the NAACP declined during the Depression—the circulation of *Crisis* was thirty thousand in 1930, whereas ten years earlier it had been one hundred thousand—other organizations emerged but followed a similar protest integrationist approach. Not only in civil rights but also in black union organizing, epitomized by Randolph's Sleeping Car Porters, the protest integrationist perspective was ascendant. Randolph noted that his union of twelve thousand members had in 1947, approximately 20 percent white membership, including Filipinos and Mexicans (Quarles 1988: 160). Protest integrationism persisted because the integrationist ideal benefited from victories won by the NAACP Legal Defense Fund. These legal victories culminated in the landmark *Brown* decision by the Supreme Court, in 1954, which legally overturned Jim Crow in the nation's public schools. In addition, the New Deal had given a second life to integrationist organizations, which extracted "concessions" (discussed earlier) from the Roosevelt administration.

Following World War II and the Korean War, a new leadership emerged—though within the dominant cast of protest integrationism—around King's SCLC, SNCC, and the major organizations of the civil rights and the early Black Power movements. King's moral suasion, SNCC's student activism, and the NAACP's legal strategies resulted in both the 1964 Civil Rights and 1965 Voting Rights acts. The preeminence of protest integrationists on a national level during this period is a point of agreement among most historians.

Nevertheless, the decline of the protest integrationists was evident even prior to the assassination of King in 1968. The movement's successes, while lauded, also exposed the incompleteness of its vision of transformation. Legal remedies for segregation were insufficient as an objective in the North, where de facto discrimination was the dominant mode of white supremacism. In the South, as well, integrationist strategies did not adequately address the economic underdevelopment of the black community wrought from a legacy of Jim Crow, sharecropping, a denial of black access to avenues of credit, and a failure of states to respect black contractual and property rights. Additionally, moral appeals met by white supremacist violence came to be viewed as ineffective for Blacks who suffered under police brutality, discrimination, and privation. As early as 1966, the movement dichotomized between King and Carmichael over the issue of black power (i.e., black nationalism). The formerly integrationist SNCC and CORE expelled Whites from their organizations by the end of that year. Although Malcolm X had been assassinated by members of the NOI in 1965, his legacy loomed larger over the black urban masses than King's influence. The Watts revolt of 1965, the Newark and Detroit revolts of 1967, and King's failed Northern Strategy spelled the demise of integrationist dominance as nationalists began to capture the hearts and minds of the black community.

1968–1975, Protest Nationalism: Black Power

By 1968, with the death of King and the failure of the Poor People's Movement, integrationists were replaced by nationalists and black power advocates (Marable 1993: 99). This was the era of SNCC's and CORE's nationalism, as well as the nationalism of Us organization, the Republic of New Afrika, and the Black Panther Party's nationalist phase. Black Congresses, Black Students' Unions, and Black Studies Programs were formed across the country. Moreover, many Blacks took to the streets in open advocacy of rebellion and black power. Marable suggests that by 1971 the old guard integrationists were discredited in much of the black community (Marable 1993: 101); however, their fall from prominence had actually occurred earlier. The National Black Political Assembly (NBPA), organized to institutionalize black power through a national political organization and political party, had three thousand delegates and five thousand alternates at its convention in Gary, Indiana, in 1972, which was dominated by nationalists.

However, the nationalists were unprepared for the magnitude and extent of repression that would be wielded against them, and their tenure would end by 1975 (Van Deburg 1992). Their organizations were infiltrated, disrupted, and often destroyed. More debilitating and destructive was the FBI's sinister COINTELPRO, which was employed in large part to wage war on black activists and their organizations. One result was the proliferation of black nationalist political prisoners, some of whom, such as Sundiata Acoli, continue to be incarcerated, primarily for their political beliefs and practices. Integrationist leaders such as King, Hamer, and Moses had been political prisoners for brief periods of time; however, nationalists were the most notable targets of this type of political repression because they often endured lengthy prison sentences (Churchill and Vander Wall 1989, 1990; O'Reilly 1989). The institutional sources of black power were also attacked on the college campuses, resulting in the halving of Black Studies programs between 1971 and 1976 (Marable 1993: 112).

The walkout of the Michigan delegation in the 1972 NBPA, led by Coleman Young, drew the line between the activists in the Black Power movement and the emergent integrationist black elected officials (BEOs). Black power retreated into an unspoken alliance with integrationists as the NBPA disintegrated (p. 114). From 1974 to 1976, the NBPA's influence was superseded by BEOs who came to prominence reaping the rewards of the black activism of the 1960s; however, the BEOs' political power was institutionalized through the vehicle of local Democratic party organizations and not through larger black nationalist formations such as the NBPA. Only a few BEOs attended the NBPA in Little Rock in 1974 (pp. 107, 109), and in 1977 only three hundred total members attended the NBPA (p. 109). Meanwhile, the number of BEOs increased from 103 in 1964 to 1,469 in 1970 to 4,311 in 1977 (p. 116).

1976–1980, Accommodationist Integrationism: BEOs, Patronage Politics, and *Bakke*

This era was marked by the ascendancy of the BEOs during the Carter Administration. Protest subsided as black leadership looked toward taking advantage of civil rights victories and affirmative action programs in order to ensure a place for Blacks in an integrated republic. Gains were sought from within tighter alignments between Blacks and the Democratic party. Even the most ardent black nationalist organization, the NOI, under the leadership of W. D. Muhammad, denounced nationalism in favor of integration, even admitting Whites to the organization. Although protests were limited during this period, the dismissal of Andrew Young as U.S. ambassador to the UN, the festering issue of U.S. support for South Africa's apartheid regime, especially after the murder of South African activist Stephen Biko, and the *Bakke* decision, the first major anti–affirmative-action decision by the U.S. Supreme Court of the post–civil rights era, began to engender a groundswell of black activism that would be manifest in the 1980s.

1981–1995, Protest Integrationism: The Resurgence of Activism

Recession, resurgent white supremacism, and Reaganomics incited an era of protest integration in this period. Early grass-roots protests in this period were initially centered on the Atlanta child murders, the Miami revolt, the murder of Michael Griffith in Howard Beach, in New York City, the lynching of Michael Donald in Alabama, and the Forsythe County incident. These and other events set the stage for a resurgence of black activism, especially among black youth. This resurgence helped to galvanize black support for Jesse Jackson's presidential runs of 1984 and 1988. Jackson's Operation PUSH and, later, his National Rainbow Coalition began a frontal attack on corporations to ensure black entrepreneurial access. In 1981 he orchestrated a national boycott of Coca-Cola. This period also saw the rise of the Free South Africa Movement and a resurgent black student movement epitomized in widespread student protests such as that at the University of Michigan, which Jackson mediated. Although this period also saw the rise of the NOI's Louis Farrakhan, it was Jackson who dominated black politics at home and abroad as he mediated the U.S.-Syrian crisis and the subsequent return of a captured U.S. Air Force pilot and provided support to Harold Washington's successful mayoral bid in Chicago. He also led the leftist wing of the Democratic party, but his efforts were stymied by rising conservatism in the country, which was evident in his own party with the growing influence of Bill Clinton's rightist Democratic Leadership Council. Finally, it was Jackson's inability to translate his national success and voter mobilization into electoral success at the national or local level that signaled his ultimate political marginalization. The result was that many Blacks came to see him only as a symbolic leader and not as one who could "deliver" in the manner of the BEOs. At the same time, Jackson resisted attempts to form local Rainbow Coalitions as an alternative party, and this "strategic indecision" undermined much of his grass-roots appeal just as rising conservatism was leaving many Blacks searching for leadership that would mobilize along their group interests.

1995, Accommodationist Nationalism: The Rise of Farrakhan

The Los Angeles revolt and the National Urban Peace and Justice Movement (the Gang Summits) demonstrated the vacuity of Jackson's purely "civil rights" focus. They also compelled the NAACP's president, Ben Chavis, to make overtures to black nationalist leaders to provide direction for the fading organization and to make appeals to end the slaughter of black and brown youth in the nation's cities. This alliance actually reflected the denuding of the integrationist ethos in the black community. In addition, following his snubbing by black leaders commemorating the thirtieth anniversary of the 1963 March on Washington, Farrakhan sought to organize a march on the Capitol that would supersede any that had come before. In that way, he would signal his ascendancy to the mantle of national black leadership. The Million Man March and Day of Atonement on October 16, 1995, did just that. Both integrationists and nationalists were outmaneuvered by Farrakhan's manipulation of a grass-roots initiative for politico-economic redress; however, Farrakhan allowed the march to degenerate into a celebration of his cult of personality in what one analyst called a "black Woodstock." While his often vulgar and reactionary ideology did not win him many converts, his scathing oratory, organizing acumen, and nationalistic appeals have provided him a solid base in the black community. Vilified by mainstream media, he made a celebratory tour of Africa and Asia, where he met with and uttered support for some of the most brutal and detestable dictators in those regions; these actions earned him the condemnation of many of his nationalist confrères. Beyond Farrakhan, it is the resurgence of black self-help initiatives and the persistence of pan-Africanist ideologies such as Afrocentrism that demonstrate the ascendant—though largely accommodationist—nationalism of the present period.

NOTES

The author thanks Harold Cruse, Hanes Walton, and Robert Packer for their comments and suggestions. Research for this article was supported by a grant from the McKnight Foundation. Previous versions of this article were presented to the Conference in Tribute to Harold Cruse, Ann Arbor, Michigan, in March 1998 and to the American Political Science Association, Boston, Massachusetts, in August 1998.

1. Cruse also suggests that black leadership has fluctuated between reform and revolution and accommodation and protest; however, national black leadership has rarely considered revolution as a viable strategy, with the exception of several large-scale slave conspiracies and the policy statements of organizations such as the Black Panther Party (BPP) and the Republic of New Africa (RNA).

2. For Cruse, this is the policy of the modern civil rights leadership, particularly the NAACP, which focuses on political transformation without a concomitant focus on economic transformation.

3. In the nineteenth and early twentieth century, many Whites resisted integrating Blacks into U.S. society, and therefore supported the nationalist efforts to repatriate Blacks to Africa.

4. The AME Church, NAACP, Urban League (UL), Randolph's Sleeping Car Porters, Terrell's National Association of Colored Women (NACW), the Nation of Islam (NOI), the Southern Christian Leadership Conference (SCLC), the Student Non-Violent Coordinating Committee (SNCC), the Congress of Racial Equality (CORE), the BPP, the RNA, and the National Rainbow Coali-

tion are examples of organizations that either vied for or obtained national leadership standing.

5. The alternations in political tactics within the respective phases, such as from accommodation to protest, represent different tactics *within* strategies and, as such, do not represent shifts in strategy.

6. Marable's analysis preceded the most recent rise of black nationalism in the 1990s.

7. Specifically, Myrdal's analysis focuses on the impact of war on black militancy.

8. The scapegoating of Blacks during wartime is doubly ironic when we recognize that many Blacks have long considered that greater citizenship rights would be conferred as a reward for their wartime sacrifice. In fact, military service was often viewed as a route for social uplift in the black community and even a stepping stone to the attainment of black leadership (Butler 1991). For example, according to Lewis (1993: 557–559), Du Bois sought an army commission in military intelligence during World War I.

9. Actually, EO 8802 was restricted to the defense industries and there it lacked teeth for enforcement, Hastie hastily resigned from his position in the War Department because of Marshall's racism, and Davis was never given operational control of troops (see Hine 1982: 250–251).

10. To be sure, integrationists have been attacked viciously and have endured even assassinations and imprisonment; however, police (often with the support of the FBI) ratcheted the levels of violence and deceit upward when it came to black nationalists, resulting in (1) ambushes and assassination, (2) extended political imprisonment, and (3) exile. COINTELPRO especially targeted those groups that Hoover labeled, "black nationalist hate groups" (Churchill and Vander Wall 1989, 1990).

11. Aptheker (1951: 792) states that "[a]ccording to the conservative figures of the Tuskegee Institute, 3,426 Negroes [were] lynched in the United States from 1882 through 1947. Of this total, thirty-six percent, or 1,217 were lynched from 1890 through 1900."

12. Most studies of civil violence capture only general levels of "repression" instead of that which is focused on a particular group. The temporal coverage of these types of studies (e.g. Gurr 1993) is restrictive, while analyses that cover a longer time period often infer repression from regime characteristics such as the extent of democracy. What is needed is an indicator that draws on documentation from black newspapers, police reports, state and federal legislatures, civil rights and advocacy organizations, over the past two centuries. Nevertheless, logistic regressions utilizing regime data from Polity III (Jaggers and Gurr 1996), which has observations for the United States from 1811 to 1993, support the findings about war and nationalism reported here. I conclude that the findings in Table 13.3 are robust.

13. The model performs best using three-year as opposed to two- and four-year lags. The findings were also consistent when we focused only on intensive wars (i.e., those wars that incurred battle deaths above the mean for all U.S. wars).

REFERENCES

Aptheker, Herbert. 1971. *Afro-American History: The Modern Era.* Secaucas, N.J.: Citadel.

———, ed. 1951. *A Documentary History of the Negro People in the United States, Vol. 2, From the Reconstruction to the Founding of the NAACP.* New York: Citadel.

Bennett, Lerone. 1965. *Confrontation: Black and White.* Chicago: Johnson.

Bracey, John, August Meier, and Elliot Rudwick. 1971. *Blacks in the Abolitionist Movement.* Belmont, Calif.: Wadsworth.

Butler, John. 1991. "The Military as a Vehicle for Social Integration: The Afro-American Experience as Data," in *Ethnicity, Integration, and the Military,* ed. Henry Dietz, Jerrold Elkin, and Maurice Roumani (pp. 27–50). Boulder: Westview.

Churchill, Ward, and Jim Vander Wall. 1989. *The COINTELPRO Papers: Documents from the FBI's Secret War on Domestic Dissent.* Boston: South End Press.

———. 1990. *Agents of Repression: The FBI's Secret War Against the Black Panther Party and the American Indian Movement.* Boston: South End Press.

Cruse, Harold 1968. *The Crisis of the Negro Intellectual.* New York: William Morrow.

———. 1987. *Plural but Equal.* New York: William Morrow.

Du Bois, W. E. B. [1903] 1961. *The Souls of Black Folk.* New York: Fawcett.

———. [1918] 1983. "Close Ranks," in *Black Protest: History, Documents, and Analyses, 1619 to the Present,* ed. J. Grant (p. 184). New York: Fawcett.

———. [1940] 1991. *Dusk of Dawn: An Essay toward an Autobiography of a Race Concept.* New Brunswick, N.J.: Transaction.

Ellsworth, Scott. 1982. *Death in a Promised Land: The Tulsa Race Riot of 1921.* Baton Rouge: Louisiana State University Press.

Essien-Udom, Essien. 1964. *Black Nationalism-A Search for Identity in America.* New York: Dell.

Evanzz, Karl. 1992. *The Judas Factor: The Plot to Kill Malcolm X.* New York: Thunder's Mouth Press.

Garrow, David. 1981. *The FBI and Martin Luther King, Jr.* New York: Penguin.

Gellner, Ernest. 1983. *Nations and Nationalism.* Ithaca: Cornell University Press.

Gurr, Ted. 1970. *Why Men Rebel.* Princeton: Princeton University Press.

——, ed. 1993. *Minorities at Risk.* Washington, D.C.: U.S. Institute of Peace.

Harding, Vincent. 1983. *There Is a River.* New York: Vintage.

Henderson, Errol. 1995. *Afrocentrism and World Politics.* Westport, Conn.: Praeger.

——. 1998. "The Farce on Washington? Crusian Pluralism, Affirmative Action, and Black Grassroots Mobilization." Paper presented to the Harold Cruse Conference, University of Michigan, March.

——. 1999. "Clear and Present Strangers: An Empirical Examination of Huntington's Clash of Civilizations Thesis." Paper presented to the International Studies Association. Washington D.C., March.

Hine, Darlene. 1982. "Mabel K. Staupers and the Integration of Black Nurses into the Armed Forces," in *Black Leaders of the Twentieth Century,* ed. John H. Franklin and August Meier (pp. 241–257). Urbana: University of Illinois Press.

Hunt, Michael. 1987. *Ideology and U.S. Foreign Policy.* New Haven: Yale University Press.

Huntington, Samuel. 1996. *The Clash of Civilizations and the Remaking of World Order.* New York: Simon & Schuster.

Jaggers, Keith, and Ted Gurr. 1996. Polity III Data. May. http://wizard.ucr.edu/~wm/polity/polity.html.

Kaufman, Robert. 1996. "Comparing Effects in Dichotomous Logistic Regression: A Variety of Standardized Coefficients." *Social Science Quarterly* 77(1): 90–109.

King, Martin Luther. 1986 [1967]. "Where Do We Go from Here," in *A Testament of Hope, The Essential Writings and Speeches of Martin Luther King,* ed. James Washington. San Francisco: HarperCollins.

Klingberg, Frank. 1979. "Cyclical Trends in American Foreign Policy Moods and Their Policy Implications," in *Challenges to America: United States Foreign Policy in the 1980s,* ed. Charles Kegley and Patrick McGowan (pp. 37–55). London: Sage, 1979.

Kryder, Daniel. 1996. "Race Policy, Race Violence, and Race Reform in the U.S. Army during World War II." *Studies in American Political Development* 10: 130–167.

——. 1997. "War and the Politics of Black Militancy in the Twentieth Century US." Paper presented to the Annual Conference of the American Political Science Association, Washington D.C., August.

Levy, Jack. 1993. "The Diversionary Theory of War: A Critique," in *Handbook of War Studies,* ed. Mannis Midlarsky (pp. 259–288). Ann Arbor: University of Michigan Press.

Lewis, David. 1993. *W. E. B. Du Bois: Biography of a Race.* New York: Henry Holt.

Marable, Manning. 1983. *How Capitalism Underdeveloped Black America.* Boston: South End.

——. 1985. *Black American Politics.* London: Thetford.

——. 1993. *Blackwater.* Boulder: University Press of Colorado.

McAdam, Doug. 1982. *Political Process and the Development of Black Insurgency, 1930–1970.* Chicago: University of Chicago.

McCarthy, John, and Mayer Zald. 1977. "Resource Mobilization and Social Movements: A Partial Theory." *American Journal of Sociology* 82(6): 1212–1241.

McCartney, John. 1992. *Black Power Ideologies: An Essay in African American Political Thought.* Philadelphia: Temple University Press.

Meier, August. 1991. *Negro Thought in America, 1880–1915.* Ann Arbor: University of Michigan Press.

——, ed. 1973. *The Transformation of Activism.* New Brunswick, N.J.: Transaction.

Meier, August, Elliot Rudwick, and Francis Broderick, eds. 1971. *Black Protest Thought in the Twentieth Century,* 2nd ed. New York: Macmillan.

Menard, Scott. 1995. *Applied Logistic Regression Analysis.* Beverly Hills, Calif.: Sage.

Mitchell, Brian. 1993. *International Historical Statistics, The Americas 1750–1988,* 2nd ed. New York: Stockton.

Moon, Henry. 1948. *Balance of Power: The Negro Vote.* Garden City, N.Y.: Doubleday.

Morris, Aldon. 1984. *The Origins of the Civil Rights Movement.* New York: Free Press.

Moses, Wilson. 1978. *The Golden Age of Black Nationalism, 1850–1925.* Oxford: Oxford University Press.

Myrdal, Gunnar. 1944. *An American Dilemma: The Negro Problem and Modern Democracy.* New York: Harper and Brothers.

Obadele, Imari. 1989. *America the Nation-State.* Washington, D.C.: House of Songhay.

O'Reilly, Kenneth. 1989. *Racial Matters: The FBI's Secret File on Black America, 1960–1972.* New York: Free Press.

Painter, Nell. 1988. "Martin R. Delany: Elitism and Black Nationalism," in *Black Leaders of the Nineteenth Century,* ed. Leon Litwack and August Meier (pp. 149–171). Urbana: University of Illinois.

Pease, William, and Jane Pease. 1971. "The Negro Convention Movement," in *Key Issues in the Afro-American Experience,* Vol. 1, ed. Nathan Huggins, Martin Kilson, and Daniel Fox (pp. 191–205). New York: Harcourt, Brace, Jovanovich.

Peeks, Edward. 1971. *The Long Struggle for Black Power.* New York: Charles Scribner's Sons.

Prather, H. Leon. 1984. *We Have Taken a City: Wilmington Racial Massacre and Coup of 1898*. Rutherford, N.J.: Fairleigh Dickinson University Press.

Quarles, Benjamin. 1968. *The Negro in the Making of America*. New York: Collier-Macmillan.

———. 1988. "A. Philip Randolph: Labor Leader at Large," in *Black Leaders of the Twentieth Century*, ed. John H. Franklin and August Meier (pp. 139–165). Urbana: University of Illinois Press.

Raboteau, Albert. 1988. *Slave Religion*. Oxford: Oxford University Press.

Russett, Bruce. 1990. "Economic Decline, Electoral Pressure, and the Initiation of Interstate Conflict," in *Prisoners of War? Nation-States in the Modern Era*, ed. Charles Gochman and Alan Sabrosky (pp. 123–140). Lexington, Mass.: D. C. Heath.

Schweller, Randall, Brian Pollins, and Michael Hannon. 1995. "Systemic Factors Affecting U.S. Foreign Activity, 1792–1995," Paper presented to the Annual Conference of the Peace Science Society (International), Ohio State University, October.

Singer, J. David, and Melvin Small. 1994. *International and Civil War Data, 1816–1992*. Correlates of War Project, University of Michigan, Department of Political Science.

Stohl, Michael. 1975. "War and Domestic Political Violence." *Journal of Conflict Resolution* 19(3): 379–416.

U.S. Department of Commerce. 1975. *Historical Statistics of the United States, Colonial Times to 1970, Bicentennial Edition, Part 1*. Washington, D.C.: U.S. Governing Printing Office.

———. 1996. *Statistical Abstract of the United States*. Washington, D.C.: U.S. Governing Printing Office.

Van Deburg, William. 1992. *New Day In Babylon: The Black Power Movement and American Culture, 1965–1975*. Chicago: University of Chicago Press.

Vincent, Theodore. 1971. *Black Power and the Garvey Movement*. San Francisco: Ramparts.

Walton, Hanes. 1985. *Invisible Politics*. Albany: State University of New York Press.

Chapter 14

Deconstruct to Reconstruct
African American Women in the
Post–Civil Rights Era

Mamie Locke

Black women have often been linked to many of American society's ills, including sexual promiscuity, welfare dependence, idleness, and poverty. Additionally, many of black America's seemingly intractable problems are inextricably linked to gender issues. Yet, the literature on black politics virtually ignores the role of gender as a viable explanatory factor. Unfortunately, scholarship mirrors reality as black women have endured sexism in their indefatigable fight against racism. This is evident in the civil rights movement, in which black women played a formidable role but one that, until very recently, has gone relatively unacknowledged.

Similarly, in the second-wave feminist movement, black women and their issues were long seen as peripheral to the overall political thrust of the National Organization of Women (NOW). While many white women were working toward the elimination of the proverbial glass ceiling, black women were fighting for jobs. While white women were fighting for more equity in the home, many black women struggled to keep their homes intact while also providing daily sustenance and shelter for their children. While white women were engaged in high-profile efforts to dismantle legislation prohibiting abortion, many black women and others were fighting for individual access to affordable and efficient health care services. Certainly, there were issues on which black and white women saw eye to eye, but the overwhelming feeling was that "color" in American society had driven an inextricable wedge between black and white women. To paraphrase the title of Barbara Smith's landmark anthology on black women's experience, "all the women were white and all the Blacks were men."

Black women, Mamie Locke argues, must break down the negative stereotypes and images rooted in centuries of oppression and proactively construct more positive images. Locke argues that the "Million Woman March" served as a starting point for this process but that black women's struggle for empowerment is fraught with challenges. Chief among them is the need to develop an ideology and a mechanism for incorporation that is attainable and practical and, at the same time, welcoming to other women of color.

On October 25, 1997, more than one million African American women from across the United States gathered in Philadelphia, Pennsylvania, for a day of "repentance, resurrection, and restoration." This Million Woman March called together African American women from all walks of life to express dissatisfaction with the deterioration in the condition and lives of African Americans. It was a call for cessation of the activities that were destroying people and communities. As stipulated in the March's mission statement, the purpose of the Million Woman March was to go beyond simply being a feel-good event. It was designed to lead African American women in the call to self-determination. "Our focus is centered around the reasons why and what it will require to eliminate this DESTRUCTION" (*Philadelphia Daily News,* October 24, 1997).

The Million Woman March was also an effort to draw attention to the alarming statistics that continue to marginalize African American women in a nation where blackness and femaleness are not considered positive attributes. The data show that 94 of 1,000 African American teenage girls are victims of violent crime. The AIDS rate for African American women is eighteen times higher than that for white women. In 1992 the high school dropout rate for African American females was 6.7 percent, compared to 3.3 percent for African American men and 4.4 and 3.8 percent for white females and males, respectively. In the area of employment and earnings, the picture remains dismal. In 1996 African American women earned thirty dollars less per week than African American men did, forty dollars less per week than white women, and $134 less per week than white men did. The median household income for African American families was $21,027, for white families $35,126. Only 19.5 percent of African American women were in managerial and professional jobs in 1992, compared to 28.5 percent of white women (*Philadelphia Daily News*, October 24, 1997). The data document the disconnectedness of African American women from the social and political system, define their condition in the aftermath of the civil rights movement, and underscore the need for a united voice to confront the issues.

As African American women joined forces in Philadelphia to raise their voices, they did so in the face of a nation suffocating from a strangling conservatism that continued to render the women voiceless and promoted stereotypical assumptions about them as welfare queens and baby manufacturing machines. On the eve of the next millennium, African American women remain shackled and marginalized despite two significant social and political movements (civil rights and women's) that reshaped the nation's thinking about African Americans and women.

This essay explores the status of African American women in the post–civil rights era. The basic premise is that if African American women are to move from "margin to center" (hooks, 1984), then American society must be transformed, eliminating the patriarchal and racist undercurrents that stand as a wall to prevent "others" from becoming an integral part of the system. Despite the many gains of the civil rights movement, African American women remain marginal and peripheral to the political and social order.

The theoretical framework that guides this work is that of black (Afrocentric/womanist) feminism. Gender is a legitimate topic of inquiry on which black feminist theory can offer many useful insights. This is true whether the research is on voting behavior, public policymaking, or, as in this instance, social and political movements. "On this score what counts as knowledge is whatever is useful in transforming the discipline of political science into one in which women and the study of women in politics are not marginalized" (Staudt and Weaver, 1997, 33).

Since its inception, black feminist theory has faced skepticism and criticism in much the same manner as theories of black politics have. Efforts to use this approach to make inroads into mainstream political science discourse are often viewed as editorializing or are seen as not a "real" academic analysis, or are met with rejection because they "do not meet established academic standards." Mack Jones, in establishing a frame of reference for black politics nearly thirty years ago, which subsequently broke new ground, points out that "one should begin by searching for those factors which are unique to the black political experience, for this is the information which will facilitate our understanding of Blacks in the American political system" (Smith, 1995, 5). This is true as well for anyone who is seeking to establish a theoretical framework for examining African American women in the political system. It is Afrocentric feminist theory, not mainstream feminist theory, that will best illuminate the condition of African Americans because of their unique history and circumstances.

Empirical data on African American women are scarce and sketchy at best. There is no cogent corpus of literature from which to draw extensive analysis and analogies, save that compiled and written by African American women over the past two decades. African American women have had to become their own historians, political analysts, theorizers, data gathers, and culture bearers. From the writings of bell hooks, Patricia Collins, Alice Walker, and others, black feminist theory (Afrocentric and womanist) has emerged as a serious field of inquiry.

Given the historical situations that created an oppressive and exploitative foundation upon which the lives of African American women have been constructed, it is only from a black feminist standpoint that a realistic analysis of African American women's lives can be understood. It is within the framework of black feminist thought that this chapter examines the condition of African American women in the post–civil rights era. Significant, too, is the women's movement, for the nuances emanating from both movements have affected the reality of African American women's lives.

The post–civil rights era has brought new and different complications for African American women. Among these are intraracial tensions over gender issues, as well as the search for an alternative to mainstream feminism. The 1970s witnessed innumerable discussions regarding African American male and female relationships. Several African American women raised the issue of male sexism and misogyny, a topic previously taboo. Seen as black male bashing, the dialogue, often contentious, continued over the next two decades. This intraracial conflict is ongoing, as is the continued subjugation of African American people overall.

African American women contend with other minority groups who compete to deconstruct the white and male power base. These groups include other minority women—Hispanic, Native American, and Asian. In an emerging multiracial society, African American women are competing for their place in society alongside these other groups.

African American women must decide if they should pursue coalition building with other women of color as a strategy to overcome race, gender, and class conflict. If they decide to do so, how can they do it in a way that preserves their unique and disparate experiences, and now that they can ensure that coalition partners accept, appreciate, and respect those differences? Gregory Rodriguez believes that the civil rights movement has fallen into a victimization trap in which all groups granted protected minority status feel aggrieved and must seek redress of those grievances. This has completely diluted the civil rights agenda as originally envisioned (*Detroit News,* March 29, 1998). The conflicts are not new.

The race, class, and gender struggle has been present since the founding of the United States as a nation. Centuries of oppression, white supremacy, and exploitation weigh heavily on the post–civil rights condition of African American women and the enduring crucible they face. The race and gender struggle manifested itself quite clearly during the American Revolution, the abolitionist period, and Civil War and Reconstruction eras.

After Reconstruction, questions remained over the status of African American people. The late nineteenth century was a period of intense social and political turmoil, particularly in race relations, a time when white supremacy and social Darwinism were the prevailing ideologies. Questions of the primacy of race over sex and other issues that marginalized Blacks and women led African American women to speak for their race. There was a self-conscious need to defend African American men and women against the inequities and widespread stereotypes that marked nineteenth-century American cultural thought (Washington, 1987, 73). Hence, African American women entered the twentieth century as race women, creating a movement to "lift as we climb."

African American women, as part of two groups that were peripheral to mainstream society, recognized their unique role in American society. Anna Julia Cooper often questioned this race/sex dichotomy, that is, the efforts of white women to make their experiences corroborative to those of all women and the view that the accomplishments of black men were those of the race. She stated that black women were "confronted by both a woman question and a race problem, and is as yet an unknown or an unacknowledged factor in both"(Cooper, 1892, 134). Her words, written more than one hundred years ago, remain hauntingly true in the late twentieth century, despite struggles for equality through the civil rights and women's movements.

For centuries a paradigm has existed "by which Blacks are reassured that there is no real inequality in the world, just their own bad dreams; and by which women are taught not to experience what they experience, in deference to men's way of knowing" (Williams, 1991, 13). The civil rights and the women's movements tackled this paradigm, demanding full and equal rights under the law for the groups they represented.

The strategy of the civil rights movement was to attack the institutional foundation of segregation and discrimination. The movement's momentum and power evolved from its moral authority, which emanated from African Americans' historical circumstances. Consequently, legal and social redress by the established political order was justified. The purpose of the movement was to eradicate the legal and social barriers that prohibited African Americans from participating as full and equal citizens in the social, economic, and political realms of society. The movement sought voting rights, educational opportunities, civil rights, and employment opportunities. As the barriers to integration tumbled, African American women availed themselves of the opportunities designed to close the gap between themselves and other groups in society.

"All the women are White, all the Blacks are men" (Hull, Scott, and Smith 1982) is part of the title of a seminal work in black women's studies that sums up the impact of both the civil rights movement and the women's movement on the status of African American women. The civil rights movement achieved many social and political gains for African Americans. Since the mid-1950s the passage of significant civil rights legislation has eliminated de jure segregation and discrimination in the nation. Affirmative action policies have opened doors for African Americans and women, particularly in the areas of education and employment. Many African Americans have ascended to electoral positions at the local, state, and national levels.

African American women have made progress in many areas as a result of the civil rights movement. However, these gains have not been substantive, radical, or dramatic. In many areas African American women are still being heralded as "firsts" long after the end of the for-mal civil rights movement. A review of rosters of elected officials and of education and employment statistics reveals that some progress has been made. However, much work remains if African American women are to reach equality.

In the electoral arena, African Americans have increased their num-ber of elected officials to 8,658. The largest growth area continues to be in education (superintendents, school boards). African American women have increased their presence significantly, moving from 160 elected officials in 1970 to 2,812 in 1997 (*Roster of Black Elected Of-ficials*, 1997). Of the forty African American members of Congress, fourteen are women. The lone African American in the Senate, Carol Moseley Braun, was defeated in the 1998 mid-term elections. Thus, in 1999, African Americans constitute a mere 7 percent of the member-ship of Congress, all in the House of Representatives. African Ameri-can women are 2.6 percent of the total membership. There are 495,000 elected officials in the United States. African Americans constitute less the 3 percent of that total (*Popularly Elected Officials in 1992*).

At the state and local levels, the numbers are not much better for African American women. The National Conference of Black Mayors reports that a total of three hundred African Americans serve as may-ors, only thirty-six of them in cities of fifty thousand or more popula-tion. Of that thirty-six, only three are African American women. Fur-ther, African American women are still accomplishing "firsts" at the dawn of the next millennium. Lynette Boggs McDonald was recently appointed as the first woman and the first African American woman to the Las Vegas city council. While the struggle for civil rights moved from direct protest to the ballot box, the rewards have not been over-whelming for African Americans overall and for African American women in particular. They continue to face obstacles and resistance to their effort to be seen as viable and electable candidates.

In the area of education and employment, there is a persistent argu-ment among white feminists and others that African American women have far exceeded the achievements of African American men and white women. The 1997 *African American Education Data Book* shows that African Americans overall must progress much more in order to obtain parity with Whites. "Although African Americans' representation in higher education has grown in the past decade, it still is significantly below the percentage they represent in the general population" (Nettles).

Over the past twenty years, the overall proportion of African American men and women who enroll in college has increased. It is the increase in African American women (60 percent) that contributes most to these overall educational gains. There are more African American women (62 percent of the total number of Blacks) than African American men (38 percent) in college. In fact, women, both African American and white, represent the majority of college and university enrollments. Ninety-one percent of African Americans enrolled in higher education are undergraduates, 8 percent are graduate students, and 1 percent are professional students. Although African American students today fare better than black students of a generation ago, their numbers do not reflect African Americans' share of the population and fall far short of the percentage of white students. African American students still drop out of college more frequently and rely more heavily on financial aid. Twenty-four percent of Whites graduate from college, compared to 13 percent of African Americans (Nettles, 1997; *Statistical Abstract of the United States, 1996*).

The educational attainment of African Americans ages 25–29 increased across all educational levels between 1971 and 1997; the percentage of those completing high school rose from 59 percent to 87 percent in those years. However, the gap between the attainment of Blacks and that of Whites decreased only for high school completion, not for higher education. Of those who graduate from high school, 46 percent of Whites go on to college, compared to 32 percent of African Americans (*The Condition of Education, 1998; Statistical Abstract of the United States, 1996*).

What accounts for the disparity between the number of African American men and the number of African American women enrolled in college? A number of theories are presented to explain this phenomenon. One argument is that prejudice impacts young black boys more heavily and at an earlier stage than girls. This prejudice manifests itself in the uneasiness of white teachers with their black male students and in the differential treatment accorded of black boys by white teachers. Many of these boys lose interest in school and are likely to succumb to negative peer pressure. Even those who are experiencing academic success are targeted as "behavioral problems" and are diverted from normal educational pursuits. A second reason given for the disparity in college enrollment is that African American men may feel compelled to seek full-time jobs to support themselves more than women. As a result, men get bogged down in the quagmire of unskilled jobs that offer few, if any benefits. Additionally, the opportunities for boys as an alternative to college appear to be greater than those for girls (*Pittsburgh Post-Gazette,* February 16, 1988).

Other reasons given include the higher arrest and mortality rates for young black men, as well as the limited resources of African American families. Furthermore, high school counselors tend not to suggest college to African American students. The differences in the rates at which African American men and women enter, persist in, and complete higher education certainly suggests that there remain many social and political challenges that must be overcome in order for educational equality to be achieved (Nettles, 1997).

The civil rights and the women's movements also focused on employment and economic opportunity as a means by which equality could be achieved. With the advent of affirmative action programs, Title VII and Title XIX of the 1964 Civil Rights Act, the doors to equal opportunity and access were opened for African American women. In the area of employment, African American women found themselves labeled "two-fors"—that is, two minorities (black and female) hired in one fell swoop. African American women have improved their economic status over the past two decades. An examination of this progress, however, shows that there are still many barriers to overcome.

Historically, African American women have had higher labor force participation rates than have white or Hispanic women. Data compiled by the Women's Bureau of the U.S. Department of Labor show that labor force participation for African American women increased from 57 percent to 60 percent between 1986 and 1996. White women have almost eliminated the gap, however, and projections show that their role of participation will be slightly higher than that of African American women by the year 2005 (62 percent for Whites to 59 percent for Blacks) ("Black Women in the Labor Force," 1997). Hence, affirmative action programs in the area of employment have clearly worked to the advantage of white women.

The number of employed African American women was lower than the number of employed African American men until 1988. However, African American women accounted for slightly more than half of the total of Blacks employed (52 percent) in 1996 ("Black Women in the Labor Force," 1997). In 1999, the employment rate for African American women age 20 or more was 62 percent, compared to 68 percent for

African American men, 58 percent for white women, and 75 percent for white men, and the unemployment rate was 7.4 percent for African American women, compared to 7.3 percent for African American men, 3.4 percent for white women, and 3.2 percent for white men (*Labor Force Statistics,* 1999). Thus, the gap in the unemployment rates for African American men and African American women is statistically insignificant but is significant when these rates are compared to those for white men and women.

Arguments that African American women earn as much as or more than white women do not hold up when occupational and employment trends are analyzed. In identified occupational categories, African American women are significantly represented only in the service, managerial, and professional specialties and in the technical, sales, and administrative support categories. An examination of the ten leading occupations for African American women shows their continued overrepresentation in traditional female fields (nurses, nurse's aids, teachers, secretaries, social workers) and service fields (janitors, cooks, maids). African American women are also heavily employed in sales and administrative support jobs. Such jobs are sometimes temporary, do not pay high salaries, and do not offer the same range of benefits as managerial, professional, and technical jobs ("Black Women in the Labor Force," 1997).

The glass ceiling does not aptly describe the barriers African American and other minority women face in corporate America. Minority women see the barrier as being concrete, not glass. Thus, they cannot see up, down, or around the corporate ladder. This was the conclusion drawn in a study conducted by Catalyst, a nonprofit research group, in its report "Women of Color in Corporate Management" (1999). The women surveyed indicated that not only did they lack mentoring but they were also dissatisfied with corporate diversity initiatives. The diversity plans, for the most part, were seen as ineffective in addressing subtle racism in the workplace.

Clearly, there is a direct correlation between education and employment. The more education one has, the more likely one is to be in the labor force. Because of the disparity between African Americans and Whites in the percentage receiving college degrees and in the highest degree field, African Americans are less likely to fill their share of new workforce positions that require degrees in the future (Nettles, 1997)). As the available jobs require more scientific and technical background and degrees, African American women will enter the market at a slower rate, because they (as well as African American men and all other women) continue to receive degrees primarily in education, nursing and health-related fields, the liberal arts, the humanities, and the social sciences. They have, however, made some advances in the fields of engineering and business (*Digest of Education Statistics*, 1997).

In 1996 the labor force participation for African American women age 25 and older with only a high school diploma was 65 percent, compared to 55 percent and 63 percent for white and Hispanic women, respectively. African American women with less than a high school diploma experienced unemployment in 1996 at a rate nearly six times that experienced by with college degrees. Most African American women in the labor force were those with a high school diploma (35 percent) or some college (24 percent). Given that college graduates and those with postbaccalaureate degrees command higher incomes, the argument that African American women's incomes are not likely to be comparable to or higher than that of white women is inaccurate. Clearly, African American women must possess postsecondary degrees to achieve higher incomes; however, 59 percent of those in the labor market do not have degrees.

In a recent essay, Derrick Bell points out that the reality of the post–civil rights era "is that blacks still suffer disproportionately higher rates of poverty, joblessness, and insufficient health care than other ethnic populations in the United States" (Crenshaw, et al., 1995, 308). This is particularly true for African American women, particularly when one looks at poverty rates. In 1995 there were 8.1 million black families in the United States, a 19 percent increase from 1985. Of the 8.1 million families, almost half (46 percent) were headed by women. Fifty-eight percent of the 8.1 million families included children under the age of eighteen, with families headed by women being more likely to include children. Furthermore, families headed by women were likely to have more children per family than other groupings (married couples, male-headed families). The median income for female-headed households was only $15,004 (U.S. Bureau of the Census, 1995).

While African American women improved their economic status between 1986 and 1996, there are several realities that must be faced. In 1996 those who worked full time earned 88 percent of the earnings of similarly employed African American men, 85 percent of comparably employed white women, and only 62 percent of the earnings of comparably employed white men. African American median family income was only 61 percent of that of white families. Of the 46 percent of African American families that were headed by women, 45 percent were living in poverty in 1995. African American women were three times as likely to live in poverty and twice as likely to be unemployed as white women. Hence, the labor market, public and private, must remove the obstacles that hinder African American women from becoming part of the economic mainstream, especially since they will constitute the largest percentage of the nonwhite labor force through 2005 ("Black Women in the Labor Force," 1997).

The activities of the civil rights movement politicized women, who began to apply some of the insights of the African American struggle to their own struggle as women. Consequently, the gender-based women's movement followed closely on the heels of the civil rights movement. The overall basis of the movement demonstrated a frustration with the existing patriarchal social and political order. Hence, the purpose of the movement, for the most part, was to obtain equality with men. Bell hooks (1995) viewed the civil rights and the black power struggles as movements that demanded an end to white supremacy, along with cultural understanding and a share in the nation's material wealth and resources. However, the women's movement that followed those struggles was co-opted to serve the interests of white patriarchy and furthered the access of white women to ruling-class wealth and power. White women did not ask critical questions about their own racial identity and racial privilege. In fact, white women appropriated the discourse on race to advance their careers, much to the detriment of African American women.

The women's movement received mixed reviews from African American women, who were not overwhelmingly accepting of feminism. The feminist movement was labeled racist by many who felt they were expected to decided which oppression was the most oppressive. African American women have often criticized the feminist movement for its exclusion of issues pertinent to the experiences of black women. While credit has been given to the women's movement for progressively reducing discrimination against women in education, laws, and workplaces, there remain many women who feel that the struggle has not touched them. These women argue that the movement has failed to broadened its base and remains made up largely of white, highly educated, middle-class women who have not adequately addressed issues that matter to the poor and struggling. These women point to child care as being more critical to them than abortion rights or lesbian issues; economic survival as more crucial than political equality; and the sticky floor of their existence as being more problematic than breaking through the glass ceiling (*U.S. News & World Report* 1994: 49).

Mainstream feminists have been accused of being elitist and of presenting their issues as those of all women when that was not the reality. This has been one of the major reasons African American women have failed to open their arms to feminism and the women's movement. The overall participation of African American women in the women's movement decreased significantly by 1975 (Taylor, 1998, 85); this is the point at which many African American women began to look inward to formulate a more positive course for themselves and the community. During the civil rights and the women's movements, African American women activists developed a distinctly feminist consciousness that provided an avenue through which they would empower themselves on their own terms. In the mid-1970s African American women struggled through the negative responses from inside (from African American men) and outside (from white women). This effort to determine their destiny was ridiculed, dismissed, or interpreted as being divisive. The popularity of conservatism further hampered the inclusion of African American women in society.

With the election of Ronald Reagan to the presidency in 1980, followed by George Bush in 1988, the veil of acceptability for "others" was slowly lowered. The twelve years spanning those presidencies was accompanied by a rising tide of conservatism and right-wing fanaticism. A political climate was created during the Reagan-Bush years that allowed women and minorities to be scapegoated as the cause of all of America's problems—increasing crime rates, illegal immigration, out-of-wedlock births, and affirmative action, to name a few. The scare tactics used by former Speaker of the House of Representatives Newt Gingrich and his Republican cohort of legislators, who rode into office in the 1990s as change agents with a Contract with America, went beyond demonstrating prejudice. Those tactics were but a continuation of race baiting that reinforced the racism and misogyny that undergird the very fabric of American society. Policies shifted in favor of those that helped to dismantle affirmative action and to reduce government protection of the rights of minorities.

African American women have borne the brunt of these policy shifts.

If the media and conservative politicians are to be believed, African American women have singlehandedly caused the moral decay of society. Lubiano (1992) asserts that African American women are seen as "the agent of destruction, the creator of the pathological, black, urban, poor family from which all ills flow; a monster creating crack dealers, addicts, muggers, and rapists—men who become those things because of being immersed in her culture of poverty" (38–39). Currently, the media, academics, and conservatives often claim that affirmative action as a program gives undeserving, underqualified African Americans an advantage over more deserving, overqualified white males.

The marginalization of African American women was never more clearly demonstrated than during the confirmation hearings on Clarence Thomas's appointment to the Supreme Court in 1991. The treatment of Anita Hill, who accused Thomas of sexual harassment, made conscious the subconscious images held by Whites of African American women as immoral women who emasculate their men. Once again an African American woman had been put in the position of defending her honor and integrity. Ironically, the farce was played out on national television with fourteen white men (members of the Senate Judiciary Committee) as judge and jury. Both race and gender bias were openly displayed for public consumption.

In her analysis of the Thomas-Hill scenario, Crenshaw (1992) states that America simply stumbled into the place where African American women reside daily, a political vacuum of erasure and contradiction maintained by the almost routine polarization of Blacks and women into separate and competing political camps. Anita Hill's status as a black woman, operating at the crossroads of the gender and the race hierarchies, was critical to the manner in which she was perceived, or, in this instance, misperceived (403). Stansell (1992) argues that Clarence Thomas merely drew upon the widespread hostilities toward women that conservatives were finding easy to drum up, especially when the women were poor and even more so when they were black. This was not a surprising tactic, given Thomas's roots in the patriarchal, conservative tradition (254, 261), which resists change and finds any shift in the political and social order threatening.

Thomas's defenders at his hearing exacerbated intraracial conflicts by relying on an attack on the collective character of African American women. Derrick Bell (Crenshaw, et al., 1995) contends that the Thomas hearings provided the most ominous evidence that African

Americans were in a period of racial rejection, a time when many Whites blocked out their justified fears about the future by indulging in blatant forms of discrimination.

The fear of what will happen to the white majority is what sustains the barriers that continue to be erected to positive change regarding race and gender. Jewell (1993) argues that this generally suppressed fear "stems from the knowledge that if the real problem, that of controlling societal resources and maintaining systems of domination is challenged, the solution becomes one of revolution rather than reform" (3). Continued questioning and attacking of racist and patriarchal modes of thinking and acting cause the dominant group to create barriers that allow them to maintain dominance. Minority groups, especially women, often find themselves held back by those obstacles. In the post–civil rights era African American women hold more political and corporate offices than ever before; however, the white male political and economic establishment still dictates governmental and political policy in the United States (Hemmons, 1996, 10).

The United States in the twenty-first century will be more racially and ethnically diverse than ever before. By the year 2000, African Americans constituted 13 percent of the overall U.S. population, and American Indians, Asians, Hispanics, and Whites constituted 1 percent, 3.5 percent, 10 percent, and 82 percent, respectively (*Statistical Abstract of the United States,* 1996). What does this mean for women? Much like African American women, Hispanic, Native American, and Asian women have had to struggle to obtain political, social, and economic equality. They have had to combat the evils of racist and sexist oppression within the broader context of nationalist struggles. They confront stereotypical images in the same manner that African American women have had to address and deconstruct the mammy, Sapphire, and welfare queen stereotypes. As Jones and Jones (1997) have observed, Hispanic women are seen as sexually promiscuous and Asian women as passive geisha girls. These women are faced with patriarchal and machismo family structures that relegate them to stereotyped gender roles. Such images continue to play "a significant and insidious role in the social, political, economic, and institutional histories of the United States" (15).

Rinku Sen (1997) paints a rather dismal picture for women of color as we begin the new millennium. She argues that the average woman of color will increasingly be forced to rely on the whims of private charity, since the standard public services will not be available; the gains of the civil rights, women's, and other progressive movements will have been slowly dismantled by the backwash of the conservative right. The conservative right is a group devoid of any social conscious because it is inherently and profoundly racist and patriarchal. As a result, women of color will face hostility that will force them to struggle for their very survival. This struggle will push and pull women of color in many directions, both within their own groups and in their relations with women of other groups. While African American women must acknowledge the commonalties they share with other women of color, they must adopt an initial selfishness that will move them and the African American community forward.

Race and gender issues remain prevalent and polarized in American society. Given African American women's interest in both issues, the battle must be waged on two fronts. Bookman and Morgen (1988) contend that the empowerment of African American women begins when they "recognize the system forces that oppress them, and they act to change the conditions of their lives"(4). They must be persistent in their challenges to racist and patriarchal ideas and practices. As a beginning, they must deconstruct political and social literature that ignores race, gender, and class issues and promotes racist and sexist notions.

African American women have centuries of racist and sexist oppression to deconstruct. The creation of black feminist theory as a new paradigm for transforming racist and patriarchal thinking is critical to the deconstruction of white-male–centered thought. Caraway (1991) posits that "black feminism deconstructs the discourse of white feminism and challenges parochial canons of acceptable knowledge and institutions" (27). Feminism that is Afrocentric allows African American women a vehicle to conceptualize difference and otherness. African American feminists such as Audre Lorde, Patricia Hill Collins, and Deborah King have developed a black feminist standpoint that has grown out of a history of struggle and solidarity, a history of multiple jeopardies. Mainstream feminist theory tends to have historical amnesia about the role of white women in the maintenance of the oppression of African American women. The struggle is about more than gender. It is about deconstructing a mindset that permeates the very fabric of the American political system. It is also about deconstructing a socialization process that promotes stereotypes and cultural images of African American women that are destructive and a means of social and political control.

Jewell further argues that, since public policies in this country are created by and designed for the protection of the privileged class, the solution becomes one of revolution rather than reform. If the goal of African American women is to reconstruct a society where the needs of individuals determine the allocation of resources, then clearly there must be an overhaul of society. There is a need to replace those ideologies that serve as the basis for patriarchy and other dominating systems with ideologies of inclusion. For African American women, there must be a recognition of the institutional and systemic forces that oppress them, for recognition of the causes of powerlessness allows them to move forward to empowerment. Lorde (1984) has stated "the master's tools will never dismantle the master's house. They may allow us temporarily to beat him at his own game, but they will never enable us to bring about genuine change" (112). Thus, the solution lies with African American women, who must create and implement their own tools for change.

Collins (1991) postulates that the key to African American women's survival lies in their ability to articulate a self-defined collective standpoint. This must be done by and for African American women. Lorde (1984) points out that "it is axiomatic that if we do not define ourselves for ourselves, we will be defined by others—for their use and to our detriment"(45). African American women must do so without feelings of guilt that they are being disloyal to African American men. One can safely say they owe no loyalty to white women. But, are coalitions with other racial minorities an immediate strategy to be pursued? What is the impact of such a strategy on African American women's efforts to achieve self-determination?

It appears logical that those racial minority groups who share common issues and goals would gravitate to each other. Women of color collectively share some common bonds. The effects of racism, colonialism, and oppression are at the base of those common bonds. Extenuating factors such as poverty and violence marginalize all women of color. How can African American women contend with other women of color in a way that allows them to continue to maximize self-determination?

An Afrocentric feminist standpoint does not preclude coalition building. Hooks (1990) contends that there can be a feminist solidarity between African American women and other women of color. Such a coalition must be constructed in a way that allows all groups to have meaningful and rigorous intellectual exchange and critique without negating each other. Sen (1997) suggests that progressive groups have at their disposal a strong power source that needs to be consolidated and nurtured. However, they will need to integrate the goal of gender equity and analysis into the movement. They must challenge patriarchy and misogyny at their core if racial and gender justice are to be achieved.

Are African American women prepared to embrace a multicultural feminist theory? Caraway's (1991) concept of multicultural feminism calls for a crossover politics of sort. All groups involved must temporarily and strategically shift their own politics if they are to survive. This means that crossover feminists must see and hear the views of others to the point of mitigating the feminist ethnocentrism that has permeated much of the women's movement. Jewell (1993) indicates that little has been done to challenge America's assumptions about African American women. The African American woman's cultural image is different from that of white women, Hispanic American women, Native American women, and Asian American women. It is an image that has changed minimally in over the years.

Multicultural feminism must be truly deconstructionist if it is to draw all women of color together. The argument here is that feminism has not reached that level. Whitaker (1999) is correct when she argues that "deconstructionist, or post-modern feminism begins with the most marginal and overlooked viewpoint . . . assumes its validity, if not its universality, then employs it to gain access to truths not available to those whose reality is more 'central'" (15). There is no one central, legitimate perspective.

African American women must contend with their own unique set of circumstances as shaped by their history in the United States. There still exists in the national psyche a deep, self-replicating strain of denial that transforms African American people into a group without any needs. Through a black feminist frame of reference, African American women have begun to challenge and deconstruct the many racist and patriarchal ideas and practices that would render them voiceless and powerless. While coalitions with other women of color must be explored as a means of consolidating and expanding their power base, African American women must strengthen themselves within their own collective initially. The Million Woman March is but one example of that effort toward expanding the black feminist power base. It is through self-definition that African American women will empower themselves to deconstruct a racist, patriarchal society and reconstruct a society based upon positive political and social change. A black and multiracial politics demands it.

REFERENCES

"Black Women in the Labor Force." 1997. *Facts on Working Women.* Washington, D.C.: Women's Bureau, U.S. Department of Labor.

Bookman, Ann, and Sandra Morgen. 1988. *Women and the Politics of Empowerment.* Philadelphia: Temple University Press.

Caraway, Nancie. 1991. *Segregated Sisterhood: Racism and the Politics of American Feminism.* Knoxville: University of Tennessee Press.

Collins, Patricia Hill. 1991. *Black Feminist Thought: Knowledge, Consciousness, and the Politics of Empowerment.* New York: Routledge.

The Condition of Education. 1998. Washington, D.C.: Bureau of the Census, U.S. Department of Commerce.

Cooper, Anna Julia. 1892. *A Voice from the South by a Black Woman of the South.* Xenia, Ohio: Aldine.

Crenshaw, Kimberlé. 1992. "Whose Story Is It Anyway? Feminist and Antiracist Appropriations of Anita Hill," in Toni Morrison, ed., *Race-ing Justice, En-gendering Power: Essays on Anita Hill, Clarence Thomas, and the Construction of Social Reality.* New York: Pantheon Press.

Crenshaw, Kimberlé, et al., eds. 1995. *Critical Race Theory: The Key Writings That Formed the Movement.* New York: New Press.

Digest of Education Statistics. 1997. Washington, D.C.: U.S. Department of Education.

Garcia, Alma M. 1994. "The Development of Chicana Feminist Discourse, 1970–1980," in Marianne Githens, Pippa Norris, and Joni Lovenduski, eds., *Different Roles, Different Voices: Women and Politics in the United States and Europe.* New York: HarperCollins.

Hemmons, Willa Mae. 1996. *Black Women in the New World Order: Social Justice and the African American Female.* Westport, Conn.: Praeger.

hooks, bell. 1984. *Feminist Theory: From Margin to Center.* Boston: South End Press.

———. 1990. *Yearning: Race, Gender, and Cultural Politics.* Boston: South End Press.

———. 1995. *Killing Rage: Ending Racism.* New York: Holt.

Household and Family Characteristics. 1995. Washington, D.C.: Bureau of the Census, U.S. Department of Commerce.

Hull, Gloria T., Patricia Bell Scott, and Barbara Smith. 1982. *All the Women*

Are White, All the Blacks Are Men, But Some of Us Are Brave: Black Women's Studies. Old Westbury, N.Y.: Feminist Press.

Jewell, K. Sue. 1993. *From Mammy to Miss America and Beyond: Cultural Images and the Shaping of U.S. Social Policy.* New York: Routledge.

Jones, Tamara, and Alethia Jones. 1997. "Women of Color in the Eighties: A Profile Based on Census Data," in Cathy J. Cohen, Kathleen B. Jones and Joan C. Tronto, eds., *Women Transforming Politics: An Alternative Reader.* New York: New York University Press.

Labor Force Statistics. 1999. Washington, D.C.: Bureau of Labor Statistics, U.S. Department of Labor.

Lorde, Audre. 1984. *Sister Outsider.* Trumansberg, N.Y.: Crossing Press.

Lubiano, Wahneema. 1992. "Black Ladies, Welfare Queens, and State Minstrels: Ideological War by Narrative Means," in Toni Morrison, ed. *Raceing Justice, En-gendering Power: Essays on Anita Hill, Clarence Thomas, and the Construction of Social Reality.* New York: Pantheon.

Klosko, George, and Margaret G. Klosko. 1999. *The Struggle for Women's Rights: Theoretical and Historical Sources.* Upper Saddle River, N.J.: Prentice-Hall.

Murray, Charles, and Richard Herrnstein. 1994. *The Bell Curve.* New York: Free Press.

Nettles, Michael T. 1997. *The African American Education Data Book.* Fairfax, Va.: Frederick D. Patterson Research Institute College Fund.

Popularly Elected Officials in 1992. 1995. Bureau of the Census. Washington, D.C.: U.S. Department of Commerce, Economics and Statistics Administration.

Rodriguez, Gregory. 1998. "With Struggle for Civil Rights Diluted, Class Agenda Needed." *Detroit News.* March 29, p. A1.

Roster of Black Elected Officials. 1997. Washington, D.C.: Joint Center for Political and Economic Studies.

Schockner, Bill. 1998. "Women Outnumber Men among Blacks on Campus." *Pittsburgh Post-Gazette,* February 16. Accessed at www.post-gazette.com/blackhistorymonth/19980216black.asp.

Sen, Rinku. 1997. "Winning Action for Gender Equity: A Plan for Organizing Communities of Color," in Cathy J. Cohen, Kathleen B. Jones, and Joan C. Tronto, eds., *Women Transforming Politics: An Alternative Reader.* New York: New York University Press.

"Separating Sisters." 1994. *U.S. News & World Report,* March 28, 49–50.

"Sisters Challenging the Stereotypes." 1997. *Philadelphia Daily News,* October 24. Accessed at www.home-phillynews.com/packages/wmill/opin/DN/S1EDIT24.asp.

Smith, Robert C. 1995. *Racism in the Post–Civil Rights Era.* Albany: SUNY Press.

———. 1996. *We Have No Leaders: African Americans in the Post Civil Rights Era.* New York: SUNY Press.

Stansell, Christine. 1992. "White Feminists and Black Realities: The Politics of Authenticity," in Toni Morrison, ed., *Race-ing Justice, En-gendering, Power: Essays on Anita Hill, Clarence Thomas, and the Construction of Social Reality.* New York: Pantheon.

Statistical Abstract of the United States. 1996. Washington, D.C.: U.S. Department of Commerce, Economics and Statistics Administration.

Staudt, Kathleen A., and Weaver, William G. 1997. *Political Science and Feminisms: Integration or Transformation?* New York: Twayne.

Taylor, Ula Y. 1998. "Making Waves: The Theory and Practice of Black Feminism." *Black Scholar* 28 (Summer): 70–90.

Washington, Mary Helen. 1987. *Invented Lives: Narratives of Black Women, 1860–1960.* New York: Anchor.

Whitaker, Lois Duke. 1999. *Women and Politics: Outsiders or Insiders? A Collection of Readings.* Englewood Cliffs, N.J.: Prentice-Hall.

Williams, Patricia J. 1991. *The Alchemy of Race and Rights: Diary of a Law Professor.* Cambridge, Mass.: Harvard University Press.

"Women of Color in Corporate Management." 1999. New York: Catalyst Research.

Epilogue
Black and Multiracial Politics:
A Look Ahead

Yvette M. Alex-Assensoh

From its conception, one of the guiding principles behind *Black and Multiracial Politics in America* was to assemble a volume that would anticipate future events and controversies and, as such, serve as a harbinger, a primer of sorts on those issues that are likely to dominate the American political scene in the years ahead. As institutions all over the country, most notably the U.S. Bureau of the Census, grapple with the practical and theoretical quandaries posed by racial categories, the need to rethink from the ground up such terms as "black," multiracial," and "biracial" is of escalating importance.

For many African Americans, being black is quite simply a question of biology: All it takes is being born with a trace, however small, of black blood in one's veins. For others, born of mixed-race parentage, racial identification becomes more complicated. Are the children of black and white or black and Asian parents "black," "multiracial," or "biracial"? Are these categories adequate to the complexities of race and ethnicity in America today? Who is to decide? Policymakers and politicians? Scientists and academics? Doctors who must enter a word or two under "Race" on a birth certificate? The individuals themselves?

The essays in this volume demonstrate the need for both flexible thinking and a central theoretical framework when considering these questions. Often transcending the black-white framework, they offer a realistic interpretation of our techno-colored American society. And yet, it is essential to acknowledge an important reality: As regional politics become more conspicuous, black politics remains a central staging area for multiracial politics and debates more generally. Although many of the preceding essays subscribe to a black-white paradigm, they also offer a discussion of the important ways in which specific political processes and outcomes affect other racial minority groups. Providing much-needed answers to queries regarding black and emerging multiracial politics in America, this volume also opens up a Pandora's box of new questions for future researchers.

For instance, what does the explosion of interethnic and interracial marriages mean for the nature and process of a political reality wherein racial categorization is related to social, political, and economic status? Tiger Woods, the golf phenomenon, provides a revealing case study. In an interview on *The Oprah Winfrey Show*, Woods, when asked if the current American categories of race were problematic for him, replied: "Growing up, I came up with this name: I am 'Cablinasian,'" an acronym of his own making that suggests his racial makeup: one-eighth Caucasian, one-fourth black, one-eighth American Indian, one-fourth Thai, and one-fourth Chinese.[1]

In the face of a growing movement among individuals of mixed-race parentage to acknowledge all aspects of their heritage, some Americans argue that it is only right that they be allowed to identify themselves in a way that genuinely reflects who they are. Toward this end, advocacy groups, like the ten-year old Multiracial Americans of Southern California, have lent support to individuals who seek to express their dual identity as well as to challenge America's current system of racial categorization. Others see the multiracial movement, especially where African Americans are concerned, as simply an opportunity for individuals to self-identify as anything other than black. In a hearing devoted to the issue of a new multiracial census category, in 1993, Arthur Fletcher, a black member of the U.S. Commission on Civil Rights, inter alia, stated:

> I can see a whole host of light-skinned black Americans running for the door the minute they have another choice. All of a sudden, they have a way of saying, in this discriminatory culture of ours, I am something other than black.[2]

Indeed, if the proponents of the multiracial category are successful, the implications for minority politics in America will be dramatic. Racial categories currently serve to track incidents of discrimination, as well as a host of social and economic indicators. They also inform the ways in which government and local authorities operate programs: For example, minority employment benefits from government contracts and contractual set-asides for minority contractors, and court-ordered school desegregation and protection for minority voting rights are based on racial tallies. The institution of an "other" or "multiracial" category would change the distribution of political benefits and possibly even the American racial-cum-ethnic hierarchy. It would add yet another dynamic component to the meaning of race in America and, as a result, change the very nature of research on American racial and ethnic groups and the extent to which behavior can be linked to racial characteristics.

Accordingly, *Black and Multiracial Politics in America* does not look beyond the important issue of interracial and interethnic relations. Cruz, Assensoh, and Jones-Correa each offer explanations for the challenges that racial and ethnic groups face in getting along with each other and in adapting to new environments and institutions. Their research also generates a host of new questions. Will increased diversity lead to increased conflict or to greater pluralism? What are the pragmatic implications of more accurate categories of classification? While Henderson forecasts an increase in separatist sentiment based on the rise in nationalism, McCormick and Franklin suggest that spurned racial and ethnic groups can endeavor to work together in the spirit of pluralism and inclusionary strategies, provided there are supportive mechanisms in the political and social arena.

Looking forward, the essays collected here also raise questions about political activities and behavior in the century to come. America's ethnic and racial minorities have traditionally relied on outside pressure and extralegal means to move their interests to the top of the policy-making agenda. The Million Man March, in 1995, and the Million Women March, in 1997, are evidence that such strategies are still considered viable political activities by African American leaders. Lien's discussion of the relationship between voter turnout and race highlights the structural barriers to voting that exist among newer immigrant groups and suggests that such barriers might lead to increased participation in unconventional forms of political activity. The increased use of violence as a form of political protest is also a subject of great concern. Recent instances of racially motivated violence on the part of white nationalists may, should they persist, lead to a backlash by racial minority groups.

In response to prevailing challenges to "majority minority" districts, the American courts may soon witness referenda and legislative appeals in support of proportional voting. Such actions might serve to ameliorate the nettlesome problem of limited representation among underrepresented racial minority groups. Either way, demographic shifts in the racial and ethnic composition of America are bound to lead to a new form of politics.

While this volume does not purport to be a definitive study of racial politics in the United States, it is an effort to present both an unusually varied and a deliberately eclectic overview of black and multiracial politics in America today, as well as to sketch the pressing issues that will face racial minorities tomorrow. As such, *Black and Multiracial Politics in America* emphasizes the need for appropriate methodological techniques, theoretical frameworks, and conceptual road maps in our efforts to chart a more inclusive course for politics in the twenty-first century.

NOTES

1. J. E. White, Tamala M. Edwards, et al., "I'm Just Who I Am," *Time* 149(18)(May 5, 1997)p. 26.

2. Ibid., p. 27.

Index